CAMBRIDGE TEXTS IN THE
HISTORY OF PHILOSOPHY

FICHTE
The System of Ethics

CAMBRIDGE TEXTS IN THE HISTORY OF PHILOSOPHY

Series editors

KARL AMERIKS
Professor of Philosophy at the University of Notre Dame

DESMOND M. CLARKE
Professor of Philosophy at University College Cork

The main objective of Cambridge Texts in the History of Philosophy is to expand the range, variety and quality of texts in the history of philosophy which are available in English. The series includes texts by familiar names (such as Descartes and Kant) and also by less well-known authors. Wherever possible, texts are published in complete and unabridged form, and translations are specially commissioned for the series. Each volume contains a critical introduction together with a guide to further reading and any necessary glossaries and textual apparatus. The volumes are designed for student use at undergraduate and postgraduate level and will be of interest not only to students of philosophy, but also to a wider audience of readers in the history of science, the history of theology and the history of ideas.

For a list of titles published in the series, please see end of book.

JOHANN GOTTLIEB FICHTE

The System of Ethics

According to the Principles of the Wissenschaftslehre

TRANSLATED AND EDITED BY

DANIEL BREAZEALE

University of Kentucky

AND

GÜNTER ZÖLLER

University of Munich

CAMBRIDGE
UNIVERSITY PRESS

CAMBRIDGE UNIVERSITY PRESS
Cambridge, New York, Melbourne, Madrid, Cape Town, Singapore, São Paulo

CAMBRIDGE UNIVERSITY PRESS
The Edinburgh Building, Cambridge CB2 2RU, UK

Published in the United States of America by Cambridge University Press,
New York

www.cambridge.org
Information on this title: www.cambridge.org/9780521577670

© Cambridge University Press 2005

First published 2005

Printed in the United Kingdom at the University Press, Cambridge

A catalogue record for this book is available from the British Library

Library of Congress cataloguing in publication data

ISBN-13 978-0-521-57140-1 hardback
ISBN-10 0-521-57140-5 hardback
ISBN-13 978-0-521-57767-0 paperback
ISBN-10 0-521-57767-5 paperback

Contents

Acknowledgments

This translation of J. G. Fichte's main work in moral philosophy, *The System of Ethics*, first published in 1798, is the collaborative work of Günter Zöller and Daniel Breazeale. Günter Zöller prepared a complete draft translation of Fichte's text, and Daniel Breazeale then revised the latter, working directly from the German text and drawing on his previous translations of most of Fichte's other works from the same period (1794–1799). The notes and introductory material are the joint work of the two editors.

Both translators would like to thank Karl Ameriks, General Co-Editor of Cambridge Texts in the History of Philosophy, and Hilary Gaskin, Senior Commissioning Editor at Cambridge University Press, for their support in bringing this project to completion. Günter Zöller would also like to thank Karl Ameriks, Wayne Martin, Scott Jenkins, and Steve Hoeltzel for comments on earlier drafts of part of the translation as well as Ursula Martin for valuable secretarial help. Daniel Breazeale would like to thank Allen W. Wood, Karl Ameriks, and Erich Fuchs for advice concerning matters of translation. He is also grateful to Janet Rocannova for her diligent proofreading of the final typescript of the translation and to Viviane Breazeale for additional assistance with proofreading and invaluable moral support throughout the duration of this project. Finally, he would also like to acknowledge the occasional inspiration he has received from Paul Naulin's fine French translation of Fichte's text, *Le système de l'éthique d'après les principes de la doctrine de la science* (Paris: Presses Universitaires de France, 1986).

Introduction

Fichte's life and works

Johann Gottlieb Fichte was born on May 19, 1762 in Rammenau, Saxony (in the eastern part of today's Germany). He studied theology and law at Jena, Wittenberg and Leipzig without taking a degree (1784–1788) and served as a private tutor in several families in Saxony, Prussia and Switzerland (1784–1793). In 1790, upon studying Kant's *Critique of Pure Reason* (1781) and *Critique of Practical Reason* (1788), he became an enthusiastic adherent and supporter of Kant's Critical philosophy. Indeed, when his first publication, *Attempt at a Critique of All Revelation* (1792)[1] appeared anonymously, it was widely assumed to be a work by Kant himself. Kant publicly declared Fichte to be the author of the latter work and thereby launched Fichte's meteoric philosophical career. He was offered a professorship at the University of Jena, where he began teaching in the Summer Semester 1794. During his five years at Jena, Fichte's widely attended lectures and numerous publications exercised a tremendous influence on German philosophical and literary culture.

Fichte's major works from his Jena period are *Concerning the Concept of the Wissenschaftslehre* (1794),[2] *Foundation of the Entire Wissenschaftslehre*

---

[1] *Attempt at a Critique of all Revelation*, trans. Garrett Green (Cambridge: Cambridge University Press, 1978).

[2] *Concerning the Concept of the* Wissenschaftslehre *or, of so-called "Philosophy,"* in Fichte, *Early Philosophical Writings*, ed. and trans. Daniel Breazeale (Ithaca, NY: Cornell University Press, 1988; Cornell Paperbacks, 1993) [henceforth = *EPW*], 94–135.

(1794–1795),[3] *Foundation of Natural Right* (1796–1797),[4] *Attempt at a New Presentation of the Wissenschaftslehre* (1797–1798),[5] and *The System of Ethics* (1798). His lectures on the *Wissenschaftslehre nova methodo* (1796–1799),[6] which are preserved only in student transcripts, are also central documents for any informed understanding of Fichte's early system. Though written shortly after he left Jena for Berlin, *The Vocation of Man* (1800),[7] represents an effort on Fichte's part to summarize the conclusions of his Jena system in a more accessible or "popular" form.

In 1799 Fichte lost his professorship in Jena over charges of atheism stemming from his publication in 1798 of a brief essay "On the Basis of Our Belief in a Divine Governance of the World."[8] He spent most of the remaining years of his life in Berlin, where he initially supported himself by giving private and public lecture courses and later assuming a professorship at the newly founded university there (1810–1814). During those years Fichte published little, and what he did publish were not the new versions of the *Wissenschaftslehre* that he was developing in his private lectures, but revised versions of his public lectures on the philosophy of history and philosophy of religion, as well as his celebrated *Addresses to the German Nation* (1806).[9] As a result, he came to share the fate he himself had helped bring upon Kant: that of being surpassed in the eyes of the philosophical public by his own followers and successors, first Schelling and later Hegel.

In fact, Fichte remained philosophically active and productive until shortly before his death from typhoid fever January 29, 1814. He left behind a large number of unpublished works and lecture notes, some of which were edited by his son, Immanuel Hermann Fichte, in the mid-nineteenth century and all of which are now being made available in the complete

---

3 Contained under the title "Foundations of the Entire Science of Knowledge," in J. G. Fichte, *Science of Knowledge With the First and Second Introductions*, trans. Peter Heath and John Lachs (Cambridge: Cambridge University Press, 1982) [henceforth = *SK*], 87–286.

4 *Foundations of Natural Right*, ed. Frederick Neuhouser and trans. Michael Baur (Cambridge: Cambridge University Press, 2000) [henceforth = *FNR*].

5 Contained in *Introductions to the* Wissenschaftslehre *and Other Writings (1797–1800)*, ed. and trans. Daniel Breazeale (Indianapolis: Hackett, 1994) [henceforth = *IWL*], 1–118.

6 *Foundations of Transcendental Philosophy (Wissenschaftslehre) nova methodo (1796/99)*, ed. and trans. Daniel Breazeale (Ithaca, NY: Cornell University Press, 1992) [henceforth = *FTP*].

7 *The Vocation of Man*, trans. Peter Preuss (Indianapolis: Hackett, 1987).

8 "On the Basis of Our Belief in a Divine Governance of the World," trans. Daniel Breazeale, in *IWL*, pp. 141–154.

9 *Addresses to the German Nation*, ed. George A. Kelly, trans. G. H. Turnbull (New York: Harper and Row, 1968).

critical edition of Fichte's writings undertaken by the Bavarian Academy of Sciences.[10] Due to this immense body of posthumous work, Fichte remains very much a philosopher to be rediscovered and, with respect to many of the previously unknown versions of the *Wissenschaftslehre* from the post-Jena period, even discovered for the first time.

Fichte between Kant and Hegel

In the overall development of modern philosophy from Descartes to Heidegger, Fichte occupies a crucial place. On the one hand, he continues the aspirations of his predecessors – especially Descartes and Kant – toward a scientific and methodologically sound form of philosophy that is free from error, illusion and doubt. On the other hand, he is the first major representative of a type of philosophy that is explicitly informed by human interests and specifically practical orientations as much as by the pursuit of pure knowledge for its own sake. Yet in contrast to later philosophers, such as Marx and Nietzsche, who criticize the very project of the pure, disinterested search for truth as a mask for hidden interests and motivations, Fichte stills seeks to preserve the ahistorical, "absolute" character of knowledge, while simultaneously acknowledging the predominantly practical nature of the pursuit of the same and the human, all-too-human obstacles to achieving it.

In more specific, historical terms, Fichte is a crucial link between Kant and Hegel. With the former he shares the critical spirit of determining the conditions as well as the boundaries of any claims to objectively valid judgments, while preparing the way for the latter's inclusion of the social and historical dimension of human existence into the domain of systematic philosophical investigation. Yet with his insistence upon the ultimate unknowability of the absolute ("God") and upon the resistance of ultimate facts to complete theoretical reconstruction ("facticity"), Fichte remains closer in "spirit" to Kant than to Hegel. Fichte approaches philosophical issues in the oblique manner of investigating what and how we can know rather than

---

[10] *Johann Gottlieb Fichtes sämmtliche Werke*, ed. I. H. Fichte, eight vols. (Berlin: Viet & Co., 1845–1846); rpt., along with the three vols. of *Johann Gottlieb Fichtes nachgelassene Werke* (Bonn: Adolphus-Marcus, 1834–35), as *Fichtes Werke* (Berlin: de Gruyter, 1971) [henceforth = *SW* and cited by volume and page number]. *J. G. Fichte-Gesamtausgabe der Bayerischen Akademie der Wissenschaften*, ed. Reinhard Lauth, Hans Gliwitzky†, and Erich Fuchs. (Stuttgart-Bad Cannstatt: Frommann-Holzboog, 1964ff.) [henceforth = *GA* and cited by series, volume, and page number].

through any purported direct insight into the nature of things. Like Descartes and Kant, and unlike Hegel, he places epistemology before metaphysics. Alternatively put, he subjects metaphysics to an epistemological turn.

Fichte's influence on the course of philosophy has been tremendous. He was among the first to move from the immediate, often piecemeal reception of Kant's work to its original appropriation and transformation into a comprehensively conceived systematic philosophy. Moreover, he single-handedly changed the character of philosophical teaching, and by extension that of other academic subject matters, by inaugurating the practice of lecturing on his own writings, often work in progress, rather than expounding an official textbook. In the process, he also contributed to changing the style of philosophical discourse from dispassionate academic language to a vigorous, rhetorically charged prose that reflects the personality of its author as much as the demands of the subject matter. Regarding the content of philosophy, in addition to his Herculean efforts to construct a new and more encompassing theory of human consciousness, Fichte did pioneering work in separating the legal and political sphere from the moral domain and in placing ethics into the larger framework of the theory of action and the theory of social relations.

Philosophy as *Wissenschaftslehre*

Fichte's technical term for his chief philosophical project is *Wissenschaftslehre*, alternatively rendered in English as "doctrine of science" and "science of knowledge" (though often left untranslated, as a technical term of art). For Fichte, this term with its emphasis on knowledge (*Wissen*), and specifically scientific knowledge or science (*Wissenschaft*), replaces the older designation "philosophy," whose literal meaning as "love of wisdom" reflects an understanding of the discipline that is at once too modest and too ambitious: too modest in its restriction to the mere *pursuit* of wisdom rather than its attainment of the same; and too ambitious in aiming at (practical) wisdom rather than (theoretical) knowledge.

The specific sort of knowledge sought by philosophy as *Wissenschaftslehre* is knowledge regarding knowledge, more precisely, knowledge concerning the grounds and conditions of all knowledge. Rather than being object-oriented and object-specific, philosophical knowledge is reflectively oriented toward the grounds or conditions of knowledge as such. It is not about this or that object to be known but rather about the very objectivity of knowledge. Philosophical knowledge is "transcendental" in the Kantian sense of that term.

Whereas Kant essentially limited transcendental philosophy to the "theoretical" realm consisting of the transcendental theory of the knowledge of objects (nature), to the exclusion of practical (moral and social) philosophy, Fichte conceives of the *Wissenschaftslehre* as a truly universal, "transcendental" science that is concerned just as much with the grounds and conditions of our knowledge of *what ought to be* or what *ought to be done* as it is with the grounds and conditions of our knowledge of *what is*. Nevertheless, the *Wissenschaftslehre* itself remains a thoroughly theoretical enterprise, even if one of its chief concerns is to produce a transcendental theory of human action and practice.

The new and broader conception of transcendental philosophy that underlies the *Wissenschaftslehre* allows Fichte to unify and to integrate into a comprehensive philosophical system elements and disciplines that remain disparate and disjointed in Kant. Fichte's move beyond Kant occurs in two main directions. In a reductive direction, or in moving from the spheres of nature and social life to their underlying grounds and conditions, Fichte traces the distinction between theory and practice to an ultimate origin that precedes but also conditions and makes necessary this seemingly elementary distinction. Whereas Kant had insisted on the irreducibility of theoretical reason (knowledge of nature) and practical reason (knowledge of morals) to each other, Fichte reveals their hidden common ground in the necessary structure of self-positing self-hood (the pure I). This unitary ground is both the source of reason's differentiation as theoretical reason and practical reason and the source of the latters' ultimate identity as reason.

Fichte also strengthens the integration of reason in a deductive direction inasmuch as his system proceeds methodically from the ultimate and intermediate grounds and conditions of all knowledge to their successive unfolding in various kinds of knowledge and their respective object domains. Unlike Kant, who had radically separated the pure principles of theoretical and practical reason from their contingent instantiations in experience and social life, Fichte insists on the gradual, methodically controlled transition from the highest principle or principles to the ever-more specific aspects and features of human mental life and its natural and social object domains. Thus, not only does his system include transcendental deductions of the first principles of theoretical and practical philosophy, but also deductions of the "applicability" of the same. This is the basis for his claim to have constructed a "real" and not merely a "formal" science of philosophy.

Fichte's radical integration of the absolute ground of all knowing with that which it grounds results in a radically unified system of the mind. It also assures the systematic unity of the philosophical reconstruction of the system of knowledge in the *Wissenschaftslehre*. Fichte was thus the first of Kant's successors to envision and to realize the systematic constitution of philosophical knowledge as well as its object, i.e., non-philosophical knowledge of all kinds. Unfortunately a series of external circumstances, chiefly the loss of his professorship at Jena, the impact of the Napoleonic wars on Prussia (his adopted homeland after 1799) and his untimely death in 1814, prevented him from completely executing the projected entire system of the *Wissenschaftslehre*.

Despite its systematic scope and methodological rigor there is a remarkable openness to the *Wissenschaftslehre*, which for Fichte is not a fixed doctrine to be laid down once and for all in teaching and in writing, but an open system animated and sustained by a spirit of continuing inquiry and self-improvement. Fichte always insisted on the freedom of the *Wissenschaftslehre* from any specific final formulation and from any specific technical vocabulary. Over the course of two decades he developed fifteen radically different presentations of the *Wissenschaftslehre*, continually reworking the "body" of his philosophy, while insisting that its "spirit" remained the same.

The systematic place of ethics within the Jena *Wissenschaftslehre*

That a complete system of philosophy would have to include a division devoted specifically to moral theory or ethics was, one might say, self-evident to a philosopher with Fichte's background and with his intensely practical orientation toward both life and philosophy. His earliest remarks concerning the systematic structure of his new system embrace a three-part organizational scheme, consisting of "universal philosophy" as well as the two branches of the same, "theoretical" and "practical" philosophy.[11] Yet even this simple scheme was somewhat complicated,

---

[11] Fichte to F. I. Niethammer, December 6, 1793 (*GA* III/2: 21).

first of all, by the fact that the first, "general" or "foundational" part of the entire system was in turn originally divided into "theoretical" and "practical" portions and, secondly, by the fact that Fichte himself sometimes referred to the practical portion of this foundational portion of the system (corresponding to Part III of the *Foundation of the Entire Wissenschaftslehre*) simply as "practical philosophy" or, more perspicuously, "*Universal Practical Philosophy.*"[12] Despite this ambiguity, it remains clear that Fichte envisioned from the first that his entire system would include a specifically "practical" sub-division, to be constructed upon the basis of a new foundation, which would in turn include theoretical and practical parts.[13] This project is first made public and explicit in the brief "hypothetical" sketch of the contours of his new system contained in Part III of *Concerning the Concept of the Wissenschaftslehre* (1794), in which Fichte confidently forecasts that the second, "practical" portion of his forthcoming presentation of the foundations of his new system will also provide the basis for "new and thoroughly elaborated theories of the pleasant, the beautiful, the sublime, the free obedience of nature to its own laws, God, so-called common sense or the natural sense of truth, and finally for new theories of nature and morality, the principles of which are material as well as formal."[14]

As the preceding, rather motley collection of topics suggests, Fichte had at this point still not worked out the precise content and details of the "specifically practical" portion of the new system. The most arresting point of this promissory note, however, is surely the claim that his new ethics – in implicit contradistinction to that of Kant – will be "material" as well as formal. What this means first becomes clear, not in the 1798 *System of Ethics*, but two years earlier in the first part of the *Foundation of Natural Right*, where he explains "How a real philosophical science is to be distinguished from a mere formulaic philosophy."[15] A "real" philosophical science has content as well as form, because content and form (object and concept) are inseparably connected in the original and necessary self-constitutive acts of the I; such a science observes and describes

---

[12] This is from Fichte's April 2, 1794 letter to K. A. Böttiger (*GA* III / 2: 92).
[13] See, e.g., Fichte's March 8, 1794 letter to G. Hufeland, in which he discloses his plans for his inaugural lectures at Jena and remarks that in his "private" lectures on the *Wissenschaftslehre* he will provide a completely new presentation of the *concept* of philosophy and will develop the first principles of the same up to the point of Reinhold's Principle of Consciousness, and "perhaps also establish the first principles of an entirely new kind of practical philosophy" (*GA* III / 2: 82).
[14] *EPW*, p. 135 (*SW* I: 66; *GA* I / 2: 151).   [15] *FNR*, pp. 3–8 (*SW* III: 1–7; *GA* I / 3: 313–318).

these very acts – with respect both to their (necessary) form and their (necessary) content. One "real" philosophical science is distinguished from another simply by the particular determinate acts it observes and describes. The foundational portion of the entire *Wissenschaftslehre*, which is also a "real" philosophical science in its own right, describes the most basic acts of the I and thus establishes the "reality" of the I itself, along with that of its domains of experience, both theoretical and practical (the "sensible" and "rational" or "spiritual" worlds). The special philosophical sciences obtain their reality or material content from those additional, necessary and determinate acts of the I that they observe and describe – with respect both to the necessary form of these acts themselves (necessary, that is, for the possibility of self-consciousness itself, or for that "real" act of ungrounded self-positing with the postulation of which the entire system begins) and to the necessary content of the same (that is, the product that necessarily emerges as an object for reflection as a result of this same originally posited action). The "real content" of the special philosophical science of natural right or law (*Naturrecht*) is provided by the concept of right itself, which is deduced or, as Fichte puts it, "genetically derived," along with its necessary object or content: a community of free, embodied individuals, each of whom must limit his external freedom and constrain his efficacious acting in specific ways in order to posit himself as one among many, and, ultimately, in order to be able to posit himself (as an individual) at all. So too, Fichte envisioned a philosophical science of ethics that would describe certain necessary acts of the I, through which it will obtain for itself a distinctive sphere of objects, as well as insight into the necessary laws (the form) of the same. Such an ethics would therefore be "material as well as formal."

When he published a second edition of *Concerning the Concept of the Wissenschaftslehre* in 1798, Fichte omitted Part III, "Hypothetical Division of the *Wissenschaftslehre*." The reason he did this was, no doubt, because he had since arrived at a clearer and more fully articulated understanding of the overall systematic structure of his own system. This new systematic conception is most fully presented in the "Deduction of the Subdivisions of the *Wissenschaftslehre*" with which he concluded his lectures on *Wissenschaftslehre nova methodo*. Beginning in the Summer Semester of 1796/97, with his first presentation of the foundations of the *Wissenschaftslehre* "in accordance with a new method," Fichte abandoned the tripartite division of *prima philosophia* that he had followed in the

Foundation of the Entire Wissenschaftslehre. Gone entirely is any preliminary discussion of the relationship between logical laws and the first principles of transcendental philosophy, along with the pretence of deriving the latter from the former. Gone too is the distinction between the "theoretical" and "practical" portions of the foundational portion of the system, an absence that eliminates the previous ambiguity regarding the meaning of the term "practical philosophy." From now on, the term "practical philosophy" designates a specific sub-division of the larger system, the first principles or foundations of which are presented in the *Wissenschaftslehre nova methodo*.

According to this new division, philosophy as a whole is divided into four major divisions: (1) the first or foundational part of the entire system, (2) theoretical philosophy, (3) practical philosophy, and (4) "philosophy of the postulates," which is in turn divided into philosophy of right and philosophy of religion. The foundational portion of the system is expounded in the lectures on *Wissenschaftslehre nova methodo*. The task of this first part of the entire system is to derive only the most basic concepts (and objects) of transcendental philosophy, the further analysis and determination of which is the subject of the "special philosophical sciences," each of which has the further task of exhaustively determining the particular concepts (and objects) that constitute its distinctive domain of inquiry.

The first of these special sciences is "theoretical *Wissenschaftslehre*, or the *Wissenschaftslehre* of cognition in the Kantian sense," which considers what we necessarily *cognize* whenever we *find* ourselves: i.e., nature or the world, as an object of objective cognition, considered both as a mechanical system and as subject to organic laws. Such a philosophical sub-discipline establishes "how the world is" and thus what we necessarily can and cannot experience. To be sure, the world (nature) is an object of philosophical interest and inquiry only to the extent that it is determined a priori by necessary laws of *thinking*, a limitation that prevented Fichte from taking seriously the project of *Naturphilosophie* as developed by Schelling and Hegel. Fichte, of course, never published any separate treatise on "theoretical philosophy" or "philosophy of nature," perhaps because – as his account of this science suggests – at least the basic features of such a science are already contained in the systematic presentation of the first principles or foundations of the entire system.[16]

---

[16] *FTP*, pp. 467–470 (*GA* IV/2: 262).

The second special philosophical sub-discipline is the "*Wissenschaftslehre* of the practical," or "*ethics* in the proper sense of the term." Of course, as Fichte notes, if the domain of "the practical" is taken to be congruent with that of acting as such, then the entire system of the *Wissenschaftslehre* is shot through with "practical" elements. As a "particular science," however, practical philosophy deals specifically with those universal laws of reason that determine how every rational person, irrespective of his individual circumstances or nature, must limit his actions and must act in a determinate manner. These universal commands are the subject of "universal ethics," a philosophical science that tells us not how the world actually is, but rather, "how the world ought be made by rational beings"; it deals not with individuals as such, but with "reason as such in its individuality," inasmuch as individuality is itself a universal condition for the possibility of reason. Viewed in this way, ethics can be characterized as "the highest abstraction in thinking," inasmuch as it involves an "ascent from the level of what is sensible to the pure concept as a motive for action."[17] This is the science expounded in *The System of Ethics*.

---

[17] "In order to find ourselves we must think of the task of limiting ourselves in a certain way. This task is different for every individual, and it is precisely this difference that determines which particular individual one actually is. This is not a task that appears to us all at once and once and for all; instead, it presents itself in the course of experience every time an ethical command is issued to us. But since we are practical beings, this summons to limit ourselves also contains a summons for us to act in a determinate way. This applies differently to every individual. Everyone bears his own conscience within himself, and each person's conscience is entirely his own. Yet the manner in which the law of reason commands everyone can certainly be established in abstracto. Such an inquiry is conducted from a higher standpoint, where individuality vanishes from view and one attends only to what is universal or general. I must act; my conscience is my conscience, and to this extent the theory of ethics is an individual matter. This, however, is not the way it is dealt with in the general theory of ethics. {If one attends only to what is universal, there arises} the practical Wissenschaftslehre, which becomes the particular [science of] ethics, {or 'ethics' in the proper sense of the term}. That is to say, what is practical is acting as such, but acting is constantly present throughout the *Foundation*, inasmuch as this entire mechanism [of reason] is based upon [acting]; consequently, the specifically practical *Wissenschaftslehre* can only be ethics. Ethics explains how the world ought to be constructed by rational beings, and its result is something ideal (to the extent that what is ideal can be a result), since this is not something that can be grasped conceptually. {[In contrast,] the theoretical Wissenschaftslehre explains how the world is, and the result of the same is pure empirical experience.} *Remark*: Both theoretical and practical philosophy are [included within] the *Wissenschaftslehre*. Both are based upon the transcendental point of view: Theoretical philosophy is based upon the transcendental point of view precisely because it deals with the act of cognizing, and thus with something within us, and it is not concerned with any sort of {mere} being. Practical philosophy is based upon the transcendental point of view because it does not deal with the I as an individual at all, but instead deals with reason as such, in its individuality. {The theory of ethics maintains that individuality is contained within and follows from reason. That I am precisely this specific individual, however, is not something that follows from reason.} The former theory is

The third special philosophical science or systematic subdivision of the entire *Wissenschaftslehre* is called "the philosophy of the postulates," because it deals with the objects of both theoretical and practical philosophy (nature and freedom), but it deals with these not in isolation from each other but in their *relation* to each other; more specifically, this subdivision of the system is concerned with the specific *demands* that practical and theoretical philosophy each makes upon the realm of the other, and hence with what each specifically "postulates" with respect to the other. The first systematic subdivision of the philosophy of the postulates, "Doctrine of Law or Natural Right," concerns itself with those postulates that theory addresses to the practical realm, that is to the domain of pure freedom as embodied in finite rational individuals. The doctrine of right or theory of natural law is the special philosophical science that demonstrates how each individual must limit his own freedom within the context of a "juridical world" and subject himself to a legal constitution, in accordance with a certain mechanical and externally enforceable connection, in order to advance toward the universal end of reason itself. Since the latter is, properly speaking, also the end of morality, Fichte concludes that this "jur-idical world must precede the moral world."[18] The theory or doctrine of right is thus equally theoretical and practical, since it deals with the *world* not as it is found, but rather, "as it ought to be found"; and it is up to us to produce such a social world, that is, to establish a just society. This is the science systematically expounded in the *Foundation of Natural Right* (1796/97).

There is also a postulate addressed by practical to theoretical reason and to the realm of the latter, that is, to nature, a postulate regarding the ways in which "the sensible world ought to accommodate itself to the end of reason."[19] This second postulate indicates the distinctive object of the other subdivision of Fichte's philosophy of the postulates, Philosophy of Religion. The distinctive task of a transcendental philosophy of religion is to describe and to deduce how nature, in accordance with a supersensible law, is supposed to be compatible with morality. Unfortunately, Fichte

---

{in a certain respect} concrete; the latter is the highest abstraction {present within thinking and involves an ascent} from the level of what is sensible to the pure concept as a motive [for action]" (*FTP*, pp. 469–470 [*GA* IV/2: 263 and IV/3: 520–521]).

[18] But note too the passage in the *Foundation of Natural Right* where Fichte says that the rule of right obtains a new sanction from moral conscience, which gives us a moral obligation to live in a human community and thus in the juridical world (*FNR*, pp. 10–11 [*SW* III: 10–11; *GA* I/3: 320–322]). The precise relationship between the disciplines of natural right and ethics is a topic worthy of further examination in its own right, inasmuch as Fichte's own comments on this topic do not appear to be always consistent with one another.

[19] *FTP*, p. 471 (*GA* IV/2: 265 and IV/3: 522).

never had the opportunity to develop adequately this final subdivision of the *Wissenschaftslehre* during his tenure at Jena, though strong hints regarding the probable contents of such a special science may be gathered from his 1798 essay, "On the Basis of our Belief in a Divine Governance of the World," as well as from portions of his introductory lectures on "Logic and Metaphysics" and from Book 3 of *The Vocation of Man*.[20]

When we compare this lucid statement of the overall systematic structure of the Jena *Wissenschaftslehre* with what Fichte was actually able to accomplish during this same period we should note that he was able to publish full, scientific presentations of only two of the various "subdivisions of the *Wissenschaftslehre*": namely, his treatises on natural right and ethics, which K. L. Reinhold accurately described, in his "Open Letter to Fichte," as the "two pillars of your philosophy."[21] Ironically enough, Fichte was forced by the Atheism Controversy to leave Jena before he was able to develop his projected philosophy of religion, and he seems never to have seriously contemplated writing a separate work on theoretical philosophy (philosophy of nature).[22] Nor was he ever able to publish a complete presentation of the new, foundational portion of the system "according to a new method," despite the fact that he thrice lectured on this topic and even began publishing a revised version of these same lectures in installments in his own *Philosophical Journal*, under the title *An Attempt at a New Presentation of the Wissenschaftslehre*.[23]

[20] See Fichte's lecture notes on §§ 933 ff. of Platner's *Philosophishe Aphorismen*, *GA* II/4: 288–353. In 1799, during the height of the Atheism Controversy, some revised excerpts from a student transcript of this portion of Fichte's Platner lectures were published anonymously under the title "Des Herrn Professor Fichte's Ideen über Gott und Unsterblichkeit. Nach einem Kollegienheft herausgegeben," in a volume entitled *Etwas von dem Herrn Professor Fichte und für ihn*. Though composed shortly after Fichte left Jena, Bk. III of *The Vocation of Man*, entitled "Faith" (*Glaube*), is obviously relevant to this topic as well.

[21] K. L. Reinhold, *Sendschreiben an Fichte und Lavater* (1799), *GA* III/3: 306.

[22] Despite its title, the 1795 *Outline of the Distinctive Character of the Wissenschaftslehre with respect to the Theoretical Faculty* (in *EPW*, pp. 243–306) does not appear to be a treatise on "theoretical philosophy" in the sense here indicated, but rather, a necessary supplement to the *Foundation of the entire Wissenschaftslehre* – a surmise that is confirmed by Fichte's insistence on publishing these works together in a single volume when he reissued them in 1802. Concerning Fichte's "philosophy of nature," see, above all, Reinhard Lauth, *Die transzendentale Naturlehre Fichtes nach der Wissenschaftslehre* (Hamburg: Meiner, 1989).

[23] Fichte's decision to abandon this project following the publication of two introductions and a single chapter raises important questions for interpreting the evolution of Fichte's philosophy and concerning the unity – or lack thereof – of the *Wissenschaftslehre*. The circumstances relevant to understanding this decision include not only the Atheism Controversy but also Fichte's ongoing debate (mainly in his correspondence) with Schelling regarding the proper limits of

On the basis of the preceding survey of Fichte's efforts to describe the overall structure of his Jena system, the systematic place of *The System of Ethics* therein would appear to be unambiguous and unproblematic: Ethics is one of several "special" philosophical sciences. Its first principles – above all, the concepts of will, freedom, and drive – are contained in and derived from the first or foundational portion of the entire *Wissenschaftslehre*. Ethics is also a "real philosophical science," which specifies and provides itself with its own, distinctive object, as well as with the formal laws that apply to the same. As the distinctively "practical" portion of the *Wissenschaftslehre*, ethics stipulates how every individual ought to determine his own freedom in accordance with universal laws of reason.

This characterization of ethics as one of several systematic subdivisions of a larger system is also repeated in *The System of Ethics* itself, where Fichte writes: "Ethics is practical philosophy. Just as theoretical philosophy has to present that system of necessary thinking according to which our representations correspond to a being, so practical philosophy has to provide an exhaustive presentation of that system of necessary thinking according to which a being corresponds to and follows from our representations" (p. 2).[24] The starting point of such a special science is the proposition that the I, in order to posit or become conscious of itself – and thus, in order to be an I at all – must *find* itself to be engaged in actual willing, and hence must become conscious of its own efficacy in the external world (p. 12). This principle, however, is not demonstrated in *The System of Ethics* itself, but must instead be derived within and thus obtained from the preceding foundational portion of the entire system, "and thus the science of ethics that we are here engaged in establishing stands firmly on common ground with philosophy as a whole" (p. 23).

---

transcendental philosophy and the relationship of the latter to *Naturphilosophie*. After arriving in Berlin in 1800 Fichte made one final effort to revise his lectures on *Wissenschaftslehre nova methodo* for publication, but this project too was quickly abandoned.

[24] References to *The System of Ethics* in this editors' introduction will be provided according to the pagination in vol. IV of *SW*. This pagination is also provided in *GA* and in most other modern editions of *The System of Ethics*, including the *Philosophische Bibliothek* edition and the present English translation.

The System of Ethics as the culmination of Fichte's early philosophy

Having considered Fichte's comments *about* the systematic place of ethics within the *Wissenschaftslehre*, let us now look more closely at *The System of Ethics* itself in order to determine the *actual* (in contrast with the intended or "official") place of the former within Fichte's early system. It was not until the Summer Semester of 1796, in a course of private lectures announced under the title "*Ethicen secundum dictata*,"[25] that Fichte was finally able to carry through on his longstanding plan to develop the "specifically practical" portion of his system. Since he had been fully occupied throughout the preceding year with the construction of his new theory of natural right, as well as with the total revision of the foundational portion of his system "according to a new method," he was unable to do much preliminary work on this new science prior to his lectures of ethics; instead, as he wrote to Reinhold on August 27, 1796, "These days I am lecturing in three different courses, one of these on an entirely new science [viz., ethics], in which I first have to construct the system as I present it."[26] These lectures on ethics were repeated in the Winter Semesters of 1796/97, 1797/98, and 1798/99. *The System of Ethics* was first issued, in printed fascicles, to students attending Fichte's lectures on ethics during the Winter Semester of 1797/98 and finally published in book form in June of 1798.

In a public appeal for subscriptions to the forthcoming *System of Ethics*, an appeal issued by Fichte's publisher, Gabler but surely written by Fichte himself, two distinctive features of the new book are emphasized: first of all, as indicated by its full title (*The System of Ethics according to the Principles of the Wissenschaftslehre*), Fichte promised that his forthcoming book would not be an *ad hoc* or freestanding treatise on ethics, but that he would instead take special care to establish the systematic connection between the principles of *ethics* and those of *philosophy in general*. According to this same announcement, one of the greatest shortcomings of all previous works on this subject lay in the failure of their authors to establish the foundations of their science

---

[25] Latin for "ethics according to his dictation." A student transcription of these 1796 lectures on ethics (presumably by Otto von Mirbach) is contained in *GA* IV/1: 7–148.

[26] *GA* III/3: 33.

securely and deeply enough, which is why most of the main concepts of this discipline – including the concepts of freedom and the moral law – remain beset with difficulties. In contrast, Fichte confidently promised that his new *Ethics* would explain the *origin* of the entire system of practical concepts.

This first point leads directly to what is described in this same announcement as the second major innovation of the new book: unlike previous treatises on ethics, *The System of Ethics* would also include a scientific demonstration of the *applicability* of the ethical principles of pure reason to actual life, "by means of a rigorous deduction of these principles from the highest principle of all knowing."[27] This, of course, is simply another way of saying what was already promised several years earlier: that the *Wissenschaftslehre* would make possible an ethical theory that is "material" as well as formal, and thus deserves to called a "real philosophical science."

It is this second innovative feature of *The System of Ethics* that is particularly stressed in Fichte's "Introduction" to the work itself (the portion of the text that was printed last, and, presumably, the part that was composed last as well). Practical philosophy, as conceived by Fichte, explicitly addresses and answers an essential question that had been largely ignored by philosophers prior to him (with the possible exception of Kant, in the third *Critique*). Whereas previous philosophers devoted ample attention to the issue of how we are able to *cognize* the external world, and thus to the problematic relationship between our representations and those objects to which they allegedly correspond, they displayed no similar curiosity concerning the equally important issue of how and with what right we are able to think of some of *our* concepts as actually *exhibited* in nature, i.e., to the question of how it is that we can actually have any *effect* within and upon the world. Moreover, according to Fichte, if they had tried to explain this possibility in a systematic fashion, this alone would have been sufficient to force them to re-examine their explanations of cognition as well, for it would have forced them to consider the previously ignored possibility that the will is a constitutive principle not merely of practical, but also of theoretical philosophy.

Another "previously unasked question" that is explicitly addressed in *The System of Ethics* concerns the basis for our everyday distinction

[27] *GA* 1/5: 6–7.

between those aspects of the external world which we can alter by means of our will and those we cannot: between the "contingent" and the "necessary" features of nature.[28] This question too, according to Fichte, forces us to reconsider the extent to which our practical freedom is not simply the principle of moral willing, but is at the same time "itself *a theoretical principle for the determination of our world*" (p. 68). Though this important point was certainly anticipated in Part III of the *Foundation of the Entire Wissenschaftslehre* and then made fully explicit in the *Foundation of Natural Right*, it still required a more complete and more deeply grounded deduction, which would be forthcoming only in *The System of Ethics*.[29]

To the extent that *The System of Ethics* really does provide a new and deeper account of the essential role of the principle of willing in the constitution of experience, it goes well beyond the limits of what is usually thought of as "ethics" or even "practical philosophy." Insofar as it does this, moreover, it is not simply a systematic *subdivision* of the *Wissenschaftslehre*, but includes material that really pertains to the *Wissenschaftslehre* as a whole and has important implications for the very *foundations* of the entire system – or at least for a proper understanding of those foundations.

In considering the systematic place of the *Sittenlehre* one must always recall that – with the exception of those students who were fortunate enough to have personally attended Fichte's lectures on *Wissenschaftslehre nova methodo* – the only full-scale, "scientific" presentation of the foundational portion of the *Wissenschaftslehre* with which potential readers of *The System of Ethics* could have been acquainted was the *Foundation of the Entire Wissenschaftslehre*, a work that, even in Fichte's own eyes, not only followed a defective method of presentation, but also failed to make clear the crucial relationship between the theoretical and practical "activities" of the I and the "equiprimacy" of both with respect to the transcendental conditions of experience.[30] This circumstance

---

[28] This question, though not mentioned in Fichte's appeal for subscriptions, is raised at the beginning of Part II of the text itself: "A thorough and complete philosophy has to explain why some things appear to us to be contingent in this manner, and in doing this it will also determine the boundary and the extent of what is contingent. To be sure, these questions have until now not even been asked, much less answered" (p. 67).

[29] "Here, however, the investigation would have to be extended even further, and the proofs of this assertion would have to reach even deeper, since we here find ourselves precisely at the ultimate point of origin of all reason" (p. 68).

[30] Regarding Fichte's dissatisfaction with the 1794/95 *Foundation of the Entire Wissenschaftslehre*, see the Editor's Introduction to *FTP*. Regarding the "equiprimordiality" interpretation of the Jena *Wissenschaftslehre*, see Günter Zöller, *Fichte's Transcendental Philosophy: The Original*

helps one understand why *The System of Ethics* includes discussions of so many issues that, as Fichte himself concedes, really belong within a scientific presentation of the first or foundational portion of the system: that is, because no remotely adequate presentation of these same foundations was publicly available to the first readers of Fichte's *Ethics*.

Accordingly, the best published account of Fichte's revised presentation of the *foundations* of the *Wissenschaftslehre* as a whole is to be found in – or perhaps, inferred from – *The System of Ethics*, which must therefore be recognized not merely as the promised presentation of that portion of the complete system that deals with the specific topic of ethics, or "practical philosophy" in the narrow sense, but also as an indispensable public presentation, however rudimentary and schematic (in comparison with the lectures on *Wissenschaftslehre nova methodo*) of the first, or "foundational" portion of the entire system. This is true not only of the Introduction and Part I ("Deduction of the Principle of Morality") but also of Part II ("Deduction of the Reality and Applicability of the Principle of Morality"); for what turns out to be required in order to establish the "reality and applicability of the principle of morality" is that one revise one's prior notions concerning "reality" in general and recognize the latter as an *appearance of the will*. It is no wonder that no author on ethics prior to Fichte had attempted such a "deduction" of the ethical law, since such a project requires a thoroughly new account of the relationship between cognition, willing, and nature, as well as the systematic articulation of a radically new doctrine of the relationship between the sensible and supersensible realms.

Fichte himself recognized that *The System of Ethics*, and particularly the first portions of the same, does much more than simply extend the principles of his previously developed system to a new domain, and, both in public announcements and in private correspondence, he recommended this new work – along with the *Foundation of Natural Right* – as providing a clearer presentation of "philosophy in general" than the one contained in the 1794/95 *Foundation of the Entire Wissenschaftslehre*.[31]

Duplicity of Intelligence and Will (Cambridge: Cambridge University Press, 1998) and Daniel Breazeale, "The Theory of Practice and the Practice of Theory: Fichte and the 'Primacy of Practical Reason,'" *International Philosophical Quarterly*, 36 (1996), 47–64.

[31] See Fichte's public "Announcement of a New Presentation of the *Wissenschaftslehre*," dated November 4, 1800 (in *IWL*, pp. 186–201 [*GA*, 1/7: 153–164]), in which he bemoans the fact that the *Foundation of the Entire Wissenschaftslehre* has been universally misunderstood by all but his own students and appears to be a text that cannot be understood properly without oral assistance.

Thus he wrote to Friedrich Johannsen on January 31, 1801: "My printed *Wissenschaftslehre* bears too many traces of the era in which it was written and of the manner of philosophizing that then prevailed. As a result, it is much less clear than a presentation of transcendental philosophy should be. I can recommend much more highly the first portions of my works on natural right and ethics (particularly the latter)."[32] Unfortunately, the eruption of the Atheism Controversy, less than six months after the publication of *The System of Ethics*, fatally distracted the attention of the philosophical public from the latter work,[33] the central importance of which for a systematic interpretation of Fichte's early *Wissenschaftslehre* as a whole has, up to the present day, seldom been recognized.

A careful reading of Fichte's *System of Ethics* forces one to rethink not only the content of philosophical ethics but also the foundations of the entire *Wissenschaftslehre* and to amend and augment some of the central doctrines of the same, particularly as these are expounded in the *Foundation of the Entire Wissenschaftslehre*. It thus plays a dual role within the overall context of the Jena system: on the one hand, it does indeed expound the "special science" of practical philosophy in the narrow or proper sense: the transcendental subdiscipline that explicitly accounts for our consciousness of the moral law and then derives material duties from this principle. On the other hand, this same text also implies and to a large extent actually furnishes a revised presentation of some – though certainly not all – of the first principles of the entire system, a presentation which, as such, belongs to no special philosophical science but to the *Wissenschaftslehre as a whole*; and to this extent *The System of Ethics* augments the first or foundational portion of the entire system. This last point was clearly grasped by Fichte himself, who concludes his deduction of the principle morality in *The System of Ethics* with the following observation (pp. 58–59):

> The perspectives upon philosophy as a whole that offer themselves
> at this point are manifold, and I cannot forego the occasion to point

Then, however, he adds: "It seems to me, however, that in my books on *Natural Right* and *Ethics* I have been somewhat more successful in presenting my thoughts concerning philosophy in general as well."

[32] *GA* III / 5: 9.

[33] Indicative of this neglect is the fact that *The System of Ethics* received only five contemporary reviews, fewer than any of the other books published by Fichte during the Jena period. See *J. G. Fichte in zeitgenössischen Rezensionen*, ed. Erich Fuchs, Wilhelm G. Jacobs und Walter Schieche (Stuttgart-Bad Cannstatt: Frommann-Holzboog, 1995), Vol. 2, pp. 204–280.

out at least some of them. – Because it is self-intuiting and finite, reason determines through itself its own acting. This proposition has a twofold meaning, inasmuch as reason's acting can be viewed from two different sides. In the context of a treatise on ethics this proposition refers only to the kind of acting that particularly merits this name: the kind of acting that is accompanied by a consciousness of freedom and is recognized as "acting" even from the ordinary viewpoint, i.e., *willing* and *acting efficaciously*. But this same proposition applies just as well to the kind of acting that is, as such, found only from the transcendental viewpoint: the kind of acting that is involved *in representation*. The law reason gives to itself for the former type of action, that is, the moral law, is not a law that it obeys necessarily, since it is directed at freedom. The law reason gives itself in the latter case, however, the law of thinking, is a law that it obeys necessarily, since in applying it the intellect, even though it is active, is not freely active. Thus the entire system of reason – both with respect to what *ought* to be and what is simply posited as existing in consequence of this ought, in accordance with the former kind of legislation, and with respect to what is immediately found as being, in accordance with the latter kind of legislation – is determined in advance, as something necessary, through reason itself. Yet what reason itself assembles according to its own laws, it also should undoubtedly be able to dissemble again according to these same laws; i.e., reason necessarily cognizes itself completely, and hence an analysis of its entire way of proceeding, that is, a system of reason, is possible. – Thus everything in our theory meshes with everything else, and the necessary presupposition is possible only under the condition of these specific results and no others. Either all philosophy has to be abandoned, or the absolute autonomy of reason must be conceded. The concept of philosophy is reasonable only on this presupposition.

The structure of *The System of Ethics*

Fichte's *System of Ethics* appeared a year after Kant published his own system of ethics, which he called the "Metaphysical First Principles of the Doctrine of Virtue" and which, together with his system of law or right, called the "Metaphysical First Principles of Doctrine of Right," make up Kant's last major work, *The Metaphysics of*

Morals.[34] Yet Fichte nowhere in his work refers to Kant's publication from the previous year, presumably because the elaboration of his own *System of Ethics* predates the appearance of Kant's parallel treatment. However, there are implicit and explicit references to other works in moral philosophy by Kant to be found in Fichte's text. Specifically, Fichte refers to Kant's earlier foundational writings in moral philosophy, which therefore form the background of Kant's own elaborated ethics of 1797 as well as the point of orientation for Fichte's parallel effort of 1798. These writings by Kant are *Groundwork of the Metaphysics of Morals* (1785),[35] *Critique of Practical Reason* (1788),[36] and *Religion Within the Boundaries of Mere Reason* (1793),[37] especially the first part of the latter, "On Radical Evil in Human Nature."

Kant's elaboration of an ethics in the "Metaphysical First Principles of Doctrine of Virtue" of *The Metaphysics of Morals* had focused on the systematic presentation of particular duties and had limited more general considerations to two comparatively brief introductions, the general introduction to *The Metaphysics of Morals* as a whole and the special introduction into that work's second part, the doctrine of virtue. By contrast, Fichte's *The System of Ethics* is for the most part an investigation into the principle of morality and the general conditions of its application. The treatment of ethics in the narrow sense is limited to the work's final thirty-some pages, amounting to no more than a ninth of the entire work.

The System of Ethics is divided into three lengthy parts (*Hauptstücke*), the third of which comprises more than half of the entire work. Part I contains the deduction of the principle of morality as a necessary condition for an individual human being's self-consciousness. Part II comprises the deduction of the applicability of the principle of morality, which proceeds by establishing our power to act in and upon a pre-existing world of objects and other human beings. On the basis of the prior deductions of the principle of morality and of its applicability, Part III demonstrates the actual systematic application of the previously deduced principle of morality by presenting, first, the formal conditions for

[34] Kant, *The Metaphysics of Morals*, in Kant, *Practical Philosophy*, ed. Allen Wood and Mary J. Gregor, trans. Mary J. Gregor (Cambridge: Cambridge University Press, 1996), pp. 363–603.
[35] Kant, *Groundwork of the Metaphysics of Morals*, in Kant, *Practical Philosophy*, pp. 41–108.
[36] Kant, *Critique of Practical Reason*, in Kant, *Practical Philosophy*, pp. 137–258.
[37] *Religion Within the Boundaries of Mere Reason*, in Kant, *Religion and Rational Theology*, ed. and trans. Allen W. Wood and George di Giovanni (Cambridge: Cambridge University Press, 1996), pp. 55–215.

the possibility of our actions (theory of the will, nature of evil) and, second, the content or material of the moral law (theory of the drives), and, third, the division of our duties into universal duties pertaining to all human beings and particular duties pertaining to groups and classes of human people (spouses, parents and children, and different estates and professions).

The philosophical contribution of *The System of Ethics*

Both chronologically and in terms of philosophical content, *The System of Ethics* lies closer to the above mentioned, second Jena presentation of the *Wissenschaftslehre* (*Wissenschaftslehre nova methodo*) than to the *Foundation of the Entire Wissenschaftslehre*. Whereas the latter had presented the absolutely first principles of knowledge in separation from their systematic unfolding and had observed a strict separation of the theoretical and practical parts of the theory of knowledge, Fichte subsequently achieved a doubly integrated presentation of the *Wissenschaftslehre*, which proceeds directly from the part containing the absolutely first principles into the general theory of what falls under those principles, within which the separation of the theoretical forms of knowledge from the practical forms of knowledge is itself grounded in and derived from a pre-disjunctive basic form of knowledge in general.

Like the first Jena presentation of the first principles of the *Wissenschaftslehre*, this second one "according to a new method" deals with the grounds of knowledge in relation to the finite subject of knowledge or human reason, which Fichte also terms "the I." The earlier version had artificially dissociated the I into the absolutely positing I (absolute I), on the one hand, and the theoretical I, which is determined by the object or the not-I (the knowing I), and the practical I, which determines the object or the not-I through its own activity (the doing I), on the other hand. By contrast, the *Wissenschaftslehre nova methodo* provides a genetic reconstruction of the development of the essential forms of consciousness along with those of its objects, starting from the minimally articulated, but infinitely differentiable basic form of the I, viz., the "original duplicity"[38] of the theoretical moment and the practical moment within the I. Fichte also characterizes the radical duality of the subject as its "ideal" (knowing) and "real" (doing) double nature and

---

[38] See *FTP*, p. 365 (*GA* IV / 2: 187 and IV / 3: 475).

uses the terms "subject–object" or "subject–objectivity" and "practical intelligence"[39] to convey the original complexity of the I.

The conception underlying this characterization is that of the I as always only active, is nothing but its activity, and is what it is only in consequence of its activity. But the I not only *is* this self-constituting activity; it also is this *for itself* or is *aware of itself as* active. In Fichte's terminology, the I "posits" or "sees" its own activity. The original duplicity of the I (or of knowledge as such) consists in the manner in which the real and ideal forms of activity reciprocally condition one another at every moment and stage in the constitution of I-hood.

The ideal–real double nature of the I not only prefigures the latter's subsequent differentiations into theoretical or cognitive and practical or volitional consciousness, it also prepares the articulation of the spheres or "worlds" that are correlated with each form of consciousness. In the one case, that of theoretical, cognitive or objective consciousness, this is the world of things ("the sensible world") and in the other case, that of practical or volitional consciousness or consciousness of doing, it is the world of other subjects (the "rational" or "spiritual" world).

In *The System of Ethics* Fichte distinguishes two possible forms under which the originally united two moments of the I (the subjective and the objective, the ideal and the real, or seeing and doing) are unfolded into relationships of succession. In the case of cognition, thinking – i.e., the conception of an object – appears to be the passively produced product of some being. In the case of willing – the conception of an end – being seems to follow or even to flow from some concept. Upon closer analysis, however, it becomes clear that the I is also active in the cognition of an object. It turns out that both the being that apparently precedes cognition and determines the latter as well as the being that is apparently first brought about by practical activity exist only in and through consciousness. For the *Wissenschaftslehre* knowing and doing, along with the aspects of the world they involve, are only finite forms for the appearance of the I's basic character, which can never appear as such and which Fichte understands as sheer "agility" – that which is absolute or infinite in the I, and which remains outside of the latter's manifold finite manifestations: "The

---

[39] See Ch. 1 of Fichte's fragmentation "Attempt at a New Presentation of the *Wissenschaftslehre*" (*IWL*, pp. 113–115 [*SW* 1: 276–278; *GA* 1/4: 527–530]). See too *FTP*, pp. 82 and 114 (*GA* IV/3: 326–328 and *GA* IV/2: 31–32 and IV/3: 346–347).

sole absolute on which all consciousness and all being rest is pure activity. [...] The one true thing is my self-activity" (p. 12).

But how does the I come to experience the pure self-activity that it is *as* its own? What is the I's original experience of itself as purely active or absolutely spontaneous, in short, as an I? According to Fichte, the I's authentic self-experience occurs in its experiencing itself as willing: "I find myself as myself only as willing" (p. 18). The proof of this first and only formally presented theorem in *The System of Ethics* can be summarized as follows (pp. 21ff.): All determinate thinking, no matter what the object that determines the act of thinking may be, is subject to the distinction, as well as the relation to each other, of what is subjective, which does the thinking, and what is objective, which is what is being thought. This also holds for the act of thinking of oneself, in which case the thinking and the thought are *materially* identical (since they concern the very same being) but in which nevertheless the *formal* distinction between what is subjective (thinking) and what is objective (thought) remains. To give up that distinction would mean the loss of any and all consciousness, whether of oneself or of anything else.

But how is the I as thinking able to grasp its material identity with the I as thought? The difficulty only increases if one realizes that this finding of itself on the part of the I must precede all self-knowledge by means of reflection inasmuch as it is supposed to render the latter possible in the first place. Only once the I has found the concept of itself can it refer reflectively to its own states and ascribe them to itself.

What is thought originally and pre-reflectively by the I in the peculiar case of the original, pre-reflective thinking of oneself (or the original finding of oneself) must be such that the I as subject (as engaged in thinking) is able to find itself for the first time only in this thought – although, to be sure, still under the form of being thought or being objective. Now the objective counterpart to the coincidence, contained in the concept of the I, the coincidence between that which is thinking and that which is being thought, is, according to Fichte, the I's own real activity insofar as the latter is directed only at itself and consists in the "real self-determining of oneself through oneself" (p. 22). Thus one could say that by means of one's acting or doing one accomplishes in a *real* way what one accomplishes in an *ideal* way by means of thinking of oneself. Yet it is essential to recall that such self-finding (or the original self-experience on the part of the ideal thinking of oneself) does not actually *precede* the doing (or the I's real acting-upon-itself), even though it *conditions* the latter.

The concept of the I – along with the original grasp of this concept *by* the I itself – is first obtained on the basis of the I's original self-experience in willing. But what is subjective (the thinking) does not find what is objective (the thought) immediately and as such, as a real self-determining activity that one simply encounters, as it were, naturally. In order for the I as subject to find *itself* in its real acting-upon-itself, the I must, or must be able to, relate this real self-determining activity to itself. It must, as Fichte likes to put it, posit this activity *as itself.* It is not simply the merely *found* real self-determining activity but the latter *as so posited*, i.e., the *understood* real acting-upon-itself, that forms the I's complete original self-experience as willing.

For Fichte the understanding or cognition of the real activity does not occur passively, as though it were a matter of observing a preexisting real activity. The original relation between thinking and willing is itself an *active* and *productive* relationship, a becoming-real of what is ideal as well as a becoming-active of the awareness of the same (the I's seeing of what is ideal). "Hence," as Fichte puts it, "in this case, the intellect is not merely an onlooker, but itself, as intellect, *becomes* – for itself [. . .] – the absolutely real force of the concept" (pp. 32–33).

Fichte's account thus subordinates the real force, insofar as it is understood or thought, to the concept. In order for practical self-determination to be an instance of willing, the real activity (force) has to be brought "under the dominion of the concept" (p. 32). Moreover, the concept that governs the practical self-determination of willing is not a concept of some objective, given being (that is, it is not a concept engendered by the reproductive power of imagination) but is instead a concept (engendered by the productive power of the imagination) of some *end* that has to be made actual or "realized" by the I itself.

In accordance with this shift from a theoretical to a practical conception of the concept in question (that is, the shift from the concept of an object to the concept of an end), a new, practical or activity-oriented form of thinking or of ideal activity emerges – one that no longer proceeds reproductively or by providing copies or after-images (*Nachbilder*), but which provides models or prefigurations (*Vorbilder*). In Fichte's terminology, the ideal activity is here engaged in "designing" or "projecting" (*entwerfen*) the concept of an end for its own real activity. This is how ideal thinking obtains practical causality in the realm of real being. Furthermore, the original status of the I's self-experience as willing lends to willing – and thus to the thinking ("designing") of ends associated with willing – primacy over mere knowledge or the thinking of objects. Only on the basis of such originally experienced and conceptually informed practical self-determination (that is, only on the basis of willing) and only by means of the material sphere involved in the exercise of willing does there come into view for the I a world of the senses or a "sensible world," to which the I can in turn relate in a narrowly cognitive, theoretical attitude.

The absolute spontaneity (or "self-activity") and independence (or "self-sufficiency") that lies at the root of the I as such and by virtue of which it is to be distinguished sharply from any Not-I or thing manifests itself in the willing I as a moment of *free* practical self-determination under the guidance of some concept of an end. After having established the basic character of I-hood in this manner, the next step is to consider how the radical freedom of self-determination and the "foreign" determination of the I's real activity by means of a concept can be successfully reconciled in the concept of *willing*. Fichte argues that the two basic elements of willing – freedom and the concept of an end – are not only compatible but mutually require each other. Only a willing that is determined by a concept, and by a quite specific concept at that, is free; and only a free willing is capable of being determined by the concept (p. 53). The basic practical concept regarding free willing is absolute self-sufficiency as such and for its own sake. The "original determination" (*Urbestimmung*, p. 53) of a finite rational being is thus its determination to absolute self-determination – to no determination other than the determination that it gives to itself (pp. 49ff.).

Accordingly, Fichte insists on the purely formal character of the moral law: "the moral law is only formal and must take its matter from elsewhere" (p. 166). For Fichte it cannot be the task of a systematic doctrine of ethics to prescribe to the practical subject laws that have been determined with respect to their content in the form of specific duties. For the identification of the latter each person is referred to his or her own conscience (pp. 156 and 173).

Nevertheless, *The System of Ethics* does have to indicate the basic and necessary *conditions* for the exercise or application of the formal and universal moral law. Fichte does this in the context of a theory of action that relates willing to the sensible (natural) as well as to the supersensible (purely rational) determining grounds of action and to this same action's sensible (material) as well as supersensible (moral) consequences. At the center of these highly original reflections on the dual natural–rational nature of human action stands the concept of drive (*Trieb*). The drive represents the medium for the practical determination or quasi-determination (to self-determination) of the subject. But determination through a drive is incomplete or only quasi-determination in that, in each and every case, a drive is able to exercise its causal power only when sanctioned by the freely choosing power of arbitrary will (*Willkür*, p. 159), which is what always occurs in completing an act of self-determination – i.e., in freely choosing to allow oneself to be determined by a drive.

In Fichte's elaborate reconstruction of the drives that practically determine (or quasi-determine, viz., determine-to-self-determine) human conduct, pure, absolutely self-determined willing is correlated with its own drive, the "pure drive," from which there ensues – under the influence of the "natural drive" – the corresponding "mixed, moral drive," which is causally effective in the natural world. Unfortunately the details of Fichte's attempt at reconciling, even integrating practical reason and nature inside as well as outside the subject remain somewhat unclear. This much is certain, however: no matter how much Fichte stresses the natural basis of all willing, including moral willing, within the drives, he always insists that it is neither nature within us nor nature outside us that acts when we act, but rather the I as reason. "*I* will," declares Fichte, "not nature" (p. 148).

Fichte then goes on to emphasize that the final goal of rational willing – namely, perfect morality – is an unobtainable ideal that ought to be infinity approached over the course of an individual ethical life. The actions of every rational individual occur as part of an "individual series," the infinite continuation of which would lead to the final goal of absolute independence. Fichte traces the coordination of the infinitely many ideal series of actions back to an alleged "pre-determination" (pp. 226ff.), which, however, is meant only to concern the content and not the actual time of occurrence of a predetermined action. This account of the external and un-free pre-establishment of the manifold of rational individuals and their actions is surely one of the more problematic aspects of the Jena *System of Ethics*. At the end of his years in Jena and during his first years in Berlin Fichte was still searching for an adequate presentation of that "transcendental system of the intelligible world"[40] in which *free* beings form part of a comprehensive whole that does not restrict their freedom but instead realizes it. This would presumably have been one of the chief topics of his projected but unwritten "philosophy of religion" from the Jena period.

---

[40] The phrase occurs in Fichte's letter to Schelling, December 27, 1800 (*GA* III/4 406).

Chronology

Titles in italics indicate works published by Fichte

1762	Born May 19 in Rammenau, in the Lower Lusatia area of Saxony in today's Eastern Germany, the first child of the ribbon weaver Christian Fichte and his wife, Johanna Maria Dorothea, née Schurich
1774–1780	Scholarship pupil in the Princely Secondary School at Pforta, near Naumburg (Schulpforta)
1780–1784	Student at the universities of Jena, Wittenberg and Leipzig, no degree earned
1785–1793	Private tutor in households in Leipzig, Zurich and Eastern Prussia
1790	Reads Kant's *Critique of Pure Reason, Critique of Practical Reason,* and *Critique of the Power of Judgment*
1792	Visits Kant in Königsberg; *Attempt at a Critique of All Revelation*
1793	Returns to Zurich; *Contribution to the Rectification of the Public Judgments About the French Revolution*; marries Johanna Rahn of Zurich
1794	Professor at the University of Jena; *Foundation of the Entire Wissenschaftslehre* (Parts I and II)
1795	*Foundation of the Entire Wissenschaftslehre* (Part III)
1796	*Foundation of Natural Law* (Part I)
1797	*Foundation of Natural Law* (Part II)
1798	*The System of Ethics* and *On the Basis of our Belief in a Divine Governance of the World*

1798	November: beginning of the atheism dispute
1799	Loses his professorship at Jena
1800	Moves to Berlin; *The Vocation of Man*
1804	Delivers three private lecture cycles on the *Wissenschaftslehre*
1805	Professor in Erlangen
1806	*Main Characteristics of the Present Age*; *Initiation to the Blessed Life*
1807	October: flees to Königsberg, then to Copenhagen after Prussia's defeat by Napoleon's forces; returns to Berlin
1808	*Addresses to the German Nation*
1810	Professor at the University of Berlin, Dean of the Philosophical Faculty
1811	First elected Rector of the University of Berlin (resigns in April 1812)
1813	Prussian uprising against Napoleon
1814	Dies January 29 in Berlin

Further reading

A detailed intellectual biography of the early Fichte is provided in Anthony J. La Vopa, *Fichte. The Self and the Calling of Philosophy, 1762–1799* (Cambridge: Cambridge University Press, 2001). See too "Fichte in Jena," the Editor's Introduction to Fichte, *Early Philosophical Writings*, ed. and trans. Daniel Breazeale (Ithaca, NY: Cornell University Press, 1988). The philosophical context of the early Fichte is explored in Frederick C. Beiser, *The Fate of Reason. German Philosophy from Kant to Fichte* (Cambridge, Mass.: Harvard University Press, 1987). A major survey of the period, including Fichte's role in it, is offered by Dieter Henrich, *Between Kant and Hegel. Lectures on German Idealism* (Cambridge, Mass.: Harvard University Press, 2003). The same terrain is covered in the form of individual essays in *The Cambridge Companion to German Idealism*, ed. Karl Ameriks (Cambridge: Cambridge University Press, 2000). Some crucial primary sources from the period leading up to Fichte's work are gathered in *Between Kant and Hegel. Texts in the Development of Post-Kantian Idealism*, trans. and ed. George di Giovanni and H. S. Harris (Hackett: Indianapolis/ Cambridge, 2000). Two book-length studies of the early Fichte, with different but complementary thematic focus, are Frederick Neuhouser, *Fichte's Theory of Subjectivity* (Cambridge: Cambridge University Press, 1990) and Wayne Martin, *Idealism and Objectivity. Understanding Fichte's Jena Project* (Stanford: Stanford University Press, 1997). Three summary assessments of Fichte's significance for philosophy past and present are Daniel Breazeale, "Why Fichte Now?", *Journal of Philosophy* 87 (1991), 524–531, Allen Wood, "Fichte's Philosophical Revolution," *Philosophical Topics* 19 (1992), 1–28, and Robert B. Pippin, *Hegel's*

Idealism. The Satisfactions of Self-Consciousness (Cambridge: Cambridge University Press, 1989), chapter 3, entitled "Fichte's Contribution."

The relation between Fichte's theoretical and practical philosophy, including his ethics, is explored in Günter Zöller, *Fichte's Transcendental Philosophy: The Original Duplicity of Intelligence and Will* (Cambridge: Cambridge University Press, 1998). Fichte's innovative and influential doctrine of recognition is presented in Robert R. Williams, *Recognition. Fichte and Hegel* (Albany: State University of New York Press, 1992). The relation between law and ethics in Fichte is discussed in Luc Ferry, "The Distinction between Right and Ethics in the Early Philosophy of Fichte," *Philosophical Forum*, 19 (1987–1988), 182–196 and in Frederick Neuhouser, "Fichte and the Relationship between Right and Morality," in *Fichte. Historical Contexts/Contemporary Perspectives*, ed. Daniel Breazeale and Tom Rockmore (Atlantic Highlands, New Jersey: Humanities Press, 1994), 158–180.

While there has been a considerable upsurge of work on Fichte in North America over the past fifteen years, a closer study of Fichte's philosophy also needs to take into account the work published on Fichte in Europe, where his philosophy has found considerable attention since the late 1960s, especially in Germany, Italy, and France. Of particular interest to readers of this book should be a collection of essays, some of them in English, devoted entirely to *The System of Ethics, Fichte. Das System der Sittenlehre (1798)*, ed. Jean-Christophe Merle and Andreas Schmidt (Frankfurt/M.: Klostermann, 2005).

Note on the text and translation

Source of the text

The present edition of *The System of Ethics* contains a new translation of Fichte's main work in moral philosophy, which was first published in 1798 under the title, *Das System der Sittenlehre nach den Principien der Wissenschaftslehre*. (In 1812 Fichte delivered a new – and very different – series of lectures under the title *Sittenlehre*, which was subsequently edited and posthumously published by his son.) The translation is based on the critical edition of *Das System der Sittenlehre nach den Principien der Wissenschaftslehre*, published under the auspices of the Bavarian Academy of Sciences, in *J. G. Fichte-Gesamtausgabe*, series 1 (= works published by Fichte himself), vol. 5, ed. Reinhard Lauth and Hans Gliwitzky (Stuttgart-Bad Cannstatt: Frommann-Holzboog, 1977), pp. 1–314.

The numbers inserted throughout the translation placed in bold print within square brackets into the main body of the text, e.g. [IV, 202], refer to the pagination of the earlier standard edition of the same work in vol. IV, pp. 1–365, of *Johann Gottlieb Fichtes sämmtliche Werke*, ed. Immanuel Hermann Fichte (Berlin: Veit & Comp., 1854/46) and are placed at the approximate place of the page breaks in the corresponding German text. The latter edition, edited by Fichte's son, who was a philosopher in his own right, has been reprinted as *Fichtes Werke*, ed. Immanuel Hermann Fichte (Berlin: Walter de Gruyter and Co., 1971). Its pagination is also contained in the margins of the edition of the Bavarian Academy listed above as well as in the separate edition of *The System of Ethics* available in the *Philosophische Bibliothek*, originally edited by Fritz Medicus and re-edited first by Manfred Zahn and most recently by Hansjürgen

Verweyen (Hamburg: Felix Meiner, 1995). Hence the parenthetical pagination permits standardizing references to Fichte's text across editions and facilitates consulting the German original in each of the editions just described.

Philosophically significant differences between the editions of Fichte's text in the modern Bavarian Academy edition and the classical edition by Fichte's son are specified in the notes to the text. The notes also record a number of marginal handwritten additions by Fichte in his personal copy of the first edition of the work from 1798. Fichte's son included those remarks in his edition, from where they were taken over into the Bavarian Academy edition and the edition in the *Philosophische Bibliothek*. These original marginalia are also included, as notes, in the present edition, with the abbreviation "*SW*" referring to Immanuel Hermann Fichte's edition as their original source.

Special care has been taken to preserve the original presentation of the text, with its many headings and subheadings, designed to guide the reader through the argumentative architecture of the work. For the same reason, the varied typography (large caps, spaced text, italics, small caps) has, insofar as possible, been reproduced as it appears in the original. An exception to this practice concerns the occasional use of gothic script that seems to have slipped into the original edition at proof stage when letters from a different font set were used to correct printing errors; all gothic lettering of the original has been rendered in regular font.

Fichte's internal references to other parts of *The System of Ethics* have been left in their original positions in the main text and have been transposed from the pagination of the original edition to that of the present translation. In addition to Fichte's printed and handwritten notes, this edition contains explanatory notes written by the editors and based, in part, on the material contained in the edition of the work by the Bavarian Academy of Sciences. Each note by Fichte is indicated as such. All other notes are by the editors.

Editorial interpolations and occasional German terms appear within the body of Fichte's text within square brackets. All material within square brackets has been inserted by the editors.

Note on the translation

The chief aim of the present edition has been to provide an accurate translation that places the modern English reader in a situation comparable to that of a reader of modern German approaching the German original. Accordingly, much of Fichte's highly original and even audacious philosophical writing style has been preserved, especially the complex syntax and the distinct vocabulary.

Particular care has been taken to render Fichte's technical terms in a consistent manner throughout the translation. But philological differences between the German and English languages place a limit on the extent to which a one-to-one correlation between a given German word and its English translation and vice versa can be achieved or is even advisable. The following list identifies those technical terms of the German original for which there is more than one English word used in the translation, distinguishing the meanings involved, as well as some English words that render more than one German technical term, indicating whether different meanings are involved or whether it is a case of practically identical meaning, as when both a Germanic and a Latin-based word are used in German to designate the same thing. In addition, the list contains information about important terminological practices adopted in the present translation. For further information concerning translation of German terms see the detailed German–English and English–German glossaries at the end this volume.

"Absolute," "absolutely," "purely and simply" render *absolute*, *schlechthin*, and *schlechtweg*, the latter occurring only rarely in the text.

"Being," used as a noun, renders both *Sein* and *Wesen*, the latter in those cases where the word has the meaning of "individual thing" (Latin *ens*). The other meaning of *Wesen* is rendered as "essence" (Latin *essentia*).

"To act" and "action" render *handeln* and *Handlung*; "to do" and "doing" are used to translate *tun* and *Tun*.

"Boundary" and its related forms ("to bound," "bounded") translates *Grenze*, *grenzen*, and *begrenzt*. *Schranke* is rendered as "limit."

"Cognition" renders *Erkenntnis*, whereas "knowledge" is used for *Wissen*.

"To design" renders *entwerfen*, a key term in this work and one that Fichte employs to designate the I's activity of constructing for itself a specific concept of an end to be achieved through its own acting. This term carries the dual sense of freely "devising" or "sketching" the concept in question and then actively "projecting" it as the concept of something that ought to exist. Such a concept serves as a "prefiguration" or "model" (*Vorbild*) of an action to be undertaken, in contrast with a cognitive concept, which is an image or "copy" (*Nachbild*) of some object of cognition.

"To determine" and its related nominal and adjectival forms ("determination," "determinable," etc.) render *Bestimmung* and its derivatives, except where *Bestimmung* has the sense of "calling," in which case it is rendered as "vocation."

"To act efficaciously," "to effect," and "to have an effect" or "to be effective" render *wirken*. *Wirksamkeit* is rendered as "efficacy" or "efficacious action."

"End" (in the sense of a goal or aim of action) renders *Zweck*, whereas *Zweckmäßigkeit* is rendered throughout as "purposiveness." *Zweckmäßig* is rendered either as "purposive" or as "appropriate."

"Ethics" and "ethical" render *Sittenlehre* and *sittlich*, respectively, while "morality" renders *Sittlichkeit* as well as *Moralität*. "Moral law" and "principle of morality" are used to translate *Sittengesetz* and *Prinzip der Sittlichkeit*, respectively. "Moral" renders *moralisch*.

"Existence" renders both *Dasein* and *Existenz*.

"Ground" and "basis" render *Grund*, except where the latter is rendered as "reason," in the sense of a reason for a conclusion.

"The I" renders *das Ich*, and "I-hood" renders *Ichheit*.

"Object" renders the both *Objekt* and *Gegenstand*.

"Power" renders both *Gewalt* – as distinct from "might" (*Macht*) – and *Kraft*, except where the latter is translated as "force." *Vermögen*, a term often translated as "faculty," is here translated as "power" or "capacity."

"Principle" renders *Grundsatz* and *Prinzip*.

"Reason" renders *Vernunft* but also *Grund* in cases where the latter word means a reason for a conclusion.

"Reflection" renders both *Reflexion* and *Überlegung*. It occasionally renders *Nachdenken* as well, though the latter is usually rendered as "meditation."

"Representation" renders *Vorstellung*, and "presentation" renders *Darstellung*.

xli

"Self-activity" is used to translate *Selbsttätigkeit*, while "self-sufficiency" renders *Selbstständigkeit*. For the former concept, Fichte also occasionally uses as a synonym "spontaneity" (*Spontaneität*) and for the latter "independence" (*Unabhängigkeit*).

The phrase "to be supposed to" renders *sollen*, except where the latter is translated as "ought."

The technical term *Wissenschaftslehre*, coined by Fichte, remains untranslated. Previous published translations of the term include "Science of Knowledge" and "Doctrine of Science."

Abbreviations

AA   *Kants gesammelte Schriften*, ed. Königliche Preußische Akademie der Wissenschaften (Berlin: Reimer/de Gruyter, 1900 ff.)

CJ   Kant, *Critique of the Power of Judgment*, ed. Paul Guyer, trans. Paul Guyer and Eric Matthews (Cambridge: Cambridge University Press, 2000)

CpR   Kant, *Critique of Pure Reason*, ed. and trans. Paul Guyer and Allen W. Wood (Cambridge: Cambridge University Press, 1998)

CprR   Kant, *Critique of Practical Reason*, in Kant, *Practical Philosophy*, ed. Mary J. Gregor and Allen Wood, trans. Mary J. Gregor (Cambridge: Cambridge University Press, 1996)

EPW   Fichte, *Early Philosophical Writings*, ed. and trans. Daniel Breazeale (Ithaca, NY: Cornell University Press, 1988)

FNR   Fichte, *Foundations of Natural Right*, ed. Frederick Neuhouser, trans. Michael Baur (Cambridge: Cambridge University Press, 2000)

FTP   Fichte, *Foundations of Transcendental Philosophy (Wissenschaftslehre) nova methodo*, ed. and trans. Daniel Breazeale (Ithaca, NY: Cornell University Press, 1992)

GA   *J. G. Fichte-Gesamtausgabe der Bayerischen Akademie der Wissenschaften*, ed. Reinhard Lauth, Hans Gliwitzky†, and Erich Fuchs (Stuttgart-Bad Cannstatt: Frommann-Holzboog, 1964ff.)

GMM   Kant, *Groundwork of the Metaphysics of Morals*, in Kant, *Practical Philosophy*, ed. Allen Wood and Mary J. Gregor, trans. Mary J. Gregor (Cambridge: Cambridge University Press, 1996)

xliii

GMS   Kant, *Grundlegung zur Metaphysik der Sitten* (1785), *AA* 4: 385–463

GNR   Fichte, *Grundlage des Naturrechts* (1796/97)

GWL   Fichte, *Grundlage der gesammten Wissenschaftslehre* (1794/95)

IWL   Fichte, *Introductions to the Wissenschaftslehre and Other Writings*, ed. and trans. Daniel Breazeale (Indianapolis: Hackett, 1994)

KpV   Kant, *Kritik der praktischen Vernunft* (1788)

KrV   Kant, *Kritik der reinen Vernunft*. As is customary, references to *KrV* will be simply to the page numbers of the A (1781) and B (1787) eds.

KU   Kant, *Kritik der Urteilskraft*

PFM   Kant, *Prolegomena to any Future Metaphysics*, trans. Gary Hatfield, in Kant, *Theoretical Philosophy After 1781*, ed. Henry Allison and Peter Heath (Cambridge: Cambridge University Press, 2002), pp. 49–161

RBR   Immanuel Kant, *Religion Within the Boundaries of Mere Reason*, in Kant, *Religion and Rational Theology*, ed. and trans. Allen W. Wood and George di Giovanni (Cambridge: Cambridge University Press, 1996)

SS   Fichte, *Das System der Sittenlehre* (1798)

SW   *Johann Gottlieb Fichtes sämmtliche Werke*, ed. I. H. Fichte, 8 vols. (Berlin: Viet and Co., 1845–1846); rpt., along with the 3 vols. of *Johann Gottlieb Fichtes nachgelassene Werke* (Bonn: Adolphus-Marcus, 1834–1835), as *Fichtes Werke* (Berlin: de Gruyter, 1971)

WLnm   Fichte, *Wissenschaftslehre nova methodo. WLnm (H)* ("Halle Nachschrift," 1796/97); *WLnm [K]* ("Krause Nachschrift," 1798/99)

The System of Ethics

According to the Principles of the *Wissenschaftslehre*

Table of contents

Introduction

1

I will begin by characterizing the task of philosophy as that of answering the following, familiar question: how can something objective ever become something subjective; how can a being for itself ever become something represented [*vorgestellten*]? No one will ever explain how this remarkable transformation takes place without finding a point where the objective and the subjective are not at all distinct from one another but are completely one and the same. Our system establishes just such a point and then proceeds from there. The point in question is "I-hood" [*Ichheit*], intelligence, reason – or whatever one wishes to call it.

This absolute identity of the subject and the object in the I can only be inferred; it cannot be demonstrated, so to speak, "immediately," as a fact of actual consciousness. As soon as any actual consciousness occurs, even if it is only the consciousness of ourselves, the separation [between subject and object] ensues. I am conscious of myself only insofar as I distinguish myself, as the one who is conscious, from me, as the object of this consciousness. *The entire mechanism of consciousness rests on the various aspects of this separation of what is subjective from what is objective, and, in turn, on the unification of the two* [IV, 2].

2

The first way what is subjective and what is objective are unified, or viewed as harmonizing, is when *I engage in cognition*. In this case, what is subjective follows from what is objective; the former is supposed to agree with the latter. *Theoretical* philosophy investigates how we arrive

7

at the assertion of such a harmony. – [The second way what is subjective and what is objective are unified is] when *I act efficaciously* [*ich wirke*]. In this case, the two are viewed as harmonizing in such a way that what is objective is supposed to follow from what is subjective; a being is supposed to result from my concept (the concept of an end [*Zweckbegriff*]). *Practical* philosophy has to investigate the origin of the assumption of such a harmony.

Up until now only the first of these questions, the one concerning how we might come to assert the correspondence of our representations with things that supposedly exist independently of those representations, has been raised. Philosophy has as yet not even so much as wondered about the second point, that is, about how it might be possible to think of some of our concepts as capable of being presented [*darstellbar*] and, in part, as actually presented in nature, which subsists without any help from us. People have found it quite natural that we are able to have an effect upon the world. That is, after all, what we do all the time, as everyone knows. This is a fact of consciousness, and that suffices.

3

Ethics [*Sittenlehre*] is practical philosophy. Just as theoretical philosophy has to present that system of necessary thinking according to which our representations correspond to a being, so practical philosophy has to provide an exhaustive presentation of that system of necessary thinking according to which a being corresponds to and follows from our representations. It therefore behooves us to consider the question just raised and, first of all, to show how we ever come to take some of our representations to be the ground of a being, and second, to indicate the specific origin of that system of those of our concepts from which a being is simply supposed to follow necessarily [IV, 3].

The goal of this introduction is to summarize briefly, from a single viewpoint, what will be presented in detail concerning these issues in the inquiry that follows.

4

I find myself to be acting efficaciously in the world of sense. All consciousness arises from this discovery. Without this consciousness of my own efficacy [*Wirksamkeit*], there is no self-consciousness; without self-consciousness, there is no consciousness of something else that is not supposed to be I myself. Anyone desiring a proof of this assertion will find a detailed proof of it in Chapter Two, below. This assertion is here presented merely as an immediate fact of consciousness, in order to connect it with our further reasoning.

What manifold is contained in this representation of my efficacy? And how might I arrive at this manifold?

Let us provisionally assume that the representation of my own efficacy includes the following: a representation of the *stuff* [*Stoff*] that endures while I am acting efficaciously and is absolutely unchangeable thereby; a representation of the *properties* of this stuff, properties that are changed by my efficacy; and a representation of this *progressive process of change*, which continues until the shape that I intend is there. And let us also assume that all these representations contained in the representation of my efficacy are *given* to me from outside (an expression which, to be sure, I do not understand), i.e., that this is a matter of *experience*, or however one may express this non-thought. Even if we make this assumption, there still remains something within the representation of my efficacy which simply cannot come to me from outside but must lie within myself, something that I cannot experience and cannot learn but must know immediately: namely, that *I myself* am supposed to be the ultimate ground of the change that has occurred.

"I am the ground of this change." This means the same as, and nothing other than, the following: that which *knows* about this change is also that which *effectuates* it; the subject of consciousness and the principle of efficacy are one. But what I assert at the origin of all knowledge concerning the knowing subject itself – what I know simply by virtue of the fact that I know anything whatsoever [IV, 4] – this is not something I could have drawn from some other knowledge. I know it immediately; I purely and simply posit it.

Accordingly, insofar as I know anything at all I know that I am active. Consciousness of myself, that is, consciousness of myself as an active subject, is contained and thereby immediately posited in the mere form of knowledge as such.

Now it might well be that this same mere form of knowledge also contains, if not immediately, then mediated by the immediate knowledge just indicated, all of the remaining manifold that lies in the above-mentioned representation of my efficacy. Should this prove to be the case, then we would rid ourselves of the awkward assumption that this manifold comes from outside, and we could do this simply by virtue of the fact that we could explain this in another, more natural way. By deriving the necessity of such an assumption immediately from the presupposition of any consciousness whatsoever, we would answer the question raised above concerning how we come to ascribe to ourselves efficacy in a sensible world outside of us.

We will endeavor to determine whether such a derivation is possible. The plan for this derivation is as follows. We have just seen what is contained in the representation of our efficacy. The presupposition is that this representation is contained in consciousness as such and is necessarily posited along with it. Our point of departure is therefore the form of consciousness as such. We will derive things from this, and our investigation will be concluded when the path of our derivations returns us to the representation of our sensible efficacy.

5

I posit myself as active. According to what was said above, this means that I make a distinction within myself between a knowing subject and a real force [*reelle Kraft*], which, as such, does not *know* but *is*; and yet I view the two as absolutely one. How do I come to make this distinction? How do I arrive at precisely this [IV, 5] determination of what is being distinguished? The second question is likely to be answered by answering the first one.

I do not know without knowing *something*. I do not know anything about myself without becoming something for myself through this knowledge – or, which is simply to say the same thing, without separating something subjective in me from something objective. As soon as consciousness is posited, this separation is posited; without the latter no consciousness whatsoever is possible. Through this very separation, however, the relation of what is subjective and what is objective to each other is also immediately posited. What is objective is supposed to subsist through itself, without any help from what is subjective and independently of it. What is subjective is supposed to depend on what is objective and to receive its material determination from it alone. Being exists on its own, but knowledge depends on being: the two must appear to us in this way, just as surely as anything at all appears to us, as surely as we possess consciousness.

We thereby obtain the following, important insight: knowledge and being are not separated outside of consciousness and independent of it; instead, they are separated only within consciousness, since this separation is a condition for the possibility of all consciousness, and it is only through this separation that the two of them first arise. There is no being except by means of consciousness, just as there is, outside of consciousness, no knowing, as a merely subjective reference to a being. I am required to bring about a separation simply in order to be able to say to myself "I"; and yet it is only by saying "I" and only insofar as I say this that such a separation occurs. The unity [*das Eine*] that is divided – which thus lies at the basis of all consciousness and due to which what is subjective and what is objective in consciousness are immediately posited as one – is absolute = X, and this can in no way appear within consciousness as something simple.

Here we find an immediate correspondence between what is subjective and what is objective: I know myself because I am, and I am because I know myself. It may well be that any other correspondence between the two – whether what is objective is supposed to follow from what is subjective, [IV, 6] as in the concept of an end, or whether what is subjective is supposed to follow from what is objective, as in the concept of a cognition – is nothing but a particular aspect of this immediate correspondence. If this could actually be demonstrated, then this would at the same time prove that everything that can occur in consciousness is posited in accordance with the mere form of consciousness – inasmuch as this immediate separation and correspondence is the form of consciousness itself, and these other separations and correspondences exhaust the entire content of all possible consciousness. How things stand in that regard will undoubtedly emerge in the course of our investigation.

6

I posit myself as active. With respect to the state of mind to be investigated, this certainly does not mean that I ascribe to myself activity in general, but rather that I ascribe to myself a *determinate* activity, precisely this one and not another.

As we have just seen, what is subjective, simply by virtue of being separated from what is objective, becomes entirely dependent and thoroughly constrained; and the ground of this material determinacy, the determinacy of what is subjective with regard to *what* it is, lies by no means within what is subjective, but in what is objective. What is subjective appears as a mere cognizing of something that hovers before it; in no way and in no respect does it appear as actively producing the representation. This is necessarily the case here at the origin of all consciousness, where the separation of what is subjective and what is objective is complete. In the progressive development of consciousness, however, by means of a synthesis, what is subjective also appears as free and determining, inasmuch as it appears as *engaged in abstracting*. It is then able, for example, freely to describe activity in general and as such, even though it is not able to perceive the latter. At this point in our investigation, however, we remain at the origin of all consciousness, and hence the representation to be investigated is necessarily a perception; i.e., in this representation what is subjective appears to be entirely and thoroughly determined, without any effort on its own part [IV, 7].

Now what does "a *determinate* activity" mean, and how does an activity become determinate or determined? Merely by having some resistance posited in opposition to it – posited in opposition: that is to say, a resistance that is thought of by means of ideal activity and imagined to be standing over against the latter. Wherever and whenever you see activity, you necessarily see resistance as well, for otherwise you see no activity.

First of all, one should not fail to note the following: that such a resistance appears is entirely the result of the laws of consciousness, and the resistance can therefore rightly be considered a product of these laws. The law itself, in accordance with which the resistance is present for us, can be derived from the necessary separation of what is subjective from what is objective and from the absolutely posited relation of the former to the latter, as has just been done. For this reason, my consciousness of the resistance is an indirect or mediated consciousness, mediated by the fact that I [here] have to consider myself purely as a *cognizing* subject and, in this cognition, entirely dependent upon objectivity.

Next, one has to develop the distinctive features [*Merkmale*] of this representation of resistance and do so merely from the manner in which it originates. This resistance is represented as the opposite of activity, hence as something that merely endures, lying there quietly and dead, something that merely *is* and in no way *acts*, something that strives only to continue to exist and thus resists the influence of freedom upon its territory only with that degree of force that is required to remain what it is but is never able to attack the latter on its own territory. In short, resistance is represented as *mere objectivity*. The proper name for something of this sort is *stuff*. – Furthermore, all consciousness is conditioned by consciousness of myself, which in turn is conditioned by the perception of my activity, which is itself conditioned by the positing of some resistance as such. Resistance of the sort just indicated thus extends necessarily throughout the entire sphere of my consciousness. It continuously accompanies my consciousness [IV, 8], and freedom can never be posited as able to do anything whatsoever about this situation, since otherwise freedom itself, along with all consciousness and all being, would fall away. – The representation of some stuff that simply cannot be changed by my efficacy, something we earlier found to be contained in the perception of our own efficacy, is thus derived from the laws of consciousness.

One of the two main questions raised above has now been answered, namely: how we come to assume something subjective, a concept, that is supposed to follow from something objective, some being, and that is supposed to be determined thereby. As we have seen, this is the necessary consequence of the fact that we separate something subjective and something objective within us in consciousness and yet regard them as one. However, the particular determinate relationship, in which what is subjective is supposed to be determined by what is objective, and not vice versa, arises from the absolutely posited relation of what is subjective as such to what is objective as such. The principle and the problem of all theoretical philosophy has thereby been derived.

7

I posit myself as active. We have said enough about what is subjective and what is objective in this positing, about their separation, their unification, and their original relation to each other. However, we have not yet investigated the predicate that is to be ascribed to the unified [*dem Einen*] and indivisible I. What does it mean to be *active*, and what do I really posit when I ascribe activity to myself?

It is here presupposed that the reader possesses some image of activity in general, of some agility, mobility or however one may want to express it in words, for this is something that cannot be demonstrated to anyone who does not discover it in the intuition of himself. As we have just seen, this inner agility absolutely cannot be ascribed to something objective as such. What is objective simply endures; it simply is and remains as it is. Agility pertains only to what is subjective, to intelligence as such, with respect to the form of its acting. I say, "with respect to its form," because, as we saw above, the material of the determination is supposed to be determined in a different respect by what is objective. With respect to its form, the act of representing is intuited as a supremely free [IV, 9] inner movement. Now *I*, the unified and indivisible I, am supposed to be active; and that which acts upon the object is without any doubt what is objective in me, the real force.[1] Taking all of this into consideration, my activity can be posited only in such a way that I start with what is subjective, as determining what is objective, in short, with the causality of a mere concept exercised on what is objective, and to this extent the concept in question is not in turn determined by something else objective but is determined absolutely in and through itself.

With this, the second of the two main questions raised earlier has now been answered, namely: how I come to assume that something objective follows from something subjective, a being from a concept; and the principle of all practical philosophy is thereby derived. This assumption arises because I have to posit myself absolutely as active, and, since I have distinguished something subjective and something objective within myself, I cannot describe this activity otherwise than as the causality of a concept. – Absolute activity is the one predicate that belongs to me purely and simply and immediately; the one and only possible way of presenting such a concept [of absolute activity], and the way that is rendered necessary by the laws of consciousness, is as causality by means of a concept. Absolute activity in this shape is also called *freedom*. Freedom is the sensible representation of self-activity [*Selbsttätigkeit*], and it arises through opposition to the constrained state [*Gebundenheit*] both of the object and of ourselves as intelligence, insofar as we relate an object to ourselves.

I posit myself as free insofar as I explain a sensible acting, or being, as arising from my concept, which is then called the "concept of an end." Therefore the fact presented above – that I find myself to be acting

---

[1] According to Fichte's account of the I, as developed, for example, in his lectures on "Foundations of Transcendental Philosophy (*Wissenschaftslehre*) *nova methodo*" [= *WLnm*], the I possesses both "real" and "ideal" force: the former is the power to engage in real, efficacious action; the latter is the power to cognize its actions, its objects, and itself. See § 3 of *WLnm*, in *J. G. Fichte – Gesamtausgabe der Bayerischen Akademie der Wissenschaften*, ed. Reinhard Lauth, Hans Gliwitzky†, and Erich Fuchs (Stuttgart-Bad Cannstatt: Frommann-Holzboog, 1964 ff.) [henceforth = *GA*], IV/2: 44–47 and IV/3: 359–363. In English, see J. G. Fichte, *Foundations of Transcendental Philosophy (Wissenschaftslehre) nova methodo*, ed. and trans. Daniel Breazeale (Ithaca, NY: Cornell University Press, 1992) [henceforth = *FTP*], pp. 139–146.

efficaciously – is possible only under the condition that I presuppose a concept designed [*entworfenen*] by myself, which is supposed to guide my efficacious acting and in which the latter is both formally grounded and materially determined. Thus, in addition to the various distinctive features [IV, 10] that were shown above to be contained in the representation of our efficacy, we here obtain a new one, which it was not necessary to note earlier and which has here been derived along with the others. It must be noted, however, that the preceding act of designing such a concept [of an end] is merely *posited* and belongs solely to the sensible aspect of our self-activity.

As has just been noted, the concept from which an objective determination is to follow, the concept of an end, as it is called, is not itself determined in turn by something objective but is determined absolutely by itself. Were this not the case, then I would not be absolutely active and would not be immediately posited in this way; instead, my activity would depend on some being and would be mediated by that being – which contradicts our presupposition. To be sure, in the course of the further development of consciousness and in connection with this same concept, the concept of an end appears as conditioned, though not determined, by the cognition of a being. Here, however, at the origin of all consciousness, where we *start* with activity, and where this activity is absolute, the matter is not to be viewed in this manner. – The most important result of all this is the following: *there is an absolute independence and self-sufficiency of the mere concept* (that which is "categorical" in the so-called categorical imperative), due to a causality of what is subjective exercised upon what is objective – just as there is supposed to be an absolutely self-posited *being* (of the material stuff), due to a causality of what is objective exercised upon what is subjective. With this we have joined together the two extremes of the entire world of reason.

(Anyone who correctly grasps at least this self-sufficiency of the concept, will view our entire system in the most perfect light, from which will arise the most unshakable conviction concerning the truth of the same.)

8

Something objective follows from a concept. How is this possible? What can it mean? It can mean only that the concept itself appears to me as something objective. But the concept of an end [IV, 11], viewed objectively, is called *an act of willing* [*ein Wollen*], and the representation of a will [*eines Willens*] is nothing other than this necessary aspect of the concept of an end, which is posited solely in order to make possible the consciousness of our activity. What is spiritual in me, intuited immediately as the principle of an efficacious action, becomes for me a will.

Now, however, *I* am supposed to have an effect upon that stuff, the origin of which was described above. But it is impossible for me to think of this stuff as being affected by anything other than something that is itself stuff. Consequently, since I do – as I must – think of myself as having an effect on this stuff, I also become for myself stuff; and insofar as I view myself in this way, I call myself a *material body*. Viewed as a principle of an efficacy in the world of bodies, I am an articulated body; and the representation of my body is itself nothing but the representation of myself as a cause in the world of bodies and is therefore indirectly only a certain way of looking at my own absolute activity.

But now the will is supposed to exercise causality, and indeed, an immediate causality upon my body; and the body as an instrument, that is, the articulated body [*die Artikulation*], extends only as far as this immediate causality of the will extends. (This preliminary survey does not include that aspect of my body known as *organization*.)[2] The will is therefore also different from the body, and it appears as not being the same as the body. This distinction, however, is nothing more than yet another separation of what is subjective from what is objective, or more specifically, it is a particular aspect of the original separation. In this relationship the will is what is subjective and the body is what is objective.

9

But what is my actual causality? What is the change that is supposed to ensue thereby in the sensible world? What is the sensible world that is supposed to be changeable by means of this causality?

---

[2] Concerning the difference between the human body as a mere organism or "organization" and the human body as an essential tool or instrument of the will, that is, as an "articulated" body, see § 11 of *WLnm* (*FTP*, pp. 250–257 [*GA* IV/2: 108–12 and IV/3: 418–422]).

Insofar as something subjective in me is transformed into something objective, the concept of an end into a decision of the will, and the latter in turn into a certain modification of my body: to this extent, I obviously represent myself as changed. But this last item that I attribute to myself, my physical body, is supposed to be connected with the entire world of bodies; and thus if the former is intuited as changed, so is the latter necessarily viewed as changed as well [IV, 12].

The thing that can be changed as a result of my efficacy, that is, the *specific constitution* or the *properties* of nature [*Beschaffenheit der Natur*], is entirely the same as that which cannot be changed; i.e., it is mere matter, simply viewed from a different side – just as, above, the causality of the concept with respect to what is objective appeared, respectively, as will and as body when viewed from different sides. Viewed subjectively and in connection with me as an active subject or agent, what is changeable is nature; what is unchangeable is this same nature, viewed entirely and solely objectively, and this is unchangeable for the reasons indicated above.

The entire manifold contained in the perception of our sensible efficacy has now been derived from the laws of consciousness, which is what was demanded. We find that the last point we have inferred is the very same as the point with which we began; our investigation has returned upon itself and is therefore concluded.

Briefly stated, the result of this investigation is as follows: nothing is absolute but pure activity, and all consciousness and all being is grounded upon this pure activity. In accordance with the laws of consciousness, and, more specifically, in accordance with the basic law that an agent [*das Tätige*] can be viewed only as a unified subject and object (as an *I*), this activity appears as an *efficacy exercised upon something outside of me*. All the things included in this appearance – from, at the one extreme, the end that is posited absolutely by myself, to, at the other extreme, the raw stuff of the world – are mediating elements of the same, and are hence themselves only appearances. Nothing is purely true but my self-sufficiency [*Selbständigkeit*][IV, 13].[3]

---

[3] In the original edition there here followed two pages of announcements of Fichte's other writings that had appeared with the same publisher and a Table of Contents of *The System of Ethics*, which has been incorporated into the Table of Contents at the beginning of the present edition.

PART I

Deduction of the principle of morality[1]

Preliminary remark concerning this deduction

It is claimed that the human mind finds itself to be absolutely compelled to do certain things entirely apart from any extrinsic ends, but purely and simply for the sake of doing them, and to refrain from doing other things, equally independently of any extrinsic ends, purely and simply for the sake of leaving them undone. Insofar as such a compulsion [*Zunötigung*] is supposed to manifest itself necessarily in human beings just as surely as they are human beings, this constitutes what is called *the moral or ethical* nature of human beings as such.

Human *cognition* can relate to this, its moral nature in a twofold manner. On the one hand, a human being may find the above-mentioned inner compulsion through self-observation, as a fact – and then it is of course assumed that this fact can certainly be found through attentive self-observation. In this case, one sticks with the sheer fact as such and is satisfied to have found that *this is simply how things are*, without asking *how* and *on the basis of what grounds* they become what they are. One might even decide, freely and from one's own inclination, to attach unconditional *faith* to this inner compulsion: i.e., one might decide actually *to think* that one's highest vocation is what is represented to one as such by this inner compulsion and to *act* unfailingly in

---

[1] *Deduktion des Prinzips der Sittlichkeit*. Regarding the translation of *Sittlichkeit* as "morality" see the editors' introduction.

accordance with this faith. [IV, 14] In this manner one obtains *ordinary* cognition both of one's overall moral nature and of one's specific duties, so long as, in the particular circumstances of one's life, one carefully pays attention to the dictates of one's conscience. Such cognition is possible from *the standpoint of ordinary consciousness*, and this is sufficient for engendering both a dutiful disposition and dutiful conduct.

On the other hand, one may refuse to remain content with the immediate perception and, in his thinking, may not stop with the facts, but may demand to know the grounds of what one has perceived. Such a person is not satisfied with factual cognition but demands genetic cognition; he wants to know not merely that such a compulsion is present within him, but he also wants to see how it originates. Were he to obtain the desired cognition, this would be a *learned* cognition; and in order to obtain it, he would have to raise himself above the standpoint of ordinary consciousness. – But how is the problem just noted to be solved? How does one go about finding *the grounds* of the moral nature of human beings or of the ethical principle within them? – Nothing absolutely excludes any question about a higher ground but this: that we are *we*; that is, the *I-hood* within us or our rational nature (although this latter phrase does not convey this point nearly as expressly as the former). Everything else, which is either *in* us, such as the compulsion noted earlier, or *for* us, such as the world we assume to exist outside ourselves, is in us and for us because we are this [i.e., because we possess I-hood or rationality]. This can easily be demonstrated in a general manner; but the kind of learned or scientific cognition of the grounds of something in or for us, which is the kind of cognition that concerns us here, involves specific insight into the manner in which this "something" is connected with and necessarily proceeds from this rationality. The presentation of these grounds constitutes a derivation or deduction [*Ableitung oder Deduktion*], since by means of such a presentation something is derived from the highest and absolute principle, that of I-hood, and is shown to follow from the latter necessarily. Thus what we have to provide here is a deduction of the moral nature of the human being or of the ethical principle therein – [IV, 15]. Rather than enumerating in detail the advantages of such a deduction, it will here suffice to note that a science of morality first comes into being thereby – and science, wherever it is possible, is an end in itself.

With respect to the scientific whole of philosophy, the particular science of ethics to be presented here is linked, by means of this deduction, with a foundation of the entire *Wissenschaftslehre*.[2] The deduction commences with propositions of the latter, and in the course of the deduction the particular science proceeds from the universal one and becomes a particular philosophical science. – In order to appreciate this deduction properly, one need only bear in mind the following: If, as has been claimed, the morality of our nature is something that follows from our rationality according to necessary laws, then for perception itself the compulsion noted above is something primary and immediate, something that manifests itself without any help from us, and we cannot freely change this manifestation in the least. Employing a deduction to gain insight into the grounds of this compulsion does not provide us with any power to change anything about the compulsion, because it is our knowledge and not our power that extends this far, and because this whole relationship is necessary; indeed, it is our unchangeable nature itself. The deduction thus produces nothing more than theoretical cognition, and one must not expect anything more from it. Just as one does not posit objects differently in space and time after one has obtained insight into the grounds of this operation than one posited them before such insight, so does morality not manifest itself any differently in human beings after its deduction than before. Even ethics [*Sittenlehre*] is not a *doctrine of wisdom* [*Weisheitslehre*] – indeed, such a doctrine is impossible as such, inasmuch as wisdom should be considered more of an art than a science; instead, like all philosophy, ethics is *Wissenschaftslehre*. More specifically, ethics is the *theory of our consciousness* of our moral nature in general and of our specific duties in particular.

---

[2] The phrase translated here as "foundation of the entire *Wissenschaftslehre*" (*Grundlage der gesamten Wissenschaftslehre*), which also occurs elsewhere in *The System of Ethics*, is the title of the presentation of the first principles or "foundations" of the entire *Wissenschaftslehre* that Fichte published in 1794–1795 [henceforth = *GWL*] and which has been translated into English under the abbreviated title "Science of Knowledge." See J. G. Fichte, *Science of Knowledge with the First and Second Introductions*, ed. and trans. P. Heath and J. Lachs (Cambridge: Cambridge University Press, 1982) [Henceforth = *SK*]. But note that Fichte refers not to "the" but rather to "a" "foundation of the entire *Wissenschaftslehre*." This is significant, because Fichte began providing a thoroughly revised presentation of the "foundations" of his system, "according to a new method," in his lectures of 1796/97 and repeated this new version in 1797/98 and 1798/99. In fact, the "foundations" to which Fichte refers in the *System of Ethics* would appear to be this new version of the foundational portion of the entire system, presented according to a "new method" (i.e. *WLnm* = *FTP*).

Enough about the meaning and end of the proposed deduction; let us now add a preliminary [IV, 16] remark concerning how this deduction is to be properly understood, a remark that is necessary only because unfamiliarity with the nature of transcendental philosophy is still very widespread.

The path of the deduction will be as follows: we will assign ourselves the task of thinking of ourselves under a certain specified condition and observing *how* we are required to think of ourselves under this condition. From those properties of ourselves that we find in this way, we will then derive, as something necessary, the moral compulsion noted earlier. At first, it may seem arbitrary that we think of ourselves under precisely this specific condition. But anyone who surveys philosophy in its entirety, as well as the systematic connection of the individual philosophical sciences, will see that this condition is necessary. Everyone else may view our way of proceeding provisionally, as an attempt to propound a scientific ethics, an attempt that may fail or succeed, until the correctness of this way of proceeding is confirmed by its success in actually establishing the desired science. This, therefore, is the least of our concerns.

A more important concern is the following, and its solution is also more instructive: Someone might say to us, "You will be *thinking* of yourself. But, as Critical philosophers you must know, and, if not, it could also be proven to you quite easily, that all of your thinking proceeds in accordance with certain inner laws of thinking, and what is thought is modified by the very manner of thinking, and thus, without your even noticing this, something becomes for you what it is for you precisely because you are thinking it. The case before us will undoubtedly be no different: by turning your thinking toward yourself, you yourself will become modified in and by this act of thinking. Hence you may not say, *this is how I am in and for myself*, for this is something you could never know unless you had some means of cognizing yourself other than through thinking. What you should say instead is simply, '*this is how I necessarily have to think of myself.*'

"Now if you remain always conscious of this, the true meaning of your conclusion, and if you limit yourself to this meaning, then there is nothing to object to in your manner of proceeding, and you may see for yourself what you have gained thereby [IV, 17]. However, it seems that you by no means limit yourself to this way of understanding the meaning of your conclusion. You want to use the result [of your deduction] to explain that compulsion that manifests itself in all of us, and hence to derive something actual from thoughts. You want to go beyond the region of thinking into the entirely different region of actual being."

We reply to this as follows: This is not at all what we are doing; we remain within the region of thinking. Indeed, this is precisely what constitutes that misunderstanding of transcendental philosophy which continues to persist everywhere: still to consider such a transition [from thinking to being] to be possible, still to demand such a transition, and still to find it possible to think of a being in itself. That compulsion within us, what else is this but a kind of thinking that forces itself upon us, a necessary consciousness? Or can we here somehow escape from a consciousness of mere consciousness and reach the object itself? Do we know anything more about this demand [*Anforderung*] than this: that we necessarily have to think that such a demand is directed at us? – What we derive from our inferences in the deduction is itself an act of thinking; and that which is within us, independent of all inferences, as something primary and immediate: this too is an act of thinking. The only difference is that we are not conscious of the grounds of the latter, immediate, kind of thinking, and thus this thinking imposes itself upon us with immediate necessity and *thereby* receives the predicate of "reality," of "perceptibility." In contrast, the former, inferential, kind of thinking occurs within a series of conscious grounds or reasons. Precisely this is the intention of all philosophy: to uncover that within the operation of our reason which remains unknown to us from the viewpoint of ordinary consciousness. Here there is no talk whatsoever of any being, as being in itself; nor can there ever be any such talk, for reason cannot get outside of itself. Except for some necessary consciousness, there is no being for an intellect, and hence no being at all, since there is being only for an intellect. When one occupies the ordinary viewpoint, this necessity of consciousness imposes itself immediately [IV, 18]. From the transcendental viewpoint, one can investigate the grounds of this necessity. The following deduction, as well as the entire system of morals that we intend to erect thereupon, sets forth nothing but a part of this [system of] necessary consciousness, and anyone who would regard the former or the latter as anything else would be regarding it quite incorrectly.

§1

Problem[3]

TO THINK ONESELF, MERELY AS ONESELF, I.E., SEPARATED FROM
EVERYTHING THAT IS NOT OURSELVES.

Solution

(1) Theorem. I FIND MYSELF AS MYSELF ONLY AS WILLING.

Explanation

(a) What does it mean to say "I find *myself*"?

The easiest way to guide someone toward learning to think and to
understand the concept I in a determinate manner is as follows:
think for yourself of some object, e.g., the wall in front of you, your
desk, or something similar. In doing this you undoubtedly assume a
thinker or a thinking subject [*ein Denkendes*], and this thinker is you
yourself. In this act of thinking you are immediately aware of your
thinking. But the object that is being thought is not supposed to be the
thinker itself; it is not identical with the thinking subject but is supposed to be something posited over against or in opposition to the latter;
and in this act of thinking you are also immediately conscious of this
counterpositing. – Now think of yourself. As certainly as you do this,
you do not posit the thinker and what is thought of in this act of
thinking in opposition to each other, as you did previously. They are
not supposed to be two, but one and the same, and you are immediately
conscious of this. The concept of the I is therefore thought when, in an
act of thinking, the thinker and what is thought are taken to be the same
[IV, 19]; and, vice versa, what arises in such an act of thinking is the
concept of the I.

Let us apply this to our present case. "I find myself" ; this would
mean that I take the finder and what is found to be one and the same;

---

[3] *Aufgabe.* This term could equally well be translated as "task" or "postulate," in the sense in which
the latter term is employed in Euclidean geometry: viz., as a summons to engage in a specific act of
thinking.

what is found is not[4] supposed to be something different from the finding subject itself.

(b)   What does it mean to say, "I find *myself*"?

What is found is here posited in opposition to what is produced by us. In particular, the finder is supposed to be engaged in an act of finding; i.e., insofar as I am engaged in this act of finding, I am conscious of no other activity beyond that of merely *apprehending* [*Auffassen*]. What is apprehended, however, is supposed to be neither produced nor in any way modified by the act of apprehending; it is simply supposed to *be*, and to *be such as it is*, independent of the act of apprehending. Without being apprehended, it is; and it would have remained as it had been, even if I had not apprehended it. As far as what is apprehended is concerned, my act of apprehending is utterly contingent and does not change anything whatsoever with respect to the essence of what is apprehended. – This is precisely how I appear to myself in the act of finding. Here we are concerned only with providing an exposition of the mere fact of consciousness, and we are not at all concerned with what may be the truth about this situation, when viewed, that is, from the highest speculative standpoint. – This point has been very expressively conveyed by saying that something is *given* to the perceiver. – In short, the finder is supposed to be purely passive; and, in the case before us [that is, the case of finding oneself], something that one recognizes as oneself is supposed to impose itself on the finder.

(c)   What does it mean to say, "I find myself as *willing*, and I can find myself *only* as willing"?

It is here presupposed that one knows what *willing* means. This concept is not capable of a real definition, nor does it require one. Each person has to become aware within himself of what willing means, through intellectual intuition, and everyone will be able to do so without any

---

[4] The "not" is missing in the original edition. It was first supplied in the version of the *System of Ethics* edited by I. H. Fichte and included in volume IV of his edition of his father's complete works: *Fichtes Werke*, ed. I. H. Fichte (Berlin: Veit, 1845–1846; rpt., including the three volumes of *Fichtes nachgelassene Werke*, Berlin: de Gruyter, 1971) [henceforth = *SW*].

difficulty [IV, 20]. The fact designated by the preceding words is this: I become aware of an act of willing. Then, by means of thinking, I add to this act of willing [the thought of] something subsisting, something that is present independently of my consciousness [of it], something that is supposed to be the willing subject [*das Wollende*], which engages in this act of willing, which *has* this will, and in which the will is supposed to inhere. (Here we are not concerned with *how* such a substrate might be added through thinking, nor with what the grounds for such an addition might be; we are instead concerned only with the fact *that* it happens, and this is something of which everyone has to convince himself by means of his own self-observation.) – I said that I become *conscious* of this willing, that I perceive it. Now I also become conscious of this consciousness, of this perceiving, and I also relate it to a substance. To me, this substance that possesses consciousness is the very same as the one that also wills; therefore, I find myself as the willing Me [*das wollende Mich*], or, I find *myself* as willing.

"I find myself *only* as willing." First of all, I do not, as it were, perceive this substance immediately. What is substantial is no object of perception whatsoever but is simply added in thinking to something that has been perceived. I can immediately perceive only what is supposed to be a manifestation of the substance. But there are only two manifestations that are immediately ascribed to the substance in question [that is, to the I]: *thinking* (in the widest sense of the term, i.e., representing, or consciousness as such) and *willing*. Originally and immediately, the former is, for itself, by no means an object of any particular new consciousness, but is simply consciousness itself. Only insofar as consciousness is directed toward something else, something objective, and is posited in opposition thereto, does it itself become objective in *this act of counterpositing*. As an originally objective manifestation of the substance in question there thus remains only the second of the two [manifestations mentioned above]; namely, willing, which, moreover, always remains *only objective* and is never itself an act of thinking, but is always only the manifestation of self-activity [*Selbsttätigkeit*] insofar as the latter is thought. – In short, the sole manifestation [of the substantial I] that I originally ascribe to myself is willing. Only under the [IV, 21] condition that I become conscious of willing do I become conscious of myself.

All this, taken together, is the meaning of the above proposition.

Proof

Note. This proof has already been conducted in the author's work on Natural Right (§ 1).[5] Nevertheless, we will not dispense with it here, but will present it anew, independent of the terms and expressions employed in the previous version. This is because we are convinced that presenting the same truth at different times and in different contexts can contribute greatly toward clarifying the insight of both the author and the reader.

(1) This proof is based, firstly, *on the concept "I."* The meaning of this concept has just been indicated by showing its genesis. That one actually proceeds in the manner indicated when one thinks of oneself, and that, conversely, such a procedure produces within one nothing other than the thought of oneself: this is something that each person has to find within himself, and no separate proof can ever be provided for this claim. (2) The proof is based, secondly, on the necessity that *something subjective is originally posited in opposition to something objective* within consciousness. In every act of thinking there is something thought that is not the act of thinking itself; in all consciousness there is something of which one is conscious that is not consciousness itself. The truth of this assertion is also something that each person has to find in the self-intuition of his way of proceeding; it cannot be demonstrated to him from concepts. – Subsequently, of course, one can become conscious of one's thinking *as* such, i.e., as an act [*Tun*]; one can become conscious of oneself while engaged in thinking, and thus turn the latter into an object. Philosophical genius is the facility and natural tendency to achieve this latter sort of consciousness, and without such genius no one can grasp the meaning of transcendental philosophy. But even this is possible only because one tacitly supplements this act of thinking with a substrate that is merely thought [VI, 22], even if the latter is entirely undetermined and even if it is only the form of an object in general. For only under this condition does one actually think an act of thinking. (3) This proof is based, thirdly, on the *original character of what is objective*: namely, that what is objective exists independently of

---

[5] See J. G. Fichte, *Foundations of Natural Right*, ed. Fred Neuhouser and trans. Michael Baur (Cambridge: Cambridge University Press, 2000) [henceforth = *FNR*], pp. 18–21 (*SW* III: 17–23; *GA* I/3: 329–334).

thinking and is hence something *real* [*Reelles*], something that is supposed to exist for itself and through itself. Here again, one has to
convince oneself of this through inner intuition. Although this relationship between what is objective and what is subjective is certainly
explicated in a *Wissenschaftslehre*, it is in no way demonstrated by
means of the concepts of what is objective and what is subjective,
concepts which themselves become possible only through such
observation.

The proof can be conducted as follows: it is the character of the I *that
the acting subject and that upon which it acts are one and the same.* As we
have seen above, this is the case when what is being thought of is the I.
Only insofar as what is thought of is supposed to be the same as what
thinks it do I take the former to be myself.

But the act of thinking is now supposed to be entirely ignored. Since
what is thought is identical with the thinking subject, I myself am
indeed the latter. According to the proposition just introduced, however,
what is thought in this case is supposed to *be something objective, an I merely
for itself and entirely independent of the act of thinking*, and yet it is still
supposed to be cognized as an I, for it is supposed to be *found as an I*.

Hence in what is thought, considered as such – i.e., insofar as it can
only be something objective and can never become subjective, that is,
insofar as it is what is originally objective – there would have to occur an
identity of the acting subject and that upon which it acts, an identity
such that it could be, as I said above, only an object. The acting in
question would therefore have to be a *real* acting [*ein reelles Handeln*]
upon itself; not a mere intuiting of oneself, as is the case with the ideal
activity, but *a real determining of oneself through oneself.* But only willing
is something of this sort; and, conversely, we can think of willing only in
this way. The expression "to find *oneself*" is therefore absolutely
identical with the expression "to find oneself willing." Only insofar as
I find myself [engaged in] willing, do I find *myself*, and insofar as I find
myself, I necessarily find myself *willing* [IV, 23].

Corollary

One can see that in order to establish anything categorically from the
proposition just demonstrated – if I find myself, I necessarily find
myself as willing – another proposition has to precede it, namely,

I necessarily find myself; I necessarily become conscious of myself. Such self-consciousness is exhibited in the foundational portion of the entire *Wissenschaftslehre*[6] – not, to be sure, as a matter of fact, for as such it is something immediate, but rather, in its connection with all the other types of consciousness, as reciprocally conditioning and conditioned by the latter. Consequently, the proposition just demonstrated, along with everything that is still to be derived from it, becomes itself a necessary consequence as well as a condition of self-consciousness. Regarding this proposition and all of its consequences, one may assert the following: just as certainly as I am, or am conscious of myself, this proposition and its consequences are certain for me and are necessarily present in me and for me. And thus the science of ethics that we are here engaged in establishing stands firmly on common ground with philosophy as a whole.

(2) WILLING ITSELF, HOWEVER, IS THINKABLE ONLY UNDER THE PRESUPPOSITION OF SOMETHING DIFFERENT FROM THE I.

In philosophical abstraction one may indeed speak of willing *as such* or *in general*, which is, for precisely this reason, something indeterminate. All willing that is actually *perceivable*, however, which is the kind of the willing that is required here, is necessarily a determinate willing, in which *something* is willed. To will something means to demand that some determinate object – which, in willing, is thought of only as a *possible* object, since otherwise it would not be willed but perceived – become an actual object of experience; and through this demand the latter is placed outside of us. Thus all willing contains within itself the postulate of an object outside of us, and in this concept [of willing] something is thought that is not ourselves [IV, 24].

Moreover, the very possibility of postulating something outside of ourselves in the act of willing already presupposes that we possess the concept of an "outside of us" as such, and the latter is possible only through experience. But such an experience, in turn, involves a relationship of ourselves to something outside of us. – In other words, what I will is never anything but a modification of an object that is actually supposed to exist outside of me. All my willing is therefore conditioned by the perception of an object outside of me. In willing, I am not

---

[6] See *SK*, p. 216 (*SW* I: 244ff.; *GA* I/2: 383ff.) and *FTP*, pp. 358 ff. (*GA* IV/3:472ff.).

perceptible for myself as I am in and for myself; instead, I perceive only how I can relate in a certain way to things existing outside me.

(3) IN ORDER TO FIND MY TRUE ESSENCE I MUST THEREFORE THINK AWAY ALL THAT IS FOREIGN IN WILLING. WHAT THEN REMAINS IS MY PURE BEING.

This assertion is the immediate consequence of the propositions that preceded it. All that is left to examine is what might remain after one has made the requisite abstraction from what is foreign in willing. Willing as such is something primary, grounded absolutely in itself and in nothing outside of itself. Let us now clarify this concept upon which everything here rests – a concept that can be grasped and explained only *negatively* (since to call something "primary" means precisely that it is not derivable from anything else, and to call it "grounded in and through itself" means precisely that it is not grounded through anything else). – Everything that is dependent, that is conditioned and grounded through something else, can, to that extent, also be cognized *mediately*, that is, through the cognition of what grounds it. If, e.g., a ball is set in motion by a push, then I can certainly see the ball move immediately; I can perceive the point from which it starts and the point at which it comes to a rest, as well as the speed at which it moves. But I could also infer all of these things, without any immediate perception, simply from the force with which the ball is impelled, provided I knew the conditions under which the ball itself stands [IV, 25]. For this reason, the movement of the ball can be considered to be something dependent or secondary. What is primary and grounded through itself would thus have to be such that it simply could not be cognized mediately or indirectly through something else, but only immediately through itself. Such a thing is the way it is, simply because this is how it is.

Insofar as willing is something absolute and primary, therefore, it simply cannot be explained on the basis of any influence of some thing outside the I, but only on the basis of the I itself; and *this absoluteness* of the I is what would remain following abstraction from everything foreign.

Remark

It is a fact of consciousness that willing, in the indicated sense of this term, *appears* as absolute. Everyone will find this within himself, and anyone who does not already know this cannot be taught it from outside. From this, however, it does not follow that this appearance itself might not need to be further explained and derived, which would mean that the appearance of absoluteness itself would be further explained, in which case it would cease to be absoluteness, and the appearance thereof would be transformed into an illusion – just as it indeed also appears to be the case that certain things exist in space and time, independent of us; and yet this appearance is further explained by transcendental philosophy (though it is not transformed into an illusion, for reasons that do not concern us here). To be sure, no one will be able to provide such an explanation of willing from something else nor even to say anything comprehensible in that regard. Nevertheless, were someone to claim that willing might still possess a ground outside of us, albeit a ground that remains incomprehensible to us, then, even though there would not be the least reason to assent to such a claim, there would also be no theoretical reason to object to it. If one nevertheless decides not to explain this appearance [of the will's absoluteness] any further and decides to consider it to be absolutely inexplicable, i.e., to be the truth, and indeed our sole truth, according to which all other truth has to be measured and judged – and our entire philosophy is based on precisely this decision [IV, 26] –, then this is not because of any theoretical insight, but because of a practical interest. I *will* to be self-sufficient, and I therefore take myself to be so. Such a taking-to-be-true, however, is *faith*. Our philosophy therefore begins with an item of faith, and it knows that it does this. Dogmatism too, which, if it is consistent, makes the claim stated above [namely, that it can explain the appearance of the will's absoluteness], starts with faith (in the *thing in itself*); but it usually does not know this. (Cf. the introduction to the new presentation of the *Wissenschaftslehre* in the fifth volume of the *Philosophical Journal*, vol. v, p. 23.)[7] In our system, one makes oneself into the ultimate basis [*Boden*] of one's philosophy, and that is why this system appears "baseless" to anyone who is unable to do this. But we can assure such a person in advance that if he cannot procure this basis for himself and cannot be content with this, then he will be unable to

---

[7] J. G. Fichte, *Introductions to the Wissenschaftslehre and Other Writings (1797–1800)*, ed. and trans. Daniel Breazeale (Indianapolis/Cambridge, Mass.: Hackett, 1994) [Henceforth = *IWL*], p. 18 (*SW* 1: 433; *GA* 1/4: 194).

find such a basis anywhere else. It is necessary that our philosophy confess this quite loudly, so that it might thereby finally be relieved of the unreasonable demand that it demonstrate to human beings from outside something they have to create in themselves.

Now how is this absolute in willing thought?

At the level of abstraction that it must receive here, this concept [of the absoluteness of willing] may well be the most difficult concept in all of philosophy, though in the future it will undoubtedly obtain the greatest clarity, since the entire science that we are now engaged in establishing is really concerned only with the further determination of this concept. In order to have something to think about with respect to this concept right from the beginning, however, let us begin our exposition of it with the following example.

Imagine a compressed steel spring. Within this spring there is undoubtedly a striving to push back against what presses upon it; hence this striving within the spring is directed outward. This would be an image of actual willing, as the *state* of a rational being [IV, 27]; but this is not what we are talking about here. Now what is the proximate *ground* (not the condition) of this striving, understood as an actually determined manifestation of the steel spring? The proximate ground in question is undoubtedly an inner effect [*Wirkung*] of the spring upon itself, a self-determination. Surely the ground for the opposing action of the spring does not lie in that body outside the steel spring, which exerts pressure upon it. This self-determination would be [analogous to] what, in a rational being, is the sheer *act* of willing. From both there would then arise – if only the spring of steel could intuit itself – a consciousness of a will to push back what exerts pressure on it. But all this would be possible only on the condition that there actually occurs a pressure on the spring from outside; just as, according to the argument given above, a rational being cannot determine itself to engage in an actual act of willing unless it stands in reciprocal interaction with something outside itself (for this is at least how it *appears* to the rational being in question). We now have to abstract from this last point, for we are here concerned just as little with it as we were with the previously indicated one. Returning to our example: if I abstract entirely from the external pressure, is there anything still left through which I can think the steel spring as such, and, if so, what is this that remains? Obviously, it is that in consequence of which I judge that the steel spring, just as soon as some pressure is exerted on it, will strive against the later; i.e., it is the inner tendency of the spring to determine itself to a counterstriving, understood as the genuine essence of elasticity and as the ultimate ground of all of its appearances, just as soon as the conditions of their manifestation are present, a ground which cannot be explained any further. – The quite essential difference between this original tendency of the steel spring and the original tendency of a rational being will become evident in the following investigations.

In the same manner that we dissected the concept that served as our example, we now have to dissect the I, as conceived through its willing [IV, 28].

First of all, with respect to its form, the problem is that of thinking the I at the requisite level of abstraction as something *subsisting* [*Bestehendes*] and fixed. From this it follows that that through which the I is here to be conceived and characterized has to be something enduring and essential. Its manifestations and appearances may change, since the conditions under which it manifests itself will change; but what manifests itself under all these conditions remains constantly the same. (Anyone familiar with the spirit of transcendental philosophy will share our presupposition that this thinking of something subsisting must itself be based on our laws of thinking and that, accordingly, what we are seeking is only the essence of the I for the I, and by no means the latter's essence in itself, as a *thing* in itself.)

Further, as to its matter, what is to be thought is supposed to be the ground of an absolute willing (for all willing is absolute). What then is it? From the start, everyone must actually have thought along with us what is demanded, must actually have carried out the prescribed abstraction, and must now intuit himself internally to see what remains, what it is that he is still thinking. Only in this way will he obtain the intended cognition. Here nothing can be rendered distinct [simply] by [giving it] a name, for the entire concept has not even been thought of until now, let alone designated linguistically. In order for it to have a name, however, we wish to designate what is conceived in this manner "the *absolute tendency* [*Tendenz*] *toward the absolute*"; or "absolute indeterminability through anything outside itself"; or "the tendency to determine itself absolutely, without any external impetus." It is not only a mere *force* [*Kraft*] or a *faculty* or *power* [*Vermögen*], for the latter is nothing actual but only what we think of as preceding actuality, in order to be able to integrate the latter into a *series* of our acts of thinking. In this case, however, what we have to think is supposed to be something actual, something that constitutes the essence of the I. But the concept of a power is contained within this [actual essence of the I] as well. With respect to and in relation to the actual manifestation, which is possible only under the condition that some object is given, it is the power to manifest itself in this manner [IV, 29]. Nor is what we have to think in this case a *drive* [*Trieb*], which is what one might call the ground of the elasticity in the steel spring that served as our example; for a drive operates necessarily and in a materially determined manner, so long as the conditions of its efficacy are present. As of yet we know nothing of the sort about the I, and we must not forestall our future investigation through some hasty determination.

Result. THE ESSENTIAL CHARACTER OF THE I, THROUGH WHICH IT DISTINGUISHES ITSELF FROM EVERYTHING OUTSIDE OF IT, CONSISTS IN A TENDENCY TO SELF-ACTIVITY FOR SELF-ACTIVITY'S SAKE; AND THIS TENDENCY IS WHAT IS THOUGHT WHEN THE I IS THOUGHT OF IN AND FOR ITSELF, WITHOUT ANY RELATION TO SOMETHING OUTSIDE IT.

Remark. One must not forget that the I is here being considered only *as an object*, and not as an *I as such*. Under the latter presupposition, the proposition just put forward would be utterly false.

§ 2

We have just shown what the I *is* in and for itself; or, to put it more carefully, how the I, when thought of only as an object, must necessarily be *thought*.

But the *I* is something only insofar as and only to extent that it posits (intuits and thinks) itself as this something; and it is nothing that it does not posit itself to be – a proposition that can be presupposed to be known and demonstrated in the foundational portion of the entire *Wissenschaftslehre*.[8]

Let us now add a few words to elucidate this proposition. The difference between a thing and the I (a rational being), which is entirely opposed to the former, is precisely this: a thing is merely supposed to *be*,

---

[8] See, e.g., *SK*, p. 241 (*SW* I: 274; *GA* I/2: 406–407) and *FTP*, pp. 112 ff. (*GA* IV/3: 345ff.).

without itself having the least knowledge of its own being. In the I, however, being and consciousness are supposed to coincide; no being of the I is supposed to occur without the latter's self-consciousness, and vice versa, the I possesses no consciousness of itself without a being of that of which it is conscious [IV, 30]. All being is related to some consciousness, and even the existence of *a thing* cannot be thought without thinking in addition of some intellect that has knowledge of this existence. The only difference is that [in the latter case] this knowledge is not located in the existing thing itself, but in an intellect outside of it. Knowledge of the being of the I, however, is located in that very substance that also *is*; and only insofar as this immediate connection between consciousness and being is posited can one say, "the I is this or that."

Applied to our present case, this means that just as certainly as what was previously established is essential to the I, then the I must have knowledge of this. Hence there is certainly some consciousness of the absolute tendency described above.

It might be important not simply to have some general knowledge of this point but to describe this specific consciousness itself in more detail. Let us proceed to this task.

Problem

TO BECOME CONSCIOUS IN A DETERMINATE MANNER OF THE CONSCIOUSNESS OF ONE'S ORIGINAL BEING.

For elucidation

One is obviously conscious of what one is talking about, and the situation will be no different in the case of philosophizing. Thus in the previous section we were surely conscious of something. The object of our consciousness was produced by freely self-determining our power to think, by means of an arbitrary abstraction.

Now it is claimed that this same object is present for us *originally*, i.e., prior to all free philosophizing, and that it imposes itself upon us just as certainly as we are conscious at all. If this is true, then there is also an original consciousness of the object in question, even if we may not be precisely conscious of it as a singular object at the same level of abstraction

35

with which we have just [IV, 31] established it. It may well occur in and be accompanied by another thought, as a determination of the latter.

Is this original consciousness any different from the one that we, as philosophers, have just produced within ourselves? How could it be, given that it is supposed to have the same object, and given that the philosopher, as such, certainly possesses no other subjective form of thinking than that common and original form that is present in all reason?

But if this so, then why are we looking for what we already possess? We possess it without knowing that we possess it. Now we simply want to produce this knowledge within ourselves. A rational being is constituted in such a way that when it thinks it does not ordinarily take into account its own act of thinking, but only what it is thinking; it loses itself, as the subject, in the object. In philosophy, however, everything depends on becoming acquainted with the subject as such, in order to judge its influences on the determination of the object. This can happen only by making the mere reflection [that is, the act of thinking of the object] into the object of a new reflection. – To the non-philosopher, the project of becoming conscious of consciousness may seem strange and perhaps even risible. This, however, merely demonstrates the non-philosopher's ignorance of philosophy and his complete incapacity for the latter.

Genetic description of the consciousness in question

(1) The I possesses the absolute power of intuition, for it is precisely thereby that it becomes an I. This power cannot be derived from anything higher, nor does it stand in need of any further derivation. If an I is posited, then this power of intuition is also posited. – Moreover, the I is and must be able to intuit what it itself is without any further ado. Therefore, the particular determination of the faculty to intuit at all, which is here postulated, also stands in no need of any [IV, 32] derivation from or mediation through external grounds. The I intuits itself purely and simply because it intuits itself. – So much for the fact as such.

(2) Let us now proceed to the determination of this fact. In doing this, we expect that each person will be able to generate for himself what we are talking about, through his own self-activity, and that he will also be able to obtain an inner intuition of what arises for him thereby.

The intuiting subject (the intellect), which becomes an intellect precisely by means of the postulated act, posits the tendency to absolute activity described above, in accordance with the postulate, as – *itself*: that is, as identical with *itself, the intellect*. The previously mentioned absoluteness of real acting *thereby* becomes the essence of an intellect and is brought under the *sway of the concept*, and this is how the absoluteness of real acting first becomes *freedom* proper: the absoluteness of absoluteness, the absolute power to make itself absolutely. – Through the consciousness of its own absoluteness the I tears itself away – from itself – and puts itself forward as something self-sufficient.

I said that it tears itself away from itself, and I will therefore begin by explaining this expression. – All intuition is, as such, supposed to be directed toward something that is there independently of it, and that is there just as it is intuited to be. The situation is no different with respect to the intuition we are now discussing, since it is, after all, an intuition. As absolute, the I is supposed to lie there and to have done so before it was grasped in intuition. The absoluteness in question is supposed to constitute its being and subsistence, independent of all intuition. In cases where what is intuited is supposed to lie outside the being of the intuiting subject, however, the intellect as such remains a passive onlooker. Here, however, the situation is supposed to be different. What is intuited is itself the intuiting subject – not, to be sure, as such,[9] but still they share a single, unified essence; they are a single force and substance. In this case, therefore, the intellect is not merely an onlooker, but itself, as intellect [IV, 33], *becomes* – for itself (as goes without saying, since it is to be hoped that no one will ask about any other kind of being) – the absolutely real force [*absolute reelle Kraft*] of the concept.[10] As an absolute force with consciousness, the I tears itself away – away from the I as a *given* absolute, lacking force and consciousness.

It is necessary to tarry a bit longer with this main thought. It is one that will seem difficult to many, yet the possibility of understanding our entire system depends upon understanding this thought correctly.

I would address the reader as follows: once again, think for yourself of that steel spring that served as our example in the previous section. This spring certainly contains within itself the ground of a particular

---

[9] "*immediately* as such." (Fichte's handwritten marginal remark, as noted in *SW*.)
[10] "*Eyes* are inserted into the unified one." (Fichte's handwritten marginal remark, as noted in *SW*.)

movement, which by no means comes to it from outside but rather resists the direction that it receives from outside. Still, you would hesitate to ascribe to the steel spring what you have always hitherto, and with complete justification, called *freedom*. What is the reason for this hesitation on your part? Perhaps you will answer as follows: the resistance results from the nature of the steel spring, without exception, according to a necessary law and from the condition under which the spring is placed, namely that some pressure is exerted on it from outside. If one posits this law and this condition, then one can certainly count on and predict the resistance of the spring, and this might be the hidden reason why one is unable to bring oneself to ascribe freedom to the steel spring. Should you respond in this manner, then allow me to remove this obstacle. I authorize you to think away the necessity and lawfulness from the steel spring and to assume that at one moment it simply yields to the pressure and that, at another, it resists it, and that one does not know why it behaves like this in either case. Do you now wish to call the steel spring, when thought of in this manner, *free*? By no means do I expect this to be the case. Far from helping you [IV, 34] connect the concept of freedom with the concept of the steel spring, something absolutely unthinkable has been suggested to you instead: blind chance. And you will continue to insist that, even though you do not know what determines the steel spring to resist the pressure, this resistance nevertheless *is* determined by something, and the spring by no means *determines itself* to do this; hence it is not to be considered free.

Now what might you be thinking when you say "*is* determined," as opposed to "*determines itself*," and what might you really demand for the possibility of the latter? Let us try to clarify this for ourselves. – Since you could not make any use whatsoever of the thought that we just tried out, that is, the thought of a free thing dependent upon blind chance, and indeed, were unable to think anything thereby, and since this did not make the attribution of freedom any easier for you, we will stick with what was established earlier. In this case, you say that the steel spring is *determined by its nature* to resist the pressure exerted upon it. What does this mean? In asking this question, we do not require that you have any acquaintance with anything that lies outside you or that you find more remote results by means of progressive inference. We are concerned here with what you are actually already thinking at this very moment and with what you have been thinking all along, well before you decided to philosophize. You only have to make clear to yourself what you are actually thinking, you only have to learn to understand yourself. – The nature of a thing lies in its fixed subsistence, lacking any inner movement, passive and dead; and this is what you necessarily posit whenever you posit a thing and its nature, for to posit something of this sort is precisely to think a thing. [In thinking of a thing,] you have already grasped along with it this passive, unchangeable subsistence; and from this it follows, as something predestined, that under a certain condition a certain change will follow – for, as you say, you have from the start been thinking of something that is *fixed* and *unchangeable*. This is the nature of a thing, which does not depend upon the thing at all; for a thing is itself its own nature, and its nature is precisely the thing [IV, 35]. Whenever you think either of these [– either the thing or its nature –] you necessarily think the other as well along with it; and it is to be hoped that you will not allow the thing *to exist in advance* of its nature, so that it may determine the latter itself. – Once you have posited the thing's nature, however, you then proceed in your thinking from one being (the [thing's] nature) to another being (its manifestation under a certain condition), and you do so through nothing but being, by way of a continuous series. Alternatively, to view this same matter subjectively and in order to observe the determination of your thinking in this process: your intuition is constantly bound and remains bound; there is no moment in this series at which it might rise to self-active producing. This is precisely that state of your thinking which you call "the thought of *necessity*" and by means of which you deny all freedom to the thing you are thinking.

We have thus found the reason why you were utterly unable to think of freedom in the case of the spring and in similar cases. Objectively expressed, every being that itself flows from being is a necessary being, and by no means is it a product of freedom. Subjectively expressed, the concept of a necessary being arises for us when we connect one being to another. From this you may infer by opposition[11] what it is that you

---

[11] In *WLnm* Fichte maintains that the basic law of all thinking is "the law of reflective opposition," also known as the "principle of determinability" or simply the "law of reflection," and he glosses this law as follows: "Furthermore, concerning the law of reflection which governs all our cognition (namely, the law that states that we *cognize* nothing – in the sense of knowing *what* it is – without at the same time thinking of what it is not): this law was not a postulate that we proposed, but was instead a matter of intuition. And it is precisely this sort of cognition, i.e., cognizing something by means of opposition, that is called 'determining' something" (*FTP*, p. 134 [*GA* IV/2: 41]).

actually require in order to think freedom, which is something that you are certainly able to think and have actually been thinking all along. You require a being – not a being without any ground, for such a thing cannot be thought of at all, but one whose ground lies not in some other being, but in something else. Other than being, however, there is nothing for us but thinking. Therefore that being that you are able to think of as product of freedom would have to be a being that proceeds from thinking. Let us see if this presupposition makes freedom any more comprehensible.

You wanted to let something count as free if it *is* not determined but *determines* itself. Is this active determining comprehensible on the presupposition that the determination in question is one that occurs through thinking? [IV, 36] Undoubtedly so, but only if one is able to think the thinking itself and does not, so to speak, transform the concept into a thing. What made it impossible to derive something free from a being – namely, the fact that a fixed subsistence was posited in that case – is completely inapplicable here. Thinking is by no means posited as something subsisting, but as agility [*Agilität*] and purely as the agility of the intellect. – In order for something to be thought of as free, you required it to determine *itself* and not be determined from outside or even by its own nature. What does this "*itself*" mean? Some duality is obviously being thought in this case. What is free is supposed to be before it is determined; it is supposed to have an existence independent of its determinacy. This is why a thing cannot be thought of as determining itself, since it does not exist prior to its nature (i.e., the total sum of its determinations). As was just said, something that is supposed to determine *itself* would, in a certain respect, have to be before it is, before it has properties and any nature at all. This can be thought only under our presupposition, under which, however, it can be thought very easily. As an intellect with a concept of its own real being, what is free precedes its real being, and the former [that is, the intellect] contains the ground of the latter [that is, its own real being]. The concept of a certain being precedes this being, and the latter depends upon the former.

Our claim, therefore, is that only an *intellect* can be thought of as *free*, and that merely by grasping itself as an intellect it becomes free; for only thereby does it subsume its own being under something higher than any being, that is, under a concept. To this someone might object as follows: even in our own argumentation in the preceding section we presupposed absoluteness as a being, as something posited; the reflection that is now supposed to accomplish such great things is itself quite obviously conditioned by this same absoluteness, which it has as its object; without presupposing some object [IV, 37] it is not a reflection at all, and without presupposing this particular object it is not this particular reflection. At the appropriate place, however, we will see that it turns out that even this absoluteness is a requirement for the possibility of an intellect as such and arises from the latter, and hence that the proposition just established can also be reversed, and one could say: only what is *free* can be thought of as an *intellect*; an intellect is necessarily free.

We now return to our project.

INSOFAR AS THE I, IN ACCORDANCE WITH WHAT IS HERE POSTULATED, INTUITS THE TENDENCY TO ABSOLUTE ACTIVITY AS ITSELF, IT POSITS ITSELF AS FREE, I.E., AS POSSESSING THE POWER OF CAUSALITY BY MEANS OF MERE CONCEPTS.

According to Kant, freedom is the power to begin a state [*Zustand*] (a being and subsistence) absolutely.[12] This is an excellent nominal explanation, but it does not seem to have done much to improve our general insight, since the concepts still in circulation regarding freedom are almost entirely false. A still higher question remains to be answered, namely: *how* can a state begin absolutely, or how can the absolute beginning of a state be thought? In order to answer this question one would have to provide a genetic concept of freedom; one would have to generate this concept before our eyes. We have just now accomplished this. It is not the case that the state that is begun absolutely is simply connected to nothing at all, for a finite rational being necessarily thinks only by means of mediation and connections. The connection in question, however, is not a connection to another being, but to a thinking.

In order to exhibit the concept in this manner, however, one certainly has to follow – and has to be able to follow – the path taken by the *Wissenschaftslehre*; that is to say, one has to abstract from all being as such (from the fact) and commence with what is higher than all being, with intuiting and thinking (with the acting of the intellect as such). The same, unique path that leads to the goal of theoretical philosophy – namely, the explanation of being ([being] for us, as goes without saying)

---

[12] See Kant, *Critique of Pure Reason* [henceforth = *KrV*], A 445/B 473.

[IV, 38] – is also the only path that makes practical philosophy possible. This also further clarifies the expression employed above, "the I posits itself as self-sufficient." We have already given a complete explanation of the first aspect of this proposition, according to which it means that the I takes up into the intuition and concept of itself everything that it originally is (but originally it is nothing but free). But this proposition asserts more than this, inasmuch as it asserts that everything that the I can be in *actuality* – in which case, the concept becomes a cognitive concept and all that is left to the intellect is to become an onlooker – still depends originally on the concept. Whatever the I is ever supposed to become, it must make itself this by means of a concept, and whatever it will ever become, it will have made itself this by means of a concept. The I is in every regard its own ground, and it *posits itself* purely and simply in the practical sense as well [as in the theoretical sense].

YET THE I ALSO POSITS ITSELF ONLY AS A POWER [*VERMÖGEN*].

This must be rigorously demonstrated, and it is capable of the most rigorous proof, as follow: – As we have seen, the tendency to absolute activity comes under the sway of the intellect. But (*as everyone has to find in the intuition of himself as intellect, something that cannot be demonstrated to anyone*) the intellect, as such, is absolutely self-determining, nothing but *pure activity*, in contrast to all *subsisting* and *being posited*, no matter how subtly the latter might be thought; hence the intellect is incapable of any determination through its nature and essence (provided it had one), incapable of any tendency, drive, inclination, or anything similar. It follows that no inclination [*Inklination*], no matter how subtly it might be thought, is possible within the active force [*Tatkraft*] that stands under the sway of an intellect, to the extent, anyway, that it does stand under the intellect's sway. Instead, this active force thereby becomes nothing but a pure *power*, i.e., only a concept of the sort to which some actuality can be connected by means of thinking – in the sense that the actuality in question is thought of as having its ground in this power – without containing within itself any information whatsoever concerning *what kind of* actuality this might be [IV, 39].

THE RESULT OF OUR PRESENT INVESTIGATION IS CONTAINED IN A DETERMINATE MANNER IN THE PROPOSITIONS ADVANCED EARLIER AND REQUIRES NO SEPARATE EMPHASIS.

§ 3

It must have seemed strange that, in the preceding section, we derived, simply from [the I's] reflection upon a tendency [*Tendenz*], a type of consciousness that does not carry with it anything resembling a tendency and that the distinctive character of this previously established tendency thus seems to have been set aside entirely. – The latter must not be allowed to happen. According to the first principle [*Grundsatz*] upon which we based our reasoning in the previous section, the I is only what it posits itself to be. The I is originally supposed to be a tendency. This is meaningless and self-contradictory unless the I is supposed to possess this character *for itself*, that is, unless the I is conscious of it. The question, therefore, is by no means *whether* such a consciousness occurs in the I; instead, careful investigation is needed in order to determine *how* such a consciousness might be constituted with respect to its form. The most expeditious way to obtain the requisite insight is to allow the consciousness in question to arise before our eyes.

Our problem therefore is as follows:

TO OBSERVE HOW THE I BECOMES CONSCIOUS OF ITS OWN TENDENCY TOWARD ABSOLUTE SELF-ACTIVITY AS SUCH.

Preliminary remark

In the previous section we proceeded by simply postulating a reflection upon the objective I, which is what was there under consideration; and we were undoubtedly entitled to postulate that the I is necessarily an intellect, and indeed an intellect that intuits itself unconditionally. We, in our philosophizing, were mere spectators of a self-intuition [IV, 40] on the part of the original I. What we established was not something we ourselves had thought, but something the I had thought. The object of our reflection was itself a reflection.

Here too, in the present section, we expect to arrive at such an original reflection on the part of the I – if, that is, we are able to solve our problem. We cannot, however, begin with such an original reflection on the part of the I. Nothing that we do not already possess can be obtained merely by postulating the occurrence of an act of reflection; and yet, for the reasons already indicated, we cannot be content with what we have already established, which is the consciousness of a mere power, but certainly not the consciousness of a tendency or drive. – The difference between the two reflections may be briefly indicated as follows: the previously described reflection was possible purely and simply; the one that is now to be exhibited must first be proven to be possible. That is to say, the grounds for the possibility of such a reflection must first be adduced, and this is precisely the task of our philosophizing, which at least for the moment, should not be taken to be anything more than philosophizing.

We now proceed to the solution of our problem:

(1) THE POSITED TENDENCY NECESSARILY MANIFESTS ITSELF IN RELATION TO THE ENTIRE I AS A DRIVE.

It is not the original I, but the philosopher who thinks in this manner, inasmuch as he states and clearly develops the preceding proposition.

This claim requires no special proof, since it follows by mere analysis from what was set forth in § 1. – The tendency in question is posited as the essence of the I, and, as such, it belongs necessarily to the I and is within the I; hence it cannot be thought away without eliminating the I itself. As a mere tendency, however, it is a *drive* [*Trieb*], a real, inner explanatory ground of an actual self-activity – a drive, moreover, that is posited as essential, subsisting, and ineradicable – a drive that drives: the latter is the manifestation of the former; the two mean exactly the same thing [IV, 41].

If we now think in a *purely objective manner* of the I that contains this drive and upon which this drive manifests itself, then the effect of the drive can be easily understood. Just as in the case of the steel spring, the drive will result in a self-activity as soon as the external conditions are present. An action will follow from the drive in the same way an effect follows from its cause. – Now if, in our thinking, we add the thought of an intellect to that of the tendency, and do so in such a manner that the intellect is dependent on the objective state [of the I] and not vice versa, then the drive will be accompanied by a longing [*Sehnen*] and the deed will be accompanied by a decision; and all of this will ensue with the same necessity with which the deed itself ensued when the conditions were present.

We are able to think of the I objectively in relation to the drive in this manner, and, in due course, we will have to think of it in this manner; at this point, however, to repeat this separation in a concept that we have already assembled would only be a distraction and would serve no purpose. In order to proceed systematically we must further determine the last thing we found, just as it was found; accordingly, the I is here to be thought of not as objective but as both subjective and objective, which is how it was established in the preceding section. This is what is meant by the expression "the *entire* I," which is employed in the above proposition. – As we have shown, the active force has come under the sway of the intellect by means of reflection; and conversely, the possibility of reflection depends, in turn, upon the presence of an active force and upon the determinacy of the latter. This is what we have presupposed. To be sure, one can grasp this concept of oneself only *partially*, as it was just set forth: that is, in such a way that one thinks only of what is objective as dependent upon what is subjective, and then thinks of what is subjective as dependent upon what is objective; but one can never grasp it as a single, unified concept in this manner.

It is necessary to go into this point in somewhat greater detail, especially since we have not dealt with it anywhere else (except for a hint in the *Philosophical Journal*, 5, p. 374: [IV, 42] "One might still demand some further explanation of this; and thus one might try to account for my limitedness ..."[13]). We said that I-hood consists in the absolute identity of what is subjective and what is objective (the absolute unification of being with consciousness and of consciousness with being). The essence of the I is neither what is subjective nor what is objective, but rather an identity [of the two], and the former is asserted simply in order to designate the empty locus of this identity. But can anyone think this identity as himself? Absolutely not; for in order to think of oneself, one has to *introduce that very distinction between what is subjective and what is objective* that is *not* supposed to occur within this concept [of the I]. Without such a distinction, no thinking is possible at all. – Consequently, we never think the two together but only *alongside* each other and *after* each other; and by means of this process of *thinking of one after the other* we make each of them reciprocally dependent on the other. This is why one is unable to avoid asking, *Am* I because *I think of myself*, or do *I think of myself* because I *am*? Yet there is no such "because" in this case; you are not one of these two because you are the other. You are not twofold at all, but are absolutely one and the same; and you are this unthinkable unity [*Eine*] purely and simply because you are.

---

[13] *IWL*, p. 74 (*SW* 1: 489; *GA* 1/4: 242).

This concept, which can be described only as a problem or task for thinking, but which can never be thought, indicates an empty place in our investigation, which we wish to designate with an X. For the reason indicated, the I is unable to grasp itself in and for itself. It is purely and simply = X.

Insofar as it is not a subject and not an object but rather a subject–object (which means nothing more than an empty place for thinking), this entire I contains within itself a tendency to absolute self-activity, which, when it is thought of apart from the substance itself and [IV, 43] as the ground of the latter's activity, is a drive that drives the substance. – Should anyone still have any doubts about whether we are entitled to relate this drive to the entire I, such doubts can be easily removed by dividing the I, a division that is certainly permissible here. This gives us the following result: according to the previous section, when the I reflects upon itself it posits what lies in its objectivity as itself; and this is also true of the I insofar as it engages in reflecting or is subjective. Now what is objective undoubtedly includes a drive, which, as a consequence of reflection, also becomes a drive in relation to what is subjective; and since the I consists in the unification of the two, this drive will become a drive related to the entire I.

Here, however, we are simply not in a position to determine *how* this drive manifests itself in relation to the entire I. And this is all the more the case since that toward which the drive is directed is absolutely inconceivable. Only this much can be said, negatively: that it cannot drive with necessity and with mechanical compulsion, since the I as what is subjective (a subjectivity which, after all, also belongs to the entire I) has placed its active force under the sway of a concept; and a concept is simply not determinable by means of a drive, nor through anything resembling a drive, but only through itself.

(2) NO FEELING RESULTS FROM THIS MANIFESTATION OF THE DRIVE, WHICH IS WHAT ONE WOULD GENERALLY HAVE EXPECTED.

Feeling as such is the sheer, immediate relation of what is objective in the I to what is subjective therein, of its being to its consciousness. The power of feeling is the proper point of unification of both, though only insofar as what is subjective is considered to be dependent upon what is objective, as follows from our description above. (Conversely, insofar as what is objective is considered to be dependent upon what is subjective, the point of unification of both is the *will*.)

46

This can be clarified as follows: what is objective in the I is moved, determined, and changed without any participation on the part of freedom, in the same way that a mere thing is also changed. The [IV, 44] I is not merely objective, but what is subjective is united with the I in the same unified and undivided essence; for this reason, any change in the former also necessarily produces a change in the latter, that is to say, a consciousness of this state, a consciousness, however, that appears to be produced just as mechanically as the state itself. A *feeling* differs as follows from a representation: in the latter, if what is represented is an actual being, then the intuiting subject finds itself to be equally passive; but in the former, in a feeling, there is no consciousness of the thinking subject, of its inner agility, whereas such consciousness is certainly present in the case of a representation, with respect to the form of the act of representing. To be sure, in the case of representation I do not produce what is represented, but I do produce the representing; in the case of feeling neither what is felt nor the feeling is produced. – These differences cannot be determined any more sharply by means of concepts, and even the determinations given here are senseless if one does not clarify them to oneself by intuiting oneself in these different states. Descriptions of this sort are not meant to replace self-intuition but only to guide it.

Further below we will indeed encounter a determination of the purely objective I by the drive to absolute self-activity, from which determination a feeling will also be derived. Here, however, according to what was said above, we are by no means supposed to be talking about the determination of the purely objective I, but rather about the determination of the *entire* I = X. Can a feeling arise from this determination?

According to the preceding description, a feeling presupposes, in part, the dependence of what is purely objective upon some stimulus [*Antrieb*], and in part, the dependence of what is subjective upon the former, upon what is objective. A dependency of the latter sort is by no means posited to be possible in this case, inasmuch as neither what is subjective nor what is objective is here supposed to be considered to be different from the other, but they are instead considered as absolutely unified [*als absolute Eins*] and are determined as absolutely unified. And yet, as was pointed out and explained above, we do not understand what this single unity [*dieses Eins*] is nor what its determination is supposed to be [IV, 45]. If we are nevertheless to understand anything at all in this case, then our only recourse is to begin with one of the two parts into which we necessarily divide ourselves, in consequence of our limits. It is most appropriate to begin with what is subjective, particularly since we are here dealing with the I insofar as what is objective is supposed be under the sway of what is subjective.

It is therefore quite certain that the I as intellect is immediately determined by the drive. A determination of the intellect is called a thought.

Hence:

(3) FROM THE MANIFESTATION OF THE DRIVE, HOWEVER, A THOUGHT NECESSARILY ARISES.

Against the argument we have just advanced for this claim, someone might raise the same objections we ourselves raised above: namely, that the intellect as such is absolute agility and is thus capable of no determination whatsoever, that the intellect *produces* its thoughts but that no thoughts can ever *be* produced in it. If so, then we will have to point out that in what follows the proposition that serves as the ground of the above claim will be restricted, and we will see that both assertions can very well stand alongside each other. There is therefore no room for any doubt *that* such a thought occurs as such, and we only have to concern ourselves with becoming precisely and determinately acquainted with this thought.

(a) We will first investigate this thought with respect to its *form*.

A *determinate* thinking, such as we have here, either appears to be determined by something that exists, as is the case when the object that is thought is supposed to be an actual object, or else it appears to be determined by another act of thinking. If it appears to be determined through the existence of the object, then the thought occurs within our consciousness in the way that it does because this is how the thing is constituted. If the determinate thinking is determined by another act of thinking, then we say that it follows from this other thinking, and we thereby obtain insight into a series of reasons [IV, 46].

Neither of these is the case here: not the first, because no objective determination is thought in this case, not even a determination of the objective I; instead, what is thought is a determination of the entire

48

I, which we are, to be sure, unable to grasp, but of which we at least know that it is not to be viewed as purely objective. Nor is this an instance of the second type, because the I thinks itself in this act of thinking, and it does so in accordance with its own fundamental essence, and not in accordance with any predicates derived from the latter. The thought of the I, however, and especially in this regard, is not conditioned by any other act of thinking, but itself conditions all other thinking.

It follows that this thought is not determined by anything outside itself, whether a being or an act of thinking, but is conditioned and determined absolutely through itself. This is a primary and immediate act of thinking. – As strange as such a claim may at first seem, it nevertheless follows correctly from the premises established above, and it is important both for the special philosophical science that we are here engaged in establishing and for transcendental philosophy as a whole. It therefore must be carefully advanced. – First of all, through this immediate act of thinking, thinking as such becomes absolute with respect to its form; we obtain a series that commences purely and simply with a thought that is itself not grounded on anything else and is not connected to anything else. Even though we have just now, in our philosophizing, grounded this thought further, by means of a drive, this has no influence on *ordinary* consciousness, which begins with this thought and is by no means a consciousness of the grounds in question, as we have also shown. From the standpoint of ordinary consciousness we know nothing more than that we are simply thinking in a certain way. – This must also be the case in any context in which being is supposed to depend on thinking and in which the real force is supposed to come under the sway of the concept. It should also be noted that this relation of what is subjective to what is objective is actually the original way in which what is subjective is related to what is objective in the I and that the opposite relationship, in which a thought is supposed to be dependent upon a being, is based [IV, 47] upon and must be derived from the former relationship. This point is demonstrated in other parts of philosophy, and it will also have to be brought into play later on in our present science. – This is particularly the case here because the thought to be described is also absolute with respect to its content: it is thought the way it is thought simply because this is how it is thought. This is of special importance for our science [of ethics], so that we can avoid being misled – as has so often been the case – into wanting to provide a further explanation of our consciousness of having duties (for this is what the thought to be described will prove to be) and wanting to derive it from grounds outside of itself, which is impossible and which would violate the dignity and absoluteness of the law.

In short, this thinking is the absolute principle of our essence [*Wesen*]. Through it we constitute our essence purely and simply; and our essence consists in this kind of thinking, for our essence is no material subsistence, like the essence of lifeless things, but is a consciousness, and a *determinate* consciousness at that – namely, the consciousness that is here to be exhibited.

We know immediately *that* we think in this manner, for thinking is just the immediate consciousness of one's determination as an intellect, and here in particular, of the determination of the intellect merely and purely as such. An immediate consciousness is called an *intuition*. In the case we are considering no material subsistence is intuited by means of a feeling, but instead the intellect is intuited immediately as such, and nothing but the intellect is intuited. For this reason, such an intuition is justifiably called an *intellectual intuition*. It is, however, the only intellectual intuition that occurs *originally* and *actually* in every human being, without the freedom of philosophical abstraction. The kind of intellectual intuition the transcendental philosopher imputes to everyone who is supposed to understand him is the mere form of this actual intellectual intuition; it is the mere intuition of inner, absolute spontaneity, in abstraction from the latter's determinacy. Without the actual intellectual intuition the philosophical one would not be possible [IV, 48], for we do not think originally in an abstract manner, but rather in a determinate manner.

(b) We will now describe the thought to be investigated with respect to its *content*.

Through the drive, the entire I is determined to absolute self-activity, and this is the determination that is thought in the act of thinking we are here considering. But the entire I cannot be grasped, and for this reason a determinacy of the entire I cannot be grasped immediately either. One can approximate the determinacy of the entire I only by means of a reciprocal determination of what is subjective by what is objective and vice versa, and this is how we shall proceed.

First of all, let us think of what is subjective as determined by what is objective. The essence of objectivity is absolute, unchangeable subsistence. Applied to what is subjective, this yields a constant and unchangeable – in other words, a lawful and necessary – thinking. The determining drive in this case is the drive to absolute self-activity. The content of the derived thought would therefore amount to this: that the intellect has to give itself the unbreakable law of absolute self-activity.

We now have to think of what is objective as determined by what is subjective. What is subjective is the positing of an absolute but completely undetermined power of freedom, as described in the previous section. What is here described as objective is determined, produced, and conditioned by this subjective power; the thought indicated [that is, the thought that the intellect must give itself the law of its own self-activity] is possible only on the condition that the I thinks of itself as free. [Finally, let us think of both what is subjective and what is objective,] of each determined by the other: the legislation in question manifests itself only on the condition that one thinks of oneself as free, but when one thinks of oneself as free, this legislation necessarily manifests itself. – With this, we have also removed the difficulty conceded above, that of ascribing any determinacy to the thinking subject as such. The thought we have described is not one that imposes itself unconditionally, for in that case it would cease to be an act of thinking and what is subjective would be transformed into something objective [IV, 49]. Instead, this thought imposes itself only insofar as one thinks something with absolute freedom: namely, freedom itself. The thought in question is not really a particular thought but only the *necessary manner* of thinking our freedom.[14] It is the same with all other necessity of thinking. Such necessity is not absolute necessity, nor can it be anything of the sort, since all thinking proceeds from a free act of thinking of ourselves; instead, the necessity of thinking is conditioned by the fact that there is any thinking at all.

An additional point to note is that the thought in question is grounded in a drive and hence must retain the character of the latter – though, to be sure, this feature of the thought is not a part of our consciousness, but follows from the preceding derivation of the

---

[14] "This is very significant." (Fichte's handwritten marginal remark, as noted in *SW*.)

thought. This character, however, is that of a postulate. – The content of the thought we have derived can therefore be briefly described as follows: we are required to think that we are supposed to determine ourselves consciously, purely and simply through concepts, indeed, in accordance with the concept of absolute self-activity; and this act of thinking is precisely that consciousness of our original tendency to absolute self-activity that we have been seeking.

Strictly speaking, our deduction is now concluded. Its proper and final goal was, as we know, to derive from the system of reason as such the necessity of thinking that we ought to act in a certain manner and to demonstrate that if any rational being whatsoever is assumed, then such a being must think such a thought. This much is absolutely demanded for the science of a system of reason, a science that is its own end.

Such a deduction also achieves several other benefits. Apart from the fact that nothing can be understood completely and correctly other than what one sees proceeding from its grounds [IV, 50], and hence that only a derivation of this sort produces the most perfect insight into the morality of our nature [*Wesen*], another benefit is that this derivation makes comprehensible the so-called categorical imperative. The latter no longer appears to be some sort of hidden property (*qualitas occulta*), which is what it previously appeared to be, though of course no positive pretext for such an interpretation was provided by the originator of the critique of reason.[15] Thanks to this derivation, that dark region of sundry, irrational enthusiasm [*Schwärmerei*], which has opened itself in connection with the categorical imperative (e.g., the notion that the moral law is inspired by the deity) is securely annihilated. This makes it all the more necessary to deploy freer and more varied ways of looking at our achievement, in order thereby to dispel completely any obscurity that might still cling to our own deduction, which was not so easy to do so long as we had to proceed under the strictures of a systematic presentation.

The upshot of the deduction just completed can be summarized as follows: a rational being, *considered as such*, is absolute and self-sufficient; such a being is purely and simply its own ultimate ground. Originally, that is, apart from its own agency [*Zutun*], it *is* absolutely nothing; through its own doing [*Tun*] it must make itself into what it is

---

[15] Immanuel Kant.

52

supposed to *become.* – This proposition is not proven, nor can it be proven. It is purely and simply up to each rational being to find himself in this manner and to grant the same.

Allow me to address the reader as follows: think of yourself in the manner I have just described. What is it you are really thinking when you do this? I do not expect you to go beyond the concept that you have posited and conceded, but simply to clarify this for yourself by means of mere analysis.

A rational being is *itself* supposed to produce everything that it is ever actually to be. You therefore have to ascribe to such a being some sort of existence prior to all actual (objective) being and subsistence, as we have already noted above. This manner of existing can be none other than existing as an intellect in and with concepts. In your present concept [of yourself] you therefore must have [IV, 51] thought of a rational being as an intellect. Moreover, you must have ascribed to this intellect the power to produce a being through its mere concept; for after all, you have presupposed it as an intellect precisely in order to find thereby a ground of being. In a word, in your concept of a rational being you have thought of what we derived above in section two under the name "freedom."

Everything now depends upon the following consideration: how much progress have you made so far toward finding your concept of a rational being to be conceivable? Are the features just described sufficient to allow you to think of self-sufficiency as the essence of reason? Certainly not; [through these features you are able to think] only of an empty, undetermined power of self-sufficiency. This merely renders your thought of a self-sufficient being possible, but not actual, which is, after all, how you have thought it. A power is something to which you merely *may* attach some actual being, as the ground of the latter, if such a being happens to be given to you in some other manner; but you do not *have to derive* any being from the concept of a mere power. This concept contains no information at all that would indicate *that* something actual has to be thought or *what sort of actuality* has to be thought. It might well be that the power of self-sufficiency is a power that can never be employed at all, or one that can be employed only from time to time; and in that case you would either possess no self-sufficiency at all, or only an intermittent self-sufficiency and by no means a self-sufficiency that endures (one that would constitute the *essence* of reason).

This, however, is not how you thought of the self-sufficiency of a rational being in the concept that is to be analyzed. You did not posit such self-sufficiency merely problematically, but categorically, as the *essence* of reason. What has been said so far is sufficient to explain what it means to posit something as essential: it means to posit it as necessary and as contained in and inseparable from the concept in question, as something already posited along with the concept and predestined. But this means that you would have posited *self-sufficiency* and *freedom* as *necessity*, which is undoubtedly self-contradictory and which you therefore could not possibly have been thinking. Hence you must have thought this being-posited-as-fixed [*Festgesetztsein*] in such a way that it also remained possible for you to think of freedom in conjunction with the same. Your determinacy in this case was a determinacy of the [IV, 52] free intellect; and a *necessary thinking* (by the intellect) of self-sufficiency as a norm, in accordance with which the intellect charges itself to determine itself freely, is such a determinacy of the free intellect. – Your concept of self-sufficiency thus contains both the power and the law demanding that one employ this power steadfastly. You cannot think of the concept of self-sufficiency without thinking of these two, [the power and the law,] as united. – As someone who has just freely decided to philosophize along with us, you are in the situation in which every rational being necessarily finds itself (assuming that you philosophize in accordance with the universal laws of reason); more specifically, your situation is the same as that of that rational being (the so-called "original I") that we are here thinking of as the representative of reason as such and whose system of thoughts it is our task to exhibit. If a rational being thinks of itself as self-sufficient – and this is precisely the presupposition with which we begin –, then it necessarily thinks of itself as free, and – this is what really matters here – it thinks its freedom under the law of self-sufficiency. This is the meaning of our deduction.

Here we began with the main point. But one can also convince oneself of the necessity of the deduced thought in another way. – Assume that a rational being thinks of itself as free in the merely formal meaning of that term, as explained above. Such a being is, however, finite; and every object of its reflection becomes limited or determinate for it merely through [this same act of] reflection. Consequently, for such a being its freedom, too, becomes something determinate. But what is a determinacy of freedom as such? We have just seen what this is.

In order to remove this point from the depths of the entire system of transcendental philosophy and to express it in the most comprehensive and incisive manner, I will put it as follows: I am an identity of subject and object = x. But I cannot think of myself in this way, since I can think only of objects, and when I do this I separate [myself as] what is subjective from them. I therefore have to think of myself as [both] subject *and* object. I connect the two by determining them reciprocally, each of them through the other (in accordance with the law of causality) [IV, 53]. What is objective in me, determined through what is subjective in me, provides [me with] the concept of freedom, as the power of self-sufficiency. What is subjective in me, determined through what is objective in me, provides the former with the concept of the necessity of determining myself through my freedom, but only in accordance with the concept of self-sufficiency. This latter thought, since it is the thought of my own original determination [*Urbestimmung*], is an immediate, primary and absolute thought. – Now neither should what is objective in me be thought of as dependent upon what is subjective (as in the first case), nor should what is subjective in me be thought of as dependent upon what is objective (as in the second case); instead, the two should be thought of as purely and simply one [*als schlechthin Eins*]. I think this as one by determining it with the aforementioned mutual determinacy (in accordance with the law of reciprocal interaction): that is, by thinking freedom as determining the law and the law as determining freedom. Neither of these is thought without the other, and insofar as one of them is thought, then so is the other. When you think of yourself as free, you are required to think your freedom under a law; and when you think of this law, you are required to think of yourself as free, for your freedom is presupposed by this law, which announces itself as the law of freedom.

Let us dwell for a moment on the last-mentioned part of the proposition we have just established. Freedom does not follow from the law, no more than the law follows from freedom. These are not two thoughts, one of which can be thought to depend upon the other; rather this is one and the same thought. This thought constitutes a complete synthesis (in accordance with the law of reciprocity), which is also how we have viewed it. In several passages Kant derives our conviction concerning freedom from our consciousness of the moral law.[16] This is to be

---

[16] See, e.g., Kant, *Critique of Practical Reason*, in Kant, *Practical Philosophy*, ed. and trans. Mary Gregor (Cambridge: Cambridge University Press, 1996) [henceforth = *CprR*], pp. 178–179 (*AA* 5: 48). *AA* = *Kant's gesammelte Schriften*, ed. Königlich Preußische Akademie der Wissenschaften (Berlin: Reimer/de Gruyter, 1900 ff.).

understood as follows: the appearance of freedom is an immediate fact of consciousness and by no means a consequence of any other thought. And yet, as was previously pointed out, one might still wish to explain this appearance further and could thereby transform it into an illusion. There is no theoretical reason for not doing this, but there is a practical one: namely, the firm resolution to grant primacy to practical reason [IV, 54], to hold the moral law to be the true and ultimate determination of our essence, and not to transform it into an illusion by means of sophistical reasoning – which is certainly a possibility for the free imagination. If, however, one does not go beyond the moral law, then one also does not go beyond the appearance of freedom, which thereby becomes for us the truth, inasmuch as the proposition, "I *am* free; freedom is the sole true being and the ground of all other being," is quite different from the proposition, "*I appear* to myself to be free." What can be derived from consciousness of the moral law, therefore, is faith *in the objective validity* of this appearance [of freedom]. "*I am actually free*": this is the first article of faith, which prepares us for the transition into an intelligible world and which first offers us firm footing therein. This faith is at the same time the point of unification between the two worlds [of doing and of being]; and our system, which is supposed to encompass both worlds, takes this as its point of departure. Doing cannot be derived from being, since this would transform doing into an illusion; and I am not *permitted* to consider my doing to be an illusion. Instead, being has to be derived from doing. The sort of reality that being receives in this manner in no way detracts from our true vocation; instead, we gain thereby. The I is not to be derived from the Not-I, life is not to be derived from death; but rather, conversely, the Not-I is to be derived from the I. That is why all philosophy has to start from the latter.

The thought just deduced has been called a "*law*" or a "*categorical imperative*"; the manner in which something is thought therein has been called an "*ought*," as opposed to a "being," and ordinary understanding finds itself expressed surprisingly well by such designations. We now wish to see how these same views of the matter also follow from our deduction.

As was indicated above, we are able to think of freedom as standing under [IV, 55] absolutely no law, but as containing the ground of its determinacy purely and entirely within itself – the determinacy of a thinking that is subsequently thought of as the ground of a being; and this is how we must think freedom if we want to think it correctly, for its essence lies in its concept, and the latter is absolutely undeterminable through anything outside itself. Since what we are thinking of is freedom, and freedom is determinable in all possible ways, we also can think it as subject to a hard and fast rule. The concept of such a rule, however, is something that only a free intellect could design for itself, and only a free intellect could freely determine itself in accordance with such a rule. The intellect could thus make for itself a great variety of different rules or maxims – for example, rules pertaining to self-interest, laziness, the oppression of others, and other similar rules – and could obey these rules steadfastly and without exception, and always freely. Let us now assume, however, that the concept of such a rule imposes itself on the intellect, i.e., that the intellect is, under a certain condition, required to think a certain rule, and only this rule, to be the rule governing its own free determinations. We may rightly assume something of this sort, since the intellect, though absolutely free with regard to the sheer occurrence of an act of thinking, still stands under determinate laws with regard to its way and manner of thinking.

In this way the intellect would be able to think of a certain way of acting as conformable to the rule and another way of acting as contradicting it. Actual acting, of course, always remains dependent upon absolute freedom; and the acting of the free intellect is not actually determined, is not mechanically necessary, for this would destroy any freedom of self-determination. Instead, all that is determined is the necessary concept of the intellect's acting. What then is the most appropriate way to designate such necessity in the mere concept [of the intellect's necessary way of acting], which is, however, by no means a necessity in actuality? I should think that the most appropriate way to do this would be to say that such acting *is fitting* [*gehöre*] or *appropriate* [*gebühre*] and *ought* to be, whereas the opposite way of acting is inappropriate and ought not to be.

As was shown above, the concept of such a rule is something purely and simply primary, something unconditioned, which possesses no ground outside itself, but is grounded completely in itself [IV, 56]. Hence the acting in question is not one that ought to occur for this or for that reason, or because something else has been willed or ought to exist; instead, this is an action that ought to occur purely and simply

57

because it ought to occur. This ought is therefore an absolute, categorical ought, and the rule in question is a law that is valid without exception, since its validity is simply subject to no possible condition whatsoever.

If it should be case that in this absolute ought one also thinks the imperative to suppress every inclination [*Neigung*], then this is a distinguishing feature of the ought that we are as yet unable to explain, since here we are relating this law merely to absolute freedom, within which no inclination or anything similar is even thinkable.

Such legislation has also and very appropriately been called "*autonomy*" or "*self-legislation.*" It can be called this in three different respects: – First of all, presupposing the law as such and considering the I merely as the free intellect, the law *as such* becomes a law for the latter when the intellect reflects on it and freely subjects itself thereto, and thus self-actively makes this law into the unbreakable maxim of all its willing. And the intellect must employ its power of judgment once again to find out what this law requires in every *particular* case (as should be obvious but will be more precisely demonstrated below, since it is not obvious to many people); and then it must yet again freely assign itself the task of realizing the concept it has found. Moral existence in its entirety is therefore nothing but an unbroken process in which a rational being continually legislates to itself; and where this legislation ceases, there immorality begins. – Furthermore [and secondly], as concerns the content of the law, nothing more is required other than absolute self-sufficiency, absolute undeterminability by anything other than the I. The material determination of the will according to the law is thus taken solely from ourselves, and all *heteronomy*, that is, any borrowing of the grounds for determining the will from anything outside of us, is an outright violation of the law. – [Third and] finally, the whole concept of our [IV, 57] necessary subjugation to a law arises solely through the absolutely free reflection of the I upon itself in its own true essence, its self-sufficiency. As has been shown, the thought that we have derived is not one that imposes itself unconditionally, which would be utterly incomprehensible and would abolish the concept of an intellect; nor does this thought impose itself by means of a feeling or anything similar; instead, it is a condition for thinking freely, the necessary *way* one must think if one is to think freely. It is therefore the I itself that brings itself into this entire relationship of lawfulness, and reason is, in every respect, its own law.

One can also clearly see here, I believe, how reason is able to be *practical*, and how this practical reason is by no means that miraculous and incomprehensible thing it is sometimes considered to be; practical reason is by no means a "second reason," but the same reason that we all surely recognize as theoretical reason. Reason is not a thing, which *is there* and *subsists*; instead, it is doing [*Tun*]: sheer, pure doing. Reason intuits itself: it is able to do this, and it does it, precisely because it is reason. Reason, however, cannot find itself to be any different than it is, namely, as a doing. But reason is *finite*, and everything that it represents becomes for it, simply by being represented by reason, something finite and determinate. Thus, merely through its self-intuition and through the law of finitude, to which such self-intuition is bound, reason's doing becomes, for reason itself, a determinate doing. The determinacy of pure doing as such, however, yields no being, but rather an ought. Thus reason *determines its own activity through itself.* But "*to determine an activity*" and "*to be practical*" are one and the same. – In a certain sense it has always been conceded to reason that it is practical – in the sense that it must find the *means* for some end given to it from outside itself, e.g., through our natural needs or by our free choice [*freie Willkür*]. Reason in this sense is called *technically practical*. We, however, maintain that reason sets itself an end purely and simply by and through itself, and to this extent it is absolutely practical. The practical dignity of reason lies in its very *absoluteness* [IV, 58], its indeterminability through anything outside of itself and its complete determinacy through itself. Anyone who fails to recognize this absoluteness – and one can only find it within oneself, through intuition – and considers reason to be nothing more than a mere power of ratiocination, which can be set in motion only if objects are first given to it from outside, will always find it incomprehensible how reason can be absolutely practical and will never cease to believe that the conditions for carrying out the law must be cognized in advance, before the law can be recognized.

(The perspectives upon philosophy as a whole that offer themselves at this point are manifold, and I cannot forgo the occasion to point out at least some of them. – Because it is self-intuiting and finite, reason determines through itself its own acting. This proposition has a twofold meaning, inasmuch as reason's acting can be viewed from two different sides. In the context of a treatise on ethics this proposition refers only to the kind of acting that particularly merits this name: the kind of acting that is accompanied by a consciousness of freedom and is recognized as "acting" even from the ordinary viewpoint, i.e., *willing* and *acting efficaciously*. But this same proposition applies just as well to the kind of acting that is, as such, found only from the transcendental viewpoint: the kind of acting that is involved *in representation*. The law reason gives to itself for the former type of action, that is, the moral law, is not a law that it obeys necessarily, since it is directed at freedom. The law reason gives itself in the latter case, however, the law of thinking, is a law that it obeys necessarily, since in applying it the intellect, even though it is active, is not freely active. Thus the entire system of reason – both with respect to what *ought* to be and what is simply posited as existing in consequence of this ought, in accordance with the former kind of legislation, and with respect to what is immediately found as being, in accordance with the latter kind of legislation – is determined in advance, as something necessary, through reason itself. Yet what reason itself assembles according to its own laws [IV, 59], it also should undoubtedly be able to dissemble again according to these same laws; i.e., reason necessarily cognizes itself completely, and hence an analysis of its entire way of proceeding, that is, a system of reason, is possible. – Thus everything in our theory meshes with everything else, and the necessary presupposition is possible only under the condition of these specific results and no others. Either all philosophy has to be abandoned, or the absolute autonomy of reason must be conceded. The concept of philosophy is reasonable only on this presupposition. All doubts and all denials of the possibility of a system of reason are grounded on the presupposition of *heteronomy*, on the presupposition that reason can be determined by something outside of itself. This presupposition, however, is absolutely contrary to reason and in conflict with the same.)

Description of the principle of morality according to this deduction

THE PRINCIPLE OF MORALITY IS THE NECESSARY THOUGHT OF THE INTELLECT THAT IT OUGHT TO DETERMINE ITS FREEDOM IN ACCORDANCE WITH THE CONCEPT OF SELF–SUFFICIENCY, ABSOLUTELY AND WITHOUT EXCEPTION.

It is a *thought*, and by no means a feeling or an intuition, although this thought is based upon an intellectual intuition of absolute activity. It is a *pure* thought, without the least admixture of feeling or sensory intuition, for it is the immediate concept that the pure intellect has of itself, as such. It is a *necessary* thought, for it is the form under which the freedom of the intellect is thought. It is the *first* and *absolute* thought, for, since it is the concept of the thinking subject itself, it is not grounded upon any other thought, as a consequence of the latter; nor is it conditioned by any other thought [IV, 60].

The content of this thought is that a free being *ought*, for the determinacy of freedom expresses itself precisely as an "*ought*." [It expresses the fact] that a free being ought to bring its freedom under a *law*, that the law in question is none other than *the concept of absolute self-sufficiency* (absolute indeterminability through anything outside it), and, finally, that this law is valid *without exception*, since it contains the original determination of a free being.

Transcendental view of this deduction

We began our reasoning by presupposing that the essence of the I consists in its self-sufficiency – or, rather, it consists in its tendency toward self-sufficiency, since this self-sufficiency can be thought of as something actual only under certain conditions, which have not yet been indicated. We have investigated how, on this presupposition, any I that thinks of itself will have to think of itself. Thus we began with the I's objective being. But is the I in itself something objective, something with no relation to a consciousness? Was, for example, the I that was set forth in § 1 not related to a consciousness? Undoubtedly it was referred to our consciousness, to the consciousness of we who were philosophizing. We now have to relate that I to the consciousness of the original I; and only in the context of this relationship can our deduction be seen from the correct viewpoint. It is not a dogmatic, but a transcendental-idealistic deduction. We do not, as it were, wish to infer an act of thinking from some being in itself; for the I exists only for and only in its knowledge. We are instead concerned precisely with an original system of thinking, an original concatenation of claims of reason among themselves and with one another. – A rational being posits itself as absolutely self-sufficient, because it is self-sufficient; and it is self-sufficient, because this is how it posits itself. In this relationship it is a subject–object = X. In positing itself in this way, it posits itself, on the one hand, as free (in the sense specified above), and, on the other, it subordinates its freedom to the law of self-sufficiency. These concepts constitute the [IV, 61] concept of its self-sufficiency, and the concept of self-sufficiency contains these concepts; the two are one and the same.

Certain misunderstandings and objections make it necessary to add the following remark: – We are not claiming that we are, from the ordinary viewpoint, conscious of the connection between the thought we have derived and the grounds of the same. It is well known that insight into the grounds of the facts of consciousness is something that pertains solely to philosophy and is possible only from the transcendental viewpoint. – Nor are we claiming that the thought in question ever occurs among the facts of consciousness with the universality and at the level of abstraction with which we have derived it, nor are we claiming that one ever becomes conscious of such a law for one's freedom as such without the further assistance of free reflection. Only by means of philosophical abstraction does one elevate oneself to such universality, and one performs this abstraction in order to be able to set forth the problem in a determinate manner. In ordinary consciousness nothing occurs as a fact but determinate thinking, and certainly not abstract thinking. Abstraction, after all, presupposes free acting on the part of the intellect. We therefore claim no more than the following: if one thinks of *determinate* actions – real and not merely ideal actions, as goes without saying – as free actions, then, along with this thought, another thought will impose itself on us: namely, the thought that such actions *ought* to be regulated in a certain way. Even if one never has such an experience when one thinks of one's *own* actions, because one is always driven by passions and desires and thus never really becomes aware of one's own freedom, one will still find this principle within oneself when one judges those actions of others that one thinks of as free. Thus if someone denies that he has any personal consciousness of the moral law, as a fact of his inner experience of himself, he may find himself to be completely in the right in a dispute with a defender of this fact [of the moral law] who does not sufficiently understand himself – who, e.g., believes that this fact is supposed to be understood as a universally expressed moral law, whereas something of this sort, by its very nature, simply cannot be an [IV, 62] immediate fact. But if the person in question were to deny what we are asserting – that is, that this law pronounces determinate utterances regarding individual, free acts –, then, so long as he remains impartial and does not keep thinking about his own philosophical system, he can easily be convinced that there is a contradiction between his claim and his behavior, at least with respect to his judgment of others. He does not, for example, become indignant toward and infuriated with the fire that engulfs his house, but is indignant toward and infuriated with the person who set that fire or who was careless. Would he not be a fool to become infuriated with this person if he did not presuppose that he could also have acted otherwise and that he ought to have acted otherwise? [IV, 63].

PART II

Deduction of the reality and applicability of the principle of morality

Preliminary remark concerning this deduction

(1) What is meant by the "reality" or the "applicability" of a principle or (which means the same thing in this context) of a concept? more specifically, what kind of reality can pertain to the concept of morality?

To say that a concept possesses reality and applicability means that our world – that is to say, the world for us, the world of our consciousness – is in some respect determined by this concept. The concept in question is one of those concepts through which we think objects; and, because we think objects by means of this concept or in this manner, the object possesses certain distinctive features [*Merkmale*] for us. To seek the reality of a concept thus means to investigate how and in what way it determines an object. – I will clarify this by means of several examples.

The concept of *causality* possesses reality, because it is through this concept that a determinate connection arises among the manifold objects of my world. In consequence of this concept, thinking proceeds from one thing to another, and one can infer from an effect, as such, to a cause [IV, 64] or from a known cause to an effect. The act of thinking of the one is already included in a certain respect in the thought of the other. The concept of *right* possesses reality. Within the infinite range of freedom (the sphere of *being free* [*des Freiseins*], as something objective, since it is only under this condition that I find myself in the domain of the concept of right), I think of my own sphere [of freedom] as necessarily limited; hence I think of freedom, or of free beings [*freie Wesen*] outside of me, with whom I enter into community by means of mutual limitation [of our spheres of freedom]. It is therefore through the concept of right that there first arises for me a community of free beings.[1]

There is, however, a noteworthy difference in the way our world is determined by each of the two concepts that have been introduced [viz., the concept of causality and the concept of right], and I wish to draw attention to this distinction at once, since this is an excellent way to prepare one for the question that we shall be trying to answer in this section. An apodictically valid theoretical proposition follows from each of these concepts: [in the first case,] every effect has its cause, and [in the second] all human beings, as such, possess rights, and they possess them precisely for right's sake. With respect to my own practice, however, it can never occur to me to deprive an effect of its cause; this is something I can neither think nor will nor accomplish. In contrast, I can very easily think of treating another human being in a manner that violates his rights; this is something I can will to do, and I very often also have the physical power to act in this manner. One should note this point carefully: I cannot deny my theoretical conviction that someone else possesses rights, despite the fact that I may treat him in a manner that violates his rights; nor can I rid myself of this conviction. Yet this conviction [concerning rights] is not accompanied by any practical compulsion. In contrast, the conviction that every effect has a cause completely eliminates any practice that might be opposed to it.

We are here dealing with the principle or concept of *morality* [*Sittlichkeit*]. This concept has already been derived, in and for itself, as a determinate form of thinking, that is, as the only possible manner of thinking our own freedom. Something [IV, 65] within our consciousness is therefore already determined by means of the concept of morality: namely, our consciousness of our own freedom. This, however, is only what is immediately determined through the concept of freedom. The concept of freedom might also determine several other things mediately or indirectly, and this is precisely the question we are now investigating.

---

[1] This is a summary of the deduction of the applicability (and hence of the "reality") of the concept of right [*Recht*] in Part Two of Fichte's *Grundlage des Naturrechts*. See *FNR*, pp. 53–84 (*SW* III: 57–91; *GA* I/3: 361–388).

In accordance with its deduction, the concept of morality by no means refers to anything that is, but rather to something that ought to be. It proceeds purely from the essence of reason, without any foreign admixture, and it demands nothing but self-sufficiency. It pays no heed to experience; instead, it resists all determination through anything whatsoever that is drawn from experience. When one speaks of the reality of the concept of morality, then this cannot – at least not *to begin with* – mean that something is immediately realized in the world of appearances simply by thinking this concept. The object of this concept, i.e., what arises in us when we think in accordance with the concept of morality (see the introduction to our *Natural Right*[2]) can only be an *idea* [*Idee*],[3] a mere thought *within us*, with no claim that anything in the actual world *outside us* corresponds to this concept. This immediately raises the question, what is this idea? Or, since ideas certainly cannot be grasped [*aufgefaßt*], how and in what way is this idea to be described? (I am presupposing that one is aware that ideas cannot be thought immediately, just as, previously, the I as subject–object = X could not be thought; but one can nevertheless indicate how one ought to proceed in one's thinking in order to grasp ideas, even if one is unable, in the end, to grasp them [adequately], just as, previously, [in the case of the I as subject–object,] we could at least indicate that the subject and the object were supposed to be thought purely and simply as one. Ideas are *problems* or *tasks* for thinking, and they occur in our consciousness only to the extent that we are able to comprehend at least this task.) Or, to formulate the same question in a more popular fashion, when we are told that we purely and simply ought to do something, *what* is it that we purely and simply ought to do?

(2) WHAT IS THOUGHT OF IN ACCORDANCE WITH THE CONCEPT OF MORALITY [IV, 66], OR THE OBJECT DETERMINED THEREBY, IS THE IDEA OF WHAT WE OUGHT TO DO. WE CANNOT, HOWEVER, DO ANYTHING WITHOUT HAVING SOME OBJECT OF OUR ACTIVITY IN THE SENSIBLE WORLD. FROM WHERE DOES THIS OBJECT COME, AND BY WHAT IS IT DETERMINED?

---

[2] See *FNR*, p. 12 note h and pp. 9–10 (*SW* III: 12 note and 8–9; *GA* I/3: 322 note and 319–320).

[3] In contrast to a concept of the understanding, which applies to the objects of experience and is involved in a possible empirical cognition, an "idea" [*Idee*], in the Kantian sense, is a "concept of reason," which can never be adequately exemplified in experience and cannot be "grasped" or "comprehended" [*aufgefaßt*] at all in the manner of an objective concept. Examples of such ideas include God, freedom, and immortality. For Kant, ideas of reason have a regulative but not a constitutive function. See *KrV*, A312 ff./B368 ff.

"I *ought* to do something" means: I ought to produce the thing in question outside of me; or even if I could never complete what I ought to do, inasmuch as an infinite goal is undoubtedly posited for me thereby, a goal I could never realize and which therefore never *is* but always only *ought to be*: in that case I at least always ought to act efficaciously in a manner that advances me along the path toward my goal. In the latter case I certainly ought actually to produce a good many things that lie along this path.

Since I am finite, however, I must always have some stuff [*Stoff*] for my activity; or, to say the same thing, what is required of me is not something I can produce from nothing.

There would therefore have to be something in the sensible world *upon which* I would have to act in order to draw nearer to or to approximate the realization of the idea in question, which is in itself infinite and unreachable. To which domain of the sensible world do the demands made upon me by the moral law refer? How am I even supposed to recognize this domain, and to do so systematically? More specifically, how am I supposed to recognize *how* I ought to treat each determinate object within this domain in accordance with the moral law – how I ought to treat precisely this A and this B, etc.?

To begin with, it is immediately evident that what I am supposed to work upon [*bearbeiten*] must be the sort of thing that *can* be worked upon by me, that I possess the physical power for the kind of work that is required. – Later on we will discuss what might, from the transcendental viewpoint, be called a physical power as such. Here, however, and to begin with, we can say only the following:

A free being acts as an intellect, which is to say that it acts in accordance with a concept of an effect, a concept designed prior to the effect in question. What is to be brought about must therefore be so constituted that it can at least be thought of by an intellect; more specifically, it must be so constituted that it can be thought of as being or as not-being (i.e., as contingent with respect to its being), in which case the free intellect, when it designs its concept of an end, chooses between the being and the not-being of the same [IV, 67]. This observation is enough to indicate to us the unique sphere in which alone we have to seek to find what is possible through our causality, inasmuch as a considerable part of what exists is excluded by the preceding observation. This is because some things in our world appear to us to be necessary; we cannot think these otherwise than as they are, and thus we also cannot will them to be otherwise than they are, inasmuch as willing is bound to the laws of thinking and is preceded by a concept. Other things, however, appear to us to be contingent with respect to their being. I cannot, for example, will to posit something outside of all space, for I cannot think of anything outside of all space; but I am certainly able to think of something as occupying a place in space that is *different* from the one it actually occupies at present, and thus I can also *will* to alter its place.

A thorough and complete philosophy has to explain why some things appear to us to be contingent in this manner, and in doing this it will also determine the boundary and the extent of what is contingent. To be sure, these questions have until now not even been asked, much less answered.

We can be guided in our investigation by noting that when something bears the distinguishing feature of contingency this is usually a sign that it is thought to be a product of our freedom; in any case, all products of our freedom are thought of as contingent (which is how this proposition is set forth and demonstrated in our *Wissenschaftslehre*).[4] Thus, for example, a representation is thought to be contingent in relation to the being of what it represents; we believe that the latter could always exist, even if it were not represented, and we believe this because we find the representation to be, with respect to its form, a product of the absolute freedom of thinking, but with respect to its matter, a product of the necessity of thinking.

From this analogy we may conclude that *everything* contingent in the world of appearances is in a certain sense to be derived from the concept of freedom and to be regarded as a product thereof. What might it mean were this proposition to be confirmed? [IV, 68]. By no means would this mean simply that the objects in question are posited by means of the ideal activity of the intellect, in the latter's function as the productive power of imagination; for here, in this treatise on ethics, we are presupposing that one is already familiar with this point, which is

---

[4] See, for example, *SK*, p. 276: "It will be apparent that what is posited as a product of the I can be nothing other than an intuition of X, an image thereof, but in no sense X itself, as is evident from theoretical principles [. . . .] That it is posited as a product of the I in its freedom means that it is posited as *contingent*, as something that did not necessarily have to be as it is, but might also have been otherwise" (translation modified) (*SW* I: 317; *GA* I/2: 442).

established in the foundational portion of philosophy as a whole and which is valid not merely for those objects of our world that are thought to be contingent, but also for those that are thought to be necessary. Nor would this mean that the objects in question are posited as products of our *real* practical efficacy in the sensible world, for this would contradict the presupposition that they are regarded as things that actually exist without any assistance from us. The proposition set forth problematically above would therefore have to mean something like the following, which occupies a middle ground [between the two extremes just considered]: namely, that our freedom itself *is a theoretical principle for the determination of our world.* Let us now add a few words to elucidate this point. Our world is absolutely nothing other than the Not-I; it is posited only in order to explain the limitedness of the I, and hence it receives all its determinations only through opposition to the I. Among other predicates, however, or rather, more than any other predicate, that of "freedom" is supposed to pertain to the I. Accordingly, what is posited in opposition to the I – namely, the world – must also be determined through this predicate. And thus the concept of *being free* [*Begriff des Freiseins*] would furnish us with a theoretical law of thinking that would necessarily govern the ideal activity of the intellect.

We have already encountered examples of this kind of determination of our objects in another science, the doctrine of right. Since I am free, I posit the objects of my world as modifiable; I ascribe to myself a body that can be set in motion purely through my will and in accordance with my concepts; I assume beings like me outside of myself, etc.[5] Here, however, the investigation would have to be extended even further, and the proofs of this assertion would have to reach even deeper, since we here find ourselves precisely at the ultimate point of origin of all reason.

Were this conjecture – that is, the conjecture that a part of the world we find is determined through freedom, as a theoretical principle – to be confirmed, and were it to turn out that it is precisely this part of the world that constitutes the sphere of the objects of our duties [IV, 69], then it would follow that the law of freedom, which addresses consciousness as a practical law, would only be a continuation of what that same law of freedom, as a theoretical principle, had already initiated, though without any consciousness thereof on the part of the intellect. This law would have determined by itself the sphere over which it has

---

[5] *FNR*, §§ 6, 5, and 3, respectively.

dominion; it could not assert anything in its current capacity [as a practical law] that it had not already asserted in its previous one [as a theoretical principle]. To begin with, this law would determine something purely and simply, and this something would thereby be *posited* as constituted in this particular way. Subsequently, by means of our practical freedom, which stands under the domain of this law, the law would also *preserve* this same thing, with the same constitution, over the course of time; and the content of this law, in its practical function, could also be expressed as follows: act in accordance with your cognition of the original determinations (the final ends) of the things outside you. For example, a theoretical consideration of the concept of my own freedom yields the proposition "every human being is free." This same concept, considered practically, yields the command, "you ought to treat a human being purely and simply as a free being." Similarly, the theoretical proposition, "my body is the instrument of my activity in the sensible world," becomes, when considered as a practical command, the injunction, "treat your body only as a means to the end of your freedom and self-activity, but never as an end itself nor as an object of enjoyment."

Were all this to be confirmed, then the principle of morality would acquire a reality and an objective meaning entirely different from what has previously been maintained, and the question raised above – namely, where do the objects for the required activity come from, and what is their principle of cognition? – would be answered. The principle of morality would itself be both a theoretical and a practical principle: in the former capacity it would provide itself with the *matter*, the determinate content of the law, and in the latter capacity it would give itself the *form* of the law, the command. This principle would revert into itself, would stand in reciprocal interaction with itself, and from a single starting point we would obtain a complete and satisfying system. Something outside of us would have the final end that it has because we ought to treat it in a certain way; and we ought to treat it in this manner because it has this final end [IV, 70]. We would thus have found both the *idea* we have been seeking – that is, the idea of *what we ought to do* – and the *substrate in which* we ought to approximate the realization of this idea.

(3) What is the meaning of the concept of a physical power to act efficaciously upon objects, and how does such a concept arise for us?

First of all, what are we really conscious of when we believe that we are conscious of our own efficacy in the sensible world? What can be contained in this immediate consciousness, and what cannot be contained in it? – We are immediately conscious [both] of our concept of an end and of actually willing, of an absolute self-determination through which the mind is, as it were, contracted into a single point. Moreover, we are immediately conscious of the reality and of the actual sensation of an object as something that is actually given in the sensible world, but which was previously only thought of in the concept of an end. (Someone might tentatively object that we are also conscious of the *work* of producing, which occupies the middle ground between the decision of the will and its realization in the sensible world. To this I would respond as follows: this is not a special consciousness, but only the previously indicated gradual consciousness of our satisfaction. The latter sort of consciousness begins with the making of the decision and continues progressively, as willing continues progressively, right up to the *complete* execution of our concept of an end. Hence the consciousness [of the "work" of producing] is only the synthetic unification of the two kinds of consciousness previously indicated: consciousness of the act of willing and consciousness of what is willed as something actual.)

We are by no means conscious of the *connection* between our willing and the sensation of the reality of what was willed. – According to our claim, our will is supposed to be the cause of this reality. How might this occur? Or, to express this same question transcendentally, as is only proper, How might we ever come to assume such a remarkable harmony between a concept of an end and an actual object outside us [IV, 71], the ground of which is supposed to lie not in the object itself but in the concept? – Let me make this question clearer by contrasting it with another one. A cognitive concept is supposed to be a *copy [Nachbild]* of something outside us; a *concept of an end* is supposed to be a *model* or *pre-figuration* [*Vorbild*] for something outside us. In the former case, the appropriate question concerns not the ground of this harmony *in itself* – for that would make no sense, given that unity and harmony between opposites exist only insofar as they are thought by an intellect –; instead, what is in question is the ground for *assuming* such a harmony *of the concept, as what comes second, with the thing, as what comes first*. So, conversely, in our present case we are asking about the ground for assuming a harmony *of the thing, as what comes second, with the concept, as what comes first.*

In the former case, the question received the following answer: both the concept and the thing are one and the same, simply viewed from different sides; the concept, provided it is a concept that is necessary to reason, is itself the thing, and the thing is nothing other than the necessary concept of it. What if we were to receive a similar answer in the present case? What if what we believe we have produced outside of ourselves were nothing other than our concept of an end, viewed from a certain side – with the proviso that this harmony occurs only under a certain condition, and that when something meets this condition we say, "we are able to do this," and when it does not, we say, "we are not able to do this"?

When what I have willed becomes actual it is the object of a sensation. There must therefore occur a *determinate feeling*, in accordance with which the object is posited, since all reality is present for me only under this condition. Therefore, in the case we are now considering, my *willing* would be accompanied by a *feeling* that refers to what is willed. An advantage of looking at the matter in this way is that the sphere of our inquiry falls solely within the I; thus we have to discuss only what goes on within us, and by no means do we have to discuss anything that is supposed to go on outside of us.

Feeling is always the expression of our *boundedness*; so too here. More specifically, in our present case there is a transition from a feeling referring to the object as it is supposed [IV, 72] to be, without any help from us, to another feeling referring to the same object as it is supposed to be modified by our efficacious acting. Since the latter is supposed to be a product of our freedom, there is here a transition from a bounded to a less bounded state.

Our question can now be expressed more precisely as follows: *how is a self-determination through freedom (an act of willing) connected with an actual extension of our boundaries*; or, expressed transcendentally, *how do we come to assume that such an extension occurs?*

This assumption of a new reality outside of me is a further determination of my world, an alteration of the latter within my consciousness. My world, however, is determined through its opposition to or contrast with me; that is, the world as I originally find it, the world that is supposed to exist without any assistance from me, is determined by its opposition to me, through its contrast with me as I necessarily find myself to be, not as I perhaps ought to make myself freely. At the basis of any change (a changed view) of my world, there would therefore have to lie some change (a changed view) of myself.

If, therefore, I were able to change something in myself by means of my will, then my world would necessarily be changed as well; and by displaying the possibility of the former that of the latter would be explained as well. "*My world* is changed" means "*I* am changed"; "*my world* is determined further" means "*I* am determined further."

The question raised above can now be phrased as follows: what might it mean to say "*I* change *myself*," and how can this be thought? If this question is answered, then the other question – how am I able to change my world? – is undoubtedly already answered along with it. – As was just noted, in any *willing* whatsoever I determine myself, I concentrate my entire being, everything indeterminate and merely determinable, into a single determinate point. Hence, *I* change *myself*. An occurrence of what is willed does not, however, follow upon every act of willing [IV, 73]. The I that can be changed through every act of willing and the I whose alteration simultaneously changes our view of the world must therefore be different I's, and the determination of the latter must not follow necessarily from the determination of the former. But what is the I in the former sense of the term? We are acquainted with this from our previous discussion (§ 2): the I in question is the I that has torn itself loose from itself by means of absolute reflection upon itself and has put itself forward as self-sufficient, i.e., as dependent only on its own concept. The I in this sense of the term can be determined *only* through[6] what can only be thought, since the I, so understood, stands completely and utterly under the sway of the concept. – But is there another I as well? According to the elucidation provided earlier, there undoubtedly is such an I: namely, that *objective*, striving and driving I *from which* the I just described – in which the intellect as such has the upper hand – has torn itself loose in order to put itself forward as self-sufficient. Let us assume that the striving in question aims at a certain specific, that is, determinate, determination of the will, as it undoubtedly must, since it can be thought of only as a determinate striving. Let us now posit a free determination of the will that does not coincide with this same striving, that is not required by the latter. One may certainly assume such a determination of the will, since the freedom of the will stands under absolutely no condition, beyond the possibility

---

[6] Following Fichte's marginal note in his personal copy of *The System of Ethics*, as recorded by Fichte's son in *SW*, which replaces "through" [*durch*] with "*only* through" [nur *durch*].

of thinking, and has expressly torn itself loose from the influence of any drive. In this case, I-hood would, so to speak, remain divided in the same way it was divided above: the drive would not coincide with the will, and I would be conscious only of my willing, of my sheer empty willing. A part of the I would be changed – namely, the state of the will – but not the entire I. The driving I [*das treibende Ich*] would remain in the same state it was in before; it would remain unsatisfied, since the kind of willing that the driving I would have demanded would by no means have been the kind of willing that was actually produced, but rather, an entirely different kind of willing [IV, 74]. If one makes the opposite assumption – namely, that the determination of the will accords with the drive – then such a separation would no longer occur; the entire, unified I would be changed, and following such an alteration of the I, our world would also be determined differently.

In order to combine the various views we have now obtained of this matter, let us review what we said earlier. We surmised that our world itself might well be determined, in some respect, in accordance with the original striving mentioned above, that is, in accordance with freedom as a theoretical principle. But anything that is supposed to determine something else must itself be determinate. In this context, therefore, we are talking about freedom as something objective, and hence, quite correctly, about the original and essential striving of the rational being. In accordance with such a surmise, our world would be originally determined through freedom as a theoretical principle; and it would also be through this same principle that contingency in particular, and hence the possibility of carrying out our free decisions, would enter into our world.

The following would be the result of everything that has been put forward problematically: the ground of the connection between appearances and our willing is the connection between our willing and our nature [*Natur*]. We can do only that to which our nature drives us, and we cannot do anything to which it does not drive us and to which we resolve ourselves only with unregulated freedom, through the power of imagination. – It should also be carefully noted that the possibility of satisfying the moral law is here found to be determined not by any foreign principle lying outside of this law (heteronomously) but by the moral law itself (autonomously).

In order to avoid all misunderstandings, we still have to point out that what drives our nature and determines our physical power need not be only the moral law itself. After all, we are also able to carry out immoral decisions. Thus a new boundary line would here have to be drawn. This much, however, can be asserted: what is commanded by the moral law must fall completely [IV, 75] within the sphere of our physical power, and with this we have warded off from the start any objection that it might be impossible to satisfy the moral law.

The intent of this remark was to determine what would have to be accomplished by the deduction here announced. This end has now been achieved. It is clear that the deduction has to prove the following main propositions.

(1) ACCORDING TO WHAT WAS SAID IN PART ONE, A RATIONAL BEING OUGHT TO POSIT ITSELF AS ABSOLUTELY FREE AND SELF-SUFFICIENT. IT CANNOT DO THIS, HOWEVER, WITHOUT ALSO SIMULTANEOUSLY DETERMINING ITS WORLD THEORETICALLY IN A CERTAIN MANNER. THESE ACTS OF THINKING OF ITSELF AND THINKING OF ITS WORLD OCCUR THROUGH ONE AND THE SAME ACT AND ARE ABSOLUTELY ONE AND THE SAME ACT OF THINKING; BOTH ARE INTEGRAL PARTS OF ONE AND THE SAME SYNTHESIS. – FREEDOM IS A THEORETICAL PRINCIPLE.

(2) FREEDOM, WHICH WAS ALSO SHOWN TO BE A PRACTICAL LAW IN PART ONE, REFERS TO THESE DETERMINATIONS OF THE WORLD AND DEMANDS TO PRESERVE THEM AND TO BRING THEM TO PERFECTION.

§4

Deduction of an object of our activity as such

First theorem

A RATIONAL BEING CANNOT ASCRIBE A POWER TO ITSELF WITHOUT SIMULTANEOUSLY THINKING OF SOMETHING OUTSIDE OF ITSELF TO WHICH THIS POWER IS DIRECTED.

[IV, 76]

Preliminary remark

All the propositions set forth in Part I are purely formal and lack any material meaning. We have the insight *that* we ought [to do something], but we comprehend neither *what* we ought to do nor *where* we have to accomplish what we ought to do.[7] We arrived at such a realization in the

---

[7] *noch* worin *wir das Gesollte darzustellen haben.*

same way that all merely formal philosophizing arises: we set forth abstract thoughts, and by no means concrete ones; we described a [certain act of] reflection as such and in general, without determining it, i.e., without indicating the conditions of its possibility. This was not a mistake on our part, since, in accordance with the laws governing any systematic presentation, this is how we had to proceed. We knew full well that we were proceeding in this manner, and we had no intention of concluding our investigation after merely setting forth these purely formal propositions, as though everything had already been accomplished.

This observation also provides us with a determinate grasp of the task now before us: we have to specify the conditions for the possibility of the reflection set forth in Part I. It will turn out that the proximate condition of the latter is, in turn, subject to another condition, which itself is further conditioned, etc. We will thereby obtain an uninterrupted chain of conditions, which we wish to set forth in a series of theorems.

From this it also follows that, even though Part II will carry us into new and different territory, this will not occur through any leap, but rather, through a gradual and progressive process of systematic reasoning; and here we are picking up the thread [of our reasoning] precisely where we left it at the end of Part I. There we claimed that, just as surely as we are conscious of ourselves at all, we ascribe to ourselves an absolute power of freedom [IV, 77]. Now we are asking how this is possible; and [once we have established this consciousness of freedom] we will then attach conditions to it that are still to be indicated and thereby attach these same conditions to immediate self-consciousness. Such a process of attachment constitutes the essence of a philosophical deduction.

As we shall soon see, the proofs to be conducted here by no means remove the need for an inner intuition of that activity of oneself through which one brings into being the concepts to be investigated. Since we do indeed rely upon observation of our own self-activity, the propositions presented in this chapter could also have been presented as tasks, and thus we could have expressed the preceding theorem as a task: namely, to think the power of freedom in a determinate manner, etc. Instead, however, we have adopted an alternative manner of presentation. This decision could be adequately justified simply by our wish to display a certain methodological freedom and, at least for the time being, to protect our system from a uniform style; but we have also adopted this alternate manner of presentation for another reason: namely, because it is our goal to indicate the precise point to which attention has to be directed in the determination of this act of thinking – for, as we shall see, there are several conditions and determinations of the latter.

Explanation

Anyone who hears the preceding words will undoubtedly understand them as follows: it is utterly impossible for anyone to think of his power of freedom without at the same time imagining something objective upon which he freely acts, even if this is not a determinate object, but simply the mere form of objectivity, the form of stuff as such, to which the acting is directed. And this is indeed how these words are meant to be understood, and in this regard they stand in no need of explanation. In a different regard, however, some explanation is needed concerning [IV, 78] the form of our claim, the condition under which it is supposed to be valid, and the matter or content of the same.

As regards the former, [that is, as regards the form of this claim,] someone might say, "Just now, in Part I, we were asked to think the sheer empty power of freedom, without any object; and if we had not actually been able to do this, then all the instruction that was supposed to have been bestowed upon us up to this point would have been lost." To this I would respond as follows: on the one hand, there is the sort of abstract thinking that is characteristic of philosophy and that is conditioned with respect to its very possibility by that experience that precedes it; we do not begin our life by engaging in speculation, but with life itself. On the other hand, there is that original and determinate thinking from the viewpoint of experience, and this is something else altogether. The concept of freedom, as we possessed it earlier, is a concept that arose for us by means of abstraction, through analysis; but we certainly could not have obtained this concept in this manner if we had not previously possessed it as something *given* and *found* at some point in time. What we are concerned with now is this latter state, viewed as a state of the original I and not a state of the *philosophizing* I; and our view of this matter is as follows: you cannot *find* yourself to be free without simultaneously finding, in the same consciousness, an object upon which your freedom is supposed to be directed.

Next, [concerning the condition under which our claim is supposed to be valid,] we are claiming that there is an absolute synthesis of thinking of a power and thinking of an object, and thus a *reciprocal* conditioning of one of these acts of thinking through the other. First of all, neither precedes the other in time, as it were, but both are thought at the same moment. If, moreover, one simply considers the fact that both are being *thought*, then one must not assume any dependency of either act of thinking upon the other; instead, consciousness finds itself irresistibly driven from the one to the other. But if one considers *how* both are thought, then thinking of freedom is an immediate or direct act of thinking, in consequence of an intellectual intuition, whereas thinking of the object is a mediated or indirect act of thinking. The former is not viewed through the latter; [IV, 79] on the contrary, it is the latter that is viewed through the former. Freedom is our vehicle for cognizing objects, but the cognition of objects is not, in turn, the vehicle for cognizing our freedom.

Finally, [concerning the content of this claim,] two different things are being claimed: first, that we are to think of an object that is supposed to lie *outside* of the free intellect; second, that the free acting [of the I] is supposed to *be related* to an object, and to be related to it in such a manner that the acting is not supposed to be determined by the object but, conversely, the object by the acting. Our proof will therefore have to demonstrate two things: first, the necessity of the *opposition*, and second, the necessity of the determinate *relationship* in question.

Proof

(1) A RATIONAL BEING CANNOT ASCRIBE TO ITSELF THE POWER OF FREEDOM WITHOUT ALSO THINKING OF SEVERAL ACTUAL AND DETERMINATE ACTIONS AS POSSIBLE THROUGH ITS FREEDOM.

The latter half of the proposition asserts the same thing as the former half; the two are identical. "I ascribe freedom to myself": this just means that I think of several actions, which differ among themselves, as equally possible for me. In order to obtain insight into the truth of this claim one need do no more than analyze one's concept of a power of freedom.

According to what was said earlier, a capacity or "power" [*Vermögen*] is absolutely nothing more than a product of sheer thinking, a product that thinking produces in order to attach to it something actual that is not originally posited, but first arises in time; and it does this because finite reason is able to think only discursively and mediately. Anyone who, in connection with the concept of a power, thinks of anything other than such a mere means of attachment does not understand what he himself is thinking. – The power in question is in this case not first to be inferred from the actuality [that is attached to thinking thereby] [IV, 80], as often happens in other cases; on the contrary, in this case thinking is supposed to commence with the power as what is primary and immediate. Even under this condition, however, the power cannot be thought of without simultaneously thinking of the actuality, since the two are synthetically united concepts; and no power – and indeed, nothing whatsoever – would be thought without thinking of the actuality. I was careful to say that the actuality must be *thought* and not that it must be immediately *perceived*; if I may so express myself, the actuality must be designed through a merely ideal function of the power of imagination, not as something *actual* but simply as something possible. Actuality is perceptibility, the capacity to be sensed [*Empfindbarkeit*]; and this is necessarily posited, not with respect to its being [*Wesen*], but with respect to its form alone. What is [here] ascribed to the I is the power to produce [something with] the capacity to be sensed, but only the power to do this, not the actual deed itself. – Here we may avoid the question concerning how reason might originally arrive at this mere form [of actuality], for this question will be adequately discussed below. It is sufficient [to have established here] that *we* can think of this form and, by means of it, can think of a sheer power.

Furthermore, the power that is supposed to be thought in this case is a *free* power; by no means are we here to think of a determinate power that contains its mode of expression within its own nature, as in the case of objects. How does a rational being proceed in order to think such a free power? We can do no more than describe this procedure, and we must leave it to each person to rely upon his own inner intuition in order to convince himself of the correctness of our description.

The I posits itself – [it posits itself in this case] only ideally [*idealiter*], it only represents itself in a certain way, without actually and in fact being like this or *finding* itself to be so. The I posits itself as freely choosing among opposing determinations of actuality. This object = A, which is perhaps already determined without any help from us, could also be determined = X, just as it could also be determined = − X [IV, 81], or in some other way as well, and so on *ad infinitum*. This is how the I announces itself, as though it were saying, "Which of those determinations I will choose, or whether I will choose none of them at all, but leave A just as it is: all of this depends solely on the freedom of my thinking. The determination that I do choose, however, will actually arise for my perception in the sensible world, so long as I determine myself through the will to produce it." – Only insofar as I posit myself in this manner do I posit myself as free – that is, think of what is actual as dependent upon my own real force, which is under the sway of a sheer concept. Anyone who wants to think this thought in a determinate manner will soon convince himself of this.

One should note that what is being thought in this act of thinking is no determinate something $= X$, which is supposed to be produced; instead, all that is being thought here is the form of determinacy as such, i.e., the mere power of the I to select this or that from the realm of what is contingent and to posit this as an end for itself.

(2) A RATIONAL BEING CANNOT THINK OF AN ACTION AS ACTUAL WITHOUT ASSUMING SOMETHING OUTSIDE OF ITSELF TO WHICH THIS ACTION IS DIRECTED.

Let us take another look at the preceding description of how we are able to think of freedom in a determinate manner. I asserted that, in this concept [of freedom], I think of myself as choosing. Now direct your attention solely to this I that is represented as choosing. This I is undoubtedly engaged in thinking and *only* in thinking; hence only ideal activity is ascribed to it in this choice. But it is undoubtedly thinking of something; the I "hovers" [*schwebt*] over something that constrains it, which is how we usually express this relationship. Here there is something *objective*, for only by means of such a relationship [to what is objective] is the I subjective and ideal. – What is objective is not the I itself and cannot be attributed to the I – neither to the *intelligent* I as such, inasmuch as what is objective is expressly opposed to the I as intellect, nor to the I that *wills* and is *really active*, for the latter has not yet been set into action [IV, 82], since there is as yet no willing but only a description of the will's choice. What is objective is not the I, nor is it nothing at all; it is something (the object of a representation as such, though we are still undecided about its true reality or capacity to be sensed). In other words, it is called the "Not-I"; it is something outside of me, something present without any help from me.

This something that is present is necessarily posited as enduring and unchangeable throughout all the modifications produced by the power that is attributed to the I by means of the concept of freedom. – The concept of freedom is based upon this: that I ascribe to myself the power to realize X or $-X$, and hence that I am able *to unite these opposite determinations, as opposites, in one and the same act of thinking.* This, however, is not possible if, in thinking of these opposites, one does not also think of something that remains *the same*, something that endures in this thinking of opposites, something to which the identity of consciousness affixes itself. This identical something is nothing other than that which makes possible thinking itself, with respect to its form: namely, *the relation to objectivity as such*; and hence it is precisely the previously indicated Not-I. It is what is thought to remain unchanged throughout all the free determinations that are thinkable, for freedom itself is thinkable only under this condition. It is therefore an infinitely modifiable *originally given stuff* external to ourselves ("originally given," i.e., posited by thinking itself, through its very form). It is that to which efficacy is directed; that is to say, it is *that* which, in the course of acting efficaciously, undergoes change in itself (as regards its form) while nevertheless remaining itself (as regards its matter).

To conclude, the stuff in question is related to real efficacy, and vice versa; properly speaking, it is nothing but the means for thinking the latter. Real efficacy is in fact limited by this stuff; it is restricted to merely forming or shaping it, and it is excluded from creating or annihilating matter; hence, like everything that limits real efficacy, this stuff too possesses reality [IV, 83]. – *It is a real object of our external activity.* We have thereby proven what was supposed to be proven.

§5

Second theorem

A RATIONAL BEING IS EQUALLY UNABLE TO ASCRIBE TO ITSELF A POWER OF FREEDOM WITHOUT FINDING IN ITSELF AN ACTUAL EXERCISE OF THIS POWER, THAT IS, AN ACTUAL ACT OF FREE WILLING.

Preliminary remark

Our deduction still remains in the same place, and we are still dealing with the same element [*Glied*] with which we began. We proved earlier that we ascribe to ourselves a power of freedom. The question we must now address is how such an ascription or attribution is itself possible. We have already indicated the *external* condition for such an attribution: namely, the positing of an object for free acting. What remains to be demonstrated is the *internal* condition of free acting, a condition of our own state, without which free acting is impossible. The above proposition requires no explanation. The words are clear, and if any ambiguity should remain, this will be sufficiently clarified by means of the proof itself. On the basis of what was said above, the following can and henceforth always will be presupposed: when, in this and in all future theorems, we assert some connection, this is to be understood as a synthetic connection in one and the same act of thinking [IV, 84]. Here, for example, what we are asserting is that the power [of freedom] can by no means be thought of and is never thought of, unless some actual exercise of this power is [also] found in one and the same state of the thinking subject.

Proof

As we know, the concept of a power of freedom is the concept, the merely ideal representation, of a free act of willing. We now maintain that this merely ideal representation is not possible without the *actuality* and *perception* of an act of willing; hence we claim that there is a necessary connection between a mere representation and an act of willing. We cannot understand this connection without becoming well acquainted with the differences between the two. The first thing we must do, therefore, is to call attention to the characteristic differences between representing and willing as such; and then, since actual willing must also appear within consciousness, we must indicate the differences between a merely ideal representation of willing and a perception of the same; only then will it be possible to prove that the former is not possible without the latter.

Mere representing, as such, is related to willing in the same way that subjectivity, as such, is related to objectivity. I originally find myself as simultaneously subject and object; and what each of these is can be grasped only through its opposition and relationship to the other. Neither is determined through itself; instead, what is absolutely determined and is common to both is self-activity as such. Insofar as they are different from each other, they are determinable only mediately: what is subjective is what is related to what is objective, that before which what is objective hovers, that which is attached to the latter, etc.; what is objective is that to which what is subjective is attached, etc. Now I am absolutely and freely active [*absolut freitätig*], and my essence consists therein: my free activity, considered immediately as such [IV, 85], is, if it is objective, my *willing*; this same free activity of mine is, if it is subjective, my *thinking* (taking this term in its widest sense as designating all the manifestations of the intellect as such). Willing can therefore be grasped only through its opposition to thinking, and thinking only through its opposition to willing. A genetic description of willing, as something that proceeds from thinking – which is, indeed, how willing must be described if it is to be represented as free – can thus be stated as follows: – Willing is thought of as preceded by a freely active comprehending of an end, that is, by an absolute producing of the end by means of a concept. In producing the concept of an end, the state of the I is purely ideal and subjective. Something is represented, and it is represented by means of absolute self-activity, since the concept of an end is only a product of an act of representing; something is represented in relation to a future act of willing, for otherwise the concept [that is represented] would not be a *concept of an end*; but what is represented is only represented and is by no means willed. I now make the transition to *actual willing*: I *will* the end, a state which, in ordinary consciousness, everyone surely distinguishes easily enough from [the state of] merely representing something that one might be able to will. But what is involved in willing? [Willing involves] absolute self-activity, as does thinking, but here it has a different character. Now what is this character? Obviously, [it involves] a relation to some knowing. My willing is not itself supposed to be a knowing; but I am supposed to *know my willing*. Consequently, the distinctive character of willing lies in its pure objectivity. Something that was previously subjective now becomes objective, and it becomes objective due to the appearance on the scene of a new subjective element, one which, as it were, leaps up from the absolute fullness of self-activity.

Note the changed order of the sequence in this case. As was noted earlier, the I is originally neither subjective nor objective, but is both [IV, 86]; but we are unable to think this identity of the two, hence we think of them sequentially, one after the other, and, by means of this thinking, we make one of them depend upon the other. In cognition, for example, something objective, the thing, is supposed to become something subjective, something represented, for the concept of a cognition is viewed as a copy of something that exists, which is how we expressed this point earlier. Conversely, the concept of an end is supposed to be the model or prefiguration of something that exists; hence what is subjective is [in this case] supposed to be transformed into something objective, and this transformation must already begin within the I, which is the sole immediate object of our consciousness. – So much concerning the difference between representing and willing.

The mere representation of an act of willing is the very representation we have just produced within ourselves: the representation of an absolute transition (accomplished by means of absolute self-activity) of what is subjective into what is objective, for this is precisely the universal form of all free willing.

How, we must now ask, is this merely ideal representation of an act of willing to be distinguished from an actual instance of willing? In the former case, the ideal activity itself freely produces this form of willing, and I am conscious of this productive action. In the latter case, the ideal activity does not posit itself as producing this form [of willing], but finds the act of willing to be something that is given and finds itself to be constrained in its representation of this willing. – Here let us also take note of this further point: in other cases, the perception of what is actual – that is, an actually existing object – proceeds from a feeling, in accordance with which something is first posited through the productive power of the imagination. This, however, is not the case when what is perceived is an actual willing, in which case I cannot say that I feel my willing – although one can hear this said by philosophers who do not pay close attention to their own expressions –, for I can feel only a limitation of my activity, whereas my willing is the activity itself. So what kind of consciousness is this consciousness of willing? [IV, 87] Obviously, it is the immediate intuition of one's own activity – but as the object of what is subjective and not as what is subjective itself, which is why the latter is not viewed as self-active [in this case]. In short, this consciousness is intellectual intuition.

Following these explanations, the proof of the above assertion will be easy.

According to the concept of the I, what is subjective is originally not present apart from something objective; for only under this condition is what is subjective subjective at all. Consciousness arises necessarily from the connection of these two [elements]. The mere representation of an act of willing, however, contains only what is subjective; what is objective for the latter, or, more precisely, the pure form of what is objective, is produced only by an act of willing. To be sure, this [production of what is objective by what is subjective] is possible in the context of philosophical abstraction, when the intellect reproduces one of its determinate states, in which case, however, the actual state is already presupposed; but it is not possible originally. For reproduction to be possible, there must already have been production. It follows that the original representation of our power of freedom is necessarily accompanied by actual willing.

Strictly speaking, our proof is now concluded. But in order not to lose what has been gained through the preceding investigations, it must be stressed that the converse of the above proposition is also true: perception of willing is not possible without an ideal representation of the power of freedom or (which means exactly the same thing) of the form of willing. We thus claim to have unified synthetically the two thoughts that we just distinguished from one another. This can easily be seen in the following way: I am supposed to become conscious of an act of willing, but the latter is an instance of willing only insofar as it is posited as free; and it is, in turn, posited as free only insofar as its determinacy is derived from the freely designed concept of an end. To this act of willing we have to ascribe the form of all willing; we must, as it were, view the former through the latter [IV, 88]. Only in this way am I the one who wills, and the willing subject is identical with the subject who perceives this act of willing.

One must not allow oneself to become confused by the fact that the act of designing the concept of an end has to be posited in a moment preceding the act of willing. As has just been shown, that is not possible, since prior to the perception of an act of willing I do not exist at all, and hence I do not comprehend anything. This act of designing the concept [of an end] does not precede [the act of willing] in time; instead, it and the act of willing occur at absolutely the same moment. The determinacy of the act of willing is only *thought* to be dependent upon the concept; there is no temporal sequence here, but only a sequence of thinking.

To summarize all of this briefly: I originally intuit my activity as an object, and to this extent as necessarily *determinate*. That is to say [when I intuit myself as an object], I ascribe to myself only a limited quantum of all the activity I could – as I am quite aware – ascribe to myself. In all human languages what is intuited in this case is called, for short, "*willing*," and this is something with which all human beings are very well acquainted; moreover, as the philosopher demonstrates, this is also the starting point of all consciousness and is that through which alone all consciousness is mediated. The act in question is an act of *willing*, however – and an act of *my* willing and an *immediately* perceivable act of willing –, only insofar as the intuited *determinacy* of the activity is not supposed to have any ground outside of me, but is supposed to be grounded utterly in me *myself*. In that case, however, according to the elucidations provided earlier (see above, pp. 51ff.), this act of willing is necessarily grounded in my own *thinking*, since beyond willing I have nothing left but thinking, and everything objective can certainly be derived from an act of thinking. In this way I necessarily think of the determinacy of my willing, just as surely as I perceive any willing at all and as such [IV, 89].

§6

Deduction of the actual causality of a rational being

Third theorem

> A RATIONAL BEING CANNOT FIND IN ITSELF ANY APPLICATION OF
> ITS FREEDOM OR ITS WILLING WITHOUT AT THE SAME TIME
> ASCRIBING TO ITSELF AN ACTUAL CAUSALITY OUTSIDE OF ITSELF.

Preliminary remark

Our deduction advances a step further. I was not able to ascribe to myself a power of freedom without finding myself to be willing. It is now claimed that I am also unable to do the latter, that I cannot find myself to be actually willing, without finding something else within me. – I.e., [it is claimed that] consciousness originally arises just as little from the representation of a sheer, impotent act of willing as from the representation of our power of willing as such, notwithstanding what might become possible in the progressive development of consciousness, by means of past experience and free abstraction. So far as we can see up to this point, consciousness arises from *a perception of our real efficacy in the sensible world*; we derive this efficacy from our willing, and we derive the determinacy of our willing from a freely designed concept of an end.

It is thus evident that the concept of freedom is mediately or indirectly conditioned by the perception of an actual causality, which now has to be derived; and, since the concept of freedom conditions self-consciousness, self-consciousness is similarly conditioned by the perception of an actual causality. Everything we have presented so far and everything we might still be able to present in the future is therefore one and the same synthetic consciousness, the individual components [IV, 90] of which can indeed be separated within philosophical reflection, but which are by no means separated in original consciousness. Let this reminder suffice once and for all.

Proof

I find myself to be willing only insofar as my activity is supposed to be set in motion by a determinate concept of the same. In willing, my activity is necessarily determinate, as has previously been sufficiently demonstrated. In sheer activity as such, however, that is, in pure activity, one can distinguish or determine nothing whatsoever. Activity is the simplest intuition; it is sheer inner agility [*Agilität*] and absolutely nothing more.

Activity cannot be determined by itself, and yet it must be determined if consciousness is to be possible at all. This means nothing else than the following: the activity is to be determined through and by means of *its opposite*, and hence by the manner of its limitation. Only in this way can one think of a manifold of activity, consisting of several particular actions.

I cannot, however, intellectually intuit, absolutely and by myself, the manner in which I am limited; instead, this is something I only *feel* in sensory experience. But if an activity is supposed to be limited, and if its limitation is supposed to be felt, then that activity itself must occur – occur for me, of course, and not, as it were, in itself. Now anything that can be intuited through the senses is necessarily a quantum, which we might provisionally describe simply as a quantum that fills a moment of time. Anything that fills a moment of time, however, is itself an infinitely divisible manifold, and thus the perceived limitation must itself be a manifold. The I is now supposed to be posited as active; and thus it would have to be posited as eliminating and breaking through a manifold of boundaries and resistance, [and it must be posited as doing this] in a succession (for there is a succession even in a single moment, since otherwise no temporal duration would arise from the combination of several singular moments) [IV, 91]. Or, which means the same, *one would have to ascribe to the I causality in the sensible world outside it.*

Corollaries

(1) In the result of our investigation we must not lose sight of the following: the intellectual intuition from which we proceeded is not possible without a sensible intuition, and the latter is not possible without a feeling; and one would completely misunderstand us and would utterly invert the sense and main goal of our system if one were to ascribe to us the opposite claim. Sensory intuition, however, is equally impossible apart from intellectual intuition. I cannot be for myself without being something, and I can be something only in the sensible world. But it is equally true that I cannot be for myself without being an I, and I am an I only in the intelligible world, which reveals itself before my eyes [only] by means of intellectual intuition. The point of union between the two [worlds] lies in the circumstance that it is only through absolute self-activity in accordance with a concept that I am for myself what I am in the sensible world. Our existence in the intelligible world is the moral law; our existence in the sensible world is the actual deed; the point of the union of the two is freedom as the absolute power to determine our existence in the sensible world through our existence in the intelligible world.

(2) The I is to be posited as an actual I, but solely in contrast with or in opposition to a Not-I. But there is a Not-I for the I only under the condition that the I acts efficaciously and feels resistance in its effective operation, which, however, is overcome, since otherwise the I would not be acting efficaciously. Only by means of such resistance does the activity of the I become something that can be sensed and that endures over a period of time, since without such resistance the I's activity would be outside of time, which is something we are not even able to think.

(3) Without causality upon a Not-I there is therefore no I all [IV, 92]. Such causality is not a contingent feature of the I, but belongs to it essentially, just as does everything in the I. – One must therefore cease trying to assemble reason from contingently connected pieces and must become accustomed [instead] to viewing it as a completed whole, as, so to speak, an organized reason. Either the I is everything that it appears to be from the point of view of ordinary consciousness, independent of all philosophical abstraction, and is as it appears to be from this point of view, or else it is nothing and does not exist at all. – Consciousness begins with sensible intuition, and the latter is thoroughly determinate. By no means does consciousness commence with abstract thinking. Philosophy has become a web of chimeras, because one has treated consciousness itself as beginning with abstractions, which is indeed how philosophy does begin, and has confused what is to be explained (actual consciousness) with the explanation thereof (philosophy).

(4) Only by representing this issue in the manner we have just represented it can one preserve the absoluteness of the I as its essential character. Our consciousness proceeds from an immediate consciousness of our own activity, and we find ourselves to be passive only by means of the latter. It is not the Not-I that acts efficaciously upon the I, which is how this issue has customarily been viewed, but the other way around. The Not-I does not intrude upon the I, but the I goes out into the Not-I, which is how we are required to view this relationship in the case of sensible intuition. The same point would have to be expressed transcendentally as follows: it is not the case that we find ourselves to be originally bounded because we become more narrowly bounded, for were that the case then, with the abolition of our reality, consciousness of our bounded condition would be abolished as well; instead, it is by expanding our boundaries – and insofar as we expand them – that we find ourselves to be originally bounded. – Even in order to be able to go out of itself, moreover, the I must be posited as overcoming resistance. We are therefore once again and in a still higher sense claiming the primacy of reason insofar as it is practical [IV, 93]. Everything proceeds from acting and from the acting of the I. The I is the first principle of all movement and of all life, of every deed and occurrence. If the Not-I exercises an effect upon us, then this does not occur within the domain of the Not-I; it

operates efficaciously by means of resistance, which it could not do if we had not first acted upon it. It is not the Not-I that encroaches upon us, but we who encroach upon it.

§7

Determination of the causality of a rational being through its inner character

Fourth theorem

A RATIONAL BEING CANNOT ASCRIBE CAUSALITY TO ITSELF WITHOUT DETERMINING IT IN A CERTAIN MANNER THROUGH ITS OWN CONCEPT.

Preliminary elucidation

The proposition set forth above is unintelligible and ambiguous. As one may conjecture at this point and as will become clearly evident later on, the efficacy of a rational being in the sensible world may well be subject to several restrictions and conditions. At first glance, however, one cannot anticipate which of these conditions might be the particular manner of determinacy that here concerns us. To be sure, the safest protection against all confusion lies in our method itself. The determinacy with which we must here concern ourselves [IV, 94] is that determinacy which conditions the perception of our efficacy first and immediately; what this determinacy is will become evident as a result of a deduction. Later on we will indicate those conditions through which this determinacy is, in turn, conditioned.

In the meantime and so that we can know what we are dealing with right from the start and can have a guiding thread for directing our attention, we will make a preliminary effort to divine what determination this might be and we will do so by inspecting ordinary consciousness. – It surely goes without saying that nothing is supposed to be demonstrated in this way and that this preliminary consideration of ordinary consciousness is intended only to prepare the way for a proof.

To begin with, as was already noted, I can neither will nor accomplish anything that violates the necessary laws of thinking, since this is something I cannot even think. I cannot produce nor annihilate matter, but I am able only to divide or to combine it; and the reason for this will become evident at the proper place. Yet even in this dividing and combining of matter, which is something that is indeed within our overall power, we are still bound to a certain order: in most cases we cannot immediately realize our end [simply] by means of our willing, but must employ various, uniquely suitable means in order to achieve our end, and what these means are is something that has been determined in advance and without any assistance from us. Let our final end be = X. Instead of directly presenting X all at once, we first have to realize, let us say, A, as the only means for achieving B, and then realize B in order to achieve C, and so on, until we finally arrive at our final end X by means of a successive series of intermediate ends, each of which conditions the one that follows. – Properly speaking, if we are at all *able to will* something then we are also able to do it; for the most part, however, we are not able to do it all at once but only in a certain order. (For example, they say that a human being is unable to fly. But why should a human being not be able to do this? One is only unable to do this immediately – in the way that, if one is healthy, one is immediately able to walk. By means of a balloon, however [IV, 95], one can indeed lift oneself into the air and can move around there with some degree of freedom and purposiveness. And as regards what our own age is not yet able to do, inasmuch as it has not yet found the means to do so: who says that *human beings* are unable to do this? I sincerely hope that an age such as ours will not take itself to be identical with humanity.)

What ordinary consciousness tells us therefore is this: in executing our ends, we are bound to a certain order of means. What does this claim mean when one views it from the transcendental viewpoint and when one attends solely to the immanent changes and appearances within the I, in total abstraction from things outside of us? – According to the preliminary elucidations provided above, whenever I perceive I *feel*. "I perceive changes outside of me" means that the state of my feelings has changed within me. "I want to act efficaciously outside of myself" means that I will that the place of one determinate feeling should be occupied by another determinate feeling, which I demand through my concept of an end. "I have become a cause" means that the feeling that is demanded actually does occur. Thus, "I proceed to my end by passing through the means" means that other feelings occur in the interval between the feeling from which I proceed to willing and the feeling demanded by my willing. "This relationship is necessary" means that a determinate, desired feeling follows another determinate feeling only under the condition that between these feelings other, intermediate determinate feelings, which are determinate as to their kind, their quantity, and their sequence, intervene.

Every feeling, however, is an expression of my limitation; and "I possess causality" always means that I expand my limits. Thus what we are claiming is that this expansion can occur only in a certain, progressive series, since we are claiming that our causality is limited to the employment of certain means for accomplishing our end. What we have to discuss now, as will emerge from our deduction, is that determination and restriction of our causality that we have just described [IV, 96]. – This portion of the deduction continues our progress through the series of conditions. The last proposition proven above was that I cannot posit myself as free without ascribing to myself actual causality outside of myself. What we now have to investigate is the condition under which such an ascription of causality is, in turn, possible.

Proof

(1) MY CAUSALITY IS PERCEIVED AS A MANIFOLD IN A CONTINUOUS SERIES.

As was noted earlier, the perception of my causality, *qua* perception, necessarily occurs in a moment of time. Through the unification of several moments there now arises a temporal duration or a filling of time. The single moment must therefore fill some time as well, for nothing can arise through the unification of several single moments of the same type that is not contained in these single moments. Now what does it mean to say, "the moment *fills* a time"? This means only that a manifold *could* be differentiated within this moment, and if one wanted to make such a differentiation one could continue differentiating it into infinity. Here, however, it is by no means asserted that the moment of time *is* being differentiated in this manner, for it is *one* moment only because no such differentiation is made. "The moment is posited as filling time" means that the overall possibility of such a differentiation is posited. – What occurs when we perceive our own efficacy is a synthesis of our activity with some resistance. Now as we know from what has already been said, our activity as such is not a manifold, but is absolute, pure identity; and it itself can be characterized only in relation to some resistance. The manifold to be differentiated would therefore have to be a manifold of resistance [IV, 97].

This manifold is necessarily a manifold of things outside of one another, a discrete manifold; for only on this condition does it fill a time. It is thought of as a series. Now what about the sequence of this manifold in this series? Does this sequence depend upon the freedom of the intellect as such, or is it also to be viewed as determined without any help from the intellect? If, for example, this manifold were A, B, C, would it have been within the power of the freedom of thinking to posit it, in contrast, as B, C, A or as C, B, A, etc.? Or did it have to be posited in precisely this sequence, so that B could by no means be posited unless A had previously been posited, etc.? It is immediately clear that the latter is the case; for the perceived efficacy of the I is something actual, and in representing what is actual the intellect is thoroughly bound with respect to the matter of such a representation and is never free.

General overview of the issue: My efficacy necessarily falls into time, since it cannot be *my* efficacy without being thought, and all of my thinking occurs within time. Time, however, is a determinate series of successive moments, in which each single moment is conditioned by another [past] moment, one that is not, in turn, conditioned by the moment that it conditions, and conditions another [future] moment, which does not, in turn, condition it. Now[8] thinking of our own efficacy is the perception of something actual, and in perception nothing whatsoever depends upon the thinker as such. – My efficacy is therefore represented as a series, the manifold of which is a manifold of resistance, and the succession of which is not determined by my thinking but is supposed to be determined independently of the latter.

(2) THE SEQUENCE OF THIS MANIFOLD IS DETERMINED WITHOUT ANY HELP FROM ME, HENCE IT IS ITSELF A BOUNDING OF MY EFFICACY [IV, 98].

It has just been proven that the sequence of the manifold in my efficacy is not determined by my thinking. Yet, as will become clear at once, it is also not determined by my acting, nor is it itself, so to speak, the product of my efficacy.

---

[8] Reading *nun* ("now") for *nur* ("only"), as proposed by the editors of the critical edition (*GA* I/5: 99).

The resistance is not my acting, but is what opposes my acting. I do not produce this resistance, hence I do not produce anything whatsoever that is contained in it and belongs to it. What I produce is my own activity, and the latter contains no manifold whatsoever and no temporal sequence, but is a pure unity. I will the end and nothing but the end. I will the means to this end only because this end cannot be achieved without these means; hence this relationship is itself a bounding [*Begrenzung*] of my efficacy.

We will now explain more clearly the result of our present investigation.

(1) The idea governing the deduced series is as follows: First of all, there has to be some starting point where the I departs from its original limitation and exercises causality for the first time and immediately; and if it were for some reason impossible to carry the analysis all the way back to this original starting point, there then might also appear to be a *plurality* of starting points. Insofar as each of these points is supposed to be a starting point, the I is at each such point an immediate cause, through its will, and there are no intermediate elements through which it first has to acquire such causality. If the I is ever to be a cause at all then there must be such starting points. As will be observed later, we call those points, when though of collectively, our "articulated body"; and our articulated body is nothing but these same [starting] points [of efficacious acting in the world], presented in and realized through intuition. Let us call this system of the first moments of our causality "group A."

To *each* of those points, moreover, several other points attach themselves, and in and through these new points, mediated through the former ones [IV, 99], the I is able to become a cause in manifold ways. I said that *several [points are attached] to each one [of the starting points]*: for if, starting from each of these points, one could act in only *one* way, then there would be no free acting beginning from the point in question, and thus there would be no second acting at all, but only a continuation of the first. Let us call this system [of secondary points attached to the original starting points] "group B." To each single point of group B there are attached, in turn, several points of a third group, group C; and thus, to illustrate this with an image, around a fixed middle point there is described an infinite circular area, within which each point can be thought of as bordering upon infinitely many others.

The world as such, including the world as a manifold, arises for us through this necessary way of viewing our own efficacy. All properties of matter – with the sole exception of those that stem from the forms of intuition – are nothing but the relationship of the latter to us, and in particular to our efficacy, for there is simply no other kind of relationship for us. Or, to express this same thought transcendentally, following the hints provided above: these properties of matter are the relations of our determinate finitude to the infinity toward which we are striving.

Viewed from the perspective of what is *ideal*, "object X lies at *such and such a distance from me* in space" means that in traversing the space from me to the object I must first apprehend and posit such and such other objects in order to be able to posit the object in question. Viewed from the perspective of what is *real*, the same proposition means that I first have to penetrate such and such an amount of space, considered as an obstacle, in order to be able to consider the space occupied by X to be identical with the space I occupy.

"This object is hard" means that in a certain *series of acting*, between two determinate members of this series, I feel a determinate resistance. – "It becomes soft" means that in the same series of acting I feel a change in the resistance I encounter at the same place. And this is the case with all the predicates of things in the sensible world.

(2) In the course of its acting, the *real*, *active* and *feeling* I describes a continuous line, in which there is no break whatsoever nor anything similar and along which there is an unnoticed progression toward an opposing point, without there appearing to be any change in the point that lies nearest, though such a change may indeed become noticeable at some point that lies further along the line [IV, 100]. The *reflecting* I, however, apprehends at its discretion parts of this progressing line as individual moments. In this manner there arises for the reflecting I a series that consists of points lying outside one another. Reflection progresses, as it were, *by fits and starts*, whereas sensation is *continuous*. To be sure, the two extreme points at each boundary of the [continuous series of] moments that succeed one another – assuming there were such a thing in an infinitely divisible line, and nothing prevents us from thinking of the matter in this way – flow into each other unnoticed. To this extent, what is contained in these two separate moments is the same; but one need merely reflect upon these opposites and then they are [viewed as] different moments and there arises a consciousness that

undergoes alteration. The identity of consciousness becomes possible because all [of these moments] also remain the same in a certain respect.

(3) From the point of view of ordinary consciousness, the fact that our efficacy is limited to the employment of certain determinate means in order to achieve a determinate end must be explained by some determinate properties of the things, by means of determinate laws of nature, which just happen to be the way they are. From the transcendental point of view, which is that of a pure philosophy – that is to say, from that viewpoint one achieves when one has abstracted from the I everything that is Not-I and has thought the I in its purity –, one can by no means be satisfied with the preceding explanation. From the transcendental standpoint it appears utterly absurd to assume a Not-I as a thing in itself, in abstraction from all reason. How then is the limitation of our efficacy to be explained from this perspective – not, to be sure, explained with respect to its *form* (i.e., why such a limitation has to be posited *at all*), for this is precisely the question we have just answered by means of a deduction, but with respect to its material (i.e., why this limitation is thought precisely in the way that it is thought, why precisely such and such means and no others are supposed to lead to the achievement of a determinate end)? Here we are absolutely not supposed to assume either things in themselves or laws of nature, understood as the laws of a nature outside of us [IV, 101]; consequently, we can comprehend this limitation [of our efficacy] only in the following manner: the I simply limits itself in this way, and does not do this freely or with any choice [*nicht etwa mit Freiheit und Willkür*], for in that case it *would* not *be* limited; instead, it limits itself in this manner in accordance with an immanent law of its own being, through a natural law of its own (finite) nature. This determinate, rational being just happens to be so constituted that it has to limit itself in precisely this way; and this constitution [*Einrichtung*] cannot be explained any further, since it is supposed to constitute our original limitation – which is something we cannot escape through our *acting*, and hence not through our *cognizing* either. To demand further explanation of this point would be self-contradictory. In contrast, one can ascertain the reasons for some of the other determinations of a rational being.

If we now combine all of these individual limitations, which occur as such only *in time*, and if we think of them as [our] original constitution *prior to all time* and *outside of all time*, we are then thinking the *absolute limits* of the original drive itself. This is a drive that just happens to be such that it is directed only at this, only at an efficacy in such a determinate series, and it cannot be directed at anything else; this is simply how it is. Our entire world, our inner as well as our outer world (only insofar as the former actually is a world), is thereby *pre-established* for us for all eternity. I said "only insofar as [the inner world] actually is a world," i.e., insofar as it is something objective within us. What is merely subjective, i.e., self-determination, is not pre-established; hence we act freely.

§8

Deduction of a determinacy of the objects without any help from us

Fifth theorem

> A RATIONAL BEING CANNOT ASCRIBE ANY EFFICACY TO ITSELF
> WITHOUT PRESUPPOSING A CERTAIN EFFICACY ON THE PART OF
> THE OBJECTS.

[IV, 102]

Preliminary remark

It has already been shown above (in § 4) that thinking our freedom is conditioned by thinking an object. There, however, this objectivity was derived as mere, raw stuff. Ordinary experience teaches us that we never find an object that is purely stuff and is not yet formed or shaped in some respect. It thus seems that consciousness of our own efficacy is conditioned not merely by the positing of an object as such, but also by the positing of a determinate form of the object. But is this experience upon which alone we are here basing everything one that is universal and necessary? And if the answer is yes, then according to which laws of reason is such an experience necessary and universal? The answer to this question should have some implications for our system.

One could easily demonstrate the universal proposition that all stuff is necessarily perceived in some determinate form. However, we are not concerned solely with this proposition, but more specifically with [acquiring some] insight into that *determinate* form we must ascribe to the objects of our efficacy, prior to the operation of our efficacy; and such insight might not be obtainable without a deeper investigation. – At this point, we are unable to explain even the words of the preceding theorem, and we must instead await the following investigation in order to obtain a complete disclosure of their meaning.

I

Thesis: A RATIONAL BEING HAS NO COGNITION EXCEPT AS THE RESULT OF A LIMITATION OF ITS ACTIVITY.

The proof of this claim is contained in everything that has been said so far, and the claim itself is simply the result of the investigations that have been pursued up to this point. I find *myself* only as free, and I do so only [IV, 103] in an actual perception of a determinate self-activity. I find *the object* only as limiting, though also overcome by, my self-activity. There is no consciousness whatsoever without consciousness of self-activity; this self-activity, however, cannot itself become an object of consciousness unless it is limited.

Antithesis: BUT SELF-ACTIVITY DOES NOT PERTAIN TO A RATIONAL BEING AS SUCH, EXCEPT IN CONSEQUENCE OF A COGNITION, AT THE VERY LEAST IN CONSEQUENCE OF A COGNITION OF SOMETHING IN THE RATIONAL BEING ITSELF.

[The fact] that something is a product of my self-activity is not something that is perceived, nor can it be perceived; instead, this is purely and simply posited, and it is posited in this way insofar as the form of freedom is posited. (See § 5, IV, p. 86.) But the form of freedom consists in the following: namely, that the material determinacy of an act of willing is grounded in a concept of an end that is freely projected by the intellect. We are here overlooking the fact that the possibility of a concept of an end itself seems to be conditioned by cognition of an object outside of us and by cognition of the latter's form, as something that exists without any help from us; for this is merely what is asserted by ordinary consciousness, and we do not yet know to what extent it will be confirmed. But even overlooking this fact, we are still presupposing, [as a condition] for the possibility of perceiving my willing, a cognition of my concept of an end as such. Yet only insofar as I perceive myself to be engaged in willing, and willing freely, is the efficacy in question *my* efficacy, my efficacy as a rational being.

As we now see, the condition is not possible apart from what is conditioned thereby, and what is conditioned is not possible apart from what conditions it. This is undoubtedly a circular explanation, and this indicates that we have not yet said enough in order to explain what we were supposed to explain: consciousness of freedom.

(One could easily solve this difficulty by conjecturing that the first moment of consciousness consists in an absolute synthesis of the designing of the concept of an end and the perception of an act of willing this end. – The sole moment of consciousness that is at issue here is the first moment of consciousness [IV, 104], since, in the course of consciousness, we are able to draw upon prior experience in order to think, without any difficulty, both the free choice and the designing of the concept of an end prior to the decision of the will. – [According to this conjecture,] the concept of an end would not be, so to speak, designed in advance, but would *only be thought of as* freely designed, and it would be thought of in this manner immediately and simultaneously with the act of willing, in order thereby to be able to find the act of willing to be free in its own right. But since no choice could precede the act of willing, a question would still remain concerning the actual origin of the determinacy of the end or of the act of willing, which are in this case entirely the same, and concerning how this is to be explained by the philosopher. – We have already seen that the I itself explains this determinacy by means of the concept of an end, which it conceives of as designed in advance. – And the difficulty will actually be resolved in just this way, and this will also provide us with an answer to the latter question. However, the rules of systematic presentation, as well as further disclosures we are expecting here, require us to seek a deeper foundation. The goal of the present note is therefore simply to indicate in advance the goal of our investigation.)

II

According to the familiar rules of synthetic method, the antithesis just set forth is supposed to be resolved through a synthesis of what is conditioned with the condition thereof, in such a way that the two would be posited as one and the same. In our present case this would mean that the activity itself would appear as the cognition we are seeking, the cognition itself would appear as the activity we are seeking, and that all consciousness would [therefore] proceed from something that absolutely unites both predicates within itself. So all that one has to do is to think the unification just described, and then the contradiction will actually be resolved.

This, however, is precisely where the difficulty lies [IV, 105]: simply understanding the thought we are supposed to be thinking and clearly thinking anything whatsoever thereby. According to the rules of synthetic presentation, we would immediately have to analyze the proposed synthetic concept [and continue analyzing it], until we understood it, which is the most difficult way of proceeding, since the synthesis in question is one of the most abstract in all philosophy.

There is an easier method, however, and since we are here concerned more with the results themselves than with cognition of the original synthetic procedure of reason – which, after all, has been sufficiently described elsewhere and which has also been applied with the utmost strictness (especially in our *Natural Right*)⁹ –, we will here employ this easier method. For we already know from elsewhere so much about this first point from which all consciousness proceeds that we can conveniently commence our investigation with these familiar distinguishing features; and we can examine whether these will permit us to resolve our present difficulty as well and whether the synthesis just described is contained in these features – which is simply to follow the same path in reverse.

III

If one originally thinks the I in an objective manner – and this is how it is found prior to all other types of consciousness –, then one can describe its determinacy only as a tendency or a drive, as has here been sufficiently demonstrated right from the start. The objective constitution of an I is by no means a being or subsistence; for that would make it the opposite of what it is; i.e., that would make it a thing. The being of the I is absolute activity and nothing but activity; but activity, taken objectively, is *drive*.

I said, "if the I is thought objectively *at all*": for once what is subjective in the I has been separated off and has been thought of, in accordance with our earlier description of the same (§ 2), as an absolute

---

⁹ See Part I of *FNR*. See too all of *FTP*.

power of freedom, then what is objective in this relationship to freedom is, for this same freedom, the moral law.

The I, however, is absolutely not something purely objective, for then it would not be an I but a thing [IV, 106]. Its original determinacy is therefore not only the determinacy of a being but also the determinacy of a thinking – taking this latter term in its widest meaning, as designating all the manifestations of the intellect. But a mere *determinacy* of the intellect, without any contribution on the part of the intellect's freedom and self-activity, is called a *feeling*; and this is also how this concept was previously determined and derived in passing (see § 3). – A thing *is* something, and this is all there is to its determinacy. The I never simply *is*; it is never something of which it has no knowledge; its being is related immediately and necessarily to its consciousness. This kind of sheer determination, one that lies [both] in being and in I-hood, is called feeling. Thus, if the I is originally posited with a drive as its objective determination, then it is necessarily posited as well with some feeling of this drive. In this way we would obtain a necessary and immediate consciousness, to which we could then attach the series of all additional consciousness. All other consciousness – reflection, intuition, comprehension – presupposes an application of freedom, and the latter, in turn, pre-supposes a number of other things. *Feeling*, however, is something I am engaged in merely through the fact that I *am*. – Let us mention in passing that this particular feeling of a drive is called "*longing*" [*Sehnen*], which is an indeterminate sensation of a need and is not determined through the concept of an object.

This original feeling of a drive is precisely the synthetic element we described above. A drive is an activity that necessarily becomes a cognition in the I, and this cognition is not, as it were, an image or anything similar of the drive's activity; it is this activity itself, immedi-ately presented. If this activity is posited, then the cognition of it is also posited immediately; and if this cognition is posited – with respect to its form, as a feeling – then the activity itself is posited. – What is objective in a representation proper is something that is always supposed to exist in a certain respect, independently of the representation itself, either as an actual thing or as a law of reason; for only thereby does it become something objective, and only because of this is it possible to distin-guish what is subjective from what is objective [IV, 107]. In feeling, what is subjective and what is objective are absolutely united; a feeling [*ein Gefühl*] is undoubtedly nothing without a feeling [*ein Fühlen*] thereof, and it is itself the latter; a feeling is always something that is only subjective.

The difficulty indicated above has been fundamentally resolved by means of this original feeling. No activity could be assumed apart from some cognition, since a freely designed concept of an end was presupposed for every activity. And in turn, no cognition could be assumed apart from some corresponding activity, since all cognition was derived from the perception of some limitation upon our acting. Now, however, something immediately cognizable has revealed itself: our original drive. Our first action is the satisfaction of this original drive, and in relation to this first action this drive appears as a freely designed concept of an end, which is also quite correct, inasmuch as the I itself has to be considered as the absolute ground of its drive.

IV

I am, as we said, completely and in every respect constrained when I am engaged in feeling. Here there is not even the freedom that there is in every representation: namely, the freedom to abstract from the object of the representation. It is not that I myself *posit* myself, but rather that I *am* posited, both objectively, as *driven*, and subjectively, as *feeling* this drive. But if only what is consciously free and self-active is posited as I – and from the point of view of ordinary consciousness this is always the case –, then, to this extent, the object and subject of the drive do not belong to the I, but are opposed to it. In contrast, my thinking and my acting belong to me and are the I itself.

The ground for distinguishing these predicates of myself, in the manner indicated, is as follows: insofar as I am free, I am not the ground of my drive, nor am I the ground of the feeling excited by the latter. How I feel or do not feel is not something that depends upon my freedom; by contrast, how I think and act is something that ought to depend purely and solely upon my freedom. The former is not a product of freedom [IV, 108], and freedom has no power whatsoever over it; the latter is purely and solely a product of freedom and is nothing whatsoever without freedom. Moreover, the drive and the feeling of the drive are supposed to exercise no causality upon freedom.

The drive notwithstanding, I am able to determine myself in a manner contrary to the drive, just as I can also determine myself in a manner that conforms to the drive; but it is always I myself that determines me, and in no way am I determined by the drive.

The ground for relating these predicates to one another[10] is the following: although a part of what pertains to me is supposed to be possible only through freedom, and another part of the same is supposed to be independent of freedom, just as freedom is supposed to be independent of it, the substance to which both of these belong is simply one and the same, and is posited as one and the same. The I that feels and the I that thinks, the I that is driven and the I that makes a decision by means of its own free will: these are all the same.

Even if, as was just noted, my first action can be none other than to satisfy the drive; and even if the concept of an end for this action is given through the drive itself, the drive is nevertheless posited with a different determination [when it is posited] as the concept of an end than [when it is posited] as a drive. When it is posited as a drive, it is posited as constituted simply as it is and as incapable of being other than it is; when it is posited as the concept of an end, it is posited as something that could also have turned out differently. To be sure, I follow the dictates of the drive, but I do so with the thought that I could also have not followed them. Only under this condition does the manifestation of my force become an instance of *acting*; only under this condition is self-consciousness – and consciousness in general – possible.

This objective view of the I (insofar as a determinate drive is originally posited in it and a feeling is derived from this drive) has already been distinguished above from another objective view of the same I, which appears as the moral law. Let us now make this distinction even clearer. These two [ways of looking at the I objectively] are *materially* distinguished from one another in that the moral law is by no means derived from any objective determinacy of the drive, but solely from the form of a drive as such [IV, 109], considered as the drive of an I – that is, the form of absolute self-sufficiency and independence from everything outside it. In contrast, some determinate material need is presupposed in the feeling of the drive. The two are distinguished *formally* as follows:

---

[10] Concerning the logical distinction between a "ground of distinction" [*Unterscheidungsgrund*] and "ground of relation" [*Beziehungsgrund*], see *SK*, p. 110 (*SW* I: 111; *GA* I/2: 272–273).

the moral law does not impose itself absolutely; it is by no means felt, nor is it in any way present independently of free reflection; instead, it first originates for us through a reflection upon freedom and by relating this form of every drive as such to freedom. In contrast, the feeling of a material drive imposes itself. Finally, with regard to their *relation*, a material drive is not related to freedom in any way, whereas the moral law is indeed related to freedom, for it is the law *of freedom*.

We have already set forth the concept of an original, determinate system of our boundedness [*Begrenztheit*] in general; drive and feeling are precisely the manifestation of what is bounded and of the boundedness within us. There is therefore an original, determinate system of drives and feelings. – According to what was said earlier, what is fixed and determined independently of freedom is called *nature*. This system of drives and feelings is thus to be thought of as nature; and the nature in question is to be thought of as *our* nature, inasmuch as consciousness of it imposes itself on us, and the substance in which this system is located is at the same time supposed to be the substance that thinks and wills freely, which we posit as ourselves.

I myself am, in a certain respect, *nature*, notwithstanding the absolute character of my reason and my freedom; and this nature of mine is a *drive*.

V

Not only do I posit myself as nature, but I also assume another nature outside my own – partly insofar as I am forced to relate my efficacy as such to some stuff that is present independently of me, and partly insofar as this stuff that is independent of me has to have at least a certain form: namely, a form that forces me to advance toward my end by means of determinate, intermediate elements. To the extent that both of these are supposed to be nature, they are necessarily thought of as *equal* [IV, 110]; but insofar as one of them is supposed to be *my* nature and the other a nature outside me, they are *opposed* to each other. Thus these two natures are thought mediately, one through the other, which is the universal relationship of all opposites that are equal with respect to one characteristic feature. In other words, my nature must be explained originally; it must be derived from the entire system of nature and grounded in the latter.

We will here add only a few words concerning the preceding claim, which is sufficiently familiar from and adequately explained in the remaining [branches of the entire system of] philosophy. What we are talking about here is an explanation and a derivation that is undertaken by the I itself when it occupies the viewpoint of ordinary consciousness; we are by no means talking about an explanation provided by the transcendental philosopher. The latter explains everything that occurs in consciousness on the basis of acting on the part of reason as such. For the purpose of explanation, the former [that is, the I of ordinary consciousness] posits objects outside of what is supposed to be explained. – Furthermore, the I does not become conscious of its own explaining as such, only of the products of this explaining; or, to express the matter somewhat differently: it is clear that perception begins from that nature that is in me and by no means from that nature that is outside of me, and that the former is what does the mediating and the latter is what is mediated, what is cognized mediately in accordance with the cognition of the former, [that is, indirectly cognized in accordance with my cognition of my own nature], or is posited in order to explain the former. In contrast, the series of what is real begins with nature outside us; our nature is supposed to be determined by nature outside us; the reason why our nature is as it is and does not have some other character is supposed to lie in nature outside us.

How, then, is our nature to be explained? Or what else do we assume following the assumption of a nature within us? Or under what conditions is it possible to ascribe a nature to ourselves? – The investigation of these questions will occupy us from now on.

My nature is a drive. How is it even possible to comprehend a drive as such? That is to say, what mediates such an act of thinking of a drive in beings such as we are, beings who think only discursively and by means of mediation? [IV, 111].

The kind of thinking that is at issue here can be made very clear by contrasting it with the opposite kind of thinking. Anything that lies in a series of causes and effects is something I can easily comprehend in accordance with the law of the mechanism of nature. Every member of such a series has its activity communicated to it by another member outside itself, and it directs its activity to a third member outside itself. In such a series a quantum of force is simply transferred from one member to the next and proceeds, as it were, through the entire series.

One never learns where this force comes from, since one is forced to ascend further with every member of the series and never arrives at an original force. The activity and the passivity of each member in this series is thought by means of this force that runs through the [entire] series. – A drive cannot be comprehended in this manner, and thus it cannot by any means be thought of as a member of such a series. If one assumes that some external cause acts on the substrate of the drive, then there would also arise an efficacious action, directed to some third thing, lying outside [this substrate, that is, lying outside the I]. Or if the cause in question does not have any power over the substrate of the drive, then nothing at all would come about. A drive, therefore, is something that neither comes from outside nor is directed outside; it is an inner force of the substrate, directed upon itself. The concept by means of which the drive can be thought is the concept of *self-determination*.

My nature, therefore, insofar as it is supposed to consist in a drive, is thought of as determining itself through itself, for this is the only way that a drive can be comprehended. From the viewpoint of the ordinary understanding, however, the very existence of a drive is nothing more than a fact of consciousness, and ordinary understanding does not extend beyond the facts of consciousness. Only the transcendental philosopher goes beyond this fact, and he does so in order to specify the ground on this fact.

Corollary

In the first of these two ways of proceeding [that is, in the kind of thinking characteristic of ordinary consciousness] the power of judgment is engaged in what Kant calls *subsuming*; in the second [that is, in the kind of thinking characteristic of transcendental philosophy] it is engaged in what he calls *reflecting*.[11] The difference is this: the law of the mechanism of nature is nothing other than the law governing the successive series of reflections and the successive determination of one

---

[11] See Immanuel Kant, *Critique of the Power of Judgment*, Introduction, Section IV, where the contrast is between a power of the judgment that is "determining" [*bestimmend*] and one that is "reflecting" [*reflektierend*] (*AA* V: 179). Kant, *Critique of the Power of Judgment*, ed. Paul Guyer, trans. Paul Guyer and Eric Matthews (Cambridge: Cambridge University Press, 2000) [henceforth = *CJ*], pp. 66–67.

reflection by another, as transferred [from the intellect] to the object. (It is through this successive series of reflections that time first arises for us [IV, 112], along with the identity of consciousness over the course of time.) In this kind of thinking the understanding proceeds along its innate course quite mechanically, and the free power of judgment has nothing else to do except reflect upon what it actually does, *qua* mechanical understanding, thereby elevating the latter to consciousness. In this [first] case comprehension occurs by means of the mere mechanism of the power of cognition, without any assistance from freedom and deliberation, and this way of proceeding is rightfully called subsuming. In the second case, comprehension by no means proceeds in accordance with any such mechanism; instead, there occurs in the mind a check [*Anstoß*] and a doubt, and a reflection then urges itself thereupon – that is, a reflection upon the fact that comprehension does not occur mechanically in this case. But even though such comprehension does not take place in *this* [mechanical] *manner*, comprehension must still occur in this case as well. (I.e., it must be incorporated into the unity of consciousness.) This means that the way of thinking must be reversed (just as the proposition, "the ground does not lie in the I, yet there is still supposed to be some ground," means "the ground lies in the Not-I"). The function of the reflecting power of judgment comes into play only where no subsumption is possible; and the reflecting power of judgment *gives itself a law*: namely, to reverse the law of subsumption.

VI

Nature *determines* itself: for the moment, to be sure, we are talking only about *my* nature, which is nevertheless in its essence nature. Nature as such, however, is characterized by its opposition to freedom, in that all the being of the latter is supposed to emerge from thinking, whereas all the being of the former is itself supposed to proceed from an absolute being. Nature as such, therefore, cannot determine itself in the manner of a free being – that is, *through a concept*. "Nature determines itself" means that it *is* determined by its being [*Wesen*] to determine itself. Formally, it *is* determined to determine itself as such; it can never be undetermined, as a free being might well be. Materially, it is determined to determine itself in *precisely this way*; unlike a free being, it has no choice [IV, 113] between a certain determination and its opposite.

My nature is not the whole of nature. There is more nature outside of my own nature, and the former is posited precisely in order to explain the determination of my nature. My nature has been described as a drive, so this must be explained from the rest of nature; and it actually is originally explained in this way. In other words, my nature's determinacy as a drive is itself [explained to be] a result of the determinacy of nature as a whole. A drive belongs to me insofar as I am *nature*, not insofar as I am intellect; for, as we have seen, the intellect as such does not have the least influence upon a drive. The concept of a drive is therefore synthetically united with the concept of nature; the former has to be explained on the basis of the latter, and everything that is thought in the concept of nature is thought of as a drive. Everything, therefore, that is thought as nature is thought of as determining itself.

Just as I have to separate my own nature from the rest of nature, so am I also able to separate other parts of that nature from the remaining parts of the same, since nature as such is a manifold. What is asserted here is merely an ideal separation. For the moment, we will leave undecided the question of whether there might also be some ground for such a separation other than the freedom of discretionary thinking, that is, *whether* there might *actually* be separate parts of nature, independent of our thinking.

A part separated off from the rest of nature in this manner will, first of all, be what it is through itself; but the reason it determines itself in this manner lies in the whole [of nature]. The whole, however, is nothing other than the reciprocal interaction of the complete sum of all its parts. – Or, in order to make this even clearer: abstract for the moment from yourself as nature, since there is a characteristic difference between your nature and the rest of nature, to the extent that the former has been posited so far – namely, the necessity of bounding it in precisely this way, of attributing to it a precise amount [of the whole of reality], neither more nor less [IV, 114]. Now reflect only on the nature that is outside you, and separate off from the latter any part you want. The reason you consider precisely this quantum of nature to be separated off [from the rest] lies solely in your own free reflection. Let us call this part [that has been separated from the rest of nature] X. X contains a drive, and a determinate drive at that. But the fact that this drive is precisely the determinate drive that it is: this is determined by the fact that outside of X there is still present a certain precise amount of nature, and this nature external to X, by its very existence, limits X's drive to be everything and leaves for X only this precise quantum of reality and leaves X with only a drive for the rest of reality. – Had we not been forced to characterize nature as such in terms of drive, then everything that X is not would have to be posited in X only as a negation; under the present condition, however, this has to be thought of as a drive. That is to say, the tendency toward reality as such is spread over the whole [of nature] and is in each part of it. But since this [i.e., X] is only a part, it lacks all the reality of the remaining parts; and in the place of this reality it is left with nothing but a drive. The reason that X is only a *drive* and is precisely *this drive* is because outside of this part there is something else, something that is specifically and precisely as it is.

At present, X is for me the precise part that it is only because I have made it into such a part through the freedom of my own thinking. Nothing prevents me from employing this same freedom in order to separate off from X in turn another part = Y. There is a drive in Y as well, determined through everything that exists outside of Y, including what I previously included in X. Nothing prevents me from going on to separate off from Y yet another part = Z, which will be related to Y just as Y is related to X. – In short, when one proceeds in this manner there is simply nothing that is first and nothing that is last. I can transform every part in turn into a whole and every whole into a part.

Something constituted in this manner, to each part of which one must ascribe determinacy through itself, yet in such a way that this determinacy *is* in turn *the result of the determinacy of the whole of all the parts through itself* is called an *organic whole*. Every part of such a whole – on into infinity – can in turn [IV, 115] be considered either an organic whole or a part. – *Nature as such is therefore an organic whole and is posited as such.*

We can display the concept with which we are here concerned from yet another side. In accordance with the concept of the mechanism of nature, every thing is what it is through some other thing and manifests its existence in some third thing. In accordance with the concept of a drive, every thing is what it is through itself and manifests its existence with respect to itself. If one now thinks of a *free* being, then the latter concept will be totally and strictly valid, without the least modification – not, to be sure, as the concept of a drive, but as the concept of absolute freedom. Freedom is *directly opposed* to the mechanism of nature and is in no way determined by the latter. If, however, what we are talking about is a *natural* drive, then the character of nature as such – namely, its character as a mechanism – must be preserved along with the character of a drive; and hence the two must be synthetically united, which furnishes us with an intermediary element or middle term standing between nature as a mere mechanism (as well as the concept of causality) and freedom as the direct opposite of all mechanism (as well as the concept of substantiality), and we badly need something of this sort in order to explain the causality of freedom in nature.

The concept of such a synthesis would be none other than the one we have just developed. Something = A is indeed what it is through itself; but the reason why what it is through itself is precisely this is a reason grounded in something else (all possible not-A). But the reason this something else is what it is and determines A exactly as it does is, in turn, grounded in A itself, inasmuch as, conversely, not-A becomes what it is through A. Necessity and self-sufficiency are thereby united, and we no longer have the simple thread of causality, but the closed circle of reciprocal interaction.

VII

According to the explanation and proof provided above, I have to posit *my nature* as a closed whole [*ein geschlossenes Ganzes*] [IV, 116], to which there pertains precisely so much [reality,] and neither more nor less than this. From the point of view of ordinary consciousness, which is where we have situated the I throughout our entire investigation, the concept of this totality can by no means be explained on the basis of the I's reflection, though this is how it is explained by the transcendental philosopher; instead, the concept of this totality is [simply] given. My nature happens to be determined and fixed in this particular way, and this totality itself is nature.

To begin with, how do I ever manage to comprehend anything in nature as a real organic whole, even though this is itself only a part of nature as such? And according to what law do I think this for myself? – This question certainly has to be raised, for up to this point we have derived nothing but nature in its entirety as a real whole, but we have by no means yet derived any part of this whole. It is nevertheless a fact that we can at least think of our own nature – which is, admittedly, only a part of the whole of nature – as a closed whole.

"A *real* whole," I said; and this determination is the chief point. I will begin by explaining this concept by means of its opposite. – In viewing nature as we did just now, it was left entirely up to the freedom of reflection to apprehend as a whole any part it liked, to divide this whole again as it wished, to apprehend the parts of the latter as wholes, etc. I had a whole, but my whole was this precise whole only because I myself had made it so; there was no ground for determining the boundaries of this whole other than the freedom of my own thinking. What I had was an ideal whole, a collective unity, by no means a real unity; an aggregate, not a compound. If my whole is to be of the latter sort, then its parts – and precisely the same parts – must unify themselves into a whole without any assistance from my thinking.

Reality is determined through a constraint upon reflection, whereas, in contrast, reflection is free in the representation of what is ideal. If a real whole is to arise for us, then this freedom to bound the whole however we wish would have to be eliminated, and the intellect would have to be required to include within the whole exactly so much [reality], no more and no less [IV, 117]. This, as we said, was the situation with the representation of *my* nature, as a closed whole.

Through which law of thinking is the necessity of determining the boundary [of a part of the whole of reality in a certain way] supposed to arise for us? – Where comprehension by means of mere subsumption is not possible, there the law of the reflecting power of judgment comes into play; and this latter law is nothing but the reversal of the former one. It might well happen, however, that once the power of judgment enters the domain of reflection it would find itself unable to achieve comprehension, even in accordance with that law that arises simply by reversing the law of subsumption. In that case, for the reason just indicated, it would have to reverse this law in turn, and we would thereby obtain a composite law of reflection, a reciprocal interaction of reflection with itself. (Concepts must arise somehow; but to say that comprehension does not occur [in a particular case such as the present one] in accordance with a certain law necessarily means that it must be achieved by following an opposing law.) According to the simple concept of reflection, every part of nature is what it is through itself and for itself. According to the concept that arises through reversal and composition [of this simple concept and law of reflection], no part [of nature] is what it is through and for itself, although the whole of which it is a part certainly is what it is through and for itself. It follows that every part of this whole is determined through all the remaining parts of the same whole, and each complete whole is itself to be considered in the same way we previously considered the universe itself – which transforms the latter from a whole of parts into a whole of wholes, a system of real wholes.

In order to connect our present line of reasoning with our earlier one, let us now continue our discussion of this new concept [of a real whole]. – According to the concept that was first set forth, everything that is apprehended possesses its own measure of reality and possesses a drive for the rest. Drive and reality stand in reciprocal interaction and mutually exhaust each other. Nothing possesses a drive for a reality that it [already] has, nor does anything possess a lack without a drive to fill that lack. It was at our discretion to continue or not to continue looking at things in this way [IV, 118]; such a mode of observation fit everything we might ever encounter, and everything was entirely uniform.

Now, however, some determinate something $=X$ is supposed to be given, something that cannot be comprehended in accordance with the preceding law. How would such an X have to be constituted? Apprehend any portion of X you wish: let us call this A. If, in the case of A, drive and reality could not be explained reciprocally, one on the basis of the other – if the drive were directed toward a reality that was not missing from A and did not pertain to A, and if, in turn, the drive were not directed toward a reality that was indeed missing in A and did pertain to A –, then A could not be explained and comprehended on the basis of itself alone, and anyone reflecting on A would be driven farther. Comprehension would not be brought to a conclusion; I would not have succeeded in comprehending anything, and it would be clear that I should not have separated at my own discretion part A from X. – Now apprehend what remains of $X=B$. Assume that the situation of B, considered in and for itself, is, with regard to its drive and its reality, the same as that of A, but that it so happens that the drive within B is directed toward the reality that is lacking in A and that the drive within A is directed toward the reality that is lacking in B: in such a case I would, first of all, be driven back from considering B to considering A, that is, to investigating whether A actually lacks that reality for which I find a drive in B. I would have to stop and review the matter; that is, I would have to reflect on my act of reflection and thereby bound it.

What would occur in this case would be a composite reflection, and, since this reflection is governed by necessity, [it would be a reflection in accordance with] a composite *law* of reflection. – Furthermore, I could not comprehend A without including B, and vice versa; hence *I would have to* unite the two synthetically in one concept, and X would therefore become a *real* whole, not merely an ideal one.

To complete the concept we are here explicating: X is nature in general and organic nature, so the universal law of the latter must therefore apply here as well. To that extent, X is infinitely divisible [IV, 119]. I can therefore divide A into b, c, d; I can divide b, in turn, into e, f, g, and so on *ad infinitum*. Simply *qua* nature, each part possesses both reality and drive and is to that extent self-sufficient. For each of these parts, however, it is also the case that the relationship between its reality and its drive cannot be explained from itself, for otherwise it would not be a part of a real whole = X. – No part can be explained before all the parts of X have been apprehended. Each part strives to satisfy the need of all of the parts, and all of them strive, in turn, to satisfy the need of this individual part. Provisionally, that is, until we might be able to find a more fitting name for it, let us call that which can be comprehended only in the manner just indicated a "real organic whole."

I myself at least am such a natural whole. Whether there are other wholes of this sort, beyond me, is not a question that can be decided in advance. A decision concerning the latter will depend upon whether or not I am able to comprehend myself as such a natural whole without also assuming that there are other wholes outside of me. – The question before us here is only how such a real whole can be explained from nature, and which new predicates might be attributed to nature through such an explanation.

As soon as one demands that something be explained from *nature*, one demands that it be explained through and on the basis of a law of physical – and by no means moral – necessity. Simply by claiming such explicability one is also claiming that nature necessarily organizes itself into real wholes, that this necessity lies in the properties that absolutely pertain to nature, and that a rational being is forced to think of nature in this manner and only in this manner.

(One should therefore not employ an argument of lazy reason in order to have recourse to an intellect as the creator or the architect of the world. Among the reasons for not doing this is the fact that in the former case it is simply unthinkable that an intellect could create matter, and in the latter case it is not yet conceivable how reason could have any influence on nature, inasmuch as this is precisely what we have to explain here in Part II. Moreover, an intellect may put things together and combine them with one another [IV, 120] forever: what results from this is aggregation, allegation, but never fusion, which presupposes an inner force in nature itself. Nor should one attempt to explain organization on the basis of mechanical laws. Mechanical laws involve an eternal pushing and shoving of matter, attraction and repulsion, and nothing else. Instead, the law in question is an immanent law of nature, a law that a rational being, in order to explain itself, must think when it thinks the concept of nature; but such a law cannot be explained any further. To do so would mean to derive it from [the law of] mechanism. – It is self-evident that it is only from the point of view of ordinary consciousness or of science that this law is supposed to be absolute, i.e., incapable of further explanation. It can certainly be explained from the transcendental point of view, that is, from the point of view of the *Wissenschaftslehre*, inasmuch as nature as a whole can be explained from the latter point of view and derived from the I.)

This, however, raised a question concerning what kind of law this might be and what determinate course of nature would necessarily have to be assumed in connection with such a law. According to the law that was set forth previously, every natural thing is what it is through itself and for itself; such a thing is nothing to any other thing, and no other thing is anything to it. What each such thing is nothing else is. – This is the principle of substantiality; and the principle of natural mechanism is the principle of causality. According to the law we are now considering, there is no possible element [*Element*] to which the former principle [of substantiality] applies: – I use the term *element* in order to be able to express myself at all, but this term must be understood in an *ideal* and by no means in a *real* sense – not as though there were elements that were in themselves indivisible, but because one has to stop dividing in order to consider something. No element, I say, is sufficient unto itself or self-sufficient by itself and for itself; it stands in need of another, and this other stands in need of it. In each element there is a drive to something foreign. – If this is so, then, in accordance with a universal law of nature, the drive that is determined in this manner extends throughout nature as a whole [IV, 121]. This law of nature can therefore be formulated as follows: every part of nature strives to unite its being and its efficacious action with the being and efficacious action of another determinate part of nature; and if one thinks of these parts as occupying space, then [this same law states that] every part [of nature] strives to unite itself in space with another part. This drive is called the *formative drive* [*Bildungstrieb*], taking this term in both the active and the passive sense: both as a drive to form or to shape or to cultivate and as a drive to allow oneself to be formed or shaped or cultivated. Such a drive is necessary in nature and is not merely a foreign addition without which nature might still continue to exist. One must not, however, think of this formative drive as having its seat here or there, in this or that part [of nature]; nor, for God's sake, should one think of the formative drive itself as some special part [of nature]. It is not a substance at all but an accident, and an accident of all the parts.

In positing the organization of the I to be the result of a law of nature, we have gained this much: [First of all,] we have at least found that the drive to organization extends throughout all of nature – for at this point we wish to leave entirely undecided the question concerning whether this drive might until now also have causality outside of us.

Within me, however, – and this is the second point – this drive has causality. Certain parts of nature have united their being and their efficacious action in order to produce a single being and a single efficacious action. In this respect, the most appropriate name for what we have until now been calling "a real natural whole" would be "an *organized product of nature.*"

There is such a thing, moreover, since, according to what was said above, I myself am such a thing. Here we are not yet talking about materiality in space, which would provide us with a real manifold (though this could be deduced easily enough); but at least the ideal manifold within me harmoniously unifies itself into a single unity [*zu Einem*]. This harmonizing is a product of the formative power of nature.

The upshot of the present investigation is therefore as follows: just as certainly as I am, I must just as certainly ascribe causality to nature; for I can posit myself only as a product of nature [IV, 122]. What was supposed to be proven has therefore now been proven as such, though it has by no means been completely analyzed as yet.

§9

Conclusions from the preceding

I

I find myself to be an organized product of nature. In such a thing, however, the being [*Wesen*] of the parts consists in a drive to preserve their union with other determinate parts. Such a drive, which is attributed to the whole, is called "the drive for self-preservation." The being of the whole is nothing other than a unification of certain parts with one another, and therefore self-preservation is nothing other than the preservation of this unification. In order to see this more clearly, consider the following: every possible part strives to unite other determinate parts with itself. This striving, however, can have causality only if mutually supporting parts are already united; for only on this condition is there an organized whole. The whole, however, is nothing other than the parts taken together. There can therefore be nothing in the whole that is not in the parts: namely, *a striving to incorporate determinate parts into itself*; and to the extent that there is supposed to be a completed whole, this striving must have causality. Its being consists in the reciprocal interaction of this striving and this causality, each of which is conditioned by the other; for it is a whole, and the comprehension of the same is completed. To this extent, the concept that was set forth earlier [– namely, that of the drive for self-preservation –] comes into play for it once again with respect to its relation to the rest of nature. "It preserves *itself*" means that it preserves this reciprocal interaction of its striving and its causality [IV, 123]. If either of these is abolished, then everything is abolished. A product of nature that no longer organizes itself ceases to be an organized product of nature; for the character of what is organized consists in its continuing formation.

Despite what seems to be usually assumed, the drive for self-preservation is not a drive directed toward mere existence as such; instead, it is a drive directed toward a determinate existence: a drive of the thing to be and to remain what it is. – Mere existence is an abstract concept, nothing concrete. There is no drive for existence in all of nature. A rational being never wants to be simply in order to be, but rather, in order to be this or that. Nor does an irrational product of nature strive and work simply in order to be in general, but rather, it strives to be and to remain precisely what it is: the apple tree strives to remain an apple tree, and the pear tree strives to remain a pear tree. In beings of the latter type the drive is at the same time the effect. This is why an apple tree can never bear pears nor a pear tree apples. Alteration of type [*Umartung*] interferes with the entire organization and sooner or later leads to extinction.

This is how things stand with me as well. There is in me a drive, one that has arisen through nature and that relates itself to natural objects in order to unite them with my own being: not to absorb them into my being outright, as food and drink are absorbed through digestion, but to relate them as such to my natural needs, to bring them into a certain relationship with me, concerning which we will learn more in the future. This drive is the drive for self-preservation in the sense indicated above: the preservation of myself as this determinate product of nature. The relation of the means to this end occurs *immediately and absolutely*, without any intervening cognition, reflection, or calculation. What this drive of mine is directed toward pertains to my preservation *because* it is directed toward this; and it is directed toward what pertains to my preservation *because* it pertains to my preservation. The connection [in this case] does not lie in freedom [IV, 124], but in the formative law of nature.

Even at this point I would like to add an important remark, the consequences of which are far-reaching and the neglect of which has occasioned considerable disadvantages for philosophy in general and for ethics in particular. – Let us say that my drive is directed toward object X. Is it perhaps the case that the stimulation or the attraction originates in X, takes hold of my nature and determines my drive accordingly? By no means. The drive originates entirely from my own nature, through which what is supposed to exist for me is already determined in advance; and my striving and longing include the latter even before it actually exists for me and even before it has had any effect on me. My striving and longing would include this thing that is supposed to exist for me even if it could not come to be all, and they would not be satisfied without it. *It is* and *must be*, however, as a consequence of the completion of nature in itself and because nature is itself an organized, real whole. – I do not feel hunger because there is food for me; instead, something becomes food for me because I am hungry. The situation is no different in the case of any of the organized products of nature. It is not the presence of the materials that pertain to the plant's substance that stimulates the plant to absorb these materials; instead, precisely these materials are demanded by the plant's inner structure, independently of their actual presence; and if such materials were not present in nature at all, then the plant could not exist in nature either. – Here there is everywhere harmony, reciprocal interaction, and not, as it were, mere mechanism; for mechanism does not produce any drive. As certainly as I am, my striving and desiring originate not from the object, but from myself; and this is true even with respect to my animal needs. If one ignores this remark at this point, then one will not be able to grasp it later, at a more crucial point, viz., in conjunction with our explication of the moral law.

II

As described above, this drive of mine is also an object of reflection, and necessarily so. As surely as I reflect at all [IV, 125], I am just as surely necessitated to perceive this drive and to posit it as mine. From the viewpoint we presently occupy, we can find no reason for this necessity; we have already indicated what is, from the transcendental point of view, the reason for this necessity. – I said, "as surely as *I reflect*": for reflection itself is not a product of nature nor can it be one. With respect to its form, reflection takes place with absolute spontaneity; only its object, as well as the necessity of attending to this object, is an effect of nature.

The first thing that arises from reflection upon this drive is a *longing* – the feeling of a need with which one is not oneself acquainted. We feel that something – we know not what – is missing. – This first result of reflection is already enough to distinguish the I from all other products of nature. What a drive brings about in other products of nature is either satisfaction (if its conditions are present) or nothing at all. No one will seriously claim that during dry weather there is a longing within plants, stemming from the lack of humidity. Either they are hydrated or they wither; no third alternative could follow from their natural drive.

III

As an intellect and as a being that acts intelligently, that is, as the subject of consciousness, I am absolutely free and depend only upon my own self-determination. This is my character. Hence my nature, insofar as this is necessarily attributed to me in the sense indicated, i.e., insofar as it is an immediate object of consciousness, must also depend only on my own self-determination.

To what extent is this nature of mine attributed to *me* as the *subject of consciousness?* The product of the reciprocal interaction of [the components of] my nature [as described above] is a *drive*. First of all, this reciprocal interaction is not *my* efficacious acting as an intellect; I by no means become conscious of the latter immediately. Nor is the drive my product; it is a product of nature, as was said above. It is given, and it does not depend upon me in any way. Nevertheless, I become conscious of this drive, and what it brings about within consciousness is something that stands within my power; or, more precisely [IV, 126], the *drive* does not act efficaciously within consciousness, but it is *I* who act efficaciously or do not act efficaciously, in accordance with this drive. Here lies the point of transition of the rational being to self-sufficiency; here lies the determinate, sharp boundary between necessity and freedom.

In a plant or an animal the satisfaction of the drive occurs necessarily, whenever the conditions of such satisfaction are present. A human being is by no means driven by the natural drive. – We have no power over digestion, metabolism, circulation of the blood, etc.; these are all the business of nature within us, as indicated earlier. *We* (the intellect) have no power over them because they do not appear immediately within consciousness. What a physician knows about these functions is something he knows by means of inferences. In contrast, we do have power over the satisfaction of our hunger and thirst; for we are conscious of the drive to food and drink. Who would wish to claim that he eats with the same mechanical necessity with which he digests?

In short, it is not within my power to sense or not to sense a determinate drive; but it is within my power to satisfy it or not to satisfy it.

IV

I reflect on my longing, and I thereby raise to clear consciousness something that was previously only an obscure sensation. However, according to the law of reflection, a law that remains constantly valid, I cannot reflect upon my longing without determining it as a longing, i.e., without distinguishing it from other possible longings. But the only way it can be distinguished from another longing is by means of its object. Thus, through this second act of reflection I now also become conscious of the object of my longing, the reality or non-reality of which does not yet concern us at this point. It is posited merely as that for which I am striving. A longing that is determined through its object, however, is called a *desiring*.

The manifold of desiring as such, unified in a single concept and considered as a power grounded in [IV, 127] the I, is called the *power of desire* [*Begehrungsvermögen*]. If there were also another kind of desiring, the manifold of which could also be unified in a power of desire, then the power of desire we have just deduced would rightly be called, following Kant, the *lower power of desire*.[12]

The form of this drive – i.e., the fact that it is a drive accompanied by consciousness – has its ground in the free act of reflection; that there is any drive at all and that the drive or the desiring is directed toward a certain precise object has its ground in nature – not, however, as was pointed out above, in any foreign nature, in the nature of the objects, but rather in my own nature; the ground in question is an immanent one. – Freedom is therefore already manifest in desiring, for an act of free reflection intervenes between longing and desiring. One can very well suppress disorderly desires by not reflecting on them, by ignoring them, and by occupying oneself with something else, especially with intellectual work, so that, as theological ethicists aptly express it, one refuses to indulge the desires in question.

V

My desiring has as its object things of nature, with the goal either of unifying these things with me immediately (as in the case of food and drink) or of placing them in a certain relationship with me (as in the case of clear air, an extensive view, good weather, and the like).

First of all, the things of nature exist for me in space, and it is here presupposed that one is familiar with this point from the theoretical portion of philosophy.[13] Consequently, anything with which these

---

[12] See *CprR*, p. 20 (*AA* V: 22).

[13] See the deduction of space, first in § 4 of Fichte's *Outline of the Distinctive Character of the Wissenschaftslehre with respect to the Theoretical Faculty* (*EPW*, pp. 291–306 [*SW* I: 390–411; *GA* I/3: 193–208]) and then in §§ 10 and 11 of his lectures on *WLnm* (*FTP*, pp. 234–257 [*GA* IV/2: 98–112 and *GA* IV/3: 410–422]).

natural things are supposed to be united or placed into a determinate relationship must likewise be in space. For only what is also in space can be united with or related to something spatial; otherwise, the latter would not remain in space, which is absurd, or else there would be no relationship with it, which contradicts our presupposition. But what is in space and fills space is matter. As a product of nature, therefore, I am matter; more precisely and in accordance with what was said above, I am organized matter that constitutes a determinate whole: I am *my body* [IV, 128].

Furthermore, my will is supposed to be able to unite with me the things of nature or to bring them into a relationship with me. This union or relationship is connected with certain parts of my organized body, and my body is the immediate instrument of my will. The parts in question must therefore stand under the dominion of my will; and, since we are here talking about a spatial relationship, then these parts [of my body], as parts, i.e., in relation to the whole of my body, must be movable, and my body itself must be movable in relation to nature as a whole. Moreover, since this movement is supposed to depend on a freely designed and indeterminately modifiable concept, my body must be movable in many different ways – Such a constitution of the body is called *articulation*. If I am to be free, then my body must be articulated. (On this matter I refer the reader to the First Part of my *Outline of Natural Right*.)[14]

Remark

Here we have arrived at one of the standpoints from which we can conveniently look around us and see whether things have become clearer in the course of our investigation.

There is within us a drive toward the things of nature, the goal of which is to bring these things into a determinate relationship with our own nature; this drive has no end outside of itself and aims at its own satisfaction solely for the sake of being satisfied. Satisfaction for satisfaction's sake is called sheer *enjoyment* [*Genuß*].

We want to be sure that the reader is convinced of the absolute character of this natural drive. Each organized product of nature is *its*

---

[14] See *FNR*, §§ 5 and 6, esp. pp. 73f. (*SW* III: 78–80; *GA* I/3: 378–379). (Fichte here inaccurately refers to his own *Grundlage des Naturrechts* as "meinen Grundriß des Naturrechts.")

own end, i.e., it forms or shapes [itself] simply for the sake of doing so, and it forms or shapes in *the way it does* simply for the sake of doing so. With this, we do not mean to say merely that the irrational product of nature does not *think* for itself an end outside itself, which is self-evident, since such a product of nature does not think at all. Instead, we also mean that an intelligent observer of such an organized product of nature cannot attribute to it any external end [*Zweck*] without being inconsistent and explaining things utterly incorrectly. In nature there is only an inner, and by no means a *relative*, purposiveness [*Zweckmäßigkeit*] [IV, 129]. The latter first arises only through the discretionary ends a free being is able to posit for itself in the objects of nature and is to some degree able to accomplish as well. – The situation of a rational being is no different than that of an irrational one, to the extent that the former is mere nature; it satisfies itself only in order to satisfy itself; and it is satisfied by a determinate object only because this is precisely the one that is demanded by its nature. Since a rational product of nature is conscious of its longing, it is necessarily also conscious of the satisfaction of this longing; the latter provides pleasure [*Lust*]; and such pleasure is the final end of such a being. The natural human being does not eat in order to sustain and strengthen his body; he eats because hunger causes him pain and food tastes good to him. – At this point one should note the following: several analysts of the feelings, especially Mendelssohn,[15] have explained delight [*Vergnügen*] as the feeling of some improvement of our bodily state.[16] This is entirely correct, so long as one is talking simply about sensory pleasure and so long as the bodily state in question is taken to be merely a state of the organized body [*Organization*].[17] To this claim, the younger Jerusalem[18] objects on the grounds that there is a sensation

---

[15] Moses Mendelssohn, 1729–1786, German–Jewish philosopher of the Enlightenment.

[16] Mendelssohn, "On Sentiments" [*Über die Empfindungen*], Eleventh Letter, in Mendelssohn, *Philosophical Writings*, trans. and ed. Daniel O. Dahlstrom (Cambridge: Cambridge University Press, 1997), p. 48.

[17] Regarding the distinction between the body as an organic, organized whole (or "organization") and the body as an articulated instrument of the will (or "articulation"), see §§ 11 and 14 *WLnm* (*FTP*, pp. 254–255 and 321–327 [*GA* IV/2: 111, 156–161 and *GA* IV/3: 420–421 and 454–457]).

[18] In his philosophical essays edited by Gotthold Ephraim Lessing, p. 61. FICHTE'S NOTE.
    This is a reference to the *Philosophical Essays* [*Philosophische Aufsätze*] of Karl Wilhelm Jerusalem (1747–1772), edited posthumously by Lessing in 1776. Fichte's specific reference is to Jerusalem's Fourth Essay, "On Mendelssohn's Theory of Sensory Enjoyment" [*Ueber die Mendelssohnsche Theorie vom sinnlichen Vergnügen*].

of pleasure even in cases where there is an obvious deterioration of our bodily state and an immediate feeling of this deterioration – such as the case of a drinker in the initial stages of intoxication. In all such examples one will note that the deterioration concerns only the state of the [body's] articulation, but that, for the moment, the state of the [body as an] organization becomes altogether better, the play and reciprocal interaction of the individual parts among themselves becomes more perfect and communication with surrounding nature becomes more uninhibited. According to the proof just conducted, however, all sensory pleasure relates to the [body as an] organization. The [body as] articulation *as* such, as an *instrument of freedom*, is not, properly speaking, a product of nature, but is a product of the exercise of freedom. The *consequences* such pleasure may have for the [body as an] organization do not come into consideration here, for what lies in the future is not immediately felt – [IV, 130]. Here a human being is entirely [the same as] a plant. A plant would feel good when it grows – if only a plant were able to reflect. But it could also overgrow and thereby bring about its own demise without thereby disturbing the feeling of its well-being.

It is within our power to give in or not to give in to this drive to mere enjoyment as such. Every satisfaction of this drive, to the extent that we are conscious of such an occurrence, necessarily occurs with freedom; and the [human] body is so constituted that through it one can exercise free efficacy.

To the extent that a human being aims at mere enjoyment, he is dependent on something *given*: namely, the presence of the objects of his drive; and he is therefore not sufficient unto himself, inasmuch as the achievement of his end depends upon nature as well. But to the extent that a human being simply reflects at all and thereby becomes a subject of consciousness (and, according to what was said above, a human being *necessarily* reflects upon his natural drive), to this extent, he becomes an I, and the tendency of reason to determine itself *absolutely by itself* – as the subject of consciousness, as an intellect in the highest sense of the word – manifests itself in him.

But first, let us raise an important question. Are my drive as a natural being and my tendency as a pure spirit two different drives? No, from the transcendental point of view the two are one and the same original drive [*Urtrieb*], which constitutes my being, simply viewed from two different sides. That is to say, I am a subject–object, and my true being consists in the identity and indivisibility of the two. If I view myself as an *object* completely determined by the laws of sensible intuition and discursive thinking, then what is in fact my one and only drive becomes for me my natural drive, because on this view I myself am nature. If I view myself as a *subject*, then this same single drive becomes for me a pure, spiritual drive, or it becomes the law of self-sufficiency. All phenomena of the I rest solely upon the reciprocal interaction of these two drives, which is, properly speaking, only the reciprocal interaction of *one and the same drive with itself*. – This immediately answers the question concerning [IV, 131] how things as opposed to each other as these two drives can occur in a being that is supposed to be absolutely one. The two are in fact one, but I-hood in its entirety rests on the fact that they appear to be different. The boundary separating them is reflection.

As a consequence of the intuition of reflection, the reflecting subject stands higher than what it reflects upon; the former rises above and includes within itself the latter. For this reason, the drive of the reflecting subject, the subject of consciousness, is rightly called *the higher drive*, and a power of desire determined through this drive is called the *higher power of desire*.

Only the object reflected upon is nature; the reflecting subject stands over against the former, and thus it is not nature and stands above all nature. The higher drive, as a drive of what is purely spiritual, is directed toward absolute self-determination to activity for activity's sake and is therefore contrary to all enjoyment, which involves a merely passive abandoning of oneself to nature.

These two drives, however, constitute only one and the same I. The I must therefore be united within the sphere of consciousness. We will see that in this unity the higher drive has to surrender the *purity* of its activity (that is, the fact that it is not determined by any object), while the lower drive has to surrender enjoyment as its end. The result of this unity is an *objective* activity, the final end of which is absolute freedom, absolute independence from all nature – an infinite end, which can never be achieved. Our task therefore can only be to indicate *how* we must act in order to *draw nearer to* this final end. If one considers only the higher power of desire, then one obtains a mere *metaphysics of morals* [*Metaphysik der Sitten*], which is formal and empty. The only way to obtain an *ethics* [*Sittenlehre*] – which must be real – is through the synthetic unification of the higher and lower powers of desire [IV, 132].

§10

Freedom and the higher power of desire

I

The final product of my nature, as such, is a drive. *I* reflect upon *myself*, i.e., upon that nature that I am *given*, which, as the immediate object of my reflection, is nothing but a drive. Our task here is to determine this reflection completely. In order to do this, we will have to consider its *form*, its *matter* or object, and the *connection* of these two with each other.

First of all, the fact *that* such an act of reflection occurs – i.e., its form – is something absolute. It is not a product of nature; it occurs simply because it occurs, because I am I. As concerns the object of this reflection, we do not need to be reminded that the object in question is our natural drive; the only question concerns the *extent to which* our nature is the immediate object of this act of reflection. This question, too, was answered earlier, albeit only in passing: [my nature is the object of this reflection] to the extent that I am *necessitated* to attribute something to myself, the reflecting subject. The connection between the subject and the object of reflection is that they are supposed to be the same. I [am a] natural being [*Naturwesen*] (for there is no other I for me); at the same time, I am also for myself the reflecting subject. The former is the substance, and the act of reflection is an accident of this substance, a manifestation of the freedom of this natural being. This is what is posited in the reflection that we now have to describe. From the point of view of ordinary consciousness no question at all arises concerning the ground of this connection. One would explain things to oneself from this ordinary viewpoint by saying, "I just happen to be such a being, a being with this particular nature and with a consciousness thereof." This explanation leaves it incomprehensible how such an agreement between two things that are completely heterogeneous and independent of each other is even possible – something that is not even supposed to be comprehensible from the viewpoint of ordinary consciousness [IV, 133]. It is comprehensible that nature, for its part, limits and determines something in the way that my nature is supposed to be determined; it can equally be understood that the intellect forms a representation of what pertains to it and determines the latter in a certain manner. What

126

is incomprehensible is how the mutually independent modes of acting of these two can be in harmony with each other and how they could arrive at *the same thing*, since the intellect does not legislate for nature, and nature does not legislate for the intellect. The former claim would lay the basis for some kind of idealism, the second for some kind of materialism. The hypothesis of pre-established harmony, as it is usually understood, does not commit itself on this issue but leaves our question just as unanswered as it was before. – We have already answered this question from the transcendental point of view above. There is no nature in itself; my nature, along with all other nature that is posited in order to explain the former, is only a particular way of looking at myself. I am limited only in the intelligible world, and my reflection upon myself is indeed limited – *for me* – through this limitation of my original drive; and conversely, my original drive is limited through my reflection on myself – also *for me*. Here there can be no talk at all of any other sort of limitation, other than a limitation of myself for myself. From the transcendental point of view we by no means have anything twofold, containing two elements independent of each other, but rather something that is absolutely simple; and surely where there is no difference there can be no talk of harmony nor any question concerning the ground of such harmony.

Right now, however, we are occupying the ordinary point of view, and this is the viewpoint from which we shall proceed. – Through the act of reflection described above, the I tears itself loose from all that is supposed to lie outside of it, brings itself under its own control, and positions itself [*stellt sich hin*] as absolutely self-sufficient. This is because the reflecting subject is self-sufficient and is dependent only on itself; but what is reflected upon [in this case, namely, the I] is one and the same as the former. This is not to say, as someone might at first blush believe, that from this point on the I observes itself and has nothing else to do than to engage in such self-observation [IV, 134]. Instead, what is asserted is the following: from this point on nothing can ensue in the I without the active determination of the intellect as such. The one doing the reflecting and the one that is reflected upon are here united and constitute one single, indivisible person. The I that is reflected upon supplies the person with real force; the I that does the reflecting supplies the person with consciousness. From now on, the person can do nothing without concepts and can act only in accordance therewith.

A reality that has its ground in a concept is called a product of freedom. Starting at the point just indicated, no reality pertains to the I except according to its own concept thereof. From this point on, therefore, the I is free, and everything that occurs through the I is a product of this freedom.

This point is crucial: for we intend to clarify very soon the doctrine of freedom. – Each member of a natural series is something that is determined in advance, in accordance either with the law of mechanism or the law of organism. When one is completely acquainted with a thing's nature and with the law it obeys, one can then predict how it will manifest itself for all eternity. What occurs in the I – beginning at the point it becomes an I and assuming that it actually remains an I – is not determined in advance and is purely and simply indeterminable. There is no law in accordance with which free acts of self-determination would occur and could be predicted, for such acts depend on the determination of an intellect, and an intellect, as such, is nothing but free, sheer, pure activity. – A natural series is continuous. Each member of such a series completely accomplishes what it can. A series of determinations of freedom consists of leaps, and such a series advances, as it were, by fits and starts. Think for yourself of a determinate member of such a series and call it A. All sorts of things may be possible starting from A; yet not everything that is possible ensues, but only a determinate part of the same = X. In the case of a natural series, everything coheres in a strict chain; but here, in a series of determinations of freedom, the connection is broken off with each link in the chain. – In a natural series each member can be explained; in a series of determinations of freedom none can be explained, for each one is a first and absolute member [IV, 135]. In a natural series the law of causality obtains, but the law that pertains in a series determined by freedom is the law of substantiality: i.e., every free decision is itself something substantial; it is what it is absolutely through itself.

Following the indicated act of reflection [of the I upon its natural drive] I cannot be driven any further by natural necessity, for following that act of reflection I am no longer a member of nature's chain. The last member in that chain is a drive, but it is also only a *drive*, and, as such, it has no causality in a spiritual being. In this way freedom can be rendered comprehensible even from the perspective of the philosophy of nature. The causality of nature has its limit; beyond this limit there necessarily lies the causality of some other force – if, that is, there is supposed to be any causality beyond this limit. What ensues from the drive is not something brought about by nature, for the latter is exhausted with the generation of the drive. Instead, this is something I bring about – employing, to be sure, a force that stems from nature, but one that is no longer *nature's* force but is *mine*, because it has come under the sway of a principle that lies above all nature, under the sway of the concept. Let us call this kind of freedom "*formal* freedom." Whatever I do with consciousness, I do with this kind of freedom. Someone might therefore follow his natural drive without exception, and yet he would still be free in this sense of the term – so long as he acted with consciousness and not mechanically; for the ultimate ground of his acting would not be his natural drive, but rather his consciousness of this natural drive. – I am unaware of anyone who has treated this aspect of the concept of freedom with sufficient care, though this is nevertheless the root of all freedom. Perhaps this is precisely why so many errors have arisen regarding this subject and so many complaints have been made concerning the incomprehensibility of the doctrine of freedom.

Corollary

No opponent of the claim that there is some freedom can deny being conscious of such states for which he can indicate no ground outside of himself. The more sagacious [among these opponents] say that what we are conscious of in these cases is by no means the fact that these states have no external ground, but only that we are not conscious of these grounds. (We will soon discuss how matters stand with regard to the immediate consciousness of freedom) [IV, 136]. They further conclude that from the fact that we are not conscious of any such external grounds it does not follow that the states in question have no causes. (Here they become transcendent right from the start. Surely what the fact that we are simply incapable of positing something means for us is that this something *is* not. Transcendental philosophy not only has no concept of what being without consciousness might mean, but it clearly shows that such a thing makes no sense.) But since everything has its cause, so these more sagacious opponents of freedom continue, those decisions that we believe to be free also have their causes as well, despite the fact that we are not conscious of these causes. Here, however, they obviously are *presupposing* that the I belongs in the series governed by the law of nature, which is what they pretended to be able to *demonstrate*. Their proof is plainly circular. To be sure, the defender of freedom, for his part, also can only presuppose I-hood, the concept of which already includes the fact that the I does not fall under the law of nature. In comparison to his opponents, however, the defender of freedom has two decisive advantages: first, that he actually is able to set forth a philosophy, and second, that he has intuition on his side, with which the opponents of freedom are unacquainted. The latter are only discursive thinkers and utterly lack intuition. One must not dispute with them but should instead cultivate [*kultivieren*] them, if that were only possible.

II

According to everything that has been said so far, I *am* free but I do not posit myself as free; I am free perhaps for an intellect outside of me, but I am not free for myself. Yet *I* am something only insofar as I posit myself as being this.

First of all, what is required in order to posit oneself as free? I posit myself as free when I become conscious of my transition from indeterminacy to determinacy. Insofar as I possess the power to act, I find myself to be undetermined. In reflecting upon this state [of indeterminacy], this is expressed by saying that the power of imagination "hovers" between opposing determinations. My perception of my freedom starts here. – I now determine myself, and along with this, my reflection [upon myself] is determined at the same time [IV, 137]. *I* determine myself: what is this determining I? Without doubt, this is the one I that arose from the union of the I that reflects and the I that is reflected upon; and this same I is, in the same undivided act and in the same regard, also what is determined. In the consciousness of freedom, subject and object are wholly and completely one. The concept (of an end) immediately becomes a deed, and the deed immediately becomes a (cognitive) concept (of my freedom). (See above pp. 83ff.) It would have been quite correct to deny that freedom can be an *object* of consciousness; freedom is indeed not something that develops by itself, without any assistance from a conscious being, in which case the latter would only have to be an observer. Freedom is not the object but the subject–object of a conscious being. – In this sense one does indeed become conscious of one's freedom through the deed: that is, by self-actively tearing oneself loose from the state of wavering and by positing for oneself some determinate end, simply because one posits it for oneself, especially if the end in question runs counter to all one's inclinations and is nevertheless chosen for duty's sake. Such consciousness, however, involves both the energy of the will and the inwardness of intuition. There are individuals who do not in fact really will, but who always allow themselves to be pushed around and driven by a blind propensity. For this reason, such persons do not possess any consciousness, properly speaking, since they never self-actively produce, determine, and arrange their representations, but merely dream a long dream, a dream determined by the obscure course of the association of ideas. When we talk about the consciousness of freedom we are not addressing such people.

Consciousness of my indeterminacy is therefore a condition for my consciousness of determining myself through free activity. Indeterminacy, however, is not simply not-determinacy ($= 0$), but is an undecided hovering between several possible determinations ($= a$ negative magnitude); for otherwise it could not be posited and would be nothing. Up to this point we have been unable to see how freedom can be directed toward several possible determinations and how it is supposed to be posited as directed toward them [IV, 138]. There is no object whatsoever for the application of freedom other than the natural drive. When the latter comes upon the scene, there is no reason at all why it should not obey freedom, but there is indeed a reason why it should. Or does one instead wish to say that several drives might operate at the same time (something which, however, we also have no reason to assume from our present standpoint) and that the stronger drive will be decisive, in which case, once again, no indeterminacy will be possible? (The drive will not be the cause of the determination of the will. According to what was said above, a drive is absolutely incapable of doing this; but freedom will always be the cause of the very thing that the natural drive would have produced if it had causality; freedom will [to this extent] stand completely in the service of the natural drive and will propagate the causality of nature.) To the extent that a free being is in this state – which, to be sure, is not an *original* state, but one that can be actual only as an *acquired* state – a *propensity* [*Hang*] is ascribed to that free being; and this is justifiably called a *blind* propensity, since it is preceded by no act of reflection and by no indeterminacy. A free being, considered as a free being, is not conscious and cannot become conscious of such a propensity.

I, however, am an I solely insofar as I am conscious of myself as an I: that is, as free and self-sufficient. This consciousness of my freedom is a condition of I-hood. (What we are about to deduce will be universally valid, since it will become evident that a rational being is not possible at all without any consciousness of this freedom, and thus also not possible without the conditions for such freedom; and since one of these conditions is a consciousness of morality, a rational being is also not possible without such consciousness. It will also become evident that the consciousness of morality is by no means anything contingent or some foreign addition, but instead pertains essentially to rationality. It is, however, certainly possible that consciousness of freedom and morality is at times, perhaps even most of the time, obscured and that a human being might sink to the level of a machine; and later on we will find the reason for this. Here we are claiming only that no human being could be absolutely lacking in *any* moral feeling) [IV, 139].

Since everything in the I is explained from a drive, there must be a drive to become conscious of this freedom (and this drive must be contained in the I's original drive); hence there also must be a drive directed toward the conditions for this consciousness of freedom. The condition for such consciousness, however, is indeterminacy. Indeterminacy is impossible if the I obeys only its natural drive. There would therefore have to be a drive to determine oneself without any reference to the natural drive and contrary to it, a drive to derive the material of one's action not from the natural drive but from oneself. Since what we are concerned with is consciousness of freedom, the drive in question would be a *drive for freedom, simply for freedom's sake.*

In contrast to the kind of freedom described earlier [viz., formal freedom], I wish to call this kind of freedom "*material* freedom." The former consists merely in the fact that a new formal principle, a new force, comes upon the scene, without making the slightest change in the material contained in the series of effects. In this case it is no longer nature that acts, but a free being, even though the latter brings about exactly the same thing that nature itself would have brought about if it could have continued to act. Freedom in the second sense [viz., material freedom] consists in this: not only does a new force come upon the scene, but there is also a completely new series of actions, with respect to the content of the same. Not only does the intellect engage from now on in efficacious action, but it also accomplishes something completely different from what nature would ever have accomplished.

We now have to deduce the drive just indicated, describe it more closely, and show how it might manifest itself.

III

First of all, we have to derive the drive in question. In the preceding section we proved that if there is no such drive, then the self-consciousness of I-hood is impossible; for in that case consciousness of an indeterminacy, which is a condition for the self-consciousness of I-hood, is impossible. That constituted an indirect proof of such a drive. A direct – that is to say, a genetic – proof [of this drive], from the concept of the I itself, must now be undertaken, not so much for the sake of certainty but for the sake of [IV, 140] the conclusions to be drawn from this.

I said above that the I places itself entirely under its own authority by means of an absolutely free act of reflection upon itself as a natural being. I need only render this proposition more intuitive, and what is required will thereby be accomplished.

First of all, this act of reflection, insofar as it is what is primary [*als erste*], is an action that is grounded purely and simply in the I. It is, I say, an *action*. In contrast to this activity, the natural drive, which is what is reflected upon and which certainly has to be ascribed to the I, is something passive, something given, something that is present without any assistance on the part of free activity. One must first consider that, in order to explain the consciousness of this first reflection, as an action, one has to posit a new act of reflection upon the subject that engages in this first act of reflection; and then one has to think about this second act of reflection. Since we are here abstracting from what is reflected upon (i.e., the natural drive), this second act of reflection contains nothing but the pure, absolute activity that occurred in the first act of reflection; and this pure activity alone is the proper and true I. The drive is opposed to this [pure, absolute] activity, and it is opposed to it as something foreign. To be sure, the drive belongs to the I, but it *is* not the I. This activity is the I. It is crucially important not to think of the two acts of reflection we have just distinguished as in fact separated from each other, as we have had to separate them just now simply in order to be able to express ourselves. They are the same action. The I becomes immediately conscious of its absolute activity by means of inner self-intuition, without which an I cannot be understood at all. One should also take note of the following: by means of the second act of reflection (I indeed have to continue separating the two acts) that which without this second act of reflection would have been nothing but the determinate activity of the reflecting subject [in the first act of reflection] becomes *activity as such*, since we are here abstracting from the object of this first act of reflection (only through the object does an act of reflection become determinate). The distinction between a merely *ideal* activity, i.e., reflection upon something given, and a *real*, absolute act of determining something that is supposed to be given occurs later.

This can be expressed more briefly and thus perhaps more clearly as follows: Starting with the act of reflection, a new force comes upon the scene, a force that propagates through itself a tendency of nature [IV, 141]. This is how we viewed the matter earlier. This new force is now supposed to come upon the scene *for me*; according to this requirement, I am supposed to be conscious of the latter as a particular force. The only way this is possible is by thinking of the latter as torn away from the power of the drive – that is, by assuming that it could also not obey the drive but resist it. At this point, this resisting is merely posited as a power; if, however, one considers it as something immanent within and essential to the I (which one has to do), then it is posited as a *drive*. It is thanks to this opposed drive that the influence of nature becomes a mere *drive*, for otherwise it would exercise causality – a point that also strengthens the proof from another side.

Let us call this [newly identified] drive of the I the "*pure* drive," since it is contained in the I only insofar as the latter is a pure I. And the other drive may retain the name it already possesses: the natural drive.

As soon as we consider the relationship of these two drives to each other, we will see how both drives – and especially the pure one, which is the one with which we are here mainly concerned – manifest themselves. To begin with, the natural drive, understood *as a drive that is determined in a certain precise way*, is *contingent* to the I itself. Viewed from the transcendental standpoint, it is the result of our own limitation. To be sure, it is indeed necessary that we be limited in some way or another, for otherwise no consciousness would be possible. But it is contingent that we be limited in *precisely this way*. In contrast, the pure drive is essential to the I; it is grounded in I-hood as such. For this very reason it is present in all rational beings, and whatever follows from it is valid for all rational beings. – Moreover, the pure drive is a higher drive, one that elevates me above nature with respect to my pure being and demands that I, as an empirical, temporal being, elevate myself above nature. That is to say, nature possesses causality and is a power in relationship to me as well; it produces in me a drive that, when it is directed at the merely formal type of freedom, manifests itself as a *propensity*. In consequence of my higher drive, however, this power has no *control* over me, nor is it supposed to have any such control; I am supposed to determine myself utterly independently of the impetus of nature [IV, 142]. In this manner I am not only separated from nature, but I am also elevated above it; I am not only not a member of the series of nature, but I can also self-actively intervene in this series. – When I see the power of nature beneath me, it becomes something that I do not respect. This is because I respect that against which I must muster all of my energy simply in order to maintain an equilibrium; but I do not respect that against which no such [expenditure of] energy is required. This is the case with nature. With a single decision I am elevated above nature. – If I succumb and become part of what I cannot respect, then I cannot respect myself from the higher point of view. In relation to the propensity that pulls me down into the series of natural causality, therefore, the [pure] drive manifests itself as a drive that fills me with respect, summons my self-respect, and determines my dignity as something elevated above all nature. The pure drive does not aim at enjoyment of any kind, but instead at disdain for all enjoyment. It renders enjoyment contemptible as such. It aims only at the assertion of my dignity, which consists in absolute self-sufficiency [*in der absoluten Selbständigkeit und Selbstgenügsamkeit*].

§11

Preliminary explication of the concept of an interest

In violation of our customary procedure, it here becomes almost necessary to insert, outside of the systematic order, a preliminary explication of a concept by means of which we hope to shed greater light on the investigation to which we now have to turn – an investigation that is as important as it is difficult [IV, 143].

It is a fact that we are entirely indifferent toward some occurrences, while others interest us; and it is here presupposed that everyone will be able to understand the way we just expressed this fact. On first blush, that toward which I am indifferent has no relationship to my drive – or since, strictly speaking, this is impossible, it possesses only a remote relationship to my drive, one that I do not even notice. In contrast, something that interests me must have an *immediate* relationship to my drive; for the interest itself is immediately felt and cannot be produced through any rational grounds. No demonstration can ever move one to be delighted or sad about something. Indirect or mediate interest (interest in something that is useful as a means for a certain end) is based upon an immediate interest.

What does it mean to say that something is related immediately to a drive? A drive itself is only the object of a feeling; hence an immediate relation to a drive could also only be felt. To say that an interest in something is immediate thus means: the harmony or disharmony of the thing in question with a drive is itself felt, prior to all reasoning and independent of all reasoning.

However, I feel only *myself*, and thus this harmony or disharmony would have to lie within me; i.e., it would have to be nothing other than a harmony or disharmony of myself with myself.

To view the same matter from another side: every interest is mediated through my interest in myself and is itself only a modification of this interest in myself. Everything that interests me is related to myself. In all enjoyment, I enjoy myself; in all suffering, what I suffer from is myself. Where does this interest in myself originate in the first place? It has its origin in nothing else but a drive, since all interest originates only from a drive, and this occurs as follows: my fundamental drive [*Grundtrieb*] as a pure and as an empirical being, the drive through which these two, very different components of myself become one, is the drive toward harmony between the *original* I, which is determined in the mere idea, and the *actual* I [IV, 144]. Now the original drive – i.e., the pure drive and the natural drive considered in their unity with one another – is a determinate drive; it is immediately directed toward something. If my actual state agrees with what is demanded by this original drive, then pleasure arises; if it contradicts it, then displeasure arises. Pleasure and displeasure are nothing but the immediate feeling of the harmony or disharmony of my actual state with the state demanded by my original drive.

The lower power of desire starts from a drive that is really nothing more than the formative drive of our nature. This drive is directed toward the self-sufficient being, in that it requires the latter to unite this drive with itself synthetically – i.e., to posit *itself* as driven. It also manifests itself through a longing. Where does this longing lie? It lies not in nature, but in the subject of consciousness, for reflection has now occurred. The longing is directed only toward what lies in the natural drive, toward a material relationship between my body and the external world. Let us assume that this longing is satisfied, without deciding the question of whether it is satisfied by means of free activity or through chance. This satisfaction is undoubtedly perceived. But why is it that we do not in this case simply deliver the cold, cognitive judgment, "our body grows and thrives" – which is what we might, as it were, expect of a plant? Why do we feel pleasure instead?

The reason for this is as follows: my fundamental drive is immediately directed toward such a judgment, and this is what ensues. What satisfies the drive and produces the pleasure is the harmony of what is actual with what was demanded by the drive.

The situation is quite different in the case of the *pure* drive. This is a drive to activity for activity's sake, a drive that arises when the I internally intuits its own absolute power. There is in this case by no means a mere feeling of the drive, as was the case above, but rather an intuition. The pure drive does not present itself as an affection; in this case the I is not *being* driven but drives *itself*. It intuits itself as it is engaged in this act of driving itself, and only to this extent can we speak

137

of a drive in this case. (Recall what was said earlier on pp. 45ff.). The aim of the drive in question is to find the acting I to be self-sufficient and determined by itself [IV, 145]. One cannot say that this drive is *a longing*, like the one arising from the natural drive, for it is not directed toward something that we would expect as a favor from nature and that would not depend upon us. It is an absolute *demanding* [*Fordern*]. If I may express myself in this way, [one could say that] the pure drive stands out more sharply in consciousness because it is not based on mere feeling but on an intuition.

Let us now set the I into action. It will, of course, determine itself through itself, independent both of the natural impulse and of the demand [*Forderung*], since it is *formally* free. What will ensue will either be a determination of the sort that was supposed to ensue in accordance with the demand or else the opposite will ensue. In the first case, the subject of the drive and the one who actually acts will be in harmony, and then there will arise a feeling of approval – things are right, what happened was what was supposed to happen. In the second case, what will arise is a feeling of disapproval connected with contempt. In the latter case there can be no talk of respect. We must respect our higher nature and the demands it places upon us; with regard to what is empirical, it is sufficient if we do not have to feel contempt for ourselves. There can never be respect for what is empirical, for the latter can never lift itself above the demand [of the pure drive].

Let us now add the following to what has already been said: feeling arises from a limitation, from a determinacy. Here, however, there is nothing on either side but sheer doing or deeds [*lauter Tat*], both in the demand and in the fulfillment of the same. How then could a feeling ensue? The harmony of the two [that is, the harmony of the original and the actual I] is not a deed, but it is something that ensues, as such, without any active participation on our part; it is a determinate state and is felt. This also makes it clear that one must not understand us to be claiming that there is any feeling of an intuition, which would be absolutely absurd. What is intuited harmonizes with what is demanded by the drive, and what is felt is this harmony of the two. (This is not an unimportant observation. If this were not the situation, then no aesthetic feeling would be possible either, for the latter is also the feeling of an intuition [or rather, it is the feeling of a harmony between a sensible intuition and a concept], a feeling that occupies a middle position between the two feelings we have described here [the feelings of enjoyment and of respect]) [IV, 146].

Could this approval or disapproval also be a cold, merely cognitive judgment? Or is it necessarily connected with some interest? Obviously, it is connected with some interest, for this demand for absolute self-activity and for harmony between the empirical I and this very demand is itself *the original drive*. If the latter harmonizes with the former, then the drive is satisfied; if they are not in harmony, then the drive remains unsatisfied. The approval in question is therefore necessarily connected with pleasure, and the disapproval is necessarily connected with displeasure. It cannot be a matter of indifference to us whether we have to feel contempt for ourselves. But this kind of pleasure has nothing to do with enjoyment.

The harmony of actuality with the natural drive does not depend on me insofar as I am a *self*, i.e., insofar as I am free. Hence the pleasure that arises from such harmony is a pleasure that tears me away from myself, alienates me from myself, and in which I forget myself. It is an *involuntary* pleasure, and this is indeed its most characteristic feature. The same is the case with its opposite: sensible displeasure or pain. – In the case of the pure drive, the pleasure and the ground of this pleasure are nothing foreign but depend upon my freedom; the pleasure in question is something I could expect to happen in accordance with a rule, whereas I could not expect this in the case of sensible pleasure. The kind of pleasure associated with the pure drive does not lead me outside of myself but rather back into myself. It is *contentment*, and this is something that is never associated with sensory pleasure; it is less arousing than the latter, but more heartfelt, while at the same time it supplies us with new courage and strength. Precisely because this is something that depends on our freedom, the opposite of such contentment is *annoyance*: inner reproach (nothing similar to which is ever associated with sensible pain, simply as such), connected with self-contempt. It would be intolerable to have to feel contempt for ourselves if we were not lifted up again by the law's continuing demand upon us, if this demand, since it issues from ourselves, did not re-instill in us courage and respect, at least for our higher character, and if this annoyance were not mitigated by the sensation that we are still capable of meeting the demand in question [IV, 147].

The name of the power of feeling we have just described, which could well be called the *higher* power of feeling, is "*conscience*." Though one can talk about the "*repose*" of conscience or the "*agitation*" of conscience, the "*reproaches*" of conscience or the "*peace*" of conscience, there is certainly no such thing as a "*pleasure*" *of conscience*. The name "*conscience*" [*Gewissen*] is well chosen, for conscience is, as it were, the immediate consciousness of that without which there is no consciousness whatsoever: the consciousness of our higher nature and of our absolute freedom.

§12

Principle of an applicable ethics

The natural drive is directed toward something material, entirely for the sake of what is material; it is directed toward enjoyment for the sake of enjoyment. The pure drive is directed toward the absolute independence of the one acting, as such, from the natural drive. If the pure drive possesses causality, then the only way we can provisionally think of such causality is as follows: thanks to the pure drive, what is demanded by the natural drive simply does not occur. This would mean that nothing could ensue from the pure drive but some *abstention*; it could produce no positive *action* beyond the inner action of self-determination.

If all of the authors who have treated ethics merely formally had proceeded consistently, then they would have had to arrive at nothing but a continuous *self-denial*, at utter annihilation and disappearance – like those mystics who say that we should lose ourselves in God (a proposition that is indeed based upon something true and sublime, as will become evident later).

If, however, one examines more closely the demand just made [i.e., the demand that the natural drive should not occur or express itself] and if one tries to determine this demand more precisely, one will see that it dissolves immediately into nothing – [IV, 148]. I am supposed to be able to posit *myself* as free, in an act of reflection; this is demanded by the drive described earlier, the one that is directed toward the subject of consciousness. Hence I am indeed supposed to *posit* my freedom as something *positive*, as the ground of some actual action, and by no means simply as the ground of a mere abstention. I, the reflecting subject, am therefore supposed to be required to refer a certain determination of the will to *myself* as the one who determines the will in this manner and to derive this act of willing solely from my own self-determination. The willing that is to be referred [to my self-determining] is therefore something perceivable, something objective in us. Everything objective, however, belongs to us only insofar as we are sensible, natural beings; through the mere act of objectifying [*Objektivisieren*] we are posited for ourselves within this [natural, sensible] sphere. – In order to indicate the relevance to our present case of this proposition, a proposition with which we are sufficiently familiar in general and which has already been adequately proven, one might add the following: all actual willing is necessarily directed toward some acting; but all of my acting is an acting upon some object. In the world of objects, however, I act only with natural force; this force is given to me only through the natural drive and is nothing other than this natural drive itself within me – the causality of nature upon itself, a natural causality that is no longer under the control of a dead and unconscious nature, but a causality that I have brought under *my* (the intellect's) control by means of an act of free reflection. For this reason, the most immediate object of any possible willing is already necessarily something empirical: a certain determination of my sensible force, which was bestowed upon me by the natural drive – and hence something demanded by the natural drive, for the latter bestows only by demanding. Every possible concept of an end is therefore directed toward the satisfaction of a natural drive. (All actual willing is empirical. A pure will is not an actual will but a mere idea: something absolute [and drawn] from the intelligible world, something that is simply thought of as the explanatory ground for something empirical.)

After all that has been said so far, it will hardly be possible to understand us to be claiming that the natural drive, as such, produces the willing. It is *I* and not nature that wills; with respect to the matter or content of my willing, however, I cannot will anything other than what nature would also will, if it could will [IV, 149].

This, to be sure, does not annul the *drive* to absolute, material freedom; but it does annul completely any *causality* of the latter. In reality, all that remains is *formal* freedom. Although I find myself driven to do something that has its material ground solely within me, I never actually do anything nor can I ever do anything that is not demanded by the natural drive, because the latter exhausts the entire sphere of my possible acting.

Yet the causality of the pure drive must not disappear; for only insofar as I posit such a drive do I posit myself as an I.

We have arrived at a contradiction, which is all the more remarkable since what is contradictory is in this case, according to the two propositions just mentioned, a *condition for consciousness*.

How can this contradiction be resolved? According to the laws of synthesis, this is accomplished as follows: the matter or content of the action must, in one and the same instance of acting, be simultaneously suitable to both the pure drive and the natural drive. The two must be united. Just as the two are united in the original drive, so are they united in the actuality of acting.

This can be comprehended only as follows: the intention, the concept that is involved in acting, aims at complete liberation from nature. But it is not as a consequence of our freely designed concept of the action that this action is and remains suitable to the natural drive; instead, this is a consequence of our limitation. The sole determining ground of the matter of our action is [the goal of] ridding ourselves of our dependence upon nature, regardless of the fact that the independence that is thereby demanded is never achieved. The pure drive aims at absolute independence; an action is suitable to the pure drive if it is also directed toward absolute independence, i.e., if it lies *in a series [of actions], through the continuation of which the I would have to become independent*. According to the proof that has been provided, however, the I can never become independent so long as it is supposed to be an I. Consequently, the final end of a rational being necessarily lies in infinity; it is certainly not an end that can ever be achieved, but it is one to which a rational being, in consequence of its spiritual nature, is supposed to draw ceaselessly nearer and nearer [IV, 150].

(Here I must attend to an objection that I would not have thought possible had it not been raised even by some good thinkers who had been properly initiated into transcendental philosophy. How, it is asked, can one draw nearer to an infinite goal? Does not every finite magnitude vanish into nothing in comparison with infinity? – In expressing such scruples, it seems as though one is talking about infinity as a thing in itself. *I* draw nearer to it *for myself*. I can, however, never grasp infinity; hence I always have before my eyes some *determinate* goal, to which I can undoubtedly draw nearer, even though, after I have achieved this determinate goal, my goal might well be extended that much farther as a result of the perfecting of my whole being, as well as of my insight, which I have achieved through this process. In this *general* regard, therefore, I never draw nearer to the infinite. – My goal lies in infinity, because my dependence is infinite. Yet I never grasp my dependence in its infinity, but only with respect to some determinate range; and within this domain I can undoubtedly render myself more free.)

There must be such a series, in the continuation of which the I can think of itself as engaged in drawing nearer to absolute independence. There must be such a series, for only on this condition is any causality of the pure drive possible. This series is necessarily determined, starting with the first point at which a person is placed through his own nature, and then on into infinity – determined, it goes without saying, in the idea. In every possible case, therefore, it is determined what is demanded by the pure drive in this case and under all of these conditions. We can call this series the "ethical vocation" [*sittliche Bestimmung*] of a finite rational being. Even though we are not yet acquainted with this series itself, we have nevertheless just shown that such a series must necessarily occur. We can therefore stand securely on this ground, and we are thus bound to announce the following as the principle of ethics: *Fulfill your vocation in every case*, even though this still leaves to be answered the question, *What then is my vocation?* – [IV, 151]. If one expresses this proposition as follows, "fulfill your vocation *as such* or *in general*," then the infinity of the final end that is imposed is already included in the proposition, since the fulfillment of our entire vocation is not possible in any time. (The error of the mystics is that they represent the infinite, which cannot be attained in any time, as something that can be attained in time. The complete annihilation of the individual and the fusion of the latter into the absolutely pure form of reason or into God is indeed the ultimate goal of finite reason; but this is not possible in any time.)

The possibility of fulfilling one's vocation *in each individual case*, singularly and in time, is indeed grounded in *nature* itself and is given in nature. The relationship of the natural drive to the principle just set forth is as follows: at each moment there is something that is suitable for our ethical vocation; this something is at the same time demanded by the natural drive (if it is natural and has not been spoiled, so to speak, through a depraved fantasy). However, it does not follow that *everything* that is demanded by the natural drive is also suitable for one's ethical vocation. Let the series of the natural drive, considered purely in itself, be = A, B, C, etc. Perhaps only a part of B will be selected and made actual as in accordance with the individual's ethical vocation; in this case, the natural drive that follows B will also be different, since what preceded it is different from what it would have been as a result of mere nature; but once again, even in what now follows B, only a part might be selected as in accordance with one's ethical vocation, and so forth *ad infinitum*. In each possible determination, however, the two drives partially coincide. Only in this way is the actual exercise of morality possible.

Here it is appropriate to explain the mutual relationship of these two drives even more clearly. – First of all, the higher drive manifests itself as the *ethical* drive that was just described, but by no means as the *pure* drive; it does not manifest itself as a drive that aims at absolute independence, but as a drive directed toward determinate actions. These actions, however, can be shown to lie in the series we just described, if this [ethical] drive is raised to clear consciousness and if the [IV, 152] actions that are demanded are examined more closely. For it has just been shown that a drive, insofar as it is a *pure* drive, a drive directed toward a mere negation, cannot appear within consciousness at all. There is no consciousness of negation anyway, because it is nothing. This is also demonstrated in experience: we feel compelled to do this or that, and we reproach ourselves for not having done something. This serves as a corrective with respect to those who will not concede any consciousness of the categorical imperative (concerning which we will have more to say later on) nor concede any consciousness of a pure drive. No such consciousness is claimed by a thorough transcendental philosophy either. The pure drive is something that lies outside of all consciousness; it is nothing but a transcendental explanatory ground of something in consciousness.

As we have now seen, the ethical drive is a mixed drive. It obtains its material, toward which it is directed, from the natural drive; that is to say, the natural drive that is synthetically united and fused with the ethical drive aims at the same action that the ethical drive aims at, at least in part. All that the ethical drive obtains from the pure drive is its form. Like the pure drive, it is absolute; it demands something purely and simply, for no end outside of itself. It is absolutely not directed toward any enjoyment, no matter what the kind. (The final end of everything that is demanded by the ethical drive is complete independence. But what, in turn, is the end of this complete independence? Is it perhaps some enjoyment, or anything similar? Absolutely not. Absolute independence is its own end. I ought to have this final end in view absolutely because I ought to have it in view – because I am an I. The inner contentment one feels on the way to this goal is something contingent. The drive does not arise from such inner contentment; instead, it arises from the drive.)

The ethical drive makes itself known as respect; and obeying or not obeying this drive provokes approval or disapproval, a feeling of contentment with oneself or a feeling of the most painful contempt for oneself. The ethical drive is *positive*; it drives one to act in some determinate manner. It is *universal*; it refers to all possible free actions, to every manifestation of the natural drive [IV, 153], which appears to consciousness within the boundaries precisely indicated above. It is *self-sufficient*; in every case it assigns itself its end. It aims at *absolute causality* and stands in *reciprocal interaction* with the natural drive, inasmuch as it receives from the natural drive its content or matter – but it receives this content only as such, and by no means as an end that has to be pursued. From its side and in turn, the ethical drive gives form to the material drive. Finally, it commands categorically. Whatever it demands, it demands as necessary.

§13
Subdivisions of the ethics

The ethical drive demands *freedom* – for the sake of *freedom*. Who can fail to see that the word freedom occurs in this sentence with two different meanings? In its second occurrence, we are dealing with an objective state that is supposed to be brought about – our ultimate and absolutely final end: complete independence from everything outside of us. In its first occurrence, we are dealing with an instance of acting as such and with no being in the proper sense of the term, with something purely subjective. I am supposed to *act freely* in order to *become free*.

There is, however, a distinction to be drawn even within the concept of freedom as it first occurs in the above sentence. In the case of a free action, it can be asked *how* this action must come about in order to be a free action, as well as *what* it is that must come about; i.e., one can inquire about the form of freedom and also about its matter or content.

Until now we have been investigating the matter of freedom; the [free] action must be part of a series, the infinite continuation of which would render the I absolutely independent. We now wish to consider briefly the *how* or the form [of free action] [IV, 154].

I am supposed to act freely; that is to say, I – as a posited I, as an intellect – am supposed to determine myself, and I am therefore supposed to act with consciousness of my absolute self-determination, with thoughtful self-awareness [*Besonnenheit*] and reflection. Only if I act in this manner do I act freely, as an intellect; otherwise I act *blindly*, in whatever manner I happen to be driven by chance.

As an intellect, I am supposed to act in a *determinate* manner; i.e., I am supposed to be conscious of that ground on the basis of which I act precisely *as* I do act. But the only ground that this can be (since I am not permitted to have any other ground than this) is that the action in question is part of a series like the one previously described. This, however, is merely the *philosophical* view of the matter, and it is by no means the view of ordinary consciousness; we can therefore also express this [in a manner more appropriate to ordinary consciousness by saying that] the only possible ground of a free action is that the action in question is a *duty*. Hence I ought to act solely in accordance with the concept of my duty, and I ought to allow myself to be determined only by the thought that something is a duty and by absolutely no other thought than this.

Let us add a few words concerning this last point: Even the ethical drive is not supposed to determine me in the manner of a sheer, blind drive – which would be self-contradictory, as though there could be anything ethical that was only a drive. Here we arrive once again at a result that we obtained earlier, though this time it is much more fully determined. We noted previously that the drive to self-sufficiency is directed toward the intellect as such, which is supposed to be self-sufficient *as* an intellect; but an intellect is self-sufficient only if it determines itself by means of concepts and absolutely not as a result of any other stimulus [*Antrieb*]. The [ethical] drive thus aims both to possess causality and not to possess it; and it possesses it solely by not possessing it, for what it demands is: *be free*. If the ethical drive acts as a stimulus [i.e., if it simply "drives" the I to act in a certain manner], then it is merely a natural drive; as an ethical drive it cannot be a stimulus, for it contradicts morality and it is unethical to let oneself be driven blindly.

(Consider, for example, the drives of sympathy, pity, and philanthropic love: we will see in due course that these drives are manifestations of the ethical drive, though they are mixed with the natural drive – just as the ethical drive is always mixed [with another drive]. Still, a person who acts in accordance with the above-listed drives certainly does act legally, though he does not act absolutely morally, and *to this extent* he acts in a manner that violates morals) [IV, 155].

A categorical imperative – which is supposed to be a *concept* and not a drive – first arises only at this point; for the [ethical] drive is not the categorical imperative, but instead drives us to form such an imperative for ourselves, to tell ourselves that something or other simply has to occur. The categorical imperative is our own product; it is *ours* insofar as we are beings capable of concepts or intelligent beings.

In the ensuing determination of the will, a rational being is, as regards its form, torn loose entirely from everything that is not itself. Such a being is not determined by the matter [or content of this determination of its will], nor does it determine itself by means of the concept of a material ought, but rather by means of the completely formal concept of an absolute ought, a concept it generates within itself. And in this way we regain, within the realm of actuality, a rational being, in the same form in which we originally set forth [the concept of] such a being: as absolutely self-sufficient. In this same way, everything that is primordial or original must present itself once again in actuality, albeit with new additions and additional determinations. – Only an action from duty constitutes such a presentation of a pure rational being; every other action possesses a determining ground that is foreign to the intellect as such. (Thus Kant says, in the *Groundwork of the Metaphysics of Morals*,[19] that it is only through the predisposition to morality that a rational being reveals itself as something *in itself*: that is, as something self-sufficient and independent, something that does not simply exist by virtue of its reciprocal interaction with something outside itself, but subsists purely for itself.) This also explains the unspeakably sublime character of duty, in that the latter places everything outside of ourselves far below us and makes it vanish into nothing when compared with our [ethical] vocation.

---

[19] See *Groundwork of the Metaphysics of Morals*, in Kant, *Practical Philosophy*, ed. Mary J. Gregor and Allen Wood, trans. Mary J. Gregor (Cambridge: Cambridge University Press, 1996) [henceforth = *GMM*], pp. 84–85 and 102 (*AA* IV: 435 and 458).

Two things follow from the form of morality:

(1) Just as certainly as I act at all, I ought to act *in general* with thoughtful self-awareness and consciousness, rather than blindly and in obedience to some mere stimulus. *More specifically*, I ought to act with a consciousness of my duty; I ought never to act without having measured my action by this concept [of duty]. – It follows that there are no indifferent actions; just as certainly as these are actually actions of an intelligent being, the moral law refers to all actions – if not materially, then it quite certainly refers to them formally. We must investigate [IV, 156] whether the concept of duty might not have some reference to such actions; and in order to ground such an inquiry, [we will show that] the concept of duty quite certainly does refer to them. It can be shown at once that the concept of duty must also refer to all actions materially as well: for I am never supposed to obey the sensible drive as such, even though, according to what was said earlier, I am subject to this drive every time I act. The ethical drive must therefore be involved in all acting, since otherwise no action could ensue in accordance with the moral law, which contradicts our presupposition.

(2) *I ought never to act against my conviction.* To do so would be utterly perverse and malicious. We will see below what it is within a human being that makes such perversion possible – even though such perversion, considered by itself, would seem impossible –, and we will at least remove from it that terrible aspect which, when considered in its true form, it possesses for everyone with an uncorrupted sense of humanity.

Combined into a single proposition, these two propositions could be expressed as follows: *always act in accordance with your best conviction concerning your duty*, or, *Act according to your conscience.* This is the formal condition for the morality of our actions, and it is what is generally meant by the *morality* of the same. We will discuss these formal conditions of morality in greater detail in the first section of our ethics proper, and then, in the second section, we will present the *material* conditions for the morality of our actions, or the doctrine of their *legality* [IV, 157].

PART III

Systematic application of the principle of morality, or ethics in the narrower sense

First section [of ethics in the proper sense of the term]: Formal conditions for the morality of our actions

§14

The will in particular

I could turn immediately to a synthetic–systematic statement of the formal conditions for the morality of our actions. But since formal morality, or what is generally meant by "morality" [*Moralität*], is also called *good will*, and since I myself intend to characterize it in this way, I first have to provide an account of my concept of the will [IV, 158].

To be sure, everything that pertains to this elucidation has already been presented under another name; but it is still necessary to address this subject explicitly under this name [i.e., "will"], in order to indicate the connection between my presentation of the same and the way it has usually been dealt with hitherto.

An act of willing [*Wollen*] is an absolutely free transition from indeterminacy to determinacy, accompanied by a consciousness of this transition. This action has been sufficiently described above. – One can distinguish the objective I, which undergoes a transition from indeterminacy to determinacy, and the subjective I, which intuits itself in this transition. In willing, however, these two are united. The will [*Wille*] is neither the drive nor the longing nor the desiring. In the case of a drive there is a propensity and an inclination; in the case of desiring there is, in addition, consciousness of the object of the inclination, but instead of any determinacy of the active I there is only

149

indeterminacy. Desiring wishes that its object would come to it, but it does not want to move either hand or foot to bring this about. Determinacy ensues as the result of an act of willing.

If one considers the overall capacity or power for undergoing such a transition accompanied by consciousness – and the laws of theoretical reason force us, when we *think, to add* [the concept of] such a *power* to the manifestation of the same [i.e., to the transition itself] – , one thereby obtains the concept of the will *as such*, as the power to engage in willing. This is an abstract concept; it is nothing actual, nothing that might be perceived, nor is it any sort of "fact," which is how some people have characterized it. If one considers an actual, noticeable movement of transition, then one has an act of willing. Willing, however, is not completed, indeed, there is no willing at all, if no determinacy is present. When such determinacy is present, it is called *a* will [*Wille*] – as when we say things such as "that is my will" – or a volition [*Wollung*]. In ordinary life one does not make this distinction between the will as such, understood as a power or capacity, and *a* will, a determinate will, understood as a determinate manifestation of the preceding power, since no such distinction is needed in ordinary life. Nor has this distinction been made in philosophy, where it would be most needed [IV, 159].

The will is free in the material sense of the term. When it wills, the I provides itself, as an intellect, with the object of its willing, and it does this by choosing one among several possible objects. In doing this, the I elevates that indeterminacy, which the intellect intuits and grasps, to a determinacy, which is likewise thought and grasped [by the intellect]. – This is not contradicted by the fact that the object might be given through the natural drive. It is given by the natural drive as an object of longing, of desiring, but by no means as an object of the will, that is, as the object of a determinate decision to realize such an object. In this respect, the will gives itself its object absolutely. In short, the will is purely and simply free, and an unfree will is an absurdity. As soon as a human being wills, he is free; and if he is not free, then he does not will but is driven. – Nature does not produce a will; nor, strictly speaking, can it produce any longing, for this too, as we have already seen above, presupposes an act of reflection. In the sort of reflection that is involved in longing, however, the I does not become conscious of itself as engaged in this act of reflecting; and thus the I itself must assume that the longing that is present in it is a product of nature, even though an observer outside of the I would find the opposite to be the case – which is what we ourselves find to be the case from our transcendental point of view.

If the will moves from indeterminacy to determinacy – and it has already been strictly proven that this is a condition for consciousness of freedom and, along with this, a condition for the I such; and hence it has also been proven *that there is a will* and that it is determined in the manner we have described – : if this is the case, I say, then the will is always a power of choosing, which is how it is quite correctly described by *Reinhold.*[1] There is no will [*Wille*] without arbitrary choice [*Willkür*]. One calls the will arbitrary choice when one attends to the feature just indicated: namely, that it necessarily chooses among several, equally possible actions.

(Some philosophers have purported to find a contradiction in the claim that it is equally possible for freedom to make either of two opposite decisions, A or not-A; and others have had difficulty exposing the circle that is offered as a proof of this contradiction [IV, 160]. Let us therefore investigate what the former presuppose and what the latter have failed to note.

Let us assume a force of nature $= X$. Since this is a force of nature, it necessarily operates mechanically; i.e., it always produces everything that it can produce as a result of its nature and under a specific set of conditions. If we say that the manifestation of this force $= A$, then it is necessarily $= A$, and it would be contradictory to assume any not-A instead.

Is this same law applicable to the will? – First of all, and this is the most important point of all and one that I had good reasons for stressing earlier: where the will comes upon the scene, indeed, wherever the I comes upon the scene at all, there the force of nature is completely at an end. Here *nothing whatsoever, neither A nor $-A$, nothing at all, is possible* through a force of nature, for the final product of a force of nature is a drive, which as such exercises no causality. A and $-A$ are

[1] See Karl Leonhard Reinhold, *Versuch einer neuen Theorie des menschlichen Vorstellungsvermögens* (*Attempt at a New Theory of the Human Power of Representation*) (Prague and Jena: Mauke, 1789). Reinhold discusses the will in the section of this work titled "Outline of the Theory of the Power of Desire" [*Grundlinien der Theorie des Begehrungsvermögens*]. See too the remarks on this topic in Reinhold's *Briefe über die Kantische Philosophie* (*Letters on the Kantian Philosophy*), vol. 2 (Leipzig: Göschen, 1792), pp. 259 and 281.

therefore equally possible, not for a force of nature but for the will, which stands in absolute opposition to any force of nature. If, moreover, one claims that the will is free, one claims that it is the first, initiating member of a series, and hence that it is not determined through any other member of the series; and one therefore claims that nature cannot be the determining ground of the will, as I have already demonstrated from [an analysis of the concept of] nature itself. One thus claims that the determination of the will has no ground outside of itself, and one further claims that the will, unlike a mechanical force, does not effect-uate everything of which it is capable, but that it consists in the power to limit itself through itself to one determinate effect – and thus, if the entire sphere [of the will's efficacy] were A + −A, it would stand in its power to determine itself to either the former or the latter portion [of this entire sphere], without having any reason or ground outside of itself for doing this. This is the presupposition that must be accepted by the [above-mentioned] opponents [of those who argue that it is contradictory to characterize the will as capable of choosing either A or −A]. Instead, however, these same opponents presuppose precisely what is here being denied: namely, they presuppose that the will lies within the series constituted by the forces of nature and that the will itself is nothing but a force of nature; and under this presupposition their conclusion [namely, that it is contradictory to say that the will could choose between A and −A] is correct. Thus they demonstrate that the will is not free by presupposing that it is not free; and if they wanted to speak correctly, they would not say that it is contradictory to claim that the will is free, but merely that such a claim contradicts [IV, 161] *their* claim that the will is not free – which is something one indeed has to grant them without any protest.

The real contradiction lies higher than they themselves believe. It contradicts their entire individual power of thinking to think of any series other than the series of natural mechanism. They have by no means yet succeeded in elevating themselves to the higher manifesta-tions of the force of thinking, which is why they make that absolute presupposition, beyond which they themselves – for their own persons, to be sure – cannot go. Everything occurs mechanically: this is their absolute first principle, since it is indeed the case that nothing presents itself within their own clear consciousness but mere mechanism. – This is how things stand with all types of fatalism. Nor can this situation be altered simply by shifting the ground of our moral decisions into the intelligible world. In that case, the ground for determining our will is supposed to lie in something that is not sensible, though something that nevertheless determines us just like a physical power, the effect of which is a decision of our will. But how is something of this sort any different from the sensible world? According to *Kant*, the sensible world is that world to which the categories can be applied.[2] In the case we are here considering, however, the category of causality is applied to something intelligible; when this occurs, the latter ceases to be a member of the intelligible world and descends into the realm of sensibility.)

This choice of the will, the necessity of which has to be conceded, is further determined as a choice between the satisfaction of a selfish drive (namely, the natural drive) and an unselfish one (the ethical drive). Let us now examine this further determination [of the concept of the will]. According to a distinction that we previously derived from its ground, freedom is not only material; it is also formal. I can become aware of formal freedom just as well as I can become aware of material freedom. To be sure, I am not originally conscious of formal freedom, and I lack in this case the sort of original consciousness upon which our previous argument was based, yet I can still become conscious of formal freedom after my self-consciousness has developed and after I have gained some experience. It is simply by becoming conscious of formal freedom that I, as an intellect, first obtain the power to postpone natural satisfaction. The natural drive, however, will continue to express itself while the satisfaction of this same drive is being postponed [IV, 162], and it will express itself in various ways; for this reason, I also acquire at the same time *the* specific ability to reflect upon the natural drive in the different ways it now presents itself to me and to *choose among several possible satisfactions of this drive*. I choose to satisfy only one need. I choose this with complete freedom of the will, for I choose with the consciousness that I am determining myself. In such a case, however, I by no means sacrifice enjoyment for the sake of morality; I merely sacrifice one enjoyment for the sake of another.

"Still," someone might reply, "you are simply surrendering to the stronger of the drives that are present within you." To this I would

---

[2] See *KrV*, B 146ff.

respond as follows: even if this were always the case, the drive in question would not exist, I would not be conscious of it, if I had not exercised self-control, if I had not deferred my decision, and if I had not freely reflected on all of my drives. Even under this presupposition, therefore, I have still conditioned the object of my will through self-determination, and my will remains materially free. – This would follow, I said, even if it were universally true that I always yield to the stronger drive; but this is not universally true. Once a certain sum of experience is present, then I can certainly use my power of imagination to represent to myself some enjoyment that is at present not in the least demanded by my nature; and I can prefer such enjoyment to satisfying any of the drives that presently exist as a matter of fact. It is true that in order to do this a stimulus [*Antrieb*] of this kind must have previously been present within me, inasmuch as I have [previously] experienced an actual enjoyment of this type, which I now merely reproduce by means of my power of imagination. In the latter case, my stimulus is the power of imagination, the objects of which are certainly products of freedom; and this means that in this case I give myself the object of my will, understanding this in the broadest sense of the term. Here again, I am not sacrificing enjoyment for the sake of virtue, but only sacrificing some actual enjoyment for the sake of another enjoyment that I am simply imagining. (This is the usual situation of a human being who is merely being *policed*, that is, of a human being who is still on the path to culture, such as the exhausted voluptuary, the avaricious person, or the person consumed by vanity: all of these pursue a purely imaginary enjoyment, for the sake of which they sacrifice true enjoyment) [IV, 163].

Only in this way is prudence possible, for prudence is nothing other than an intelligent choice between several satisfactions of a natural drive. According to the alternative concept of the will,[3] when applied most broadly, prudence would not be possible at all, but only morality or immorality.

---

[3] Though Fichte does not here name any of the exponents of "jenem Begriff vom Willen," this would appear to be an allusion to the concept of the will that is often, albeit controversially, attributed to Kant, according to which one can act freely *only* when one acts in accordance with the moral law.

§15

Systematic presentation of the formal conditions for the morality of our actions

I

As we have now seen, the formal law of morals [*Sitten*] is as follows: act purely and simply in accordance with your conviction concerning your duty. One can attend both to the form and to the content of this law, or perhaps it might here be clearer to say that one can consider either the condition or what is conditioned by this law. What is contained in the former [i.e., in the form of the moral law, or the condition of the same] is, as we have already seen, the following: in every case seek to ascertain for yourself what is your duty. What is contained in the latter [i.e., in the content or matter of the moral law, or what is conditioned thereby] is the following: do what you can now regard with conviction as a duty, and do it solely because you have convinced yourself that it is a duty.

II

To this someone might object as follows: "But what if my conviction is mistaken? In this case, then what I have done is not my duty, but is what goes against my duty. How then can I be satisfied with this?" Obviously, I can be satisfied with this [way of characterizing the moral law] only insofar as and to the extent that I do not regard it as even possible that my conviction might be mistaken nor that I might ever come to regard it as mistaken, even if I were to live forever [IV, 164]. Hence I do not simply hold up to my action the concept of my present conviction, but I, in turn, hold up to my present conviction the concept of my possible conviction as a whole – that is, I hold up to the concept of my present conviction the concept of the entire system of my convictions, to the extent that I can represent the latter to myself at the present moment. Such a comparison and examination is a duty, for I *ought* to acquire conviction. It is not a matter of indifference to me whether I act in accordance with duty or not, for I consider this to be the supreme concern of my life; for this reason I also cannot be indifferent to whether my conviction might be true or might be mistaken. – The correctness of my conviction in any particular case is therefore guaranteed by the agreement of this conviction with every conviction I can think of; and it is itself a duty to investigate whether such agreement is present or not.

III

The entire system of my convictions, however, cannot itself be given to me in any way other than by means of my present conviction concerning this system. Just as I can err in my judgment of an individual case, so can I also err in my judgment concerning my overall judgment as such: that is, in my conviction concerning my convictions as a whole.

From this it follows that my morality, and hence my absolute self-sufficiency and peace of conscience, remains forever dependent upon chance. When I consider all of this – and it is my duty to take it into consideration –, I must either take a chance and act, or else I am not permitted to act at all but must spend my entire life in a state of indecision, constantly swaying back and forth between pro and con – if, that is, there is no absolute criterion for the correctness of my conviction concerning duty.

(The latter is an important observation, which, to the best of my knowledge has not yet been adequately discussed by anyone. By elucidating this observation we will knit our theory more tightly together and facilitate an easier transition from the formal conditions of morality to the material ones) [IV, 165].

IV

In order for dutiful conduct to be possible at all there must be an absolute criterion for the correctness of our conviction concerning duty. A certain conviction must therefore be absolutely correct, and for duty's sake we have to stick with this conviction. – One should first of all note the kind of inference that is involved here. If dutiful conduct is to be possible at all, then there must be such a criterion. But according to the moral law, dutiful conduct is purely and simply possible; therefore, there is such a criterion. From the presence and the necessary causality of the moral law we therefore infer that there is something present in the power of cognition, and in making this inference we assert a relationship between the moral law and theoretical reason: the *primacy* of the former over the latter, as *Kant* puts it.[4] That without which there could be no duty whatsoever is absolutely true, and it is a duty to regard it as such.

In order to avoid gravely misinterpreting this proposition, one should note the following: the moral law indeed demands and authorizes a certain determinate conviction = A. The moral law, however, is not a power of cognition, and therefore, by virtue of its very essence, it cannot produce [*aufstellen*] this conviction by itself; instead, it expects it to be found and determined by the power of cognition – the power of reflecting judgment – and only then does the moral law authorize this conviction and make it a duty to stick with it. The opposite claim would imply a material duty of belief, i.e., a theory according to which certain theoretical propositions would be immediately contained in the moral law, propositions which one would then have to consider to be true without any further examination and regardless of whether or not one could convince oneself of them theoretically. On the one hand, a claim of this sort would be utterly self-contradictory for the simple reason that the practical power is not a theoretical power; on the other, such a claim would open the door wide to every kind of deceitfulness and to all sorts of ways of suppressing and subjugating conscience [IV, 166]. The theoretical powers pursue their own course until they hit upon something that can be approved. They do not, however, contain within themselves any criterion for the correctness of the latter; instead, this criterion lies in the practical power, which is what is primary and highest in human beings and constitutes their true essence. The present claim is the same one we encountered earlier, simply taken here in its broader determination: the moral law is purely formal and must receive its content from elsewhere; but *that* something is its content: the ground for this can lie only in the moral law itself.

This only raises a far more difficult question: how does the moral law's confirmation of a theoretical judgment concerning duty manifest itself, and how does one recognize such a confirmation? – When applied to an empirical human being, the domain of the moral law has a determinate *starting point*: namely, the determinate state of limitation in which every individual finds himself when he first finds himself at

---

[4] See *CPrR*, First Part, Second Book, Second Chapter, III, pp. 236–238 (*AA* 5: 119–121).

all. It also has a determinate goal, which can never be achieved: namely, absolute liberation from every limitation. Finally, it guides us along a completely determinate *path*: namely, the order of nature. From this it follows that for every determinate human being, in each situation, only one determinate something is in accord with duty, and one can therefore say that this is what is demanded by the moral law as it applies to this temporal being. Let us call this determinate action or abstention from acting [*Handlung der Unterlassung*] "X."

As was just pointed out, the practical power is not a theoretical power. The practical power is therefore unable to provide us with this X; instead, the latter has to be sought by the power of judgment, which is here reflecting freely. But since we possess a drive simply to act in one way or another and, indeed, to realize through our action this determinate X, it follows that this drive determines the power of judgment – not materially, not by giving something to the power of judgment, which is something this drive is unable to do –, but formally: i.e., it determines the power of judgment to search for something. The moral drive [*das sittliche Trieb*] thus manifests itself in this case as a drive toward a determinate cognition. Let us assume that the power of judgment were to find X, a discovery that seems to depend upon good luck: the original I [IV, 167] and the actual I will now be in harmony, and from this there will arise a feeling – as there always does in such cases, according to the proof provided earlier.

The only question is: what kind of feeling might this be, and what distinguishes it from other feelings? All aesthetic feelings are similar to the feeling to be described here in that they arise from the satisfaction of a drive in accordance with a determinate representation. But aesthetic feelings are unlike the feeling we are now discussing inasmuch as the drive underlying them does not absolutely *demand* satisfaction, but simply *expects* it, as a favor of nature. The cognitive drive [*das Trieb nach Erkenntnis*], however, which is what we are talking about here, is itself the moral drive, and the latter demands absolutely. Thus there cannot arise in this case what arises in the case of aesthetic feeling – namely, an unforeseen pleasure that surprises us – but only [a feeling of] *cold approval* of something that was to be expected and simply had to be found, so long as reason is not to abandon itself. What is approved in this manner is in the case of actions called *right* and in the case of cognitions called *true*.

The absolute criterion for the correctness of our conviction concerning duty, which is what we have been seeking, would therefore be a feeling of truth and certainty. We will now describe this important feeling in more detail. – As long as the power of judgment continues to search, the free power of imagination continues to hover between opposites; and since this act of searching is undertaken at the instigation of a drive and since the latter is not yet satisfied, there is present a feeling of doubt, which is connected with concern [*Besorglichkeit*], since the matter in question is of the utmost importance. (I know, for example, that I *doubt*. But on what basis do I know this? Surely I do not know this on the basis of the objective constitution of some judgment I have made. Doubt is something subjective; like its opposite, certainty, it can only be felt.) As soon as the power of judgment finds what was demanded, the fact that this is indeed what was demanded reveals itself through a feeling of harmony. The power of the imagination is now bound and compelled, as it is in the case of everything real. I cannot view this matter in any way other than in the way I do view it: constraint is present, as it is in the case of every feeling [IV, 168]. This feeling provides cognition with *immediate certainty*, with which *calm* and *satisfaction* are connected.

(In Part 4, second section, § 4 of *Religion Within the Boundaries of Mere Reason*, Kant says, quite splendidly, that the consciousness that an action I am about to undertake is right is an unconditional duty.[5] But is such consciousness even possible, and how do I recognize it? Kant seems to leave this up to each person's feeling, which is indeed that upon which such consciousness must be based. Transcendental philosophy, however, is obliged to indicate the ground of the possibility of such a feeling of certainty, which is what we have just done. Yet Kant also elucidates his thoughts on this topic by means of an example, an example that also serves very well to elucidate what we have just presented. – An inquisitor who condemns to death someone who seems to him to be a heretic can never be entirely certain that, in doing this, he is not acting unjustly.[6] If he were perhaps to ask himself,

---

[5] See Kant, *Religion Within the Boundaries of Mere Reason*, in Kant, *Religion and Rational Theology*, ed. and trans. Allen W. Wood and George di Giovanni (Cambridge: Cambridge University Press, 1996) [henceforth = *RBR*], p. 203 (*AA* 6: 186): "So the *consciousness* that an action *which I want to undertake* is right, is unconditional duty."

[6] See *RBR*, pp. 203ff. (*AA* 6: 186ff.).

"Would you dare to maintain the truth of these statements in the presence of him who scrutinizes the heart and at the risk of relinquishing everything that is valuable and holy to you?" Faced with such a question, says Kant, even the boldest teacher of the faith would be likely to tremble. Or, as Kant puts it in another place: a person who steps forward and says "any among you who does not believe everything I say to you is eternally damned" would also have to possess the courage to add, "but if what I say is not true, then I myself want to be eternally damned." Yet it is to be hoped that most people would hesitate to run such a risk; and from this Kant concludes that they are able to see that they themselves are not so firmly convinced of this belief that they want to impose upon others. Following this analogy, we could say that whoever is completely certain of his own cause [*Sache*] has to stake even his own eternal damnation thereupon, and he betrays his uncertainty through his unwillingness to do this.

If one were now to ask what it might mean for someone to want to be eternally damned, then the only rational meaning one could extract from this would be as follows: [this would have to mean that one would want] *to relinquish for all eternity one's own improvement* – [IV, 169]. This is the greatest evil, and it is one that no human being whatsoever can seriously consider; indeed, the serious thought of the same would annihilate anyone. Even in the case of the most wanton sinners against their own conscience, there is always somewhere in the background an empty promise that they will continue behaving in this manner only this one time more or only for such and such a period, and that they will in due course improve themselves. So long, therefore, as one either specifically intends to alter one's manner of acting at some future time or at least considers it to be possible to do this: so long as this is the case, one can be assured that one does not [yet] possess a clear conscience. A person who is certain of his affairs [*Sachen*] accepts the risk of not being able to alter either his manner of acting or the principles in accordance with which he is acting in this manner – the risk that he will lose his freedom completely concerning this point and that he will be forever confirmed in this decision. This is the sole sure criterion of true conviction.

The proof of this is as follows: such a conviction transposes the person in question into a state of harmony with the original I. The latter, however, is elevated above all time and all temporal change. It follows that in this state of unification [with the original I] the empirical I likewise elevates itself above all temporal change and posits itself to be absolutely unchangeable. This is the source of the imperturbability of firm conviction.)

From what has just been said one may draw the following conclusion: it is not by means of any argumentation that I know whether I am in doubt or am certain, for this would require a new proof to establish the correctness of my first argument, and this new proof would require in turn yet another proof, and so on *ad infinitum*; instead, this is something I know through immediate feeling. Only in this way can we explain subjective certainty as a state of mind. The feeling of certainty, however, is always an immediate harmony of our consciousness with our original I – nor could things be otherwise in a philosophy that begins with the I. This feeling never deceives us, since, as we have seen, it is present whenever there is complete harmony of our empirical I with the pure I, and the latter is our sole true being, all possible being and all possible truth [IV, 170].

Certainty is possible for me only insofar as I am a moral being, since the criterion of all theoretical truth is not itself, in turn, a theoretical one. – The theoretical power of cognition cannot criticize and confirm itself. Instead, the criterion of all theoretical truth is a practical one, and it is our duty to stick with the latter. Moreover, this practical criterion is a universal one, a criterion that is valid not only for the immediate cognition of our duty but is valid in general and as such for every possible cognition, inasmuch as there is also in fact no cognition that is not at least indirectly related to our duties.

V

As we have now seen, the criterion for the correctness of our conviction is an inner one. There is no outer, objective criterion, nor can there be one, since it is precisely here, where the I is regarded as a moral being, that it is supposed to be entirely self-sufficient and independent of everything that lies outside it. This, however, does not preclude us from indicating the general type of convictions that will be sanctioned by this criterion, and this is the final thing we have to do in this section.

Only because of the practical drive are there any objects for us at all: this is a proposition with which we are quite familiar and which has been sufficiently proven on several occasions.[7] Here we will attend only to the following circumstance: my drive is limited, and as a result of this limitation I posit an object. Obviously, I cannot posit and characterize this object without [also] characterizing in some determinate manner the drive that it limits; for a determinate object is nothing else whatsoever and cannot be described in any other way than as what limits a determinate drive. This is how I obtain the given properties of the thing, since I place myself and the thing in mutual states of rest or repose. But I can also reflect upon freedom, and when I do this my limitation by means of the object becomes something that can be expanded in a regular manner and in a certain order; moreover, such an expansion of my own boundaries would also serve to change the object. I posit, e.g., that the object can be modified in a certain way [IV, 171], and in doing this I determine its purposiveness [*Zweckmäßigkeit*], *its usefulness for certain freely chosen ends* [*beliebigen Zwecken*] that one might set for oneself with regard to this object.

In this context, one will notice, first of all, that the determination of purposiveness is nothing other than a determination of the inner properties of a thing in a state of repose, nor can it be any other kind of determination. This determination is simply undertaken from a different point of view [than the previously mentioned determination of the given properties of the thing]. In both cases, the object is determined by means of the drive that it is supposed to limit; the difference is that in the previously discussed case one pays no attention to the possible liberation [of the drive from the boundaries associated with the object], whereas in the second case one does attend to this. In the first case, the drive is at rest; in the second, it is set in motion. – One should also not lose sight of the fact that I have derived the concept of purposiveness from the relation of an object to freedom as such, and not simply from its relation to my own freedom. Something might be thought of as purposive even if it has not become clear whether I or another free being could accomplish those possible ends that are present in this object. To be sure, the latter [presupposition] underlies – albeit in an obscure manner – every assumption of purposiveness.

---

[7] See, for example, the famous declaration from Part III of *GWL*, "No striving, no object" (*SK*, p. 231 [*SW* I: 262; *GA* I/2: 397]).

Now it may be the case that I am conscious of my drive – and here I am referring to the drive as such or in general – only *in part*. In this case I will have grasped the purposiveness of the thing only in part; I do not cognize this thing's proper end but only, so to speak, an arbitrary one – one end among others for which the thing can be employed. The aim of my drive as a whole is absolute independence and self-sufficiency; and until I have grasped it as such, I have not yet completely determined myself nor have I completely determined, in opposition to myself, the thing – neither with respect to its properties nor with respect to its ends. If the thing is completely determined in the manner indicated, then I am aware of the full range of its ends, i.e., its final end. All complete cognitions, all cognitions with which one can rely and rest content, are therefore necessarily cognitions of the final end of objects; a conviction is not sanctioned by conscience until it includes an insight into the final end of the thing, and such cognitions [of the final end of objects] are at the same time those that guide moral conduct. The moral law therefore aims to treat every thing in accordance with its final end [IV, 172]. This furnishes us with an easy way to present scientifically the content or material of the moral law.

I still have to point out that we have just presented a closed whole of cognition, a complete synthesis; for we have shown that the ethical drive and theoretical knowledge stand in reciprocal interaction with each other and that all morality is conditioned by this reciprocal interaction. The ethical drive, insofar as it appears within consciousness, demands some concept $= X$, which is, however, insufficiently determined *for the ethical drive*; and to this extent the ethical drive formally determines the power of cognition: i.e., it drives the reflecting power of judgment to search for the concept in question. The power of cognition is, however, also determined materially with regard to concept X by the ethical drive, insofar as the latter is viewed as what is original; for, as we have just seen, X arises through the complete determination of the object by means of the entire original drive. It follows from this that all cognition, considered objectively as a system, is thoroughly determined in advance and that it is determined by means of the ethical drive. (To begin with, therefore, a rational being is determined absolutely through itself and through nothing whatsoever outside of itself – with respect to both the matter and the form of all its possible cognitions. We here arrive once again, in a more determinate fashion and indeed as the result of a genetic deduction, at something we could otherwise have asserted simply on the basis of the principle of I-hood. Moreover, all of the I's cognition is determined by its practical being [*Wesen*] – as indeed it has to be, since this is what is highest in the I. The only firm and final foundation of all my cognitions is my duty. This is the intelligible "in itself," which transforms itself by means of the laws of sensible representation into a sensible world.)

Conversely, cognition has an effect within consciousness upon the ethical drive, inasmuch as it supplies the latter with its object. – The ethical drive thus reverts back into itself through the intermediary of cognition, and the reciprocal interaction in question is really the reciprocal interaction of the ethical drive with itself. Everything that constitutes a rational being comes together in the reciprocal interaction described in detail above [IV, 173], and this coming together manifests itself in the feeling of certainty.

To summarize all that has gone before: the formal condition for the morality of our actions, or of what properly deserves to be called the morality of the same, consists in deciding to do what conscience demands, purely and simply for conscience's sake. Conscience, however, is *the immediate consciousness of our determinate duty*. This is not to be understood in any sense other than in the sense in which it has here been derived: consciousness of something determinate is, as such, never immediate, but is found through an act of thinking. (With respect to its content, the consciousness of our duty is not immediate.) Once something determinate has been given, however, the consciousness *that* this determinate something is a duty is an immediate consciousness. With respect to its form, the consciousness of duty is immediate. This formal aspect of consciousness is a sheer feeling.

(Kant says in the passage previously cited that conscience is a consciousness that is itself a duty.[8] This is a correct and sublime pronouncement, which contains two assertions: first of all, it is, according to the proof provided earlier, absolutely a duty to acquire such consciousness. Everyone is simply supposed to convince himself of what his duty is; and everyone is in every case able to do this. This is, so to speak, the constitutive law of all morals: the law that one give a law to oneself. Moreover, this state of consciousness is nothing whatsoever

---

[8] See *RBR*, p. 202 (*AA* 6: 185): "*Conscience is a consciousness which is of itself a duty.*"

but a consciousness of duty. A content of consciousness is a duty because it is the content of *this* kind of consciousness. In other words, conscience, the power of feeling described above, does not provide the material, which is provided only by the power of judgment, and conscience is not a power of judgment; conscience does, however, provide the evidential certainty,[9] and this kind of evidential certainty occurs solely in the consciousness of duty.)

Corollaries

(1) The preceding deduction has forever removed and annihilated any possible appeal to the possibility of an *erring conscience* – an evasion that still remains possible according to most moral systems [IV, 174]. Conscience never errs and cannot err, for it is the immediate consciousness of our pure, original I, over and above which there is no other kind of consciousness; it cannot be examined nor corrected by any other kind of consciousness. Conscience is itself the judge of all convictions and acknowledges no higher judge above itself. It has final jurisdiction and is subject to no appeal. To want to go beyond conscience means to want to go beyond oneself and to separate oneself from oneself. All material moral systems (i.e., all those that still seek some end for duty beyond duty itself) do go beyond conscience and are caught up in the fundamental error of all dogmatism, which searches outside the I in order to discover the ultimate ground of all that is in and for the I. Moral systems of this sort are possible only in consequence of an inconsistency, since for a consistent dogmatism there are no morals [*Moral*], but only a system of natural laws. – Nor can the power of judgment err about whether conscience has spoken or not. What would force a human being to act before the power of judgment has become completely certain that conscience has spoken? No action takes place *through or by means of a human being* unless the human being in question has determined himself to act in this way. If, therefore, one acts without being certain

---

[9] *aber die Evidenz gibt es her*. The German term *Evidenz*, particularly as used by Fichte and other philosophical authors of this period, has a meaning close to that of the English "self-evidence." Kant, for example, identifies "evidence" [*Evidenz*] with "intuitive certainty" [*anschauende Gewißheit*] (*KrV*, A 734/B 763).

of the pronouncement of one's conscience, then one acts unconscionably [*gewissenlos*]; one's guilt is clear, and one cannot pin this guilt on anything outside oneself. There is no excuse for any sin; it *is* a sin, and it remains a sin.

I have to stress this last point as strongly as possible because of its importance both for morality and for the science of morality. A person who says the opposite [of what was asserted above] may well find in his own heart some reason for doing this – the error can lie only in his heart, not in his understanding –, but it is amazing that he dares to admit to this so loudly, in the presence of himself and others.

(2) In order to prevent the word *feeling* from occasioning dangerous misunderstandings, I also wish to stress the following: a theoretical proposition is not felt and cannot be felt; what is felt is the certainty and secure conviction that unites itself with the act of thinking this theoretical proposition [IV, 175], an act that is accomplished in accordance with theoretical laws. Thus when one is engaged simply in thinking one should not concern oneself in advance with how conscience might fare as a result of this thought. This would result in an inconsistent thinking, the goal of which would be pre-determined. Thinking should rigorously pursue its own course, independently of conscience. The opposite way of thinking amounts to a kind of cowardice, which truly places little confidence in one's conscience. – The allegedly "objective" instructions of feeling are unregulated products of the power of imagination, which cannot stand up to an examination by theoretical reason; and the feeling that unites itself with instructions of this sort is the feeling of the free self-activity of our power of imagination. This, however, is not a feeling of ourselves in our original wholeness, but only a feeling of a part of ourselves. A proposition produced in this way can be recognized by the fact that it contradicts the laws of thinking, something that can never occur in the case of any conviction confirmed by conscience; and the feeling that accompanies a proposition of this sort can be recognized by the fact that, even though it may possess strength, sublimity, and fervor, it still lacks security. No mere fanatical enthusiast would ever dare act upon his feeling if this meant being stuck with this same conviction for all eternity, with no possibility of ever altering this conviction.

(3) The feeling of certainty arises from the concurrence of an act of the power of the imagination with the ethical drive. A necessary

166

condition for the possibility of such a feeling is therefore that the subject has actually judged [this concurrence] for himself. This is why there can be no certainty nor any conviction whatsoever in the case of alien judgments and why conscience can absolutely not allow itself to be guided by any authority, which would involve a clear and obvious contradiction – a self-feeling of something that I myself neither am nor do.

It follows that anyone who acts on authority necessarily acts unconscionably; for, according to the proof just provided, such a person is uncertain. This is an extremely important proposition, and it is quite necessary to present it in its full rigor [IV, 176].

One can, to be sure, guide human beings in their investigations; one can provide them with the premises for an adjudication that they are supposed to make, and they might accept these premises provisionally, on the bases of authority. This is more or less the story of all human beings: by means of education they receive, as premises for their own judgments, what the human species has agreed upon up to this point and what has now become a matter of universal human belief; and for the most part they accept this without any further examination. It is only the true philosopher who does not accept anything without examination, and his meditating proceeds from the most absolute doubt concerning everything.

Before arriving at the point of acting, however, everyone is bound by his conscience *to judge for himself* on the basis of those premises he has accepted in good faith; that is, each person, purely and simply on his own, has to draw for himself those final conclusions that will immediately determine his acting. If his conscience subsequently confirms what follows from those premises, then it thereby also confirms indirectly the *practical validity* of the premises in question, though this does not confirm their theoretical validity; for the moral element [*Zusatz*] in these premises, which reveals itself only in the result and which is approved by conscience, can be right, even while the theoretical element is entirely false. If one's conscience disapproves of those premises, then they are annihilated and it is an absolute duty to relinquish them. Something that has no practical consequences is morally indifferent, and one can calmly leave as it is. To be sure, for humanity as such no cognition is indifferent; anything that is supposed to be true and with respect to which conviction is supposed to be possible must necessarily be related to what is practical. For individual human beings in their limited situations, however, a large portion of theory can remain indifferent throughout their entire lives.

For the sake of conscience, every human being must judge for himself and must compare his judgment to his own feeling: otherwise he acts immorally and unconscionably. There is therefore absolutely no external ground nor external criterion for the binding force of an ethical command. No command, no dictum is unconditionally binding because it is stated in one place or another [IV, 177] or because it is uttered by a certain person – even if it is allegedly a divine dictum or command. A command is binding only on the condition that it is confirmed by our own conscience and only *because* it has been confirmed in this way. It is an absolute duty not to accept any command or dictum without examining it for oneself, but first to test it through one's own conscience; it is absolutely unconscionable to omit this test. Nothing whatsoever can be advanced against this categorical dictum of reason, which is valid without exception; and all excuses and exceptions and modifications of the latter must be rejected out of hand. It is impermissible to say, "I have found this and this to be true, hence something else, something perhaps that is stated in the same place, will also be true." The first two were true because they were found to be true, not because they were stated in this place, and to accept the third with the risk that it might yet be false is an instance of unconscionable carelessness. Anything that does not have its origin in faith, in confirmation by our own conscience, is an absolute sin.

§16

The cause of evil in a finite rational being

The following investigation is not without its own intrinsic interest, in that it has to answer some questions that are customarily introduced and answered quite incorrectly; in addition, it can also, by way of contrast, shed considerable light on what was said in the previous section.

I

What pertains to any rational being whatsoever is necessarily to be found – wholly and without any omission – in each rational individual

[IV, 178], since otherwise the individual in question would not be rational. It cannot be too strongly stressed that a rational being is not something arbitrarily composed from heterogeneous pieces but is a whole; if one removes one of its necessary components, then one removes all of them. – Here we are talking about a rational being as considered with respect to its original condition or with respect to its origin [*ursprünglich betrachtet*]. Now, according to the moral law, an empirical temporal being is supposed to become an exact copy of the original I. This temporal being is the conscious subject; something is in this subject only insofar as it is consciously posited by means of a free act of the subject's own self-activity. Moreover, one can comprehend that this positing, these acts of reflecting upon what originally constitutes us [as rational beings], have to fall into a successive temporal series, since they are all limited; and thus it will take some time until everything that is originally in us and for us is raised to the level of clear consciousness. To describe this temporal course of the I's reflections is to provide the history of an empirical rational being. Note, however, that everything that occurs along this course seems to ensue contingently, since it is all dependent on freedom and by no means on any mechanical law of nature.

II

If a human being is to possess any consciousness at all and is actually to be a rational being, then he must be conscious of something or other. For reasons indicated above, the first thing a human being becomes conscious of within time is the natural drive; and he acts in accordance with the demands of this drive – freely, to be sure, but only in the formal sense of the word and without any consciousness of his own freedom. When a human being occupies this standpoint then he is free for an intellect outside of himself; but for himself – if only he could be something for himself – he is only an animal.

It is to be expected that he will reflect upon himself in this state. When he does this he raises himself above himself and steps onto a higher level. – This reflection does not ensue according to any law, but occurs through absolute freedom [IV, 179], which is why we described it only as something that is to be expected. It ensues because it ensues. It *ought to* ensue because the empirical I ought to correspond to the pure I, but it does not *have to* ensue. (The society in which a human being lives can provide him with an occasion for this reflection, but it is absolutely unable to cause it to occur.)

As was described above, the individual tears himself loose from the natural drive by means of this reflection and positions himself as a free intellect independent of the natural drive. The individual thereby obtains for himself the power to defer his self-determination and, along with this power, the power to make a selection between *multiple* ways of satisfying the natural drive, a multiplicity that arises precisely through the act of reflection and through the postponement of the decision.

Let us reflect a bit more upon this possibility of choosing. – A free being determines itself only through and only in accordance with concepts. Its choice therefore presupposes a concept of that choice, of what is to be chosen thereby. Let the choice be between A, B and C. If the free being in question chooses, let us say, C, then can it prefer C for no reason and without any ground – that is, without any intelligible ground in a concept? Absolutely not, since in that case the choice would not occur through freedom but through blind chance. Freedom acts in accordance with concepts. There simply must be something in C that makes it stand out. Let us call this something X.

Another question arises now however: why is the choice in question decided precisely by X, and not by some possible non-X? The reason for this can lie only in a universal rule that the rational being already possesses. This rule must be the major premise of a syllogism that would go as follows: whatever is of such and such a kind ($=$X) must be preferred to everything else; now C is of this kind; hence, etc. The major premise contains the rule. Kant designates such a rule quite felicitously as a *maxim*.[10] (This would be the major premise in a theoretical syllogism; but theory is not what is highest for a human being [IV, 180], and every possible major premise has a still higher proposition above itself. What is highest for an empirical human being – his maximum – is the rule for his acting.)

Let us dwell for a moment on this concept of a maxim. First of all, with respect to its form, a maxim is a maxim precisely through an act of my own freedom. Were it not a product of my freedom, then all other

---

[10] See *CPrR* § 1, p. 153 (*AA* 5: 19).

freedom would be abolished, since everything else follows necessarily and according to a fixed rule from the maxim in question. This is how Kant argues.[11] Moreover – and this is what I would prefer to build upon – it is absolutely contradictory [to claim] that something is given to the I from outside. The I could never become immediately conscious of anything that were to come to it from outside. A maxim, however, is an object of the most immediate consciousness.

Thus, if one should find an evil maxim, then this can be explained only on the basis of the freedom of the human being himself [who formulates such a maxim for himself], and the latter cannot blame this on anything outside himself. – A principle [*das Prinzip*], moreover, is not a maxim; and since there is, properly speaking, no principle of acting other than the moral law, the moral law is not a maxim, for this law does not depend *upon the freedom of the empirical subject*. Something becomes a maxim only insofar as I, the empirical subject, freely make it the rule of my acting.

If we now consider the human being occupying the point of reflection at which we left him above, what could his maxim be? Since the only drive that occurs within his consciousness at this point is the natural drive, and since the latter aims only at enjoyment and has pleasure as its incentive, the maxim in question can be none other than the following: one must choose that which promises the greatest pleasure, in terms both of intension and of extension – in short, [he will adopt] the maxim of his own happiness. Because of the sympathetic drives, one may of course also seek one's own happiness in the happiness of others, but in this case the ultimate goal of acting still remains the satisfaction of these drives and the pleasure that arises therefrom, and hence one's own happiness. At this level the human being becomes an intelligent animal [IV, 181].

I have *proven* what the maxim must be at the present point of reflection, and I therefore assume that this maxim is determined through a theoretical law and can be derived from it. Shortly prior to this, however, I said that the maxim is determined through the absolute spontaneity of the empirical subject. How can these two assertions coexist? – Though I raise this question only at this point, the answer is valid for our entire present inquiry. – *If* a human being continues to

[11] See *RBR*, p. 70 (*AA* 6: 21).

171

occupy this point of reflection, then this is the only maxim that is possible for him. Under this condition he cannot have a better one. This maxim can therefore be derived theoretically from the point of reflection we are now presupposing. It is, however, by no means necessary *that* a human being remain at this point of reflection; instead, this is something that depends upon his freedom. He absolutely *ought to have* raised himself to a higher level of reflection, and he also *could have done* this. He is to blame for not doing this, and hence he is also to blame for the unworthy [*untaugliche*] maxim that flows from his failure to raise himself to a higher level of reflection. We therefore cannot say in advance at which point of reflection an individual will remain, for this is not something that follows from any theoretical law. Hence one is quite correct to judge as follows: in this situation, i.e., with this way of thinking and with this character, this human being could simply not have acted any differently from how he did act. Yet one would be wrong to rest one's judgment at this point and to want to claim that the person in question could not have had a different character than the one he has now. If a human being's present character is unworthy, then he is absolutely supposed to form for himself another character; and he is able to do this, for it depends purely upon his own freedom.

There is something incomprehensible here, and it cannot be otherwise, since we are now standing at the boundary of all comprehensibility: namely, the doctrine of freedom as it applies to the empirical subject. So long as I do not yet occupy a higher standpoint of reflection, then this standpoint does not exist for me, and hence I cannot have a concept of what I am supposed to do before I actually do it. Yet it nevertheless remains the case that this is what I absolutely ought to do [IV, 182]. That is to say, when judged from the perspective of another person, one who is acquainted with the higher standpoint of reflection, the act in question is something I ought to do; and for me as well it is something I ought to do, once I have become familiar with this same higher standpoint. Once I have attained this standpoint I will no longer excuse myself by appealing to my own incapacity, but will blame myself for not having done what I ought to have done much sooner. – I ought to do this in relation to my original character, which, however, is itself only an idea.

The situation could not be otherwise, for an act of freedom is purely and simply because it is, and it is what is absolutely primary [*ein absolut erstes*], something that cannot be connected to anything else and cannot be explained on the basis of anything else. Only if one fails to take this into account does one encounter those difficulties that so many people encounter when they arrive at this point. "To comprehend" means to connect one act of thinking to another act of thinking, to think the former by means of the latter. Wherever such mediation is possible there is no freedom but only mechanism. It is therefore absolutely contradictory to want to comprehend an act of freedom. Were we able to comprehend it, then – precisely for this reason – it would not be freedom.

All the particular acts of reflection that are demanded here are therefore also absolute starting points of a completely new series, and one cannot say where these acts of reflection come from, since they do not come from anywhere at all. – This already clarifies, in a preliminary fashion, something that *Kant* says: namely, that radical evil is inborn in the human being and yet has its ground in freedom.[12] To be sure, it can be predicted and comprehended that a human being will remain at the lower points of reflection for a long time, perhaps even for his entire life, since there is absolutely nothing that drives him higher; and experience confirms that the former is at least generally the case. To this extent, evil is inborn in human beings. It is nevertheless not necessary that a human being remain on this lower point, since there is also nothing that *keeps* him there. It is just as possible for him to transport himself at once to the higher point of reflection; and if he has not done this, then this is because he has failed to use his freedom, even if, in his current state, he does not become conscious of his obligation [IV, 183]. To this extent, the evil in human beings has its ground in freedom.

The maxim deduced [above, i.e., the maxim of one's own happiness], is indeed lawless, but it is not yet a perversion of the law nor enmity against the latter. It is both to be hoped and to be expected that the human in question will sooner or later raise himself to the higher viewpoint, if he is only left to himself. This however will be made extremely difficult if this unworthy maxim is sophistically transformed into a principle, as happens in the case of so many so-called philosophers. In saying this, I am not referring to the exponents of the principle

---

[12] *RBR*, pp. 83ff. (*AA* 6: 37ff.).

of happiness and perfection among the Germans. In their case it was mainly a matter of misunderstanding and incorrect expression; what they meant to say was for the most part more innocent than their words. Instead, my remark is aimed especially at those materialistic and atheistic teachers of ethics who were formerly so favored abroad, such as Helvetius[13] and others, who said that a human being simply does everything out of self-interest, and that his nature contains no other motive for action [*Bewegungsgrund*] but this. According to such teachers, this is man's vocation; he cannot be different, and he is not supposed to be different; and anyone who wants to be better is a fool and a fanatical enthusiast who misjudges the limits of his own nature.[14] For anyone who places confidence in such reasoning – and for anyone who views this matter in purely natural terms – all striving after something higher is spoiled and rendered impossible.

Even in the absence of such a false philosophy, however, this mode of thinking is powerfully confirmed by general custom and by the experience (which might well be the same in every age) that the vast majority of human beings around us are no better [than they are described as being by this materialistic ethics]. This may also be the source of the prejudice that those who seem better when judged by their outward actions – which is all that one can observe – may, in the depth of their hearts, be of the same mind as everyone else and simply possess greater prudence and knowledge of the world. – It is equally important to note, moreover, that it is *natural* for a human being [IV, 184] to borrow his maxim from the general practice or at least from the practice that seems to him to be the most common and to judge what *ought to* happen on the basis of what *actually happens*; and without the occurrence of an act of spontaneity he will remain in this condition. The reason for this is as follows: it is through education in the widest sense, that is, through the influence of society in general upon us, that we are first cultivated [*gebildet*] in a manner that makes it possible for us to employ our freedom. If we do not raise ourselves above it, then the matter rests with that cultivation we have received from society. Were society better, then we would be better as well, though without any merit on

---

[13] Claude-Adrien Helvétius (1715–1771), French philosopher, author of *De l'esprit* (*Concerning the Mind*) (Paris: Durand, 1758).

[14] See Helvétius, *De l'esprit*, VIII, XII.

our part. This does not abolish the possibility of obtaining merit on one's own, but such a possibility first arises only at a higher point.

III

If, however, a human being is left to himself and is fettered neither by the example of his age nor by a ruinous philosophy, it is then to be expected that he will become conscious of that drive to absolute self-sufficiency that is always enduring and active within him. He then raises himself to a completely different kind of freedom; for though he is formally free within the domain of the maxim just described, materially he is wholly and completely dependent upon the objects of nature. He has no other end than the enjoyment they afford.

If only a human being is left to himself, I said, then he might raise himself higher. Anyone can see that there is no continual process of transition from that state of thoughtlessness and inattentiveness, in which this drive [toward absolute self-sufficiency] is simply not present for a human being, to reflection upon the latter; accordingly, this reflection upon the drive occurs through a special act of spontaneity, and we have no intention of contradicting this truth with our assertion that the individual might perhaps advance further. We are here viewing the matter as determined only by laws of nature, and we cannot view it otherwise if we want to consider it in a coherent manner. Despite all the evil examples and all the perverted philosophical arguments [IV, 185], it remains true that a human being ought to raise himself above the laws of nature,[15] and he is also capable of doing this; and it always remains his own fault if he does not do so. For after all, none of these external circumstances exercise any causality upon him; it is not *they* that operate in him and through him, but it is he himself who determines himself in response to a stimulus from the latter. It also remains true that, in spite of all hindrances, actual individuals do manage to raise themselves above these hindrances. *How* they manage to do this remains inexplicable; i.e., it can be explained only on the basis of freedom. By analogy with an outstanding degree of intellectual capability, one could call the capacity in question the *genius for virtue*.

---

[15] Reading *dieselben* as referring to *Naturgesetze*, though it might also refer to "evil examples and perverted philosophical arguments."

It is not sensitivity, as a certain author says,[16] but self-sufficiency, and anyone who wants to teach virtue has to teach self-sufficiency.

Were we somehow, in some incomprehensible manner, to become conscious of this drive toward self-sufficiency – conscious of it, that is, as a blind drive, since it has not [yet] been reflected upon intentionally nor with any consciousness of this reflection –, then it would necessarily appear to us to be something contingent, something that is present within us simply by chance and for no higher reason. We can see in advance that the character of the individual would be determined further and determined differently by such an appearance [of the blind drive toward self-sufficiency], and it is this [new] determinacy of the individual's character that we now have to examine.

The distinguishing features revealed by an examination of this character are as follows: the drive [toward self-sufficiency] appears only as a blind drive and neither as a law nor as a drive governed by a law; furthermore, since the character in question is already determined through the previously described maxim of self-interest, the drive appears to be contingent, something that is not essential to our nature – something that does not have to exist. We must draw our inferences from these two distinguishing features. It is by no means necessary that anyone should arrive at this point [of understanding himself to be acting in accordance with a blind drive to self-sufficiency] nor is it necessary that one remain there; but *if* anyone does arrive at this point, then his character is necessarily determined in a certain manner.

First of all, to the extent that our actions are to be explained from that fact that we occupy this level [IV, 186], then we are acting in accordance with a mere drive, and not in accordance with a *maxim*. There thus arises a manner of acting that the one who is acting does not and cannot explain to himself and that appears to involve something contradictory. It is no accident then that the exponents of the previous mode of thinking, which is entirely sensory, point to the contradiction contained in this manner of acting, confuse it with true morality, and then characterize both as absurd. This feature alone is sufficient to establish the reprehensibility of the manner of acting we are now examining. – The previously established maxim of self-interest remains in force as a

---

[16] Joachim Heinrich Campe (1746–1818), author of *Über Empfindsamkeit und Empfindelei in päda-gogischer Hinsicht* (*On Sensibility and Cult of Sensibility in a Pedagogical Regard*) (1779).

maxim in this state as well; this maxim is always followed whenever one acts with consciousness of an end. An action motivated by the blind drive [to self-sufficiency] is only an exception to this rule; and this is why one makes an artificial connection between the maxim of self-interest and this blind drive when, after the fact, one tries to account for the incentives of one's action and attempts to derive one's way of acting from this maxim – thereby doing oneself an injustice, so to speak.

In terms of the matter or content of willing, what arises from the preceding is the maxim of *unrestricted and lawless dominion over everything outside us* – a maxim which, to be sure, is not clearly thought, but which offers to an observer who occupies a higher standpoint the only ground for explaining [such a way of acting]. It is not that the human being intends to bring everything outside of him under the absolute sway of his will – he does not intend anything at all, but is only driven blindly –, but he acts as though he had this intention, and he does so for absolutely no other reason than because he wills to do it. It is quite clear that this is the manner of acting that must arise from the blind and lawless drive to absolute self-sufficiency. The way to evaluate this maxim is by comparing it to the genuinely moral maxim. For the latter certainly wants freedom and independence as well, but it wants to obtain these ends only gradually and in accordance with certain rules; hence it does not want to possess unconditional and lawless causality, but a causality that stands under certain restrictions. The drive we are speaking of here, however, demands unconditional and unlimited causality [IV, 187].

The most conspicuous and common manifestations of this way of thinking are the following: one certainly wants to possess a good will and wants everyone outside of oneself to allow everything to depend upon one's own good will; but one wants to hear absolutely nothing about duty, obligation, and law. One wants to be magnanimous and considerate, but one does not want to be just. One feels benevolent toward others, but one does not esteem and respect their rights. In short, our empirical will, which again depends upon nothing beyond our own will, and which is therefore an absolute empirical will, is supposed to be the law for all of nature outside us, both the irrational and the free parts of the same.

Anyone can see that these character traits cannot be explained on the basis of the mere drive for enjoyment. Every attempted explanation of this sort is forced and is unable to accomplish what it is supposed to accomplish – provided that one really does will the happiness of others outside of oneself and that this unworthy end is not merely a disguise for an even more unworthy one, namely, the desire for mere enjoyment. The object of our will is by no means determined by some possible enjoyment, but is determined absolutely through the will. With respect to its form, therefore, there is no difference between this way of thinking and the genuinely moral way of thinking.

Furthermore, this drive necessarily retains its character of demanding respect. – *Either, on the one hand*, no sacrifice of enjoyment is required in order to act in accordance with this way of thinking, either because one has no desires or because the circumstances do not require any sacrifice from us. In this case one approves coldly, and what one approves of is not one's own conduct, for one has not reflected upon the latter as something subject to a rule; instead, what one approves of is the course of nature itself or our fellow human beings' manner of acting. One believed that one could demand that everything bow to one's will – for that is precisely the character of the drive to self-sufficiency; and thus, according to this mode of thinking, what happened in this case of approval was nothing more than what is right and in order. No true pleasure nor joy is connected with such success, since we did not expect any favor from nature but were only demanding that nature fulfill its obligation [IV, 188]. If, however, we fail to obtain what we desired, what then arises is not pain and suffering, which is a sad and disheartened feeling, but annoyance, which is an invigorating emotion; and we feel annoyed because we were driven by a propensity toward self-sufficiency and because we decisively demanded what we wanted. In this case we will accuse God and nature of violating and denying justice, and we will accuse human beings in particular of ingratitude and ungratefulness.

Or else, on the other hand, some sacrifice is required in order to act in accordance with this way of thinking. It is quite possible that one makes the greatest renunciations in order to act in accordance with this way of thinking, for this drive [toward self-sufficiency] is higher than the drive toward mere enjoyment. Since this drive has retained its character, that is, since it still aims at respect, what ensues is *esteem* for oneself. The following is to be noted in this regard: first of all, what we esteem in this case is not so much our free acting through absolute self-activity as it is our own character, considered as something passive and given to us. We are overjoyed to find ourselves to be so good and so noble – indeed, better and more noble than we could even have imagined. That this must actually be the case is evident from the following: we act in accordance with a blind drive; hence we do not really act with freedom and self-awareness. We have not reflected upon our action prior to acting but only find it, as something given, once it has occurred. Only after we have acted do we find the rule according to which we might have acted. Our action thus is and remains something given, not something self-made; and since this action is supposed to be something good, it is a given, innate good. This feature often reveals itself both in ordinary life and in philosophical reasoning. The claim concerning the original goodness of human nature, for example, is based on experiences of the sort just described, and even the defenders of this claim do not maintain anything different. (This claim, however, is utterly false. Human nature is originally neither good nor evil. Only through freedom does it become either of these) [IV, 189].

Furthermore, this assessment of ourselves is not an instance of cold, calm approval, as is the case with moral self-assessment, but is connected with joy, which always arises from what is unexpected – with joy concerning ourselves, joy that we are so good. The following observation will show that this has to be the case: we have acted in accordance with a blind drive and have demanded nothing of ourselves. The median on which we consciously place ourselves, alongside all others like us, is the maxim of self-interest. "This is just how human beings are," we think, "and nothing more can be demanded of them." Yet we find ourselves to be elevated quite a bit above this ordinary measure of humanity; we possess very special merits. It is not as though we find ourselves to be as we would find ourselves to be if we were to consider ourselves in accordance with the moral law, that is, *as we purely and simply ought to be*; instead, we here find ourselves to be incomparably better than we had to be. For us, there are in this case only great and noble and meritorious actions, only *opera supererogativa*.[17] – To characterize this way of thinking in a single stroke: everything that God, nature, and other human beings do for us is merely what they are absolutely obliged to do; they can never do too much and are always

---

[17] Latin for "supererogatory acts."

useless servants. Everything we do for them, however, is a matter of goodness and grace. No matter how we act, we can never be wrong. If we sacrifice everything to our own enjoyment, then this is entirely in order and is no more than an exercise of our good and justified right. If we renounce our enjoyment even in the slightest degree, then we have acquired thereby extraordinary merit.

Hardly anyone will deny that such a way of thinking, reduced to its principle, is irrational. Anyone, however, who is familiar with human beings and who is capable of entering into their inner life will also not deny that this way of thinking is very widespread, even among people who are considered to be very righteous and virtuous, though, to be sure, it usually occurs in an obscure manner and is not raised to the level of concepts. Here we are not thinking of any particular individuals, but of humanity in its entirety. Almost all of human history is nothing else but a proof of our assertion; and only by presupposing such a way of thinking can human history be rendered comprehensible [IV, 190]. For how else can we explain the subjugation of the bodies and the conscience of nations, the wars of conquest and the religious wars, and all those other misdeeds through which humanity has been dishonored from time immemorial? What made the suppressor expend labor and risk danger in pursuit of his end? Did he hope that the sources of sensible enjoyments would be enlarged thereby? By no means; the only principle that animated him was this: what I will is what ought to happen; what I say should settle things once and for all.

We showed earlier that the aim of this way of thinking is not enjoyment. The self-conceit that accompanies it is based on the consciousness of sacrifices, which one believes one could also have spared oneself. Afterwards, to be sure, the satisfaction one derives from those sacrifices is the source of another, non-sensible kind of enjoyment, enjoyment of the pats on the back one gives oneself; but such enjoyment is certainly neither the intended end of our actions nor the incentive for the same. The end that obscurely guides our actions, even though, to be sure, we never clearly think it as such, is this: that our lawless, arbitrary choice should have dominion over everything. It is to *this* end that we sacrifice enjoyment, and then later we flatter ourselves regarding our disinterestedness.

If we consider human beings as natural beings, then this way of thinking has an advantage over the one described earlier, which evaluates everything according to the sensible enjoyment it provides. Viewed from this [natural] standpoint, this way of thinking evokes admiration, whereas in contrast we despise the human being who has to calculate what he stands to gain before he will move a finger. [The end of] the way of thinking we have just discussed is and always remains independence from everything outside us, self-reliance. One could call it *heroic*, and it is also the usual way of thinking for the heroes of our history. – If, however, one considers this way of thinking from the perspective of morality, then it does not possess the least value, because it does not issue from morality. Indeed, this way of thinking is even more danger-ous than the first, purely sensible way of thinking. To be sure, it does not falsify and render impure the principle of morality (for no such principle is present for this way of thinking), but it falsifies and renders impure the adjudication [IV, 191] of the material actions that issue from this principle, inasmuch as this way of thinking accustoms one to viewing what is one's duty as something meritorious and noble. The publican and sinner may indeed have no greater value than the Pharisee who believes himself to be just, for none of these have even the slightest value; but the former are easier to improve than the latter.

IV

A human being has only to raise to clear consciousness this drive to absolute self-sufficiency – which, when it operates as a blind drive, produces a very immoral character – and then, as was shown earlier, simply by means of this very act of reflection, this same drive will transform itself within him into an absolutely commanding law. Just as every act of reflection limits that upon which one is reflecting, so too is the drive [to self-sufficiency] limited through this reflection, and as a result of this reflection the blind drive for absolute causality becomes a law of conditioned causality. The human being in question now knows that he absolutely ought to do something.

If this knowledge is to be transformed into action, then the human being must make it his maxim to do always and in every case what duty demands, *because duty demands it*. – The latter is already implicit in the concept of a maxim, which is, after all, the highest and absolute rule and which recognizes no other rule above itself.

It is absolutely impossible and contradictory that anyone with a clear consciousness of his duty at the moment he acts could, in good consciousness, *decide not to do his duty*, that he should rebel against the law, refusing to obey it and making it his maxim not to do his duty, because it is his duty. Such a maxim would be diabolical; but the concept of the devil is self-contradictory and therefore annuls itself. – We can prove this as follows: to say that a human being is clearly aware of his duty means that he, as an intellect, absolutely demands of himself that he do something [IV, 192]; to say that he decides to act in good consciousness contrary to his duty means that, at the same undivided moment, he demands of himself that he not do the very same thing. At one and the same moment, therefore, these contradictory demands would be placed upon him by one and the same power – a presupposition that annuls itself and involves the clearest and most patent contradiction.

It is, however, quite possible for one to *render obscure* within oneself the clear consciousness of what duty demands; for such consciousness arises only through an act of absolute spontaneity, and it endures only through the continuation of this same act of freedom. If one ceases to reflect, then this consciousness disappears. (The case here is the same as it is with many of the concepts of transcendental philosophy: as soon as one descends from that higher point of view, from which alone these concepts are possible, they vanish into nothing.) The situation is thus as follows: if one constantly reflects upon the demand of the law, if this demand always remains before one's eyes, then it is impossible not to act in accordance with this demand or to resist it. If the law disappears from our attention, however, then it is impossible for us to act in accordance with it. Necessity thus reigns in both cases, and we seem to have become caught up in some kind of intelligible fatalism, though of a somewhat lower degree than the usual kind.[18] In the ordinary kind of intelligible fatalism, either the moral law, which is present without any assistance from freedom, produces a consciousness of itself within a human being,

---

[18] The term "intelligible fatalism" [*intelligibler Fatalismus*] designates the doctrine that human action is completely determined at the (unknowable) non-empirical, "intelligible" or "noumenal" level, at which the human being has the status of a thing in itself. The term was introduced into the critical discussion of Kant's theory of freedom by Carl Christian Erhard Schmid in the First Part of his 1790 *Versuch einer Moralphilosophie* (*Attempt at a Moral Philosophy*). Fichte explicitly criticized Schmid's intelligible fatalism in one of his earliest published writings, his 1793 review of Leonhard Creuzer's *Skeptische Betrachtungen über die Freiheit des Willens* (*Skeptical Reflections on the Freedom of the Will*), (*SW* VII: 417–426; *GA* 1/2: 7–14); English trans. Daniel Breazeale, *The Philosophical Forum* 32 (2001): 289–290.

as well as a corresponding action, or else the moral law does not possess such force, and, in the absence of such an incentive, one's action is determined by a lower incentive. This system is already averted by means of the important insight that the moral law is by no means the sort of thing that could ever be present within us without any assistance from us, but is instead something that we ourselves first make. In the system we are now considering, however, either one remains continually conscious of the moral law, in which case a moral action necessarily ensues, or else such consciousness disappears, in which case it is impossible to act morally. The appearance of fatalism disappears as soon as one notices that it is up to our freedom whether such consciousness continues or becomes obscured. The situation here is the same as it was in the case of the various points of reflection discussed above [IV, 193].

One should also note that this act of freedom, through which this consciousness [of the moral law] is either clearly retained or else allowed to become obscure, is an absolutely primary and therefore inexplicable act. That is to say, it is certainly not by means of any maxim, and hence not with any consciousness of what I am doing nor of the freedom with which I am doing it, that I obscure within myself the demand of the law. This would be a revolt against the law, the same kind of revolt that was previously shown to be contradictory. This obscuring of consciousness of the moral law is something that simply happens, just because it happens, absolutely without any higher reason. Or, to view this same matter from another side: the disappearance of the consciousness of duty is an *abstraction* from the latter. There are, however, two quite different kinds of abstraction: I can either engage in an act of abstraction with clear consciousness that I am doing so and in accordance with a rule, or else, simply as a result of *indeterminate* thinking, the abstraction can arise in me by itself, even in a case where I was not supposed to engage in abstraction, and this is how, for example, all purely formulaic philosophy[19] comes into being. The disappearance that here concerns us is an instance of the latter sort of abstraction, an indeterminate

---

[19] *Formular-Philosophie*. Fichte first introduced this term in 1794 in § 4 of *GWL*, where he describes the *Wissenschaftslehre* as a "system of real thinking," which establishes *Fakta* by means of a genetic deduction, and explicitly contrasts this kind of philosophy with an "empty formulaic philosophy" (*SK*, p. 197 [*SW* I: 220; *GA* I/2: 363]). This contrast is elaborated in the first section of the introduction to *FNR*, "How a real philosophical science is distinguished from a merely formulaic philosophy" (*FNR*, pp. 3–8 [*SW* III: 3–7; *GA* I/3: 313–318]).

thinking that works against duty, inasmuch as a determinate consciousness of duty is itself a duty. – In contrast, I obtain a clear consciousness of duty by means of an act that is itself an absolute beginning. This is all that can be said about it. As a result of that thoughtlessness and inattentiveness to our higher nature which is the condition in which our lives necessarily commence, we become accustomed to this thoughtlessness and continue along in our ordinary rut – which, however, does not mean that we could not freely raise ourselves above this state. We are equally able to *become accustomed* to steadily meditating on attending to the law, though no necessity is involved in this. Exercise and attentiveness, keeping watch over ourselves: these must be constantly continued; and without continued effort no one is secure in his morality for even a single second. No human being – indeed, so far as we can tell, no finite being – is ever *confirmed* in the good.

The determinate clear consciousness [of the moral law] disappears. Here we can think of two possible cases [IV, 194]: either this consciousness disappears for us completely, and no thought of duty remains, right up to the point of acting. In this case we will act either in accordance with the maxim of self-interest or in accordance with the blind drive to make our lawless will reign everywhere. Both of these two character types were described above.

Or else we retain some consciousness of duty as such, though only an indeterminate consciousness. – The main thing at this point is to gain some general appreciation of how a determinate consciousness can be transformed into an indeterminate and wavering consciousness. – All of our consciousness commences with indeterminacy, for it commences with the power of the imagination, which is a power that hovers and wavers between opposites. It is only by means of the understanding that the product of this hovering, a product that does not yet possess any sharp outlines, is determined and fixed. Even after it has been determined, however, the sharp boundary can easily be lost again, in which case the object will be retained only in the power of the imagination. This occurs consciously whenever we engage in arbitrary acts of abstraction, when [for example] I form an ordinary concept. When I do this, I omit the individual determinations and thereby raise my concept to the level of universality. To be sure, in this case too the concept is determined. Its determinacy consists precisely in the fact that it is indeterminate to such and such a degree. – The loss of determinacy that interests us here, however, is the kind that occurs without consciousness, as a result of distraction and thoughtlessness. Only very few human beings grasp objects determinately and sharply. For most people, objects simply float by, as in a dream, and are enveloped in fog. Does this mean that their understanding has not been active at all? No, it has been active, for otherwise they would not be conscious at all. It is simply that the determinacy immediately escapes them once again, and the passage through the regions of the understanding is quickly over. A concept that arises in this way is indeterminate, even with regard to its own indeterminacy. It oscillates between more or less indeterminacy, without any contribution from the power of judgment. – We are here assuming that this is the case with the concept of duty; it becomes obscure because I do not hold it fast [IV, 195].

Three kinds of determinacy are involved in the concept of duty when it is thought of in any determinate case, and it can lose each of these three types of determinacy. – First of all, among all the actions that are possible in each determinate case, only one of these determinate actions is a duty, and all other actions are contrary to duty. Only the concept of *this* action is accompanied by the feeling of certainty and conviction described above. This determinacy of the action escapes us, even while the form of the concept of duty remains. We then seize upon something other than duty, something which, so far as we know, we might even be able to do for the sake of duty, but which, unbeknownst to us – assuming that we set to work honestly – is demanded and must be determined by some inclination, since we have already lost the genuine guiding thread of conscience. In such a case we deceive ourselves about what is our duty and we act, as one usually puts it, from an erring conscience. The error in question, however, is and remains our fault. Had we only held on to our insight into duty, which was already present (and which depends upon nothing but our freedom), then we would not have erred. Quite a dangerous self-deception is involved here, against which one has to be very much on the alert. – I said above, "assuming only that we set to work honestly," for it is entirely possible that someone only pretends in front of others that he does something from duty, while he himself knows very well that he does it from self-interest, that it is by no means demanded of him by duty, and that he does not care one whit about duty, because he is a dogmatic non-believer. Someone of this sort is a coarse hypocrite and does not belong among the class of human beings we are here considering.

Second, in the cognition of duty it is determined that one ought to act in a certain way *in precisely this case*. This determinacy of the present time can [also] escape us, and when this happens the command appears to be one that does not apply to any determinate time, a command that certainly continues to demand obedience, just not right now; and thus it appears to be a command with which one does not have to hurry to comply. This leads one to defer the process of improvement [IV, 196], and it fosters the thought that one first wishes to continue enjoying this or that pleasure or to continue pursuing this or that blameworthy plan, and only then will one think about one's own improvement. – Such a way of thinking is utterly *reprehensible*; the moral law does not grant time for reflection and delay, but it demands instant obedience in every case, just as soon as it speaks. This way of thinking is also dangerous, because once one has learned to delay in this manner, one will easily continue to do just that. There will never come a time when one has no more favorite wishes, the fulfillment of which one would first like to await; for a human being always wishes. – A person who thinks in this way is lazy and begs to be thrown by some foreign power from the passivity[20] in which he happens to find himself; but there is no such power. Not even the Almighty himself is capable of granting what such a person desires.

Third and finally, the demand of duty is determined *as duty*, that is, it is determined with respect to its form; it demands obedience absolutely and demands that all the other drives be set aside. If one allows this determinacy to become obscured, then the command of duty no longer appears to us to be a command, but merely something similar to a good piece of advice, which one can follow if one wishes and if it does not require one to renounce too much, and which can even be bargained down a bit. When one is in this state one makes for oneself a mixed maxim. One does not always aim at the highest enjoyment and demand only the latter; instead, one is content with having to do one's duty here and there, and one might even sacrifice to duty those enjoyments that do not otherwise entice one – such as greediness, in the case of a spendthrift, and pleasures that might deprive one of honor, in the case of an ambitious person – , but one reserves for oneself one's favorite

---

[20] *Ruhe*. The editor of *SW* IV (I. H. Fichte) suggests that this might be a misprint for *Reihe* ("series").

enjoyments. In this manner one makes a contract between conscience and desire and believes that one has come to terms with both.

This way of thinking insolently pretends that one *cannot* live as the moral law demands, that the precise execution of the latter is impossible – a pretense [IV, 197] that is quite common in ordinary life, but which has also insinuated itself from there into philosophical and theological systems. What kind of impossibility could one be talking about in this case? It may well be that, because of external hindrances, we are often unable to realize in the world outside us what we have willed most firmly, but the moral law does not unconditionally demand the execution [of what we have willed], but only that we apply all of our strength and only that we do what we are able to do. And why should we not be able to do what we are able to do? The moral law demands only that we not do the opposite of our duty. And why should we not be able to refrain from the latter? What power might be able to force free beings like ourselves to act? – What this pretense really means to say is this: if we want to hold on to this or that enjoyment, possession, etc., if we want to satisfy this or that inclination, then we are not able to [refrain from doing the opposite of what duty commands]. Duty demands such sacrifices from us. We cannot have both of these together. – But who says that we are supposed to hold on to the former? Everything is supposed to be sacrificed for duty: life and honor and all that can be dear to a human being. We have by no means claimed that the satisfaction of self-interest and the fulfillment of duty can coexist always and in every case. The former ought to be surrendered. It therefore comes down to this: we simply do not *will* to do this [i.e., what duty demands]; we simply cannot bring ourselves to will to make such sacrifices. This, however, means that what is lacking is obviously the will and not the ability. – If there is any glaring evidence of the wide distribution of human corruption and the shamelessness of the same, then it is this contradictory and utterly irrational excuse, which is offered again and again and is echoed and defended by the most intelligent people, and which has actually been endorsed by several ethical theorists who have taken it seriously, as if it possessed any degree of rationality.

(The situation is the same elsewhere, for example, when one speaks of the technical and practical aspects of executing what is demanded by pure reason; and the proposition, "we are not able to do this," always means the same thing. If, for example, what is demanded is a thorough improvement of the constitution of the state [IV, 198], then the response is, "these proposals cannot be carried out" – meaning, of course, they cannot be carried out *if the old abuses are to remain in place*. But who says that the latter are to remain?)

These three different ways of circumventing the strength of the moral law can occur together. The last one, however, is a special danger to the human condition. Once one has persuaded oneself that one can make some accommodation with the rigor of the law, one will very easily continue to proceed in this manner throughout one's entire life, unless one experiences some powerful external jolt, which provides one with an occasion for going back into oneself; and to this extent it is far easier to improve a sinner than it is to improve someone who belongs to this last group and imagines himself to be just.

Appendix

In order to shed the clearest light on the doctrine of freedom and in order to pursue fatalism into its last refuge, we will now direct our attention specifically to Kant's claim concerning *the radical* evil in human beings.[21]

We have explained the evil in human beings as follows: anyone who is supposed to be able to be called a human being has to achieve a consciousness of himself. This demands nothing more than that he become conscious of the freedom that is involved in his choice of actions. This consciousness already arises simply by virtue of the fact that a human being learns to make the selection from the manifold that is demanded of him by the purely natural drive. When he does this he will be acting according to the *maxim of* self-interest, either obscurely or, if he possesses more understanding and engages in more reflection, clearly; and to that extent one can, with *Reinhold*,[22] attribute to him a selfish drive, which, however, he has made selfish only through his own freely chosen maxim. For the purely natural drive is by no means a selfish or blameworthy drive; instead, as we shall see in due course, the satisfaction of this drive is itself a duty. It is easy for a human being to remain at this level, for nothing drives him any further, and there is no necessity for him to reflect on his higher predispositions [IV, 199].

---

[21] See *RBR*, pp. 69ff. (*AA* 6: 19ff.).
[22] See Reinhold, *Versuch einer neuen Theorie des menschlichen Vorstellungsvermögens*, pp. 571ff.

If only we had said that a human being *can* remain at this level if he wants to do so, then this claim would merit no further thought. We would have made a purely problematic claim. But how did we arrive at the categorical and positive claim that though it may not be necessary, it is nevertheless to be expected that a human being will remain at this level? What are we really asserting here, and what *positive* element are we tacitly presupposing?

What we are presupposing is that a human being will do nothing that is not absolutely necessary and will do nothing that he is not forced to do by virtue of his own being [*Wesen*]. We are therefore presupposing an original laziness or inertia [*Trägheit*] with respect both to reflection and to what follows therefrom: namely, acting in accordance with such a reflection. – This, therefore, would be a truly positive radical evil, and not simply a negative one, which is what it has seemed to be so far. This is also how it had to be. We had to have something positive simply in order to be able to explain what is negative.

And what entitles us to make such a presupposition? Is it merely a matter of experience? This is what *Kant* seems to assume,[23] despite the fact that he also makes the same inference we are about to make. Mere experience, however, would not entitle us to make such a universal presupposition. There must therefore be some rational ground for this claim, though one that does not yield necessity, since that would destroy freedom, but only explains this universal experience.

We have to ascribe to nature in general, as such, a force of inertia (*vis inertiae*). This follows from the concept of the efficacy of a free being, an efficacy that necessarily has to fall into time if it is to be perceivable; but this efficacy could not fall into time were it not posited as kept in check [*aufhalten*] by objects. To be sure, the concept of a force seems to stand in contradiction to inertia, but this concept is nevertheless real; what matters is simply that we grasp it correctly. – Nature as such, as not-I and as object in general, possesses only passivity, only being; it is what it is, and to that extent no active force whatsoever is to be ascribed to nature [IV, 200]. Simply in order to endure, however, nature possesses a quantum of tendency or force [sufficient] to *remain* what it is. If it did not have this tendency or force, then it would not endure for a single moment in its [present] shape; it would change constantly; it would not

[23] See *RBR*, p. 80 (*AA* 6: 32).

really have any shape at all and would not be what it is. If an opposing force now operates upon it, then it will necessarily resist this with all its force in order to remain what it is; and only now, through its relation to the opposing activity, does what was previously only inertia become an activity. The two concepts have been synthetically united, which is exactly what *a force of inertia* is supposed to mean.

From the point of view just indicated we ourselves are nothing more than nature. Our forces are forces of nature; and though these forces are animated by freedom, since the causality of nature came to an end with the drive, their direction is still absolutely none other than the direction that nature too would have taken had it been left to itself. Moreover, even the fact that we are occupying the indicated point of reflection must also be viewed as a consequence of the mechanism [of nature], since it is necessary that we occupy this point of reflection. Considered from every angle, therefore, we are nature. But what pertains to nature as a whole must also pertain to the human being insofar as he is nature: namely, a reluctance to leave his state, a tendency to remain on the habitual track.

(This is the only way to explain a universal human phenomenon and one that extends to all human acting: *the possibility of* habituation and the propensity to stick with that to which one is accustomed. Every human being, even the strongest and most active one, has his beaten path (if we may be permitted to use this vulgar but very telling expression), and he will have to fight against it his whole life long. This is the force of inertia of our own nature. Even the regularity and order of most human beings is nothing other than this propensity toward repose and toward what is habitual. It always requires some effort to tear oneself loose. Even if we succeed every once in a while and if the jolt we received continues to [IV, 201] reverberate, the human being still falls back soon enough into his habitual inertia, just as soon as he stops watching over himself.)

Let us consider a human being in the state we have just described. Since he is, in accordance with his original being [*Wesen*], free and independent of nature, even if he is not free in actuality, he always ought to tear himself loose from this state [of inertia]; and if one considers him to be absolutely free, then he is also *able* to do this. Before he can freely tear himself loose, however, he must first be free. But it is precisely his freedom itself that is fettered; the very force through which he is supposed to help himself is allied against him. No balance is established here; instead, there is [only] the weight of his nature [*Natur*], which is what holds him in check, and there is no counterweight from the side of the moral law. It is indeed true that a human being absolutely ought to step onto the other side of the scale and decide this conflict; and it is also true that he actually possesses within himself the force to give himself as much weight as is necessary, up to infinity, in order to outweigh his own inertia and that he can, at any moment, release this force from himself by putting pressure on himself, through sheer will. But how is he ever supposed to arrive at this act of willing, and how does he first become able to place such pressure on himself? Such a state [of willing] by no means emerges from the state he is in, which instead yields the opposite state, one that holds him in check and fetters him. It is also true that this initial impulse [*Anstoß*] is not supposed to emerge from his present state, nor can it do so, but instead it emerges absolutely from his self-activity. But where in his state is there a place from which he could produce this force? – Absolutely nowhere. If one views this matter in purely natural terms, then it is absolutely impossible that a human being should be able to help himself; he cannot improve at all in this way. Only a miracle could save him – a miracle, moreover, which he himself would have to perform. (Those who have claimed a *servum arbitrium*[24] and have characterized the human being as a stick and a block, unable to move himself from the place he occupies by means of his own force and therefore needing to be animated by some higher force, were entirely right; and they were also consistent, so long as what they were talking about was the *natural* human being, which is in fact what they were talking about) [IV, 202].

The true, inborn radical evil lying in human nature itself is therefore inertia or *laziness*, which infinitely reproduces itself through long habit and soon becomes a complete incapacity for what is good; and such radical evil can be explained quite well on this basis. As Kant very correctly says, human beings are by nature lazy.[25]

---

[24] Latin for "bonded will." See Martin Luther, *De servo arbitrio* (*On the Bondage of the Will*) (1525).
[25] See Immanuel Kant, *Idea for a Universal History with a Cosmopolitan Purpose*, Fourth Proposition, in Kant, *Political Writings*, ed. H. Reiss, 2nd edn (Cambridge: Cambridge University Press, 1991), p. 44 (*AA* 8: 21).

The first fruit of this laziness is *cowardice*, which is the second fundamental vice of human beings. Cowardice is that laziness that prevents us from asserting *our freedom* and *self-sufficiency* in our interaction *with others*. Everyone has sufficient courage in the face of someone of whose weakness he is already firmly convinced; but if one lacks such conviction, if one encounters someone whom one suspects to possess greater strength – of whatever kind one imagines – than one possesses oneself, then one is terrified to apply the force that might be needed in order to maintain one's self-sufficiency and therefore yields. – This is the only explanation for slavery among human beings, both physical and moral, the only explanation for submissiveness and parroting. I am terrified by the physical exertion required for resistance, and therefore I subjugate my body; I am terrified by the difficulty of thinking for myself that is inflicted upon me by someone who seems to me to be making bold and complicated claims, and therefore I prefer to believe in his authority in order thereby to rid myself of his demands all the more quickly. (There are always human beings who want to dominate in such situations, and we have seen the reason for this above. These are the few and the stronger. They possess a robust and daring character. But why do individuals who would, when united, be stronger than they are subjugate themselves to such human beings? This happens as follows: the trouble that would result from resisting those who are stronger seems to such individuals to be more painful than the slavery to which they subjugate themselves and within which they hope to be able to endure. The least exertion of force is far more painful to the ordinary human being than a thousand-fold suffering, and he would rather endure anything than act even once. In this manner he remains in a state of repose and becomes accustomed to it. This is similar to the case of the sailor who preferred to console himself with the hope that he might be able to bear up in hell rather than having had to improve himself in this life [IV, 203]. In hell he was merely supposed to suffer, whereas in this life he would have had to do something.)

In this state of subjugation, which he certainly does not enjoy, the coward consoles himself particularly by means of cunning and deceit; for the third fundamental vice of human beings, one that naturally arises from cowardice, is *falseness*. A human being is not quite so able to deny his concern for himself [*Selbstheit*] or to sacrifice it to someone else as he might pretend to be in order to avoid the trouble of having to defend it in open combat. He therefore says that he will do this, but he says this only in order to await a better opportunity to combat his oppressor when the latter is no longer paying any attention to him. All falseness, all lies, all spite and perfidy exist because there are oppressors; and anyone who subjugates others must be prepared for the same. – Only the coward is false. The courageous human being does not lie and is not false – because of his pride and strength of character, if not because of his virtue.

This is the image of the ordinary natural human being – of the ordinary one, I say, for the extraordinary human being, the one eminently favored by nature, possesses a robust character without being the least bit better with respect to morality. He is neither indolent nor cowardly nor false, but in his exuberance he tramples upon everything around him and becomes the lord and oppressor of those who prefer to be slaves.

Such a description may seem ugly and repugnant. Upon hearing this, however, one should not start in with the usual sighs or slanders concerning the imperfection of human nature. – The very fact that these traits appear to you to be so ugly is proof of humanity's nobility and sublimity. Do you find it equally ugly that the stronger animal eats the weaker one and that the weaker one outwits the stronger one? Certainly not, for you find this to be natural and in order. You feel differently in the case of human beings only because it is by no means possible for you to regard a human being as a mere product of nature, and because you are forced to think of a human [IV, 204] as a free and supersensible being, elevated high above all nature. Even the fact that a human being finds himself capable of vice indicates that he is destined for virtue. – For what would virtue be if it were not an actively engendered product of our own freedom, if it were not an elevation into a completely different order of things? – Finally, following the *account of these traits that has been provided here*, who could think that they are valid only for the *human* species, that they are first cast into human beings as something foreign by a malevolent demon, and that some other kind of *finite* rational being could be any different in this respect? These traits are not the result of any particular condition of our nature, but follow from the concept of finitude as such. One may think of cherubim and seraphim; and these may well be thought of as different from human beings in their further determinations, but not with respect to their basic traits. There is only one Holy One, and every creature is by nature necessarily unholy and impure and is able to elevate itself to morality only through its own freedom.

So how is a human being supposed to be helped, given his deeply rooted inertia that immobilizes the one force through which he is supposed to help himself? – What is it that is really missing? What is lacking is not the force, which he surely possesses, but the consciousness of this force and the stimulus to use it. For reasons that have already been stated, this stimulus cannot come from inside. As long as the stimulus in question is supposed to arise through natural means, and not through a miracle, then it has to come from outside.

A human being could receive such a stimulus only through his understanding and through his entire theoretical power, which can surely be cultivated [*gebildet*]. The individual would have to see himself in his contemptible shape and feel disgust toward himself; he would have to see exemplars who elevate him and provide him with an image of how he ought to be, who infuse him with respect, along with a desire to become worthy of respect himself. There is no other path toward cultivation. This path provides us with what was previously missing: consciousness and a stimulus. It goes without saying, however, that the improvement and the elevation always depend upon one's own freedom [IV, 205]. Anyone who in this case still does not make use of his own freedom cannot be helped.

From where, however, are these external stimuli within humanity supposed to come? – Since each individual, regardless of his inertia, is always able to elevate himself above the latter, we may assume that among the large number of human beings a few really will have elevated themselves to morality. For those who have done this it will be a necessary end to influence their fellow human beings and to influence them in the manner described.

What we have just described is *positive religion*: institutions arranged by excellent human beings for the purpose of influencing others to develop their moral sense. Such institutions, by virtue of their age and their general use and utility, might also be invested with special authority, which may be very useful to those who need it. – First and foremost, however, this sort of authority is useful only to attract attention; for such institutions cannot have any other end – such as establishing faith on the basis of authority and blind obedience – without making human beings at root immoral, as was shown earlier.

In the case of these human beings in whom the moral sense – which they may well not have encountered in any of their contemporaries – has developed from inside, through a true miracle and not as a result of any natural cause, it is, as we have seen, quite natural that they should have interpreted this miracle as brought about by a spiritual and intelligible being outside of themselves; and if they understood "themselves" to mean *their empirical I*, then they were entirely correct. It is possible that this interpretation has endured right up to our present time. Indeed, when it is understood in the sense just indicated, this interpretation also possesses theoretical truth; moreover, even if it is not determined as precisely [as we have just determined it], it is still quite harmless – just *so long as it is not supposed to enforce any blind obedience*. As for belief in this interpretation, each person will deal with this in a manner consistent with his own convictions. Practically speaking, however, this is a matter toward which most human beings are utterly indifferent [IV, 206].

Second section of ethics in the proper sense of the term: The material content of the moral law, or systematic survey of our duties

§17
Introduction, or elucidation of our problem

We have to know what we are inquiring about; we have to draw up in advance some plan for answering our questions. This is the intent of the present section. First, however, let us recall some points that were previously established.

I

As we now know, "I have causality" means that what I propose as an end for myself is something that occurs in experience. We have seen that this harmony of perception and will is, when considered from the transcendental point of view, ultimately nothing other than the harmony of our empirical being, as determined through absolute spontaneity, with our original drive. If I determine myself to do something that is actually demanded by my original drive, then I, the I that is determined in time, am placed into harmony with myself, with the original I that is present without any consciousness thereof on my part. From this there arises a feeling of constraint; for I now feel myself to be a *whole*, and this feeling is a perception, as was explained in more detail above [IV, 207].

This original drive aims at many different things, for it is given to me for all eternity; all of my existence occurs within all eternity, and all my experience is nothing but an analysis of this same drive. According to what was said above, to be sure, this drive can be satisfied only gradually, through intermediary states, and this is true even in individual cases [of satisfying specific ends]. Even in individual cases the end of the original drive can be divided into a manifold by free reflection. (At every possible moment the original drive strives after something determinate = X, which is determined *by everything that preceded it*, as well as by its *own nature*. This determinate X, however, is a quantum, which absolutely free reflection can divide infinitely into a, b, and c; and a, in turn, can be divided into d, e, and f, and so forth.) Only in this manner does a manifold acting [*ein mannigfaltiges Handeln*] arise. Since, however, X as a whole (which is what is demanded by the original drive) is *possible*, then all the parts of X are also possible as well. Even in each individual case, several different actions are *possible*. – In order for something to ensue, however, it must not merely be *possible*, but I must also determine myself to act in this way. Nothing occurs through my drive that I do not will; and among everything that is possible, nothing occurs but what I will.

II

Let us dwell a bit upon the concept of the manifold of what is possible in this case, and let us consider it purely as such – i.e., ignoring the relationship of these [possible] actions to one another and not asking whether they exclude one another or contain and comprehend one another as parts of themselves, since such questions that do not yet pertain to our inquiry. Among this manifold of actions that are possible in a particular case, there is absolutely only one (a determinate part of this manifold) that is dutiful, and everything else is contrary to duty. (In passing, one should note that what is commanded *always* lies within the sphere of what is possible, for it lies within the sphere of what is demanded by the original drive, since the moral law is itself based on the original drive. Something impossible is never a duty, and a duty is never impossible.) [IV, 208]

Which of these possible ways of acting is the one that duty demands? In the previous section we answered this question by referring to an inner feeling within our conscience. In every case, whatever is confirmed by this inner feeling is a duty; and this inner feeling never errs so long as we simply pay heed to its voice. This would suffice for actual acting, and nothing more would be required in order to make possible such acting. The educator of the people [*Volkslehrer*], for example, can leave it at that and can conclude his instruction in morals at this point.

This, however, is not sufficient for the purposes of science. We must either be able to determine *a priori* what conscience will approve of in general, or else we must concede that ethics [*eine Sittenlehre*], as a real [*reelle*], applicable science, is impossible.

Let us now view this same matter from another angle. Feeling decides. This decision on the part of feeling is surely based on some law that is *grounded in reason*, a law that cannot, however, be an object of consciousness so long as one continues to occupy the standpoint of ordinary human understanding. To do so would involve a contradiction, since all that occurs in [ordinary] consciousness is a feeling, which is how this law manifests itself in a specific case. From the transcendental point of view, however, it must certainly be possible to discover this law [of reason]. Instruction of the purely popular sort remains at the standpoint of ordinary consciousness, and thus nothing that lies within the transcendental standpoint is present for this sort of instruction. Instruction becomes philosophical only insofar as it elevates itself to the transcendental standpoint.

Reason is thoroughly determined; therefore, everything that lies within the sphere of reason, and this includes the system of conscience, which manifests itself through feelings, must also be determined. – Later on we will also find external grounds for the necessity of this law of reason upon which the feelings of conscience are based. Once we have exhibited this law we will at the same time have an answer *a priori* (that is, prior to any immediate decision on the part of conscience) to the question, What is our duty? [IV, 209].

III

One could give a preliminary answer to the above question, an answer that is, to be sure, tautological, and hence not decisive, but which still might point us toward the path of further investigation.

The final end of the moral law is absolute independence and self-sufficiency, not merely with respect to our will, for the latter is always independent, but also with respect to our entire being. This goal is unachievable, but there is still a constant and uninterrupted process of approximation to this goal. Accordingly, there must be a constant, uninterrupted series of actions by means of which one draws nearer and nearer to this goal, a series that starts from the initial standpoint occupied by each person. In each case, conscience can approve only of those actions that lie in this series. One can think of this with the help of the image of a straight line. Only the points lying along this line can be approved, and absolutely nothing that lies outside it. – Our question can therefore be restated as follows: what are the actions that lie on the line we have described? – In order to facilitate some insight into the overall connections [between the various steps of our inquiry], I will add the following: our inquiry picks up at the very point we dropped it at the end of Part II, which dealt with *the applicability* of the ethical principle. At that point we were quite unable to see how we could determine *a priori what* our duty is; we possessed no criterion at all for determining this, beyond the approval or disapproval of our conscience *following* the deed. Doing our duty would therefore have had to have been a matter of trial and error, and the only way we could have acquired any moral principles would have been through long experience, involving many false steps. In such a case the moral law, understood as a properly practical law that determines our actions, would nearly have fallen away completely and would have become, for the most part, a mere law of adjudication [*Beurteilung*]. – In the first section of Part Three we indeed discovered such a criterion, namely, the feeling of conscience; and with this we guaranteed the practical applicability of the moral law. This is sufficient for the purposes of acting in the course of life, but not for the purposes of science [IV, 210]. The question before us now is whether there is an even higher principle – if not within consciousness, then at least within philosophy – , a unitary ground of these feelings themselves. Our investigation has proceeded steadily along its path in a regular manner, and we are therefore entitled to hope that we can now extend it even into areas we were previously unable to penetrate.

IV

Considered in terms of their *matter* or *content* [*Materie*], which actions lie in that series of actions that approaches [the end of] absolute self-sufficiency? This is how we have formulated our current problem. Regarding this, it was shown earlier (§ 15, subsection v) that the actions in question are those in which one treats each object according to its final end. – Let us briefly summarize what was said there: a determinate object is posited only in consequence of some determinate limitation of a drive; it is posited in order to explain this limitation. If the drive itself, *qua* drive, is posited (as a longing or desiring) and is referred to the object [of this longing or desiring], then one obtains [the concept of] what the I wants to bring about in the object, [the concept of] what the I might use the object for; i.e., one obtains [the concept of] the thing's original, determinate end – which is by no means the same thing as an end one has arbitrarily posited for the object. It follows from the preceding remark, however, that every arbitrary end is at the same time an original one; or, to put it more clearly, it follows that I am at least unable to achieve any end that is not demanded by an original drive. But it is quite possible for me to apprehend only a part of my original drive when it aims at an object, and in that case, I grasp only a portion of the thing's purposiveness. If, on the other hand, I apprehend my entire drive in relation to this object, then I have apprehended the total purposiveness of the thing or its final end.

V

Let us reflect upon the meaning of what was just said. I am supposed to apprehend the *totality* of my drive. Every totality is complete and hence limited [IV, 211]. What is claimed, therefore, is an original limitedness [*Beschränktheit*] of the drive.

One should note that what we are talking about here is a limitedness of the *drive* itself, and not any limitation of its power to realize that for which it is striving. We are saying that the drive, as an original drive, is unable to aim at certain things.

What kind of limitedness could this be? It could certainly not be any limitedness of the drive with respect to its form, for, as we know, the aim of the drive is absolute self-sufficiency. This goal, however, is infinitely distant and can never be achieved; and thus the drive itself can never come to an end. The limitedness in question would therefore have to be a material one: the drive would have to be unable to strive after certain things.

Now this limitedness is supposed to be an original and necessary limitedness, grounded in reason itself, and by no means an empirical and contingent limitedness.

There is, however, no other kind limitedness of reason through itself than that limitedness that follows simply from the fact that the rational being is an I. The original limitedness of the drive, the limitedness grounded in reason itself, would therefore be the limitedness that proceeds from I-hood itself; and the drive would be apprehended in its totality when one assumes absolutely no other limitedness of the same, beyond, that is, its previously indicated limitedness by virtue of I-hood itself.

There can be no drive within the I to cease being an I, to become a not-I; for in that case the I would aim at its own annihilation, which is contradictory. Conversely, moreover, any limitedness of the drive which does not follow immediately from I-hood is not an original limitedness, but is a limitedness that we have inflicted upon ourselves by means of our incomplete reflection. We have allowed ourselves to be satisfied with less than we could have demanded.

In short, the aim of the drive, when apprehended in its totality, is the absolute self-sufficiency of the I as such. The way to discover the material content of the moral law is by synthetically uniting the concept of I-hood and the concept of absolute self-sufficiency. I am supposed to be a self-sufficient I; [IV, 212] this is *my* final end. I am supposed to use things in any way that will increase this self-sufficiency; that is *their* final end. With this we have discovered a level path for advancing into the inquiry before us. All we have to do is provide a complete presentation of the conditions of I-hood and show how these conditions are related to the drive for self-sufficiency and how this drive is determined by these conditions: by doing this we will have provided an exhaustive account of the content of the moral law.

§18

Systematic elucidation of the conditions of I-hood in their relationship to the drive for absolute self-sufficiency

I

The (reflecting) I must find itself as an I; it must, as it were, be given to itself. As we have indicated earlier, when the I reflects upon itself in this way it finds itself as possessing a drive, which is posited as a natural drive precisely because it is found only as something given and because no self-activity reveals itself when the I finds itself in this way.

As the object of a reflection, what is found is necessarily a finite and limited quantum. If the natural drive, which in itself is a single unity, is divided by free reflection in the manner indicated (in the previous §), there then arises a multiplicity of drives, which, since this is a finite multiplicity or manifold, constitutes a complete system of drives. I cannot view these drives – or rather, this drive – as *something foreign*, but must relate it to myself; I must locate it, as an accident, in the very same substance that at the same time also freely thinks and wills [IV, 213].

Even though I have to refer this drive to myself and posit it as *my* drive, it still remains in a certain respect something objective for *me*, to the extent that I am *a genuinely free and self-sufficient I*. What ensues from this drive is a mere longing, a longing that I can freely satisfy or not satisfy and that therefore always lies outside of me and below me, since I am free. What ensues for me, as a free intellect, is simply the cognition that this determinate longing is present within me. – As a force, as a stimulus, etc., this longing remains something foreign to me. If, however, I freely determine myself to satisfy this longing, it then becomes "mine" in a completely different sense: it becomes mine insofar as I am free and insofar as I am freely posited and determined. In this case I appropriate this longing not merely ideally, not merely by means of theoretical cognition, but I appropriate it in reality, by means of self-determination. Even from the viewpoint of ordinary consciousness I consider myself to be twofold, I divide myself from myself, I berate myself, etc.

(In the latter case I myself posit me, and I am nothing but what I make of myself. This extends to the point that I do not really appropriate or make my own anything that I find within myself in the manner indicated above, but I appropriate only what is present within me in consequence of an act of self-determination. Even in ordinary life we make an important distinction between those aspects of ourselves that are part of our personality but are not present as a result of freedom – e.g., birth, health, genius, etc. – and what we are as a result of freedom, as was expressed, for example, by the poet who wrote, "*genus, et proavi, et quae non fecimus ipsi, vix ea* nostra *puto*".)[1]

---

[1] Ovid, *Metamorphoses*, XIII: 140–141. "Race and ancestors, and those things that we did not make ourselves, I scarcely consider to be our own." This same passage was cited by Kant in section IV of Book One of *RBR*, p. 86 (*AA* 6: 40), which is presumably where Fichte encountered it.

What is demanded by the original drive is always supposed to occur within experience if I freely determine myself to this end. This is here the case: the natural drive belongs to the original drive. What will ensue if I determine myself to satisfy this drive? Answering this question will also help to clarify the distinction we just made [between those parts of ourselves that are products of freedom and those that are not].

The natural drive is a mere driving [*Treiben*] on the part of nature, and the causality of this drive comes to an end exactly at the point where I posit a drive as my own. The latter drive, since it ensues from self-determination, is truly *my* driving; it is grounded within me as a free being. [IV, 214] To say that this [natural drive] can be encountered within experience means that I feel it as a tendency of nature to exercise causality on itself.

All of my force and efficacious action within nature is nothing other than the efficacious action of nature (of nature within me) upon itself (upon nature outside of me).

My nature, however, stands under the sway of freedom, and nothing can ensue through the former unless it is determined through the latter. In the case of a plant, the nature of the plant operates immediately upon itself (upon nature outside the plant); in my case, however, nature operates only by passing through a freely designed concept. To be sure, everything that is required for a successful outcome on the part of nature is given prior to the self-determination through freedom; yet in this case nature by itself is by no means sufficient to produce an efficacious action. What is required on the part of the subject for a successful outcome is not given prior to the [free act of] self-determination. Instead, this is given through and by means of the act of self-determination, and with this we have assembled everything needed in order to produce an efficacious action. Self-determination provides the force of my nature with the requisite principle, that prime mover that my nature itself lacks; for this reason, its driving is from now on *my* driving, as a genuine I, which has made itself into what it is.

This is the first and most important point, upon which our entire argument rests. Now we need only remind ourselves of something with which we are already familiar and that has previously been proven: all of nature is posited as a result of reflection; it is posited necessarily, as contained in space and as filling space, and hence as matter [*Materie*]. Since we have posited the system of our natural drives as a product of nature and as a part of nature, we necessarily must also posit it as matter.

This system of our natural drives becomes a material body. The driving of nature is concentrated and contained in our material body. This driving possesses no causality in itself, but obtains its causality immediately as a result of our will. For the reason stated above our will becomes an immediate cause in our body. We only have to will, and what we have willed ensues in our body [IV, 215]. To employ an expression I used earlier, the body contains those first points from which all causality issues. – Unlike everything outside our body, our body is [already] subject to our power, without first having to be brought under it. It alone has already been placed under our power by nature, without any free assistance from us.

Our body is engaged in sensing [*empfindend*]; that is to say, the natural drive that is concentrated within it is necessarily posited as our own, as belonging to us; and, everything that follows from this, including the satisfaction and non-satisfaction of the drive, is also accessible to us (and, as we know, this alone provides the basis for our entire system of sensory cognition). The body, moreover, is immediately set in motion by the will and can act causally upon nature. Such a body, a body determined in precisely this way, is a condition of I-hood, since such a body follows directly from that reflection upon itself through which alone the I becomes an I.

From this we can draw the following further implications:

All possible acting is, with respect to its material content, acting that is demanded by the natural drive. This is because all our acting occurs within nature; [only] in nature is our acting possible, and only in nature can it become actual for us; yet external nature as a whole is present for us only in consequence of the natural drive. The natural drive addresses itself to me only through my body, and this drive is realized in the world outside me only through the causality of my body. The body is the instrument of all of our perceptions, and hence of all cognition, since all cognition is based on perception. It is also the instrument of all our causality. This *relationship* is a condition for I-hood. The natural drive aims at preservation, cultivation, and well-being – in short, at the perfection of our body – and does so just as certainly as it is a drive and is aimed at itself (since it itself is our body, inasmuch as the latter is an embodiment of this drive). The natural drive, however, extends no further than this, for nature cannot elevate itself above itself. The end of nature is nature itself. *Our* nature has our nature as its final end; but our nature is contained and enclosed in our body, and hence the sole end of nature – *our* nature and *all* nature – is only the body.

My highest drive is the drive for absolute self-sufficiency. I can approach or approximate this goal only by means of acting [IV, 216], but I can act only by means of my body. A condition for the satisfaction of this [highest] drive – that is to say, a condition for all morality – is therefore the preservation and maximal perfection of the body. Conversely, the sole end of my conscious acting is supposed to be self-sufficiency; morality is supposed to be the sole end of my acting. Hence I have to subordinate the former end to the latter: I must preserve and cultivate my body purely as an instrument of moral acting, but not as a end unto itself. The sole end of all my care for my body absolutely ought to be and must be to transform this body into a suitable instrument of morality and to preserve it as such.

In this manner we obtain the following three material commands of ethics. The first of these commands is a negative one: our body absolutely may not be treated as a final end; i.e., it absolutely may not become an object of enjoyment for enjoyment's sake. The second command is a positive one: to the extent that it is possible, the body ought to be cultivated in a manner that will make it suitable for all the possible ends of freedom. – Mortification of sensations and desires, weakening of force is absolutely contrary to duty. The third command is a limitative one: every enjoyment that cannot be related, with sincere conviction, to our efforts to cultivate our body in a suitable manner [in order to make it an instrument of freedom] is impermissible and contrary to the law. It is absolutely contrary to the moral way of thinking to care for our body if we are not convinced that we are thereby cultivating and preserving it for dutiful acting; i.e., it is absolutely contrary to the moral way of thinking to do this for any reason other than for the sake of conscience and with the latter in mind. – Eat and drink in order to honor God.[2] A person to whom such an ethics appears austere and painful is beyond help, for there is no other ethics. –

To facilitate our survey, one should note that the condition of I-hood that was just indicated is a condition for the I's *causality*, a causality that is demanded by the moral law. It will become evident that there is also a second condition [for the possibility of the I], one concerning the substantiality of the subject of morality, as well as a third condition,

[2] 1 Cor. 10:31.

one concerning a certain, necessary reciprocal interaction [*Wechselwirkung*] of the latter. This will furnish us with an *external* proof that we have provided an exhaustive account of the conditions of I-hood [IV, 217]. The *internal* proof of the same follows from the systematic connection or coherence of what is to be presented here.

II

The preceding investigation commenced with the claim that the I must find itself as an I. The present investigation begins with the same claim; the only difference is that, whereas we previously attended to the passivity of the I in this act of self-reflection, that is, to the object of reflection, we will now be attending to the activity of the I, to the subjective pole of this same act of reflection. In order to produce freely an inner image or copy [*nachzubilden*] of what is given, the I must possess the power of reflection. We have called this kind of activity on the part of the I the "ideal activity" of the same. It is immediately clear that this is a condition of I-hood. An I is necessarily an intellect.

But how is the drive for self-sufficiency, or the moral law, related to this determination of the I?

The moral law addresses itself to the intellect as such. I am supposed to draw ever nearer to self-sufficiency, and I am supposed to do this consciously and according to concepts. There is a moral law only insofar as I am an intellect, to the extent that I, as an intellect, promulgate the moral law, make it into a law or a principle. The entire being (the substance, the subsistence) of the moral law — and not just the causality of the same, which was the case when the being of the body was posited — is therefore conditioned by the intellect. Only if I am an intellect and only insofar as I am an intellect is there a moral law; the latter extends no further than the former, since the intellect is the vehicle of the moral law. A material subordination of the intellect to the moral law is therefore impossible (though a material subordination of the natural drive to the moral law was indeed possible). Though I may not give in to certain inclinations and pleasures because this runs counter to my duty, it is not the case that I must will not to cognize certain things because this might perhaps run counter to my duty.

Our highest end, however, is self-sufficiency (morality), and hence theoretical cognition is [IV, 218] formally subordinated to duty.

Cognition of my duty must be the final end of all my cognition, of all my thinking, and of all my inquiring. The following three moral laws follow from this:

1. Negative: never subordinate your theoretical reason as such [to anything higher], but continue to inquire with absolute freedom, without taking into account anything outside your cognition. (Do not set for yourself in advance some goal that you want to reach – for from where might you obtain such a goal?)
2. Positive: cultivate your power of cognition just as much as you are able. Learn, think, and inquire just as much as you possibly can.
3. Limitative: but, with respect to its form, refer all of your reflecting to your duty. While engaged in reflecting, always remain clearly conscious of this end. – Inquire from duty rather than from mere, empty curiosity or simply in order to keep yourself busy. – Do not think in a certain way in order thereby to discover precisely *this* or *that* to be your duty – for how could you know your duties in advance of your cognition? – but only in order to cognize *what* your duty is.

III

We have already established elsewhere (namely, in my *Natural Right*[3]) that the I can posit itself only as an individual. It follows that consciousness of individuality would [also] be a condition of I-hood. Ethics lies higher than any other particular philosophical science (hence, it also lies higher than the doctrine of right). Accordingly, the proof [that individuality is a condition for I-hood] must here be conducted on the basis of some higher principle.

(a) Everything that is an object of reflection is necessarily limited, and it becomes limited simply by becoming an object of reflection. The I is supposed to become the object of a reflection; hence it is necessarily limited. – The I, however, is characterized by a free activity as such; hence this free activity must also be limited. For a free activity to be limited means that a certain quantum of free activity is posited over against or in opposition to free activity as such or in general, and to this extent it is posited in opposition to another free activity. In short

---

[3] *FNR*, §§ 1–4, pp. 18–52 (*SW* III: 17–56; *GA* I/3: 3299–3360).

[IV, 219], the I is absolutely unable to appropriate to itself any free activity unless the latter is a quantum, and – given that every quantum is necessarily limited – the I is therefore unable to appropriate to itself any free activity without at the same time positing, along with this act of thinking [of its own activity], another free activity, one which, to this extent, does not belong to the I.

(b) This alone would imply nothing whatsoever regarding the positing of individuality, for it could well be possible that the I posits this free activity outside of its own free activity only through *ideal* activity, as a free activity that is merely *possible* – perhaps as a free activity that is possible for the I itself, even if, for the moment, it might voluntarily abstain from this activity; or it might also be a free activity that is possible for other free beings, something that occurs often enough in the course of consciousness. Whenever I ascribe an action to myself, I *thereby* remove this action from all [other] free beings – but not necessarily from all [other actual] determinate free beings, but perhaps only from possible beings that one might perhaps be able to imagine.

(c) The following point, however, is decisive: I cannot originally determine myself by means of free ideal activity but must *find* myself as a determinate object; and since I am an I only insofar as I am free, I must *find* myself *to be free*; I must be given to myself as free – as strange as that may seem at first blush. This is because I can posit something *possible* only by contrasting it with something actual with which I am already familiar. All mere possibility is based upon abstraction from some familiar actuality. All consciousness therefore begins with something actual – a fundamental proposition of any real philosophy [*einer reellen Philosophie*] – and this applies to consciousness of freedom as well.

In order to facilitate insight into the overall connection [between the preceding propositions], the following should be noted: – [1.] Previously, [that is, in Part III, section 1] the proposition, "I find myself as an object," meant "I find myself as a natural drive, as a product of nature and as a part of nature." It is obvious that I have to reflect in order to find this, and thus that I have to be an intellect. We are not, however, conscious of this reflection as it occurs; we do not become conscious of it at all without a new act of reflection. I am nevertheless supposed to ascribe this natural drive to *myself*; moreover, as we saw in the first section of this §, I am supposed to posit this drive as something that does indeed belong to me, even though it does not properly constitute *me*. Which *I* is it then to which I am supposed to appropriate the natural drive? [IV, 220] [This natural drive is to be ascribed to] the genuinely substantial I, not [to] the intellect as such; and we have just seen the reason for this. Hence [it is to be ascribed] to the *freely acting* I. – Just as surely as I am supposed to find myself – both in general and in particular – to be a product of nature, I also have to find myself to be freely active; for the former discovery is impossible without the latter. The former is conditioned by the latter. And, since I simply have to find myself, it follows that I have to find myself as freely active. What can this mean, and how is it possible?

First of all, I cannot find, as something given, the genuinely real [act of] self-determination, the one that occurs by means of spontaneity; instead, this is something I have to give to myself. It would be an utter contradiction to say that this could be given to me. It is therefore only by means of ideal activity that I could find a certain self-determination, that is, only by copying [*Nachbildung*] something that is present without any help from me. – [2.] To say, "my self-determination is present without any help from me," can mean only that it is present as a *concept*, or, in short, that I am summoned [*aufgefordert*] to determine myself in this way. Just as surely as I understand this summons, I also think of my self-determination as something given in this summons; and I am given to myself as free in the concept of this summons. Only in this way does the postulate set forth previously make any sense.

As surely as I comprehend this summons, I also ascribe to myself a determinate sphere for my freedom, though it does not follow that I immediately make any use of this sphere and fill it up. If I fail to comprehend the summons, no consciousness will arise; despite the fact that all the conditions for such finding are present, I do not yet find myself – though I might find myself at some other time. Precisely because I am free, [the presence of] all these conditions does not compel me to reflect; instead, I still reflect with absolute spontaneity. If, however, these conditions were not present, then I would not be able to reflect, despite all my spontaneity.

(d) I cannot comprehend this summons to self-activity without ascribing it to an actual being outside of myself, a being that wanted to communicate to me a concept: namely, the concept of the action that is demanded [of me], [IV, 221] and hence a being capable of [grasping] the concept of a concept. A being of this sort, however, is a rational being, a being that posits itself as an I; and hence it is an I. (Here lies the sole sufficient reason for inferring that there is a rational cause outside of us – and not simply because we can conceive of the influence of such a being, for this is always possible. See my *Natural Right*.)[4] It is a condition of self-consciousness, of I-hood, to assume that there is an actual rational being outside of oneself.

I posit myself over against or in opposition to this rational being, and I posit it over against myself; *this*, however, means that I posit myself, as an individual, in relationship to this other rational being, and I posit the latter in relationship to myself. It is therefore a condition of I-hood that one posit oneself as an individual.

(e) It can thus be proven strictly *a priori* that a rational being does not become rational in an isolated state, but that at least *one* individual outside it must be assumed, another individual who elevates this being to freedom. But, as we will soon see in more detail, beyond the influence of this *one*, absolutely necessary individual, we cannot demonstrate [the necessity] of any additional influences, nor of several [other] individuals.

From what has been deduced there already follows a limitation of the drive toward self-sufficiency and hence a more detailed material determination of morality, and now we wish to provide a provisional account of the latter. My I-hood, along with my self-sufficiency in general, is conditioned by the freedom of the other. It follows that my *drive to self-sufficiency* absolutely cannot aim at annihilating the *condition of its own possibility*, that is, the freedom of the other. Now I am purely and simply supposed to act only in accordance with the drive for self-sufficiency and by no means in accordance with any other stimulus. This limitation of the drive [for self-sufficiency] therefore contains within itself an absolute prohibition against disturbing the freedom of the other, a command to consider the other as self-sufficient, and absolutely not to use him as a means for my own ends. (The natural drive was subordinated to the drive for self-sufficiency. The theoretical power is not materially subordinated to the latter drive, but neither is the drive to self-sufficiency materially subordinated to the theoretical power. That to which the drive to self-sufficiency is subordinated is the freedom of the other. I am not allowed to be self-sufficient at the expense of the other's freedom.)

---

[4] *FNR*, § 3, pp. 29–39 (*SW*, III: 19–40; *GA* I/3: 340–348).

(f) The mere fact that I have posited even *one* individual outside of myself means that, among all the free actions that are possible, several have become impossible for me: namely, all of those that are conditions of the freedom I ascribe to the other. Moreover, even as I continue along a course of acting, I must constantly, in accordance with the concept of freedom, make some selection from among all of the actions that still remain possible for me. According to our presupposition, however, the entire sphere that is excluded from [the sphere of] my own freedom is, so to speak, occupied by [other] possible individuals, even if it is not occupied by actual ones; and from this presupposition it also follows that I determine *my individuality further* through each action – [IV, 222].

This is an important concept, which I will now explain more clearly and which resolves a major difficulty associated with the doctrine of freedom.

Properly speaking, who am I? I.e., what kind of individual am I? And what is the reason for my being *who* I am? To this question, I respond as follows: from the moment I become conscious, I am *what I freely make myself to be, and this is who I am because this is what I make of myself.* – At each moment of my existence, my being is through freedom, if not with respect to its conditions, then at least with respect to its *ultimate* determination. This being limits in turn the possibility of what I can be at some future moment (because I am this at the present moment, there are some things I cannot be at some future moment). Among everything that still remains *possible* at some future moment, however, the possibility I will choose depends once again upon freedom. My individuality, however, is determined through all of this, and in this way I become, materially speaking [*materialiter*], the one who I am.

Under the present presupposition, however, – namely, that there is only one individual outside of me and that I am affected by only a single free influence – my first state, which is, as it were, the root of my individuality, is not determined through my freedom [IV, 223], but through my connection with another rational being. What I become or do not become from this point on, however, depends purely and simply and completely on me alone. At every moment I have to choose among several things, but there is no reason outside of me why I have not chosen any of the other things that are possible.

(g) There could, of course, be *several* individuals outside of me who influence me. As we have already seen, it cannot be demonstrated *a priori* that this is the way things have to be, but we still have to prove that things at least *can* be this way.

In any case, as we have seen, I am required by virtue of the very essence of freedom itself to limit myself every time I act freely, thus keeping open the possibility that other possible free beings might act freely as well. Nothing prevents these free beings from being actual. From this provisional consideration of the matter it seems that such beings could actually exist without any harm to my freedom, which had to be limited whether such other free beings were actual or not.

Can they, however, be actual *for me*? I.e., can I perceive them as actual beings, and if so, how can I perceive them? This question could be easily answered on the basis of the principles stated above: they can exercise an immediate influence upon me, as one free being acting upon another; they can summon me to free activity.

It is, however, by no means necessary that there occur any immediate influence upon me. It is also possible that all that occurs is an efficacious acting upon nature [on the part of these other free beings]; and yet I can still infer, simply from the character of this efficacious acting, the existence of a rational being – *once I have merely acquired the concept of actual rational beings outside me*. It would not be possible to infer this originally. The way of acting efficaciously upon mere nature to which we are here referring is that through which a product of art or an artifact [*Kunstprodukt*] comes into being. Such an artifact exhibits the concept of a concept, which is what was previously identified as the criterion of a rational being outside me. This is because the end of a product of art, unlike that of a product of nature, does not lie in itself, but lies outside it. An artifact is always an instrument, a means toward something else. Its concept is something that is not present in mere intuition but something that can only be thought, and it is thus *merely* a concept [IV, 224]. The person who manufactured the art product, however, had to have thought this concept that he wanted to present; hence he necessarily had a concept of this concept. As surely as I cognize something as a product of art, I have to posit some actually existing rational being as the originator of the same. This is not the case with a product of nature; to be sure, there is a concept present in this case [as well]; but one cannot establish the presence of the concept of this concept, unless one perhaps presupposes it to be present in advance in a creator of the world.

I said, "as surely as I recognize it to be a product of art." This, however, is possible only on the condition that I am already thinking of a rational being outside of me, an assumption that is by no means a consequence of the perception of a product of art – which would amount to a circular explanation – but is instead a consequence of the summons to free action described above.

Such an inference is valid from the point of view of ordinary consciousness, which explains a perception within us by means of the presence of a thing outside us. What is assumed from the viewpoint of ordinary consciousness, however, must itself be explained from the transcendental viewpoint; and from the transcendental point of view it is not permissible to begin with something outside us; instead, what is supposed to be outside us must itself first be explained on the basis of something within us. We must therefore address the higher question: how do we first arrive at the assumption that artifacts or products of art exist outside us?

Everything that is supposed to be outside us is posited in consequence of a limitation of the drive. This also holds true for the product of art, insofar as it is an object at all. But what is the origin of the particular determination of the latter? Why is it posited precisely as an artifact? This question allows us to infer that there must be a particular and characteristic limitation of the drive [in this case]. – In short, our being is limited by an object as such; or better still, we infer an object as such from some limitation of our *being*, but the drive can perhaps aim at the modification of this object [IV, 225]. In the present case, however, what we are dealing with is not simply a limitation of our *being*, but also a limitation of our *becoming*: we inwardly feel that our acting is being repulsed. In this case, even our drive toward acting is limited, and from this we infer that there is *freedom* outside of us. (This point is expressed very well by *Schelling*, in the *Philosophical Journal*, Vol. 4, p. 281, § 13, where he writes: "Where my *moral* power encounters resistance, there can no longer be *nature*. I shudder and stop. I hear the warning: here is *humanity*! I *am not permitted* to proceed any farther.")[5]

---

[5] Friedrich Wilhelm Joseph Schelling, "Neue Deduction des Naturrechts," *Philosophisches Journal einer Gesellschaft Teutscher Gelehrten* 4/4 (1796), § 13, in Schelling, *Ausgewählte Werke. Schriften von 1794–1798* (Darmstadt: Wissenschaftliche Buchgesellschaft, 1975), p. 129. See too the English translation by Fritz Marti, "New Deduction of Natural Right," in Schelling, *The Unconditional in Human Knowledge: Four Early Essays (1794–1796)* (Lewisburg, PA: Bucknell University Press, 1980), p. 13.

As we have just seen, something of this sort can indeed occur. – If it does occur, then I am limited still further than I am limited merely through the fact of I-hood; for as we have shown, this new limitation is not contained in I-hood [as such]. – When this occurs, I am no longer merely a rational being in general, which I could be if there were only a single individual outside of me and if this individual had manifested itself only once in relationship to me; instead, I am [now] a *particular* rational being. This particular limitation cannot be derived *a priori* from the universal one, since if it could, then it would not be a particular limitation, which would contradict our assumption. This particular limitation is the foundation of what is merely *empirical*, though even this must, with respect to its possibility, still be grounded *a priori*. – This [particular] limitedness is, to be sure, an original limitedness, and one should therefore by no means think of it as something that first occurs within time. Nevertheless, there is a certain sense in which it does arise within time, as we will now see.

The propositions that have now been established allow one to conclude the following: individuality can also be determined in the further course of its development, and determined not only through freedom but also through original limitedness; the latter, however, cannot be deduced but is a particular limitedness, and in this respect it is for us, viewed from the standpoint of experience, something *contingent*. – This *can* be the situation, and a pure philosophy must be content to leave it at that. If such a philosophy deals with a science that is influenced by this presupposition [of a particular limitedness of the I], then any inferences it draws from this presupposition must be put forward as *conditional* assertions. Ethics is just such a science, and its material portion thus includes something conditional. If we renounce pure philosophy and permit ourselves to appeal to facts, then we can say: "This *is* the situation [IV, 226]. – I cannot be nor can I become everything; nor am I permitted to do so, since there are several others who are free as well."

I am originally limited, not only formally, by virtue of I-hood, but also materially, through something that does not necessarily pertain to I-hood. There are certain points beyond which I should not proceed with my freedom, and this *ought-not* [*Nichtsollen*] reveals itself to me immediately. I explain to myself these points [beyond which I ought not to proceed] by appealing to the presence of other free beings and their free effects in the sensible world.

(h) In embracing such a theory we seem to be caught up in a contradiction and driven to a very dangerous conclusion. I wish to deal with this issue, in part in order to promote clarity, and in part because this will settle a difficult philosophical dispute. This will also serve to clarify the doctrine of freedom, upon which everything in ethics depends.

The free actions of others are supposed to lie originally within me, as border points of my own individuality; hence, to express this in popular terms, these free actions are supposed to be predestined from all eternity and are by no means first determined in time. But does this not abolish my freedom? By no means, so long as how I will respond to these free actions of others is not determined in advance; and, according to everything that has been said so far, I still retain this freedom to choose among all the courses of action that are possible. Let us now lift ourselves to a higher point of view. The others in the sensible world, those upon whom *I* exercise an influence, are also rational beings, and their perception of *my influence* on them is predestined *for them*, just as my perception of *their influence* on me is predestined *for me*. *My* actions are not predestined for me; I perceive them as consequences of my own absolute self-determination. But for all the others who live in society with me these same actions are predestined, just as their actions are also not determined in advance for them, though they are for me. From this it follows that my own free actions are indeed determined in advance. But if this is the case, then how can there be any freedom? [IV, 227].

Here is where the matter stands: *predetermination* cannot be removed, for if it were removed then the reciprocal interaction of rational beings – and hence rational beings as such – could not be explained. Freedom, however, can also not be removed, for then rational beings themselves would cease to be.

The solution is not difficult. – *For me* (I will use this expression for the time being, simply in order to be able to express myself, in spite of the fact that an important remark still has to be made on this subject) all the influences of free beings are determined *a priori*. But does one not recall the meaning of the term "*a priori*"? The *a priori* involves no time nor temporal sequence, no *one-after-another*, but everything *at once* (this seems to be how one has to express this point). Thus it is by no means determined that I make events follow one another in such and such a way in time, or that I attach one thing to a particular determinate individual series and another thing to another series. What is determined is *what* I will experience, but not *from whom* [this experience will come]. The others outside me remain free.

For others, the influences that [other] free beings would have upon them is certainly determined, and thus the influences that *I* in particular would have upon them was also determined for them. In truth, however, it was not determined that *I*, the same individual who was originally determined in such and such a manner, was supposed to be the one to exercise these influences. Had someone else exercised these influences [upon these others] before I did, then I would not have exercised them; and had I not exercised them, someone else would have exercised them later than me; and if these others had freely made themselves what I am, then no one at all would have exercised these influences on them. – Who am I, as such? It remains true that I am what I make myself to be. – Up to this point I have acted in such and such a manner, and as a result I am this and that: that is, I am the individual to whom the series of actions A, B, C, etc. pertains. From this moment onward there again lies ahead of me an infinite number of *predestined* actions, among which I can choose. Both the possibility and the actuality of all these actions are predestined; but it is by no means predestined that the precise action I choose is supposed to be attached to the entire series (that is, to actions A, B, C, etc.) that constitutes my individuality up to this point, and so on *ad infinitum*. What comes first are determinate points of individuality, and from then on an infinity lies ahead of each of these points [IV, 228]; and of all the individuals who are possible from this point on, the one that any individual will become is entirely up to the freedom of that individual.

My claim is therefore as follows: all free actions are predestined through reason for all eternity – i.e., outside of all time – , and with regard to perception every free individual is placed in harmony with these actions. For reason as a whole there is an infinite manifold of freedom and perception, which is, so to speak, shared by all individuals. The temporal sequence and the temporal content, however, are not predestined, for the sufficient reason that time is nothing eternal and pure but is merely a form of intuition for finite beings – and by "time" I here mean a point of time at which something happens – , and it is not predestined who will act in this way. The question that seemed so unanswerable thus resolves itself when one examines it carefully: predestination and freedom are perfectly united.

Any difficulties one might find in this solution are due solely to the basic error of all dogmatism, which makes being into something primary, and thus separates being and acting from each other (if, indeed, dogmatism recognizes acting at all) and allocates to each individual his entire being, independently of his action. To be sure, if one pursues this line of thinking with sufficient precision one thereby abolishes all freedom and all genuine acting. No human being in the world is able to *act* in any way other than the way he does act, even though he may very well be acting badly – given that he simply *is* this human being. Nothing is more true than this; indeed, this claim is a tautology. Yet he should precisely not be this human being, and he could also be an entirely different one; indeed, *there ought not to be such a human being in the world at all.* – Or does one imagine that a determinate person is supposed to be this person before he is this person, that his relationships and his destiny are determined from the day of his birth until his day of death, but not his acting? But what else are relationships and destinies if not the objective aspect of acting? If the latter depends upon freedom, then the former would surely have to depend upon freedom as well. I am, after all, only what I do. If I now think of myself in time [IV, 229], then I am not determined in a certain respect before I have acted in this respect. – To be sure, this theory of freedom will never be illuminating to anyone who cannot cure himself of the previously mentioned basic ill of dogmatism.[6]

IV

As has often been pointed out, self-sufficiency, which is our ultimate goal, consists in everything depending on me and my not depending on anything, in everything that I will to occur in my entire sensible world occurring purely and simply because I will for it to occur – just as happens in my body, which is the starting point of my absolute causality. The world must become for me what my body is. This goal is of course unreachable; but I am nevertheless supposed to draw constantly nearer to it, and thus I am supposed to fashion everything in the sensible world so that it can serve as a means for achieving my final end. This process of drawing ever nearer to my final end is my finite end.

---

[6] In the draft of a letter to Reinhold of September 18, 1800 (*GA* III/3: 314), Fichte asserts that he has explicitly retracted the preceding speculations on freedom and predestination, first in his lectures at Jena, and then in Part III of *The Vocation of Man* (1800).

The fact that nature placed me at one point or another and that nature instead of me took the first step, as it were, on this path to infinity does not infringe upon my freedom. Nor is my freedom infringed upon by the fact that a rational being outside of me provided me from the start with a sphere for my possible progression by means of freedom; for this is how I first obtain freedom, and it certainly cannot be infringed upon before I have obtained it. Nor is my freedom infringed upon by the fact that I must go on to assume that there are additional free and rational beings outside of me, for their freedom and rationality is, as such, by no means the object of a perception, which would limit me, but is a purely spiritual concept.

Furthermore, my freedom is not infringed upon by the fact that, in accordance with the concept that was subsequently presented, I have to choose among several possible actions; for such a choice is a condition for my consciousness of my own freedom and hence a condition for this freedom itself; and the content of what is chosen is always in my power, since all possible ways of acting freely [IV, 230] are under my sway. Nor does it limit my self-sufficiency if, in accordance with the presupposition made on the same occasion, other free beings choose among the remaining possibilities of acting. *They* are limited by me; *I* am not limited by them.

If, however, in accordance with our subsequent presupposition as well as with universal experience, that which certainly lies in my way (since it is encountered within the world of my experience) and which therefore limits me (as do all objects of my experience) has already been modified by free beings outside me, then my freedom is indeed limited if I am not permitted to modify this same object in accordance with my own end. But according to the indicated prohibition of the moral law I am not permitted to modify such objects in this manner. I am not permitted to disturb the freedom of rational beings, but if I alter the products of their freedom then I disturb that freedom, for these products are, for them, means to further ends. If I deprive them of these means, then they cannot continue to exercise their causality according to those concepts of an end that they have designed.

Thus we encounter here a contradiction of the drive to self-sufficiency – and hence of the moral law – with itself. The latter demands:

(1) That I subordinate everything that limits me (or, which means the same, everything that lies within my sensible world) to my absolute

final end; that I make it into a means for drawing myself nearer to absolute self-sufficiency.

(2) That I do not subordinate to my own end some of those things that certainly do limit me (since they lie within my sensible world), but that I leave them as I find them. Both of these are immediate commands of the moral law: the first, when one considers this law in general or as such; the second, when one considers a particular manifestation of the same.

V

The only way to resolve this contradiction and to establish the agreement of the moral law with itself would be to presuppose that all free beings necessarily share the same end [*Zweck*] [IV, 231], which would mean that the purposive [*zweckmäßige*] conduct of one person would at the same time be purposive for all others and that the liberation of one would at the same time be the liberation of all the others. – Is this the case? I will now delve deeper into this matter, since everything – and everything for us in particular, i.e., the distinctive character of our presentation of ethics – depends upon the answer to this question and depends especially upon the grounds upon which this answer is based.

The drive for self-sufficiency is the drive of I-hood; I-hood is the sole end of this drive.[7] The I alone is supposed to be the subject of self-sufficiency. As we have now seen, it is certainly a necessary feature of I-hood that each I is an individual – but only that it be an individual as such or in general, not that it be the determinate individual A or B or C, etc. As we have seen, all determinations of our individuality, except for the first and original determination, depend upon our own freedom; and therefore when I talk about "[individual] A, etc." I can be referring only to that original limitation of freedom that I previously called "the

---

[7] *Der Trieb nach Selbständigkeit ist Trieb der Ichheit, er hat nur sie zum Zwecke.* Whereas the pronoun *er* in this clause clearly refers to "the drive" [*der Trieb*], *sie* could refer either to "self-sufficiency" [*Selbständigkeit*] or to "I-hood" [*Ichheit*]. Moreover, the phrase "drive of I-hood" [*Trieb der Ichheit*], both here and in the discussion that follows, could also mean "drive for I-hood" or "drive toward I-hood." Indeed, this would appear to be precisely Fichte's point: the basic drive *of* the I (that is, of a free being) is its drive *to become* an I (or to become self-sufficient).

root of all individuality." Since it is for I-hood as such a contingent fact that *I*, individual A, am precisely A, and since the drive for self-sufficiency is supposed to be a drive of I-hood, essentially as such, the aim of this drive is not the self-sufficiency of [the individual] A, but rather, the self-sufficiency of reason as such. Our ultimate goal is the self-sufficiency of all reason as such and thus not the self-sufficiency of one rational being [*Einer Vernunft*], insofar as the latter is an individual rational being.

For my person, however, I, [individual] A, *am* only insofar as I am A. A, therefore, is for me my empirical self; only in the empirical self is there any consciousness of the drive for self-sufficiency and of the moral law; only by means of A can I act efficaciously in accordance with this law, since it is only through A that I can act efficaciously at all. For me, A is an exclusive condition for the causality of this drive. In a word, A is not an *object*; it is for me the sole *instrument and vehicle* of the moral law. (Previously, this tool was the body, now it has become the *entire sensible and empirically determined human being*; and with this we have at the same time sharply distinguished the empirical I from the pure I, which is very beneficial both for ethics in particular and for philosophy as a whole) [IV, 232].

If the aim of the drive for self-sufficiency is the self-sufficiency of reason as such or in general, and if the latter can be presented [*dargestellt*] only *in* and *through* individuals A, B, C, etc., then it is necessarily a matter of utter indifference to me whether I present this drive or it is instead presented by A or B or C; for reason in general is presented in each of these cases, since these latter individuals also belong to the one undivided realm of reason. In each case my drive is satisfied, for it did not want anything other than this. What I will is morality as such; it does not matter in the least whether this is *in* me or is *outside* me. I will morality from myself only insofar as it pertains to me, and I will it from others insofar as it pertains to them; my end is achieved in the same way through the one as through the other.

My end is achieved if the other person acts *morally*. He, however, is free, and by means of his freedom he is also able to act immorally. If he does act immorally, then my end has not been achieved. Do I in that case not have the right and the obligation to abolish the effect of his freedom? Here I am not resting this claim upon the negative proposition that was provisionally stated above; instead, I am now engaged in a thorough deduction of this proposition itself, and this is the appropriate place to do this.

Reason is supposed to be self-sufficient. But reason addresses this demand to the determinate individuals B, C, etc.; and there is no such demand at all and no (material) self-sufficiency except by means of the formal freedom of all individuals. The latter, therefore, is the exclusive condition for the entire causality of reason as such. If freedom is abolished, then *all* the causality of reason is abolished, including its causality with respect to self-sufficiency. No one who wants self-sufficiency, therefore, can fail to want freedom. Freedom is the absolute condition for all morality, and without it no morality whatsoever is possible. This also confirms the moral law's absolute prohibition on disturbing and abolishing the freedom of another free being under any condition. Here too, however, the contradiction remains. One can say, "I will and can will that the other person be free, but only on the condition that he use his freedom to advance the end of reason; otherwise, I certainly cannot will that he be free" [IV, 233]. This, too, is quite correct. If the wish for universal morality is my ruling wish, as it surely ought to be, then I absolutely must wish to abolish any use of freedom that violates the moral law.

At this point, however, the following additional question arises: which use of freedom violates the moral law, and who is able to be the judge who passes universally valid judgments on this question? – If *the other person* claims to have acted according to his best conviction, and if *I* act differently in the same situation, then according to *his* conviction *I* am acting immorally, just as *he* is acting immorally according to *mine*. Whose conviction is supposed to guide that of the other? The answer is that neither conviction can play this role, so long as they remain in conflict with each other; for each person ought to act purely and simply in accordance with *his* conviction, and this constitutes the formal condition of all morality. – Could we not therefore simply part ways, so that everyone would allow all the others to follow their own paths? Absolutely not, at least not so long as we do not wish to relinquish all our interest in universal morality and in the rule of reason – something that would be utterly reprehensible. Therefore, we must seek to make our own judgment harmonize with that of the other. Yet just as surely as neither party lacks conscience each will presuppose that *his* opinion is correct (for otherwise he would have acted contrary to his conscience when he acted upon this opinion); and hence each of them will aim at, and will have to aim at, convincing the other while not allowing himself to be convinced by the other. Ultimately, of course, they must arrive at one and the same result, since reason is simply one; but until then, in consequence of an absolute prohibition, it is the duty of each party to preserve the external freedom of the other. – It follows that everyone can and is permitted to will to determine only the convictions of the other and by no means the other's physical behavior [*Wirkung*]. The former is the only kind of constraint that free beings are permitted to exercise upon free beings.

Let us now go over this again more carefully.

(a) As we have seen, the moral final end of every rational being is the self-sufficiency of reason as such, and hence the morality of all rational beings. We are all supposed to act the same way. This is the reason for the Kantian proposition, Act in such a way that you could think of the maxim of your will [IV, 234] as a principle of a universal legislation.[8] – From my point of view, however, the following has to be noted in this regard: first of all, Kant's proposition only talks about the *idea* of an agreement and by no means about any *actual* agreement. We will see that this idea has real use, that one ought to seek to realize this idea of agreement and must, to some degree, act as though it were realized. Moreover, this proposition is purely *heuristic*: I can very well and very easily employ it as a test to determine whether I might have erred in my judgment concerning my duty. It is, however, by no means *constitutive*. It is by no means a principle [*Prinzip*], but only a consequence of or an inference from a true principle, that is, a consequence of the command concerning the absolute self-sufficiency of reason. The relationship in question is not that something ought to be a maxim of my will because it is a principle of a universal legislation, but conversely, because something is supposed to be a maxim of my will it can therefore also be a principle of a universal legislation. The act of judging begins purely and simply with me. This point is also clear from Kant's proposition, for who is it that judges in turn whether something could be a principle of a universal legislation? This is surely I myself. And according to which principles does one make this judgement? It is, is it not, surely made in

---

[8] See *CprR*, § 7, p. 28 (*AA* 5: 30): "So act that the maxim of your will could always hold at the same time as a principle in a giving of universal law."

accordance with principles contained within my own reason? This formula, however, has a heuristic use for the following reason: a proposition from which an absurdity follows is false; now it is absurd that I ought to do X if I cannot think that all human beings also ought to do X in the same situation. In the latter case, accordingly, I certainly ought not to do X, and I have erred in my prior judgment [that I should act in this way].

(b) Everyone ought to produce outside of himself absolute agreement or harmony with himself; he ought to produce such harmony in everything that is present for him, for he himself is free and independent only on the condition of such harmony. The first implication of this is that everyone ought to live in society and remain in society, since otherwise one could not attain agreement with oneself, which is, however, absolutely commanded of everyone. An individual who separates himself from others surrenders his end and is completely indifferent to the spread of morality [IV, 235]. An individual who wants to take care only of himself does not, in a moral sense, even manage to take care of himself; for it ought to be his final end to care for the entire human species. His virtue is no virtue at all, but is instead a servile egotism, intent upon gain. – We are not charged with the task of seeking society on our own and bringing it into existence by ourselves; if a person were, let us say, born in the wilderness, he would surely be permitted to remain there. Everyone, however, with whom we are in any way acquainted becomes assigned to our care simply by virtue of this acquaintance; he becomes our neighbor and a part of our rational world [*Vernunftwelt*], just as the objects of our experience belong to our sensible world [*Sinnenwelt*]. We cannot abandon him unless we lack conscience. This also refutes the opinion, which is still to be encountered among us in many guises, that one can satisfy one's duty – and do so in a more meritorious manner at that – by living the life of a hermit, by separating oneself from others, and simply by entertaining sublime thoughts and speculations. In fact, one can by no means satisfy one's duty in any of these ways. One satisfies one's duty only by acting, not by means of fanatical enthusiasm but only by acting in and for society. – To be sure, each person's end is only to convince the other person, and certainly not to allow himself be convinced by the other. This follows from the very nature of the situation. Anyone who dares to act in accordance with his conviction and seeks to get others to act in this way as well has to be certain of himself, otherwise he would be acting unconscionably.

(c) This end [of convincing others] is not the exclusive end of one or another individual, but is a communal end. Everyone is supposed to have this end; and precisely this – namely, to enable everyone else to posit this same end for themselves – is the end of each person, just as surely as he wills universal moral cultivation [*allgemeine moralische Bildung*]. First of all, this serves to unite human beings; everyone wants only to convince the other of his opinion, and yet, in the course of this conflict of minds, he is perhaps himself convinced of the other's opinion. Everyone must be ready to engage in this reciprocal interaction. Anyone who flees from such interaction, perhaps in order to avoid any disturbance of his own belief, thereby betrays a lack of conviction on his own part, which simply ought not to be the case [IV, 236]. From this it follows that such a person has an even greater duty to seek such engagement in order to acquire conviction for himself.

This reciprocal interaction of everyone with everyone for the purpose of producing communally shared practical convictions is possible only insofar as everyone starts from the same shared principles; and it is necessary that there be such principles, to which their additional convictions must be connected. – Such a reciprocal interaction, in which everyone is obliged to engage, is called a *church* or an ethical commonwealth, and that upon which everyone agrees is its *symbol* or *creed*.[9] – Everyone is supposed to be a member of the church. If, however, the church community is not to be entirely fruitless, the *symbol* in question must be constantly changed, because as these different minds continue to engage in reciprocal interaction the area upon which they all agree will gradually expand. – (Instead of symbolizing that upon which everyone agrees, the symbols of certain churches seem to contain something that is an object of dispute for everyone, something that no one sincerely believes because no one can even think it.)

(d) The necessary goal of all virtuous people is therefore unanimous agreement concerning the same practical conviction and concerning the uniformity of acting that ensues therefrom.

This is an important point and is a characteristic feature of our presentation of morals, and yet this same point has in all likelihood

---

[9] *Symbol.* This German term also carries another meaning, derived from the Latin: "creed" (as in *Symbolum Nicaeum*). But it also carries the meaning of the English "symbol," and Fichte here seems to be using this term in both of these sense.

raised many doubts. Let us therefore examine it more closely on the basis of the principles set forth previously.

The object of the moral law within me, as an individual, is not simply me alone but *reason as a whole*. I am the object of this law only insofar as I am one of the instruments of its realization in the sensible world. All it demands of me as an individual, therefore, and all for which it holds me alone responsible is that I should be a capable instrument [of the moral law]. This development [*Ausbildung*] of my capacities as an instrument of the moral law is a matter that is referred exclusively to my own private conviction, and by no means to the communal conviction of everyone. As an individual and as an instrument of the moral law, I possess both an understanding and a body. I alone am responsible for the development of these [IV, 237]. First of all, the development of my understanding depends solely on my own conviction. I possess absolute freedom of thought – not external freedom (which is already included within the very concept of thinking), but freedom before my own conscience. I simply must not allow any scruples to prevent me from inwardly doubting everything and from continuing to investigate everything, no matter how holy it may appear; nor may the church force me to have such scruples. Such an investigation is an absolute duty, and when something is undecided in one's own mind then it is unconscionable to continue to allow it to occupy its place. With respect to my body, I have the absolute freedom to nourish it, develop it, and take care of it in the manner that, according to my own conviction, I can best preserve it, keep it healthy, and make it into a suitable and capable instrument. I am not bound by conscience to do any of these things in the same way that others do them; indeed, it is unconscionable of me to make the way in which I tend to the preservation and cultivation of my own body dependent upon the opinions of others if I myself am not convinced regarding such matters.

What lies outside my body, and hence the entire sensible world, is a common good or possession [*Gemeingut*], and the cultivation of the same in accordance with the laws of reason is *not* mandated of *me alone* but rather of *all rational beings*. This is because responsibility for what lies outside my body is not mine alone, and with regard to this I am by no means permitted to proceed on the basis of my private conviction; for I cannot act efficaciously within this sensible world without having some influence upon others and hence without infringing upon their freedom (which occurs whenever my influence upon them is not in accordance with their own will), and this is something I am simply not permitted to do. I am absolutely not allowed to do anything that influences everyone unless I have everyone's consent and thus act in accordance with fundamental principles that are approved by everyone and are in accord with our shared convictions. – If, however, such communally shared conviction and agreement concerning the manner in which everyone ought to be permitted to influence everyone else were impossible, then it would follow from what we have been saying that there could be no acting at all, which contradicts the moral law. Yet acting without universal agreement is no less contradictory to the moral law. It therefore follows, by virtue of an absolute command of the moral law, that such universal agreement simply must be achieved. – Agreement [IV, 238] concerning how human beings are permitted to influence one another – i.e., agreement concerning *their communal rights* in the sensible world – is called the *state contract* [*Staatsvertrag*]; and the community that has achieved such agreement is the state. It is an absolute duty of conscience to unite with others in a state. Anyone who does not want to do this is not to be tolerated within society. This is because one cannot in good conscience enter into community with such a person; since he has not declared how he wants to be treated, one always has to worry about treating him in a manner contrary to what he wills and in a manner that violates his rights.

Since no acting is possible at all before a state has been erected, and since it might nevertheless be difficult to obtain the explicit consent of everyone, or even of a considerable number of people, the higher and more cultivated human being is forced by necessity [*durch die Not getrieben*] to take the *silence* of others regarding certain regulations and their submission to them as a sign of consent. One also cannot calculate and weigh reciprocal rights so precisely, given that one individual may not submit to *any* order from which he does not obtain considerable advantages, whereas another individual may be silent about *everything*. This is how a *makeshift state*[10] [*Notstaat*] arises, which is the first condition for the gradual progress toward a rational and just state. – It is a matter of conscience to submit unconditionally to the laws of

---

[10] *Notstaat*. More literally, "state of necessity," "necessary state," or perhaps "emergency state," this term is translated "makeshift state" in *FNR*, a rendering that calls attention to the fact that such a state represents a first and unavoidable response to a situation of pressing *need*, an arrangement with which one must therefore "make do."

one's state; for these laws contain the presumptive general will, against which no one may influence others. Everyone receives moral permission to have an effect on others only by virtue of the fact that the law declares their consent to be influenced in this way.

It violates conscience to overthrow the state unless I am firmly convinced that the *community* wills such an overthrow, which could be the case only under a condition that will be discussed later. This remains true even if I were to be convinced that most of the state's institutions are contrary to reason and right, for my action of overthrowing the state affects not simply myself alone, but the entire community. My conviction that the constitution is contrary to what is right may perhaps be entirely correct, considered in itself (that is, when judged from the point of view of pure reason [IV, 239] – if only there were a visible tribunal of pure reason), but it is still only a private conviction. In matters that concern the whole [community], however, I am not permitted to act in accordance with my private conviction; instead, I must in such cases act in accordance with communal conviction, as follows from the proof that was provided earlier.

There is a contradiction here. I am inwardly convinced that the constitution is contrary to right, and yet I help maintain it, even if only through my submissiveness. I may even hold some constitutional office that is contrary to right. Am I then at least supposed to refrain from holding such an office? On the contrary, this is something I ought to do; I ought not to withdraw from holding such an office, for it is better that the wise and just govern than that the unwise and unjust reign. What Plato says about this in his letters[11] is incorrect and even contradictory. I ought never to remove myself from my fatherland. – One might say, "I, for my own part, do not want to commit any injustices," but this is an egotistical way of talking. Do you then want to allow these same injustices to be committed by someone else? Were you to see that such injustices occur, you would still have to prevent them.

I am therefore acting contrary to [my own] better conviction [when I continue to cooperate with what I am convinced is an unjust state constitution]. – Considered from another side, however, it remains a

---

[11] See Plato's *Seventh Letter*, 324b–326b, where Plato argues that until such time as philosophers become rulers the wise man should not become involved in public affairs and uses this principle to justify his own departure from Athens for Syracuse.

correct and dutiful conviction that, in communal matters, I ought to act only in accordance with the presumptive general will. It is no injustice whatsoever to treat another in the manner he wants to be treated, and hence [when I act in accordance with a constitution that I am convinced is unjust] I am also acting according to my own best conviction. – How can this contradiction be resolved? Let us see which conviction is at issue in each of these two propositions. The first proposition concerns my conviction regarding some *ought*, some state of affairs that is supposed to be brought about. The second one concerns my conviction regarding that *actuality* to which I myself belong as a member of society. Both of these convictions have to be united in my maxim, and this is easily done. As a means for bringing about the rational state, I have to take into account the present condition of the makeshift state [*Notstaat*], and I must act solely in order to accomplish this end (that is, in order to establish the rational state). I must not take any measures that would allow things to remain forever as they are now, but I should instead act in such a way that things have to become better [IV, 240]. This is purely and simply a duty. Any acting within the state that is not based on this end may be materially legal, in the sense that it may nevertheless further the end of establishing the rational state, but it is nevertheless formally contrary to duty. Any acting that aims directly at the opposite end is both materially and formally evil and unconscionable. – After acting according to these principles for a period of time, it may well happen that the common will is completely contrary to the constitution of the state. Were this to happen the continuation of this state would be an instance of unjust tyranny and oppression; the makeshift state would then collapse by itself, and a more rational constitution would take its place. In such a case every honorable person could then in good conscience endeavor to overthrow this [makeshift] state entirely, but *only if he has ascertained the common will.* (In passing, I will add the following: in recent times some extremely unintelligent people – I will not call them people without a conscience, since that is something they will have to judge for themselves, before their own conscience – have raised a hue and cry and have suggested that belief in the unlimited perfectibility of humanity is something extremely dangerous, utterly contrary to reason, and the source of God knows what horrors. In order to put an end forever to such idle talk, let us situate our inquiry at the correct point of view. First of all, the question is not whether one has to decide on the basis of purely theoretical rational grounds for or against the perfect-ibility of humanity. This is a question we can totally ignore. The moral law, which extends to infinity, absolutely commands us to treat human beings *as if they* were forever capable of becoming perfected and remaining so, and this same law absolutely prohibits us from treating human beings in the opposite manner. One cannot obey such a com-mand without believing in perfectibility. Consequently, the latter con-stitutes the first article of faith, something one cannot doubt without surrendering one's entire moral nature [*sittliche Natur*]. Consequently, even if it were to be proven that the human species had not advanced a single step from its first beginnings to the present day, but had instead always fallen further behind; even if one could derive from the *natural* predispositions of the human species a mechanical law, according to which our species always had to relapse (which, however, is far more [IV, 241] than could ever be established): even if all this were the case, we would still not be permitted nor be able to give up that belief [in human perfectibility] that is implanted in us inwardly and inextinguish-ably. Nor would this involve any contradiction on our part; for this belief is by no means based on any *natural predispositions*, but rather on *freedom*. Let everyone judge for himself what kind of people these are who consider a belief that is absolutely commanded by the moral law to be a piece of folly. It is true, moreover, that nothing is more dangerous to the tyranny of despots and clerics nor more destructive to the very foundations of their reign than this belief [in human perfectibility]. The only semblance of an argument these critics of the belief in human perfectibility can adduce, and one which they never tire of adducing, is this: one absolutely cannot deal with humanity in any way other than the way in which they deal with it; humanity just is the way it happens to be, and it will forever remain as it is; and therefore the situation of human beings must also forever remain as it is.)

(e) To repeat: as surely as all human beings take their own vocation to heart, all of them necessarily aim at imparting their own convictions *to everyone*; and the union of everyone for this end is called the *church*. This process of reciprocally convincing one another is possible only on the condition that one can proceed from something upon which both sides agree; otherwise neither understands the other at all, and they do not influence each other but remain isolated from each other, with each person speaking his piece only for himself, while the other does not listen to him. If we are dealing with only two or three people, and if the people in question are mutually able to explain their opinions to one another, then it ought to be easy for them to reach agreement on a communal point, since, after all, they all find themselves in the same domain of common human understanding. (In philosophy, which is supposed to elevate itself to the domain of transcendental consciousness, this is not always possible. Here it may well be the case that philosophizing individuals cannot agree on even a single point.) According to our requirement, however, each person is supposed to act efficaciously upon *everyone*, even though all of these others would most probably diverge greatly from one another in their individual convictions. How then can one become aware of that upon which everyone agrees? This is not something one can learn simply by asking around; hence it must be possible to presuppose something [IV, 242] that can be viewed as the creed of the community or as its *symbol*.

It is implicit in the concept of such a symbol or creed that it presents something not in a very precise or determinate manner, but only in a general way, for it is precisely concerning the further determinations of this symbol that individuals disagree among themselves. Moreover, since the symbol is supposed to be appropriate for everyone, including the most uncultivated among them, it is also implicit in the concept of the same that the symbol does not consist in abstract propositions but rather in sensory presentations of the latter. The sensible presentation is merely the costume; what is properly symbolic is the concept. That precisely this presentation had to be chosen is something that was dictated by need, since unless there was unity concerning something or other no reciprocal communication would have been possible; yet it was impossible to unite human beings concerning anything else, because they were not yet capable of distinguishing the costume that the concept had received by chance from the essence of the concept. To this extent, therefore, every symbol is and remains a *makeshift symbol* [*Notsymbol*]. – Allow me to explain myself more clearly by means of an example: what is most essential about every possible symbol or creed is expressed in the proposition, "there is something or other that is supersensible and elevated above all nature." Anyone who does not earnestly believe this cannot be a member of a church; such a person is completely incapable of all morality and moral cultivation. What this supersensible something may be, the identity of this truly holy and sanctifying spirit, the character of the truly moral way of thinking: it is precisely concerning these points that the community seeks to determine and to unify itself more and more, by means of mutual interaction. This is also the end and the content of, for example, the symbol of our Christian church. The only difference is that the latter symbol, understood as a symbol realized in the sensible world and as the creed of an *actual, visible* community, arose among members of the Jewish nation [*Nation*], which already had its own customs, types of representation, and images. It was natural that they [that is, the early Christians] thought this proposition [concerning supersensible reality] in terms of the images to which they were accustomed. It was natural too that it was only in the shape in which this proposition appeared to them that they could communicate the supersensible to other peoples [*Völkern*], who, as peoples, (for here we are not talking about their educated public) were first elevated to a clear consciousness of the supersensible by members of the Jewish nation [IV, 243]. Another religious founder, Mohammed, gave this same supersensible something a different form, one more suitable to his nation, and he did well in so doing, if only the nation of his faith had not met the misfortune of coming to a standstill due to the lack of an educated public (concerning which we will have more to say at the appropriate time).

What do those enveloping images [that is, these costumes for the concept of the supersensible] have to say? Do they determine what is supersensible in a universally valid manner? By no means, for why would there then be any need for people to combine in a church, the end of which is none other than the further determination of what is supersensible? As surely as a church exists – and it exists just as surely as human beings are finite but perfectible – what is supersensible is not determined but is now, for the first time, supposed to become determined, and it continues to become further determined in a process that continues for all eternity. It can therefore be presumed that these costumes are merely the manner in which a community expresses for itself and for the time being the proposition, "*there is something supersensible.*" Without agreement on something or other no reciprocal interaction for the end of producing communally shared convictions would be possible; the latter, however, which is what is conditioned in this case, is commanded absolutely, and thus so too is the condition that makes it possible. It is therefore an absolute duty to establish something, no matter what it might be, about which at least most people agree, as a *symbol*; i.e., it is an absolute duty to bring together, to the best of one's ability, a visible church community. Moreover, I cannot act efficaciously upon everyone without proceeding from what they all agree upon. But I ought to have such an effect on them; hence I ought to proceed from what they all agree upon and certainly should not begin with something that is in dispute among them. This is not, as it were, a demand of prudence; it is a duty of conscience. As surely as I will an end, I also will whatever is the sole means to this end. Anyone who acts otherwise certainly does not will the end of instruction for the purposes of moral cultivation; instead, he seeks to dazzle others with his erudition, and he turns himself into the teacher of a theory, which is something very different indeed.

Note that I am saying "I ought to *proceed from* this, as from something presupposed," and not, "I ought to *aim at* this, as at something still to be established" [IV, 244].

At this point we might encounter the following objection to this doctrine: someone might say, "If I am not convinced of the truth of those representations from which I am supposed to proceed, do I not then speak in violation of my own better conviction; and how could I be permitted to do that?" – But what is it that really violates my stronger conviction in this case? One hopes that what violates my conviction is not the underlying concept of something supersensible; so perhaps what violates my conviction is only the manner of *designating* what is supersensible, understood as a *fixed determination* of the same. But who says that this manner of designation is an actual determination [of what is supersensible]? Personally, I determine what is supersensible in a different manner; but I cannot proceed from *my* determination, nor ought I to proceed from it, for it is *contested*. Instead, I ought to proceed from that upon which everyone else can agree with me, and this, according to our assumption, is the church's symbol. It is my *aim* to elevate everyone to my *conviction*, but this can occur only gradually and in such a way that we always remain in agreement, beginning with the first point indicated. Insofar as I actually and sincerely regard the symbol in question only as a means to elevate the others gradually to my conviction, my teachings are surely totally in accord with my conviction – just as my acting in the makeshift state had to be viewed as a means for bringing about the rational state. It is ignorant to insist that this costume constitutes a determination [of the concept of the supersensible]. It is unconscionable to make it one's end, in violation of one's own conviction, to get others to retain a certain belief; indeed, this constitutes true and genuine priestcraft [*Pfaffentum*] – just as the striving to keep human beings in a makeshift state constitutes true and genuine despotism. – The symbol is [only] the starting point. It is not something that is *taught* – that is the spirit of priestcraft – instead, teaching begins with the symbol, which is presupposed. Were it not to be presupposed, then there would be another starting point, one that would be higher and closer to my conviction, from which I could proceed and which I would prefer. Since, however, there is no other place to start, I can make use only of this starting point.

It is therefore a duty of conscience for anyone who aims to exercise some effect upon the practical conviction of the community to treat the symbol as the foundation of his instruction, but it is by no means a duty of conscience to believe inwardly in this same symbol [IV, 245]. We have already seen earlier that the opposite is the case. The symbol is changeable, and it is supposed to be constantly changed by means of good, purposefully effective teaching.

In passing, I will add the following: this further progression, this process of raising the symbol to a higher level is precisely the spirit of Protestantism, if this word is supposed to have any meaning at all. Sticking with the old, bringing universal reason to a standstill: this is the spirit of papism. The Protestant starts with the symbol and then proceeds into infinity; the papist proceeds toward the symbol as his final goal. Anyone who behaves in the latter fashion is a papist, in both form and spirit, even though the propositions that he does not want to allow humanity to rise above may be, with respect to their matter or content, genuinely Lutheran or Calvinist or something similar.

(f) Not only am I permitted to have my own private conviction concerning the constitution of the state and the system of the church, I am even obliged by my conscience to develop this same conviction just as self-sufficiently and as broadly as I can.

Such development [*Ausbildung*], or at least the continuation of the same, is possible, however, only by means of reciprocal communication with others. The reason for this is as follows: there is simply no criterion for the objective truth of my sensory perceptions other than the agreement of my experience with the experience of others. In the case of reasoning, the situation is somewhat different, though not by much. I am simultaneously a rational being in general and an individual. Only by being an individual am I a rational being. To be sure, I argue in accordance with universal laws of reason, but I do this by employing my powers as an individual. So how can I guarantee that the result of my reasoning has not been falsified by my individuality? I do indeed assert that this is not the case, and I will fight for this claim, and this too has a basis within my own nature. But even as I make such a claim, I may still not yet be, in the most secret depths of my own mind, completely certain of my own cause [*Sache*]. If my conviction is rejected by one person after another to whom I present it [IV, 246], then even though this may not immediately cause me to abandon that conviction, it may still make me somewhat dubious and provoke me to examine and to re-examine the conviction in question; if so, this reveals that I am not completely certain of my own cause. For why would I do this if I were already completely certain of my cause in advance? If I wanted to stand completely on my own, and if I were able to do this, then how could the doubts of another person exert any influence on my own way of proceeding? On the other hand, when I believe that another person sincerely agrees with me, then this serves to confirm me in my conviction. I am not satisfied when someone concedes that I am right, so long as I cannot presuppose any inner conviction on his part, which goes to show that I am not interested in the external appearance of being right.[12] On the contrary, I am rather annoyed by this, because it casts suspicion on this criterion [namely, the agreement of others with my conviction], which is the only criterion I still retained. – Deep in my mind, even if I am not clearly conscious of it, I harbor that doubt to which we pointed earlier, a doubt concerning whether my individuality might not have had some influence on the result I found [by means of my reasoning]. What is required in order to remove such doubt is not the complete agreement of everyone. The honest agreement of even one single person can be enough to satisfy me, and it actually does satisfy me. The reason for this is as follows: I was afraid that the basis for my opinion might lie in my individual manner of thinking. This fear is removed as soon as even one other individual agrees with me, for it would be extremely odd for such an agreement, as such, of two

---

[12] *daß es mir nicht um das äussere Rechtbehalten zu tun ist.*

individuals to occur simply by chance. Nor does the removal of my doubt on this score require that this other individual and I agree *on everything*. If only we are in agreement concerning first principles, concerning a certain way of looking at the matter in question, then I can easily tolerate the fact that the other individual might not be able to follow me in all the inferences I go on to draw [from this first principle]. From this point on the correctness of my propositions may be guaranteed by universal logic, the universal validity of which cannot be doubted by any rational being. One need only think of the example of philosophy: this involves a state of mind that is so contrary to nature that the first person who elevated himself to this state of mind surely could not have had confidence in himself until he had observed a similar elevation in others.

It is therefore by means of communication that I first obtain certainty and security for the cause or matter itself [*die Sache selbst*] [IV, 247]. Yet even if my propositions are actually in accord with universal reason and hence are universally valid, the particular presentation of any proposition still always remains something individual; this clothing for the proposition is the best available, above all for me. But even as it is within me, my proposition would come closer to the universal and be modified by the way in which everyone thinks if it had a less individual form. My proposition obtains a less individual form when I communicate it to others and when they respond to it and present their own counterarguments, which, if the proposition is, in itself, correct, spring from their individual ways of thinking. I correct the latter, and in doing so I develop my own representation in a way that is more generally comprehensible, even in my own eyes. The wider this reciprocal interaction extends, the more truth (objectively considered) gains thereby, and the more I gain as well.

From this it follows that the exclusive condition for the further development of my particular convictions is that I be allowed to communicate them, and hence that I *proceed* from them.

And yet, according to what was said above, in a community I am by no means supposed to proceed from my private conviction, but instead I am supposed to begin with the symbol. As far as the constitution of the state is concerned, I am supposed to comply with this constitution and even help carry it out, if it is my office to do so. Thus, if my private conviction concerning this constitution is opposed to what has to be presupposed to be the conviction of the community, then I am also not permitted to express this private conviction, since in doing so I would be working to overthrow the state. But if I am not permitted to communicate my convictions, then how could I ever confirm and develop them by means of communication?

If something conditioned is commanded, then the condition thereof is also commanded. Now the former, the development of my convictions, is absolutely commanded, and therefore the latter is absolutely commanded as well. The communication of my private convictions is an absolute duty. –

Yet we have just seen that the communication of my private convictions is [in the case before us] contrary to duty. How can we resolve this contradiction? It is immediately resolved if we take note of the premises from which we have derived the duty to keep to oneself one's private convictions concerning the system of the church [IV, 248] and the constitution of the state. We presupposed that in this case *everyone* whose convictions one could not learn by asking them would be affected [by one's decision to express one's own private convictions].

If, therefore, we were not dealing with everyone, but instead with a determinate, limited number [of individuals], whose convictions we could indeed come to know, since they too would be engaged in communication from their side and would be capable of doing so, then I would not be prohibited from making my private convictions known [to them] nor from proceeding from the same. The synthetic link that unites the two sides of the contradiction would be a society of the sort just indicated. The concept of such a society includes the following: first of all, the society in question is supposed to be limited and determinate, and thus it is not supposed to include everyone (which is an indeterminate concept), but only a certain number [of individuals] who are selected from the totality and, to that extent, separated from the latter. Secondly, in such a society the previously discussed freedom to doubt everything and to examine everything freely and independently, a freedom that everyone has *before himself and in his own consciousness*, is supposed to be *realized and presented externally as well*. The society in question is the forum of a communal consciousness, before which any conceivable thing can be thought and investigated with absolute, unlimited freedom. Just as everyone is free before himself, so is everyone free within this domain. From what has been said so far it follows, finally, that each member of this association must have thrown off the fetters represented by the symbol of the church and by the legal concepts sanctioned by the state. To be sure, one does not have to have thrown these things off *materially*, since one may well consider much of what is presented in this symbol and in these concepts to be the final and highest determination of the truth, but one must certainly have thrown them off *formally*; that is, one must not ascribe any authority to them and must not consider anything to be true or correct simply because the church teaches it or because the state practices it. Instead, one must have some other reason for calling something true or correct; for the end and the essence of this society is precisely to investigate matters beyond these limits [represented by the symbols of the church and the laws of the state]. But anyone who considers these to be limits will not pursue his investigations beyond them, and thus such a person is not a member of a society of the sort we have just described, the name of which is "the *learned public*" or "*the republic of scholars*" [*das gelehrte Publikum*].

Everyone who has elevated himself to absolute non-belief in the authority of the communal conviction of his age has a duty of conscience to establish a learned public [IV, 249]. Having rejected the confirmation of the communal conviction of his age, he now lacks a guiding thread. As surely as he thinks morally, he cannot be indifferent to whether he errs or not; and yet, according to the proofs presented earlier, he can never arrive at complete certainty before himself on this point by means of theoretical propositions (which, however, will always exercise a stronger or weaker influence upon morality). Furthermore, he has a duty to communicate his convictions in order thereby to make them publicly useful; yet he is not permitted to communicate them immediately to everyone. Hence he has to seek out a like-minded individual, one who, like him, has thrown off belief in authority; and he cannot rest easy with his own conscience until he has found such a person – and found in him a confirmation of his conviction, as well as a means for *recording* the same, until such time as it may be of some use for the whole. It is also a duty of conscience for others who find themselves in the same situation with regard to their own convictions to associate with the former person. When several persons are of such a mind, they will soon find one another, and through their communication they will establish a learned public.

It follows from what was said earlier that it is a duty of conscience to communicate to this learned public any new discoveries one might make, as well as to communicate to this same public any unusual convictions that diverge from the common judgment or lie beyond the common sphere – if one possesses or believes that one possesses such convictions – and thereby to own up to them.

The distinguishing and characteristic feature of the learned public is absolute freedom and independence of thinking. The principle of its constitution is absolutely not to subject oneself to any authority, to base everything upon one's meditations, and to reject utterly everything that is not confirmed by the latter. The learned person is distinguished from the unlearned person in the following way: the latter surely also believes that he has convinced himself through his own meditations, and indeed he has. But if one looks further than the latter person himself does, one will discover that his system concerning the state and the church is the result of the most up to date opinion of his age. All he has done is convince himself that it is precisely this that represents the up to date opinion of his age [IV, 250]. Though he may have drawn conclusions on his own from his premises, these premises are formed by his age, without any contribution from him, though he does not actually know this. The learned person notices this and seeks his premises within himself, [and in doing this] he consciously and on the basis of a free decision establishes for himself his own reason as the representative of reason as such.

For the learned public there is no possible symbol, no plumb line, no restraint. According to the concept of such a learned public, within the republic of scholars [*gelehrte Republik*] one must be able to put forward anything of which one believes one has convinced oneself, just as one is also allowed to dare to admit this same thing to oneself. – (Universities are learned schools. Hence in them as well one must be allowed to put forward anything of which one is convinced, and for universities too there is no symbol or creed. Those who recommend restraint when one is speaking from the lectern and who believe that here too one is not permitted to say everything, but must first consider what might be useful or harmful, what might be interpreted correctly or misinterpreted, are quite wrong. A person who cannot examine matters for himself and is incapable of learning how to do this is himself guilty of having wrongly intruded into a university. This is of no concern to the others, for they act in accordance with their full rights and according to their duty. In material terms, a lecture is absolutely no different from what is presented in scholarly writings; they differ only in their methods.)

Since scholarly inquiry is absolutely free, so must access to it be open to everyone. If a person can no longer believe sincerely in authority then it is a violation of his conscience to continue in this belief, and it is a duty of conscience for such a person to join the republic of scholars. No earthly power has the right to issue commands regarding matters of conscience, and it is unconscionable to deny entrance into the learned public to anyone whose own mind calls upon him to join the same.

The state and the church must tolerate scholars; otherwise they would be applying compulsion in matters of conscience, and no one could live with a good conscience in a state or in a church that behaved in such a manner, for if a person in such a state or in such a church were to begin to doubt the authority of the same, no recourse would be available to him [IV, 251]. Furthermore, no progress toward perfection would be possible in such a state and yet such progress absolutely ought to be possible. Instead, the people in such a state would remain forever at whatever stage they now happen to occupy. The state and the church must tolerate scholars, and this means that they must tolerate everything that constitutes the essence of the latter, including the absolute and unlimited communication of thoughts. One must be allowed to put forward anything of which one believes oneself to be convinced, no matter how dangerous or terrible it might seem. If someone has gone astray and is not allowed to communicate his errors, then how is he to be helped, and how are others to be helped in the future if they should go astray in the same fashion?

I maintain that the state and the church must *tolerate* scholarship or learned inquiry [*Gelehrsamkeit*] as such. They cannot do anything more for scholarship than tolerate it, however, since they occupy completely different spheres. (In what follows we will discuss a certain relationship the state has to scholars, insofar as the latter are indirectly *officials* of the state, but this is not a relationship to them as *scholars* per se.) The state as such can neither support nor advance scholarly inquiry as such; the latter occurs only through free investigation, and the state, as such, does not engage in investigation at all, nor is it supposed to do so. Instead, it regulates and stipulates. As for those *statesmen* who are themselves scholars, i.e., regarding any use the state wishes to make of scholars as persons: that is a different question.

The scholarly republic is an absolute democracy, or, to put it even more precisely, the only law [*Recht*] that applies within this republic is the law of the stronger mind. Everyone does what he is able to do, and he is right if his position is eventually confirmed. The only judge [in the scholarly republic] is time and the progress of culture [*Kultur*].

According to what was said above, both religious teachers and state officials are working for the perfection of humanity, and therefore they themselves must be further advanced [along the path to perfection] than the community; i.e., they themselves must be learned and must have enjoyed a scholarly education. The scholar in the proper sense of the term, that is, the person who is only a scholar, is himself indirectly an official of the state inasmuch as he is the educator of its teachers of the people and of those who serve directly as state officials [IV, 252]. Only to this extent can the scholar receive a salary, and only to this extent does he stand under the supervision of the state. It is not as though the state could prescribe for the scholar *what* he ought to teach; indeed, this would involve a contradiction, since the scholar would no longer remain a scholar at all [if the state told him what to teach], and this would mean that the education of future state officials would not be a scholarly education after all, but an ordinary, symbolic education – though perhaps one involving a somewhat different symbol. Instead of this, it is the business of the state to see to it that the scholar actually does freely communicate the best things that he believes himself to know and that he does this in the best way he is able. – Scholarly institutions or learned schools are not the sort of schools in which one learns the future trade of the teacher of the people or of the civil servant. Such things must also be learned, but this requires a different kind of instruction. The official and the teacher, moreover, are not supposed to be mere craftsmen or tradesmen but scholars. They are thus both scholars and officials or teachers. And yet, according to the preceding principles, it is a duty of conscience for the teacher of the people and for the state official, as they go about their business, to separate these two roles precisely: where one is a teacher or an official one is not a scholar, and where one is a scholar one is not a teacher of the people nor an official of the state. It is a coercion of conscience to prohibit a preacher from advancing his heterodox convictions in scholarly writings, but it is quite proper to prohibit him from broadcasting them from the pulpit; and if only he is sufficiently enlightened about those matters, he will realize that it is unconscionable for him to do so.

The state and the church have the right to prohibit the scholar from realizing his convictions within the sensible world, and they have the right to prevent him from doing this. If he nevertheless does this – if, e.g., he does not obey the laws of the state – then he is rightfully punished, no matter what he may inwardly think about the laws in question. Moreover, he has to reproach himself in his conscience [for acting in this manner], for his action is immoral.

And thus the idea of a learned public or republic of scholars, entirely by itself, is able to overcome the conflict between, on the one hand, an established [*fest*] church and state and, on the other, the individual's absolute freedom of conscience. The realization of this idea is therefore commanded by the moral law.

(g) In conclusion, let us summarize the complete final end of the human being, considered as an individual [IV, 253].

All of a person's efficacious acting within society has the following goal: all human beings are supposed to be in agreement; but the only matters that all human beings can agree on are those that are purely rational, for this is all they have in common. Under the presupposition of such agreement the distinction between a learned and an unlearned public falls away, as do the church and the state. Everyone has the same convictions, and the conviction of any single person is the conviction of every person. The state falls away as a *legislative and coercive power*. The will of any single person is actually universal law, for all other persons will the same thing; and there is no need for constraint, because everyone already wills on his own what he is supposed to will. This ought to be the goal of all our thinking and acting, and even of our individual cultivation: our final end is not ourselves but everyone. Now if this unachievable goal is nevertheless thought of as achieved, what would then happen? Employing one's individual force in accordance with this common will, each person would do his best to modify nature appropriately [*zweckmäßig*] for the usages of reason. Accordingly, anything that any one person does would be of use to everyone, and what everyone does would be of use to each individual – and this would be so in actuality, for in actuality they all have only a single end. – Now this is already how things stand, but only in the *idea*. In all that one does, each person should think of everyone. And this is precisely why one is not allowed to do certain things: because one cannot know that this is something *everyone* wills. Then, [when the unachievable final end of humanity has actually been achieved,] everyone will be allowed to do everything he wills because all will will the same [IV, 254].

Third section of ethics in the proper sense of the term: Doctrine of duties in the proper sense of the term

§19
Subdivisions of this doctrine

I

In the preceding sections we have already made a distinction between individuality and what is pure in a rational being. The latter manifests and presents itself in the moral law, whereas what is individual in such a being is what distinguishes each person from all other individuals. What unites what is pure and what is empirical is the fact that any rational being simply has to be *an individual*, albeit not precisely *this or that determinate individual*. That someone is this or that determinate individual is something contingent, and hence something that has an empirical origin. What is empirical [or individual] is the *will*, the *understanding* (in the widest sense of this term – that is, the intellect or the power of representation [*Vorstellungsvermögen*] as such) and the *body*. The object of the moral law, i.e., that in which it wants its end to be presented, is by no means anything individual, but is reason as such; in a certain sense, the moral law has itself as its object. As an intellect, I posit this reason as such as something outside me: the entire community of rational beings outside me is this presentation of reason as such [IV, 255]. I have thereby – that is, in accordance with the moral law, considered as a theoretical principle – posited reason as such outside me. – Now that this externalization of what is pure within me has occurred, I will from now on use the term "I" to refer only to the empirical or individual I, and this is how this term must be employed in ethics [*Sittenlehre*]. Thus, whenever I employ the word "I" from now on, it always means the person.

(Our ethics is therefore extremely important for our entire system, since it provides a genetic account of how the empirical I arises from the pure I and finally shows how the pure I is posited entirely outside the person.[1] Considered from our present point of view, the presentation of the pure I is the totality of rational beings, i.e., the "community of saints.")

Now how do I – as a person – relate to the moral law? I am the one to whom the moral law addresses itself and to whom it assigns the task of its execution; but the end of the moral law lies outside me. Hence I am *for myself* – i.e., before my own consciousness – only an instrument, a mere tool of the moral law, and by no means the end of the same. – Driven by the moral law, I forget myself as I engage in action; I am but a tool in its hand. A person who is looking at the goal [of his action] does not see himself, for the goal in question lies outside that person. As is the case with every intuition, so in this case as well: the subject loses itself and disappears into what is intuited, into its intuited final end. – Within me and before my own consciousness, the moral law does not address itself to other individuals outside me but has them only as objects. Before my own consciousness, these others are not means but the final end.

We must begin by addressing some objections that might be raised against this proposition.

Kant has asserted that *every human being is himself an end*,[2] and this assertion has received universal assent. This Kantian proposition is compatible with mine, when the latter has been further elaborated. For every rational being outside me, to whom the moral law certainly addresses itself in the same way that it addresses itself to me, namely, as the tool of the moral law, I am a member of the community of rational beings [IV, 256]; hence I am, from his viewpoint, an end *for him*, just as *he* is, from my viewpoint, an end *for me*. For everyone, all others outside of oneself are ends, but no one is an end for himself. That viewpoint from which all individuals without exception are a final end is a standpoint that lies beyond all individual consciousness; it is the viewpoint from which the

---

[1] *und zuletzt das reine Ich aus der Person gänzlich herausgesetzt wird.*
[2] See Kant, GMM, Section II, pp. 78–79 (*AA* 4: 428).

consciousness of all rational beings is united into one, as an object. Properly speaking, this is the viewpoint of God, for whom each rational being is an absolute and final end.

Yet someone might object that everyone expressly ought to be an end for himself; and we can concede this point as well. Everyone is an end, in the sense that everyone is a *means* for realizing reason. This is the ultimate and final end of each person's existence; this alone is why one is here, and if this were not the case, if this were not what ought to happen, then one would not need to exist at all. – This does not diminish the dignity of humanity; instead, it elevates it. Everyone is, for himself and before his own self-consciousness, charged with the task of achieving the total end of reason; the entire community of rational beings is dependent on the care and efficacious action of each person, and he alone is not dependent on anything. Everyone becomes God, to the extent that one is permitted to do so – that is, so long as one preserves the freedom of all individuals. It is precisely by means of this disappearance and annihilation of one's entire individuality that everyone becomes a pure presentation of the moral law in the world of sense and thus becomes a "pure I," in the proper sense of the term; and this occurs by means of free choice and self-determination.

That this forgetfulness with regard to oneself occurs only in the course of actual acting in the sensible world is something that was sufficiently discussed above. Those who think that perfection lies in pious meditations and devout brooding over oneself and who expect such exercises to produce the annihilation of their individuality and their merger with the godhead are very mistaken indeed. Their virtue is and remains egotism; they want only to perfect *themselves*. True virtue consists in acting, in acting for the community, by means of which one may forget oneself completely. – In the application [of the principle of morality] I will be forced to return very frequently to this important point [IV, 257].

II

I can forget myself in my efficacious acting [*Wirken*] only insofar as the latter takes place without impediment and I thereby become a means to obtaining an end that has been previously set. If this does not occur, then I will thereby be driven back into myself and will be forced to reflect upon myself, in which case I will be given to myself as an object by means of this [external] resistance.

In such a case, the moral law addresses itself immediately to me and makes me an object. I am supposed to be a means; but it turns out that I am not a means [for the end of the moral law], and I therefore ought to make myself into such a means.

One must carefully note the condition just set forth. In the ethical mood [*Stimmung*] – and I ought always and steadfastly be in such a mood –, to the extent that I cannot be a means I become for myself an object of reflection as well as an object of the acting that is commanded. My concern for myself is thus conditioned by the fact that I am unable to realize my end outside myself. Under this condition, however, such concern with myself becomes a duty.

This is how the concept of a duty *toward* [*auf*] myself arises – not, properly speaking, a duty *with respect to* [*gegen*] myself and *for the sake of* myself, which is how one customarily puts it; for in this situation as well I am and remain a means for a final end outside of myself. This concept of a duty toward myself is the concept of an acting in accordance with duty, the immediate object of which is I myself. I therefore do not wish to call such duties "duties to ourselves," which is what they are customarily called, but rather *mediate* and *conditioned* duties: "mediate" or "indirect" [*mittelbare*], because they have as their object the means for all our efficacious acting; "conditioned" [*bedingt*], because they can be derived only from the following proposition: if the moral law wills something that is conditioned (namely, the realization through me of the dominion of reason outside of me), then it also wills the condition (namely, that I be a fit and capable means for this end).

There is *for me* no other means for the realization of the law of reason, which absolutely has to be realized, than myself; and for this reason there can be no other mediate duties, in the strict sense of this term, than those [IV, 258] with respect to myself. In contrast, duties with respect to the whole, which are ultimately the highest duties and which are commanded absolutely, are to be called *immediate* (or *direct*) [*unmittelbare*] and *unconditioned* duties.

III

There is yet another division of duties, the basis of which is as follows: – Each individual is commanded to do all he can to further reason's self-sufficiency. Now if every individual responds to this command simply by doing the first thing that occurs to him or by doing whatever seems to him to be especially needed, then many different things will happen in many different ways, and some things will not happen at all. The effects of all of these actions of many different people will reciprocally hinder and cancel each other, and the final end of reason will not be advanced in an orderly manner. But the moral law absolutely commands that the latter should occur, and hence it is a *duty* for everyone who is aware of the hindrance described above to help remove it (and anyone who reflects on this situation at all can easily become aware of this hindrance). But the only way the hindrance in question can be removed is if different individuals divide among themselves the various things that have to happen in order to further reason's final end, with each person assuming responsibility on behalf of everyone else for a determinate portion of what needs to be done, while they turn over to him the responsibility for doing another determinate portion of the same. – Such an arrangement can arise only by means of agreement, through the union of several different individuals for the end of such a distribution [of responsibility]. Everyone who grasps this point has a duty to bring about a union of this sort.

Such an arrangement involves the *establishment of different estates.*[3] There ought to be different estates, and it is everyone's duty to work for the establishment thereof – or, if different estates have already been established, to select a specific estate for oneself. Everyone who selects an estate thereby selects the particular manner in which he will assume responsibility for furthering the self-sufficiency of reason [IV, 259].

Some such tasks [*Geschäfte*] can be delegated or transferred to someone else, but others cannot. What cannot be delegated is a *universal* duty. What can be delegated is a *particular* duty of the individual to whom it is transferred. From this it follows that there are universal and particular duties. The two ways of dividing duties, the one just indicated and the one provided earlier [viz., the distinction between conditioned or mediate and unconditioned or immediate duties], overlap with and mutually determine each other. We thus have to deal both with *universal* and *particular conditioned* duties and with *universal* and *particular absolute* duties.

---

[3] *Stände.* Fichte uses the term "estates" both in the sense of parliamentary estates ("estates of the realm") and that of social groups or classes, but always with reference to particular professions or trades (scholars, public officials, farmers, merchants, etc.).

§20

Universal conditioned duties

I am a tool of the moral law in the sensible world. – But I am a tool in the sensible world only on the condition, first, that there is a continuous reciprocal interaction between me and the world, the manner of which is to be determined only through my will, and second, that there is a continuous reciprocal interaction between me and [other] rational beings, since we are here dealing specifically with the effect of rational beings upon the world. (This proposition is proven in my *Natural Right*.[4] Since I would simply have to repeat the same things here, I will [instead] refer to that proof as the *proof* [of the proposition in question]. This however in no way diminishes the distinctness and clarity of our present science; for the meaning of the postulated interaction [between rational beings themselves and between rational beings and the world] will gradually become clear.) – If I am to be a tool of the moral law, then the necessary condition for my being such a tool must pertain; and if I think of myself as subject to the moral law, then I am commanded to realize to the best of my ability the condition necessary for the continued interaction between me and the world (both the sensible world and the rational world[5]) [IV, 260], for the moral law can never command the impossible. It follows that all we have to do is analyze the concept in question and relate the moral law to the particulars contained in this concept [of the continued interaction between me and the sensible and rational worlds]. In this manner we will arrive at that universal duty of which we ourselves are the immediate object; i.e., we will arrive at our universal conditioned duties – since the condition in question is a universal one, which is valid for every finite rational being.

First of all, the interaction is supposed to be *continuous*; the moral law demands our *preservation* as members of the sensible world. In my treatise on natural right, which takes no account whatsoever of any

---

[4] See *FNR*, § 3, pp. 29ff. (*SW* III: 30ff.; *GA* I/3: 340ff.).

[5] See *WLnm* for a detailed account of the complex relationship between the "sensible" and "rational" worlds – the world of material objects in space and time and the world of freely acting individuals. Both of these worlds are necessarily posited by the finite I in order to posit itself at all. These two "worlds" or "spheres" are the two extremes of a "fivefold synthesis," the central element of which is pure self-consciousness and the other two elements of which are the original determinations of the same as an finite individual material and rational being. On this point see esp. § 17 (*FTP*, pp. 354–425 [*GA* IV/2: 178–233 and *GA* IV/3: 470–499]).

moral law and knows nothing of the commands of the latter, but only has to establish the will of a free being that is determined by natural necessity, the necessity of willing our own continued existence [*Fortdauer*] was proven in the following way:[6] to say that "I will something = X" means that the existence of this object [= X] is supposed to be given to me in experience. But just as certainly as I *will* this object, it is not given to me in my present experience but first becomes possible in the future. Hence, just as certainly as I will this experience, I also will that this same *I*, the experiencing subject, exist in the future as this same identical being. When my will is viewed from this perspective, I will my continued existence only for the sake of a satisfaction that I expect in the course of this continued existence.

The will that is determined by the moral law does not will the continued existence of the individual for the same reason [as the will that is determined by natural necessity]. When guided by the moral law I am by no means concerned with whether something will be given to me in some future experience. In this case, X is something that absolutely ought to exist, apart from any relationship to me; whether or not *I* may perhaps experience X ought to be a matter of utter indifference to me, just so long as it becomes actual and just so long as I may safely presuppose that it will at some point become actual. The demand on the part of the natural human being that the object [of his willing] should be given to him is always a demand for some enjoyment; but enjoyment is, as such, never the end of the ethical way of thinking. If someone were able to tell me in advance and with complete certainty, "The end you are aiming at will indeed be realized, but you will never have any share in it; annihilation awaits you, even before it occurs" [IV, 261], I would still have to work with just as much effort for the realization of this end. I would be guaranteed that my true end would be achieved, for sharing in the enjoyment of the same was never permitted to be my end. When I am guided by the moral law I do not want to continue to exist for the sake of experiencing the end at which I am aiming, and therefore such an experience is not the reason why my own preservation is a duty. How then could the latter become my duty?

---

[6] See *FNR*, § 11, pp. 106ff. (*SW* III: 117ff.; *GA* I/3: 408ff.).

Nothing I am able to realize in the sensible world is ever the *final end* commanded by morality; this final end lies in infinity, and anything I may realize in the sensible world is only a means of approaching the latter end. Thus the proximate end [*nächste Zweck*] of each of my actions is a new acting in the future; but a person who ought to act in the future must exist in the future. Moreover, if this person is supposed to act [in the future] in accordance with a plan that he has already designed in the present, he must be and must remain the same person he is now; his future existence must develop in a regular way from his present one. When I am animated by the moral disposition, I consider myself to be simply a tool of the moral law; and therefore I will to continue to exist, and the only reason I will to continue to exist is so that I can continue to act. This is why self-preservation is a duty. We must now further determine this duty of *self-preservation*.

What is demanded is the preservation and orderly further development of the empirical self, which is viewed as intelligence (soul) and as body. The object of this command is the health and orderly further development of both the soul and the body, each considered in itself and apart from the other, and the continuation of their unhindered reciprocal influence on each other.

What is demanded by the moral law in this case is to be considered, on the one hand, *negatively*, as a prohibition: *do not undertake anything that could, in your own estimation, endanger your own self-preservation (in the sense indicated)*. On the other hand, this demand is also to be viewed *positively*, as a command: *do everything that, in your own best estimation, furthers this preservation of yourself.*

I

Let us begin with the prohibition: the preservation and well-being of the empirical self can be endangered either internally, *by disturbing the course of its natural development* [IV, 262], or *by some external force* [*Gewalt*]. As far as the former is concerned, our body is an organized product of nature, and its preservation is endangered whenever anything hinders and opposes its orderly course of operation. This is what would occur if the body were denied necessary nourishment, as a result of *fasting*, or if it were provided with too much nourishment, as a result of *intemperance*, or if the overall tendency of nature to preserve the machine were to be turned in the opposite direction, as a consequence of *sexual depravity*.[7] All these excesses violate the duty of self-preservation, especially with respect *to the body*. They [also] disturb the development of the *mind*, the activity of which depends on the well-being of the body. Fasting weakens the mind and puts it to sleep. Intemperance, gluttony, and especially the lack of chastity plunge the mind deeply into matter and deprive it of all its ability to raise itself aloft.

The development of the *mind* is immediately disturbed by the *inactivity* of the same, for the mind is a force that can be developed only by exercise; or it is disturbed by too *great an exertion*, accompanied by neglect of the body that has to support it; or it is disturbed by the mind's own *disorderly activity*, or by the blind enthusing of the imagination, without aim or rule, or by learning alien thoughts purely by rote and without exercising one's own judgment, or by sterile brooding unaccompanied by any living intuition. The mind as a whole must be trained [*ausgebildet*] completely and from all sides and by no means one-sidedly. One-sided cultivation [*Bildung*] is no cultivation at all; instead, it is the suppression of the mind. All the things just mentioned are not simply imprudent and inappropriate [*Zweckwidrig*] (that is to say, in opposition to a freely chosen end), but they also work against the absolute final end and are absolutely contrary to the duty of anyone who has acquired insight into the end of his empirical existence. Everyone, however, ought to acquire such insight.

Regarding the second danger, namely, that my preservation can be endangered by objects outside of me, the prohibition of the moral law is as follows: do not expose yourself needlessly to dangers to your health, your body, and your life. And such an exposure to danger is always (IV, 263) needless unless it is demanded by duty. If duty demands that I do something, then I am supposed to do it absolutely and regardless of any danger; for to fulfill my duty is my absolute end, and my self-preservation is only a means to this end. How there could be a command of duty that requires one to endanger one's own preservation is a question

---

[7] *Unkeuschheit*. Though *Keuschheit* would normally be rendered as "chastity" and *Unkeuschheit* as "lack of chastity," Fichte often gives this term a rather more specific sense. See, e.g., his *Staatslehre* of 1813, in which he defines *Unkeuschheit* as "the employment of the reproductive power for mere pleasure, without any attention to the end of the same and without intentionally willing this end" (*SW* IV: 478).

that does not belong here, but will be considered as part of the doctrine of absolute duties.

What does belong here is an investigation of the morality of *suicide*.

I am not supposed to expose my life to danger needlessly, i.e., without being summoned to this by a command of duty; hence the prohibition against taking my own life must be all the stronger – unless, someone might add, duty were to demand such self-destruction, just as, by your own admission, duty can demand that you expose your life to danger. A thoroughgoing solution to this problem [of whether suicide can ever be morally justifiable] thus depends upon the answer to the [prior] question concerning whether it is possible that duty could demand that one kill oneself.

Note first of all the great difference between a demand of duty that one expose one's life to danger and a demand that one destroy it. The former makes it my duty only to forget myself, to pay no regard to my own safety; and the action that is absolutely commanded and in the course of which I am supposed to forget myself aims at something lying outside of me. In this case, therefore, there is no immediate command to expose oneself to danger but only a command that one absolutely must do something that might well expose one to danger. The exposure to danger is thus commanded only indirectly and conditionally. In contrast, the immediate object of the action of committing suicide is oneself, and thus one would have to show that there is an immediate and unconditional command of duty to commit suicide. We will now see whether such a command of duty is possible.

Briefly expressed, a decision [concerning whether there can ever be a duty to commit suicide] is based on the following consideration: my life is a necessary condition for my carrying out the [moral] law. Now I am absolutely commanded to carry out this law [IV, 264], and therefore I am absolutely commanded to live, to the extent that this is something that depends upon me. My destruction of my own life would flatly contradict this command. – Such self-destruction is therefore absolutely contrary to duty. – I certainly cannot destroy my own life without removing myself, to the extent that I am able to do so, from the dominion of the moral law. But this is something the moral law can never command, since by doing so it would place itself into contradiction with itself. If my disposition is considered to be moral – and that is how it *ought* to be and how it ought to be considered when judging the morality of an action – then the only reason that I will to live is in order to do my duty. Thus to say that I do not will to live any longer is to say that I no longer will to do my duty.

The only way one might attempt to object to this conclusion would be by objecting to the major premise of our syllogism. One might then maintain the following: this present life on earth, which is all that is relevant in this context, is not for me the sole and exclusive condition of my duty. I believe in a life after death, and thus [by committing suicide] I do not end my life as such, and I do not remove myself from the dominion of the law. Instead, I only alter the *mode* [*Art*] of my life; I only move from one place to another, as I also do in this life, and as I am permitted to do. – In responding to this objection, I will stick with this simile. When I think of myself as standing under the command of the moral law is it ever really the case, even in this life, that I am merely *permitted* to alter my situation, that this is something I am free to do or not to do? Is it not the case instead that it is always either a *duty* or *contrary to duty* [to alter my situation]? Certainly the latter is the case, since, according to what was said earlier, the moral law does not leave any leeway at all for my arbitrary choice. Under the dominion of the moral law there are no indifferent actions; in every situation of my life I either ought or ought not [to do something]. What would have to be shown in this case is therefore not merely that the moral law grants us the permission to depart this life and to move on to another one, which is all that would follow from the argument stated above, but that it commands us to do this. But the impossibility of such a command can be strictly demonstrated [IV, 265]. – To begin with, the command of duty never demands immediately that I live simply for the sake of life itself, whether in this life (which is the only life with which I am familiar) or in some possible other life. Instead, the immediate command of duty is always directed at some determinate action. But since I cannot act without being alive, this first command of duty also commands me to live. (Considered as a natural human being, I do not *will* to live simply for the sake of living, but rather for the sake of some determination of my life; considered as a moral being, I *ought* not to will simply for the sake of living, but rather for the sake of some action for which I need to be alive. Just as, according to Kant, being as such is by no means a property or determination of a thing, but only the condition for its having any determinations at all,[8] so too, for a spiritual being, is life itself simply a condition [for acting in accordance with duty].) Thus it follows that I could not be directly commanded to make a transition into another life, but could be commanded to do so only indirectly, by means of a command that I engage in some determinate action not in this life but in the other one. Under no condition is it permissible – and, since there are [from a moral point of view] no actions that are merely permitted, under no condition can there be a duty – to depart this life unless we have some determinate task in the other life. This, however, is something no one still in possession of his rational powers will assert; for the laws of our thinking force us to determine what is our duty by means of that with which we are already acquainted. The state and constitution of any future life, however, is something that is entirely unknown to us, and our knowable duties fall entirely into this life. Far from ever referring me to another life, the moral law always demands, in every hour of my life, that I continue my present life, for in every hour of my life there is something for me to do, and the sphere in which this has to be done is the present world. Thus, not only actual suicide but even the mere wish not to live any longer is a violation of duty, for this is a wish to discontinue working in the only manner in which we can conceive of working [IV, 266]; it is an inclination that stands opposed to the truly moral way of thinking; it is a weariness and listlessness, which a moral human being should never allow to arise within himself. – If the joy in departing life simply signifies one's willingness to leave life as soon as one is commanded to do so by the ruler of all human fate (in whom, from this point of view, we believe), then this is quite right; and such a way of thinking is inseparable from true morality, since life, in and of itself, does not possess the least value for true morality. If, however, such joy in departing life were indicative of an *inclination* to die and to arrive at a connection with beings in another world, then such joy would be a pernicious and fanatical enthusiasm, which has already determined and depicted the future world. Such a determination of the future world is not only groundless, inasmuch as the data for such a determination can only be imagined, but it is also a violation of duty; for how can a person with a

---

[8] See Kant's demonstration, in the Dialectic of the first *Critique*, of the impossibility of an ontological proof of the existence of God on the grounds that being is not a "real predicate" (*KrV*, A 592/B620–A602/B630).

truly moral disposition have any time left over for pious fanatical enthusiasm? At each hour true virtue is completely immersed in what it has to do during the hour in question; anything else is of no concern to it, and it leaves that to those whose concern it is.

Let us examine every possible reason for this deed [of suicide], in order to convince ourselves [of the preceding argument against the morality of suicide] even as this applies to the details. The first motive to be considered, of which there have allegedly been examples, would be that one kills oneself out of despair, in order to win victory over certain vices that have become habitual and, as it were, second nature. – But precisely such despair constitutes an immoral way of thinking. If only one really and truly wills something, then one is certainly able to do it.[9] For what could compel our own will? Or what, except for our own will, could set into motion that force of ours through which we sin? In this case, therefore, one admits to oneself that one does not really and truly will to do something; one cannot bear life without exercising the vice in question, and one would rather come to terms with the demand of virtue by means of an easy death, which the latter does not demand, than by means of the difficult duty of living a blameless life, which virtue does demand. – Another possible motive might be that one kills oneself in order not to endure something shameful and vicious [IV, 267], in order not to serve as the object of another person's vice. In this case, however, what one is fleeing is not really vice; for what we suffer – if only we really suffer it; i.e., if, despite the utmost effort of all our physical force, we are still unable to resist it – does not make us guilty; only what we do can make us guilty. In such a case, therefore, what one is fleeing is the injustice, the violence, and the disgrace that is done to one and not the sin, which one does not commit oneself and which one cannot prevent the other person from committing. One kills oneself because one has been deprived of a certain enjoyment, and one cannot bear living without this enjoyment. In doing this, however, one has not renounced oneself, which is what one ought to do, and one has not sacrificed everything else to virtue. – Now that the impermissibility of such motives has been shown, is there any further need to examine others, all of which share this in common: that they are ways of evading

---

[9] *Wenn man nur recht will, kann man gewiß.*

life's purely physical sufferings? It is never the goal of a person with a moral disposition to flee life's physical sufferings.

Note. Some have accused those who commit suicide of cowardice, while others have praised their courage. Both parties are right, as is usually the case in disputes among reasonable people. This issue has two sides, and each party has viewed it only from one of these two sides. It is necessary to view it from both sides; for one must not do injustice even to the most repulsive side, since this would serve only to generate contradiction.

The decision to die is the purest presentation of the supremacy of the concept over nature. In nature there is only the duty to preserve oneself, and the decision to die is the exact opposite of this drive. Every suicide that is undertaken with cool and thoughtful self-awareness is an exercise of such supremacy, a proof of the strength of the soul, and, when viewed from this side, it necessarily occasions respect. (Most suicides occur during an attack of mindlessness, and nothing reasonable can be said about such a state.) A suicide undertaken with cool and thoughtful self-awareness issues from the previously described blind drive to self-sufficiency [IV, 268] and occurs only among those with a robust character. Courage is resoluteness toward a future that is unknown to us. Since the person who commits suicide destroys any future for himself, one cannot really attribute courage to him – unless he assumes that there is a life after death and faces the latter with the firm resolve either to fight or to endure whatever he might encounter there.

Yet no matter how much strength of soul might be required in order to decide to die, it requires far more strength to endure a life from which one expects, from this point on, nothing but suffering – a life, moreover, to which one assigns no value in itself, even if it were to be filled with the greatest joy – and not to do anything unworthy of oneself. If the former [decision to commit suicide] reveals the supremacy of the concept over nature, then the latter [decision to endure a life of suffering] reveals the supremacy of the concept itself over the concept: the autonomy and absolute self-sufficiency of thought. What lies outside the latter lies outside myself and does not concern me. If the former represents the triumph of the thought, then the latter represents the triumph of the law of thought, the purest presentation of morality; for nothing higher can be demanded of a human being than that he endure a life that has become unendurable for him. Such courage is lacking in the person who commits suicide, and only in this respect he can be called uncourageous and cowardly. He is a coward in comparison with the virtuous person; but in comparison with the abject person who subjects himself to shame and slavery simply in order to prolong for a few more years the miserable feeling of his own existence he is a hero.

II

Viewed as a command and hence *positively*, the prescription of the moral law with regard to ourselves commands us to respect our *body* and to promote its health and well-being in every way. It goes without saying that this is permitted to occur in no other sense and with no other end than in order to live and to be a fitting tool for furthering the end of reason [IV, 269].

If I am supposed to nourish myself and to promote my own bodily well-being I must possess the means required in order to do this. Hence I must economize, save, and in general maintain order and regularity in my pecuniary circumstances. This, too, is not merely a good counsel of prudence; it is a duty. Anyone who is unable to cover on his own the costs of his own maintenance is punishable.

As regards the *mind*, it is a positive duty to exercise it constantly and regularly and to keep it occupied – to the extent, of course, that this is permitted by each person's particular duties and by the duties of the estate to which one belongs (which is what we will discuss next). This is the appropriate function of aesthetic pleasures and the fine arts, the moderate and appropriate employment of which enliven both body and soul and strengthen them for further efforts.

There is nothing we can do immediately in order to further the unhindered mutual influence of body and soul upon each other; but if the body and the soul are each maintained properly in and of themselves, then such mutual influence will follow on its own.

III

All these duties are only conditioned duties. My empirical self is only a means for achieving the end of reason, and it is to be preserved and cultivated [*erhalten und gebildet*] only as such a means and only insofar as it can be such a means. It must therefore be sacrificed if its preservation comes into conflict with this end.

Before the forum of my own conscience the only thing that is contrary to reason's end is my acting in violation of an unconditioned duty. Hence the only case in which my self-preservation must be sacrificed would be one in which the only way I could maintain my life would be to violate such an unconditioned duty. I am not permitted, for the sake of life, to do anything that violates duty; for life itself is an end only for the sake of duty, and the final end is fulfilling one's duty. The usual objection to this runs as follows [IV, 270]: if, just this one time, I make an exception to the rigor of the law, an exception that allows me to save my own life, then afterwards I can still do much good, which otherwise would have remained undone. Am I not, in such a situation, bound to make such an exception for the sake of the good that I could still do? – This is the same pretense that is normally employed to defend evil in general, namely, for the sake of the good that is supposed to arise from it. In arguing in this manner, however, one forgets that we are by no means in a position to select those good works that we might want to do and to select others that we not want to do. Everyone ought to do and everyone simply must do whatever his situation, his heart, and his insight order him to do – this, and nothing else; and one simply must not do anything one is prohibited from doing by one's situation, heart, and insight. Thus, if the moral law withdraws its permission for me to *live* even before I can accomplish certain future good actions, then it is certain that these future good actions are not commanded *of me*; for I will no longer exist at the future time in question, or at least I will no longer exist under the conditions of this sensible world. Furthermore, it is already clear, simply when considered by itself, that if a person does something that is contrary to duty, purely in order to preserve his own life, then duty as such, and especially those duties he still wants to exercise after [choosing to preserve his life rather than to do his present duty] are not his absolute final end; for if duty alone were his end and if he were enlivened and animated by the moral law alone, then it would be impossible for him to do anything that would violate the moral law, just as it is impossible for the moral law to command anything that violates itself. Such a person's final end was living, and it was only after the fact that he devised the pretext that he had been concerned about the possibility of good works in the future. – Yet another remark: I am not permitted to consider or to authorize my death as a means for some good end. It is my life that is a means, not my death. It is *as an active principle* that I am a tool of the law, and not as a *thing* that serves as the law's means. It is already clear from what was said above that I am not, in this respect, permitted to kill myself (as one might consider the suicide of Lucretia[10] a means for liberating Rome). Moreover, I am also not permitted [IV, 271] willingly to allow myself to be murdered, if I can prevent it, and still less to seek the occasion for that or to provoke others to kill me (as is related, e.g., of Codrus),[11] even were I to believe that in doing this I would insure the salvation of the world. Such behavior is itself a kind of suicide. – Here we need to make some careful distinctions: not only am I permitted to expose my life to danger when duty demands this, this is what I ought to do. That is to say, I ought to *forget* my concern for my own self-preservation. But I absolutely ought not to *think* of my own death as a *end*.

§21

Particular conditioned duties

As was indicated earlier (§ 19) when we deduced the necessity of establishing estates, particular duties are the duties of one's estate. *Conditioned* particular duties are those that have as their object our-selves, our empirical selves, insofar as we belong to this or that particular estate. The following is to be noted concerning such duties.

I

Where there are particular estates, it is the absolute duty of each individual to be a member of one of these estates, i.e., to further the goal of reason in a particular way. We demonstrate this as follows:

Were there no established estates, then it would be the duty of everyone who saw the necessity of such estates to establish them as a necessary condition for the complete and methodical furtherance of the end of reason, as was shown earlier [IV, 272]. It is therefore all the more one's duty to choose a determinate estate where such estates have already

---

[10] Lucretia, wife of Lucius Tarquinius Collatinus, killed herself after having been raped by Sextus Tarquinius. Traditionally, her death was considered the occasion for the overthrow of the Roman kingdom in 510 BC.

[11] According to tradition, Codrus was the last king of Athens. The Delphic oracle had informed the invading Dorians that they would be victorious so long as they did not kill the Athenian king. Codrus, dressed as a peasant, killed a Dorian and was killed in return. When the Dorians discovered his identity, they withdrew.

been established; for where this is the case no one can any longer act efficaciously "in general," without thereby doing what others have already taken upon themselves and thereby either hindering them and injuring the furtherance of reason's end, or else doing something that is superfluous and in vain, which equally violates the moral law. The only option remaining is that everyone choose an estate for himself and make this choice known to his fellow human beings in a universally valid way.

II

It is a duty to base one's choice of an estate not upon inclination, but rather upon one's best conviction concerning the estate that is most precisely appropriate for one, taking into account the quantity of one's forces, one's education, and those external conditions over which one has some control. The aim of our lives is not to satisfy inclination but to further the end of reason, and every force in the sensible world ought to be employed for this aim in the most advantageous manner. To this one might object as follows: very few human beings choose their estate themselves. Instead, it is chosen for them by their parents, by circumstances, and so forth; or, in cases where it can indeed be said that they themselves choose their estate, they do so prior to attaining the requisite maturity of reason and before they are really capable of serious reflection and of being determined purely by the moral law. To this I reply that such a situation should not exist and that anyone who recognizes it has to work, wherever possible, for this situation to become different. Until the maturity of humanity as such has been developed within them, all human beings should be educated in the same manner and should educate themselves in the same manner; and only then should they choose an estate. We are not denying that for this to occur many other aspects of human affairs would have to be different than they are at present. But what is established by an ethics [*ein Sittenlehre*] is always the ideal, even if the latter should not be realizable under all conditions. Indeed, what is established by an ethics cannot be realizable under all conditions, for then ethics itself would be something vacillating and indeterminate [IV, 273]. Ethics, however, is not supposed to conform to the circumstances, but the circumstances are supposed to begin to conform to it.

Perhaps this is an appropriate place for a reminder that the hierarchy of the estates, their rank, etc. is a purely civil arrangement [*bürgerliche*

Einrichtung], though such an arrangement is necessary. The manifold activities of human beings are subordinated to one another as what is conditioned and its condition, as end and means; and thus so must those who engage in such manifold activities be subordinated to one another in the same manner. From the standpoint of moral judgment all estates have the same worth. Reason's end is furthered in each estate, beginning with that estate that wrests from the soil its fruits, which is a condition for the preservation of our species in the sensible world,[12] through the scholar, who thinks of future ages and works for them, and including the legislator and the wise ruler, who establishes institutions that embody the thoughts of the researcher for the well-being of the most remote generations. If everyone dutifully does all that he is able to do, then everyone is of equal rank before the tribunal of pure reason.

III

I cannot, however, choose an estate without the consent of all other human beings, for reason's plan ought to be furthered completely and purposively. Others, however, have already distributed among themselves the particular tasks that are necessary for furthering this plan, and thus I have to inquire if there is space remaining for me, and, in case my effort is needed, [indicate] where I want to exert it. I have the right to apply to do this, and society has the right to turn me down. But if there were no institution established for the purpose of making such an adjudication, then I would have to judge for myself, as conscientiously as possible, where my assistance is most needed.

An individual's estate is therefore determined through the reciprocal interaction between him and society, a reciprocal interaction that has to be initiated by the individual. He has to apply [for membership in a particular estate] [IV, 274].

IV

It is one's duty to cultivate one's mind and body in the particular ways that will make them of use to the estate to which one has dedicated oneself. The farmer requires, above all, strength and physical

---

[12] *Durch welche die sinnliche Erhaltung unseres Geschlechts bedingt ist.*

endurance; the artist or craftsman [*Künstler*] particularly requires skill and dexterity. Whereas theoretical cultivation of the mind is only a means for the farmer and the artist, the scholar's end is the all-around cultivation of the mind, and for him the body is only a means for supporting and preserving the mind in the sensible world. – This aspect of the scholar seems to have exercised a harmful influence on popular opinion. It is the duty of the scholars to reflect and to cultivate their understanding systematically, for that is what is required of them by their estate. But many [scholars] wanted to transform into a duty for humanity in general what was [only] a duty for their estate, and the meaning of this demand seemed to be more or less that all human beings ought to become scholars. This was most clearly visible, and in part it still remains visible, in the tendency of theologians to transform all human beings into theologians as good as themselves and to view their science as necessary for blessedness. This is why a much too lofty value was attributed to theoretical enlightenment, even in the absence of other good qualities, and why even virtue and godliness were associated with solitary meditation and speculation. To be sure, this is a virtue for the scholar, but only if he retains the goal of communicating with others. Other estates require only as much theoretical culture as is needed in order to understand and to judge what pertains to the affairs of their estate and is required in order to perfect their skills – but, above all, they require that cultivation that enables them to elevate themselves to acting from duty, and this requires less cultivation of the understanding than of the will [IV, 275].

Overview of universal immediate duties

§22

Subdivisions

The final end of all the actions of any morally good human being, and especially of all the external effects of his actions, can be summarized in the following formula: *he wills that reason and reason alone should have dominion in the sensible world.* All physical force ought to be subordinated to reason.

Reason, however, can have dominion only in and through rational beings. Hence moral acting, even if it is perhaps aimed directly at non-rational nature, always refers, at least indirectly, to rational beings and has only them as its [ultimate] aim. Just as there are no rights with regard to non-rational nature, so too are there no duties regarding nature. As we will see later, there does arise a duty to fashion [*bearbeiten*] nature, but only for the sake of rational beings.

The morally good person therefore wills that reason and morality should have dominion within the community of rational beings.

The aim is not merely that nothing should occur except what is good and in accordance with reason, i.e., that legality alone should rule, but rather that this should occur freely, in consequence of the moral law, and hence that genuine, true morality should rule. – This is a major point and one that must not be overlooked. Neglect of this point has introduced much that is harmful and corruptive into [the realm of] theory and from there into life, as we shall show at the proper point by means of examples [IV, 276].

But no action is moral that does not occur with freedom; hence every morally good human being's goal is the formal freedom of all rational beings; and thus we must begin by discussing [in § 23] *duties in relationship to the formal freedom of others*.

Everyone, without exception, ought to be formally free. But it can happen that someone uses his own intrinsic freedom to suppress the freedom of others. We must investigate what duty demands in such a case; therefore we must also discuss [in § 24] *duties with respect to conflict between the formal freedom of rational beings.*

Finally, every morally good person wills that everyone employ his freedom to do his duty; the good person's end is to promote a dutiful disposition within all rational beings. We must therefore conclude by discussing [in § 25] *duties regarding the immediate dissemination and promotion of morality.*

§23

Duties regarding the formal freedom of all rational beings

The formal freedom of an individual consists in the continuous reciprocal interaction between his body, both as a tool and as a sensory organ [*als Werkzeug und Sinn*], and the sensible world – an interaction that is determined and determinable only through the individual's freely designed concept concerning the character of this reciprocal interaction. This demands two different things: [1] the continuation of absolute freedom and the inviolability of *the body*, that is, that nothing should be able to exercise a direct influence on the body by means of physical force, and [2] the continuation of one's free influence upon the *entire sensible world* [IV, 277]. (See my *Natural Right*, § 11.)[13]

I

The prescription [*Verordnung*] of the moral law with respect to the bodies of rational beings outside us can on the one hand be considered negatively, as a prohibition, and on the other positively, as a command.

The principle of adjudication in this case is the following: for a person with a moral disposition, every human body is a tool for the realization of the moral law in the sensible world. A body, however, can be such a tool only on the condition that it remain free, that is, on the condition that it remain entirely and solely dependent upon the free will of the person in question. – Just as soon as anyone catches sight of a human body, the moral law issues to him a command regarding this determinate body. – I have good reason for adding this point and for emphasizing it as well; for someone could claim that even if one thing or another were not the case, the end of reason would nevertheless still be realized, inasmuch as the realization of reason's end really cannot depend on one thing more or less. The reply to such a claim is as follows: this is a matter that simply does not concern us at all, and we are by no means permitted to think in this manner. It suffices that this individual also exists, and that he is free; as soon as we perceive him, the moral law commands us to consider him as a member of the community of rational beings, and thus as necessarily one of the tools for realizing the moral law. (It should be noted, if only in passing, that here we already have some idea of the dominion of the moral law within nature, independent of us, and of the purposiveness of nature for the moral law – an idea [*Idee*] that is realized in the idea of the godhead, though this is not something we need to discuss here.)

---

[13] See *FNR*, pp. 103 ff. (*SW* III: 113ff.; *GA* I/3: 405ff.)

This prescription, viewed negatively, is an absolute prohibition: *never exercise any immediate influence over the body of the other.* A human body is supposed to be dependent upon the will of the person, and absolutely not dependent upon any external force. To be sure, I may determine the [other's] body indirectly, by determining the will of the other person through rational grounds in order thereby to bring about this or that modification in his body and thereby to produce some modification of the sensible world.

I may not employ the body of the other as a tool, as a means for my will – which is certainly the most impractical way of proceeding as well [IV, 278]. I may not seek to move the other person's will by constraint, beatings, hunger, withdrawal of freedom, or imprisonment. I may influence the will of the other only through rational grounds and in absolutely no other way.

I may not immediately impede another person's causality within the sensible world. Later on, we will consider exceptions to this universal prohibition.

I am absolutely prohibited from ever intentionally killing anyone; the death of a human being is never permitted to be the aim of my action. This may be rigorously proven as follows: every human being is a means for the realization of the moral law. Now in the case of any specific human being, I either consider it to be possible that this person could nevertheless be or become such a means or else I do not consider this to be possible. If I consider this to be a possibility, then how can I, without renouncing obedience to the moral law and without being indifferent to the realization of the same, destroy this person who, according to my own presupposition, is destined to contribute to the realization of the moral law? If I do not consider this to be a possibility, if I consider a certain person to be an incorrigible villain, then, precisely because I think of him in this way, I am engaging in an immoral way of thinking. This is because the moral law absolutely obliges me to cultivate him to [the standpoint of] morality as well and to assist in the effort to improve him.[14] If I take it to be an established fact for me that he is incorrigible, then I shirk a task that is absolutely commanded; but since I am not permitted to shirk such a task, I also am not permitted to consider any

---

[14] *Denn es ist mir durch das Sittengesetz schlechthin aufgegeben, ihn zur Moralität mit zu bilden, und an seiner Besserung arbeiten zu helfen.*

person to be incorrigible. The moral law simply demands that I believe that every human being can improve himself. But if such a belief is necessary, then the first part of our argument once again proves to be valid: I cannot take a human life without abandoning my own end and without also destroying the end of reason in him, to the extent that this concerns me [IV, 279]. If a person is supposed to become moral, then he has to remain alive.

Our inference was as follows: it is absolutely commanded of me to promote the morality of every individual. But I cannot do this without assuming that it is possible to do so; hence, etc. The minor premise of this syllogism, which alone might stand in some need of proof, can be proven as follows: to say that I adopt something as my end – in this case, my end is the improvement of some individual – means that I postulate the actuality of this end at some future moment; but to postulate this means to posit it as possible. But since the end in question here is one that I necessarily must, according to the moral law, posit for myself, I necessarily have to think as well of everything that is contained in this end. – Just as we previously demonstrated the necessity of believing in the perfectibility of the human species in general or as such, so here we have demonstrated the necessity of believing in the improvability of each individual in particular.

Consequently, just as premeditated suicide is under no condition compatible with a truly moral disposition, so too is the latter never compatible with the premeditated murder of someone else, and indeed for the same reason. In each of these cases, what is destroyed is a possible tool for accomplishing the end of reason. To be sure, just as there can arise a duty to expose one's own life to danger, so can there also arise a duty to expose someone else's life to danger. We will see under what circumstances this might occur. (In my *Natural Right*[15] I addressed the alleged right of the state to punish a criminal by taking his life, and there I explained that the state, as a judge, can do no more than totally abrogate the civil contract with the criminal, as a result of which the criminal loses all of his rights and becomes a mere thing [*Sache*]. This, however, concerns only his relationship to the state, which is not a *moral* but is merely a *juridical* person. The killing of the criminal may well ensue, following the abrogation of all of his [civil] rights – not as a

---

[15] See *FNR* (Part II, § 20, V, sects. d–f), pp. 242–247 (*SW* III: 279–284; *GA* I/4: 73–78).

punishment, however, but rather as a means of security. It is therefore not an act of the *juridical* power at all, but only of the *police power*. An individual may well risk his own security for the sake of the [IV, 280] duty never to take a human life; indeed, this is something one ought to do. But the [civil] authorities do not have this same right to risk the security of everyone.

In this same work we also declared our views concerning the killing of an armed enemy during warfare, which is something that can certainly be in accord with right and duty.[16] The aim of war is by no means to kill the citizens of the state upon which we are making war. Its aim is only to repulse the enemy or to disarm him, to render the state upon which war is being made defenseless and to force it to enter into a lawful relationship with our state. In hand-to-hand combat an individual may kill the enemy, not in order to kill him but in order to defend his own life against him; and in doing this he is not acting in accordance with any [alleged] right to kill, conveyed to him by the state (a right that the state itself does not possess), but rather, in accordance with his own right and duty of self-defense.)

Considered *positively* and as a command, the disposition of the moral law with respect to the bodies of rational beings outside us, is as follows:

Our end is supposed to be the health, strength and preservation of the other's body and life; not only ought we not to hinder this preservation, we also ought to further it, to the extent that this is something that lies within our power and to the same degree that we further the preservation of our own bodies. – This may be rigorously proven as follows: every human body is a tool for advancing reason's end. Now if the latter is indeed my highest final end, then the preservation and the greatest possible fitness of each tool for accomplishing this goal must necessarily be my end as well, for I cannot very well will something conditioned without also willing the condition thereof. The preservation of every person outside me is a cause that will lie just as close to my heart as does my own preservation, because my reason for willing each of these is the same. I preserve and care for myself only as a tool of the law of reason. But every human body is such a tool; hence I must demonstrate the same concern for everyone, if indeed I am driven by nothing but the moral law – which is how it ought to be [IV, 281].

---

[16] See *FNR*, pp. 327–328 (*SW* III: 377–378; *GA* I/4: 157–159).

Here we arrive for the first time at a proposition that, from this point on, will regulate all [our] positive duties toward others: demonstrate just as much concern for the well-being of each of your neighbors as you do for your own well-being; love your neighbor as yourself.[17] The basis for this assertion has already been indicated. I am permitted to care for myself only because and only insofar as I am a tool of the moral law; but every other human being is also a tool of the moral law. – This also furnishes us with an unfailing test for determining whether concern for ourselves is moral or is merely [an expression of] the natural drive. If it is the former, then one will demonstrate the same concern for others; if it is the latter, then it will be directed exclusively toward oneself. The natural drive is directed purely toward oneself; and the effect of sympathy, which is a natural drive that stirs one to share in the fate of others, is far weaker than that of the immediate drive for self-preservation. Here one always thinks of oneself first, and only afterwards of one's neighbor.

I ought to be just as concerned about the preservation of others as of myself. But according to what was said earlier, I am not concerned with my own preservation and I do not think about myself at all unless I am reminded of myself, either by feelings of weakness and exhaustion or when my self-preservation is endangered. Concern for the preservation of others is no different. We are not claiming that I ought to do nothing but pursue or seek opportunities for saving someone else's life and health – unless, perhaps, to do so constitutes my particular profession. But as soon as someone is in danger, I absolutely ought to go to his assistance, even if this should endanger my own life and regardless of whether the danger stems from the non-rational physical power of nature or from an attack by some rational beings.

I just said, "even if this should endanger my own life"; and, despite what one might believe, there is no conflict of duties whatsoever in such a case. My self-preservation is conditioned by the preservation of the other, and his preservation is conditioned by mine. The two are completely equal; they possess the same value and for the same reason. It is not my intention that either I or the other should perish, but rather, that we both should be preserved. If, however, one or both of us should in

---

[17] Lev. 19: 18; Math. 22: 39.

fact perish [IV, 282], this is not something for which *I* have to take responsibility; I will have done what was required by duty.

(It is a vain excuse to appeal to the duty of self-preservation when another person is in danger; in such a case the duty of self-preservation ceases. Translated correctly, such an appeal asserts that we want to save the other person, but only if we ourselves can remain safe in the process. And this is supposed to be something special and grand! Not to want to save human lives even when we could do this with no danger to ourselves would obviously be murder. – Furthermore, and despite what some moralists believe, we are not, in such cases, first supposed to calculate which life might possess more value, whose preservation might matter more. Judged by the moral law, every human life possesses equal value; as soon as any human being is endangered, all other human beings, no matter who they may be, no longer have the right to be safe until this person's life has been saved. – The words of the late Duke Leopold[18] are forthright, grand, and totally in line with the ethical disposition: "What is at stake here are human lives, so why should I count any more than you?")

II

The second element of the other person's formal freedom, which, according to the moral law, we are supposed to preserve and promote, consists in the latter's free influence upon the sensible world, i.e., his influence upon the same to the extent that this is determined merely through a concept of his. His efficacious action is supposed to produce what he is thinking of when he acts in this way, for only on this condition is he free.

(a) First of all, a condition for exercising such causality is that one possess correct knowledge of that upon which one is exercising an effect. I can by no means act efficaciously upon anything of which I do not possess a concept. My concept of an end is determined by my concept of the actual being and constitution of the thing as it is, apart from any contribution from me. My concept of an end proceeds from the present constitution of the thing and conforms to the natural laws pertaining to that thing. If I have an incorrect concept of the object of

---

[18] Duke Maximilian Julius Leopold of Brunswick (1752–1785), major general in the Prussian army, died while trying to save flood victims in Frankfurt/Oder.

my action, then what will follow from the same will be something utterly different than what I thought, and my causality will therefore not be free [IV, 283].

I must will something conditioned: the free causality of my fellow human beings in the sensible world; therefore I must also will the condition for the same: that others have a correct cognition of the sensible world, a cognition sufficient for the causality in question. The correctness of the other person's practical cognition must therefore be my goal as well, just as much as and for the same reason that the correctness of my own practical cognition is my end.

This disposition [*Disposition*] of the moral law, considered *negatively*, leads to the absolute prohibition against ever leading another person into error, that is, to the prohibition against lying to or deceiving the other – whether this occurs in an outright manner (by categorically asserting something I myself do not consider to be true) or by means of circumlocution (by providing him with ambiguous reports intended to deceive him). The latter is just as much a lie as the former, for what matters is not my words themselves but my intention in using them. If I will to deceive, then I am a liar – regardless of whether I tell a boldfaced lie or merely mislead the other into making a false inference. Whether the latter is actually my intention, or whether, instead, it is simply by chance that my statement happens to be ambiguous: this is something for which I must answer before my own conscience. In short, absolute sincerity and truthfulness is something I simply owe everyone; I am not permitted to say anything that contradicts the truth. We will examine below whether and to what extent I also owe [others] openness, that is, to what extent I am obliged to tell all the truth that I know.

The preceding proposition can be rigorously proven as follows: if I have a dutiful disposition [*Gesinnung*], then I consider the other person to be a tool not, as it were, of mere legality, but of morality; that is, I consider him to be someone who always ought to choose what is best, according to his own insight and from his own good will. But if I furnish him with an incorrect cognition, and if he then proceeds to act in accordance with this criterion, then what ensues is not something that was chosen by this other person himself; instead, he has been made into a means for my end, and this contradicts a dutiful disposition. If I thereby mislead him into performing an illegal action – an action he might consider to be moral, since he is acting on the basis of incorrect presuppositions – , then my wrongdoing is obvious [IV, 284]: I have aimed to accomplish an immoral end and have used the other as a tool, perhaps contrary to his own way of thinking. Even leaving out of account my misuse of the other person, it is as if I myself had committed the immoral deed that I deceived him into performing. Properly speaking, I am the author of this deed. But even if the action that I was counting on and that was accomplished by the other person were legal, I would still have acted completely in violation of duty. The other person is not supposed to do what is right on the basis of some error, but ought to do it out of love for the good. I am by no means permitted to aim at mere legality; instead, morality is my final end. I cannot make legality my sole aim without renouncing morality, which violates my duty. – And yet, a defender of such an immoral ethics [*Sittenlehre*] might reply, I knew very well that this was the only way that the other person could be brought to do the good. To this I would respond as follows: first of all, this is not something you can ever know, nor is it anything you ought ever believe; for giving up on the other's rationality in this way is a violation of duty. Furthermore, even if we were to assume that you are correct about the situation and that unless you had deceived him the other would not have accomplished that good that you allege to have had as your sole end, you would bear no guilt whatsoever for this state of affairs. For you are by no means charged simply with realizing this good, regardless of the means. It is supposed to be realized on the basis of morality; otherwise it is not good. Precisely by renouncing the form, which alone constitutes the essence of the good, and by aiming solely at the matter or content, you make it obvious that what concerns you with respect to the good in question is not the interest of morality, but some advantage. For it is only the latter that is satisfied through the mere content. The same reasons apply against anyone who might seek to excuse a lie by saying that he told it because he thereby wanted to prevent some wrongdoing.[19] He ought to hate the wrongdoing and to prevent it because it is immoral, and by no means for the sake of the action as

---

[19] In September 1797 Immanuel Kant had published in a Berlin journal a brief essay entitled, "On an Alleged Right to Lie From Philanthropic Love." Earlier that year a German translation of a work by the French writer and political theorist, Benjamin Constant (1767–1830), had appeared, in which the latter had argued against Kant's position that it would be wrong not to tell the truth to a prospective murderer who asks me whether a friend of mine, whom he is pursuing, is hiding in my house. In his response to Constant in the essay, "On the Alleged Right to Lie," Kant defends his position by rejecting the very notion of a "right to lie."

such. He can tell the truth to someone who asks him for it with an evil intent, but if he is aware of the other person's evil intent then he ought to remonstrate with him and seek to convince him of the [IV, 285] blameworthiness of his intention. How could he ever presuppose that these remonstrations will be of no help? But even if they were actually to prove to be of no help, the option of resistance by physical means still remains open to the person in question. Thus we have here cut off forever the pretense of lying with good intent; what ensues from a lie is never good.

The information [I provide the other in this case] could concern either nature (which, in this context, also includes the dispositions [*Dispositionen*] of other free beings, concerning which nothing in particular is here to be noted) or my own disposition. In the latter case, I make a promise to the other. I must keep my promise, unless I have promised to perform some immoral action.

To this one might respond that I may change my opinion and my operating assumptions [*Maßregeln*] regarding what I have promised. Our reply to this is as follows: with respect to a matter upon which I have given another person grounds to depend, I am no longer dependent only upon myself, but also upon the other person. With respect to this matter, I am in his service; I cannot take back my word without frustrating those actions of his which he undertook in view of my promise, and hence without destroying his causality in the sensible world. – I can remonstrate with him in order to persuade him to release me from my promise, and I am rid of this promise only when he releases me from it of his own good will. In doing this, he gives me a gift. Good advice for avoiding the difficulties arising from such a situation in community with others is not to make promises lightly regarding matters concerning which one fears one may be able to change one's opinion and which are in any way dependent upon some future outcome.

I said that I must keep my word unless I have promised something immoral. This proposition needs to be determined more precisely. For everything concerning which I know better or concerning which I am merely undecided is immoral for me; and from this it would seem to follow that I would not be permitted to keep [IV, 286] my word the moment I became of a different mind or even if I were simply to begin to harbor doubts concerning the promised achievement. My response to this is as follows: for the other person's sake I have to do everything that lies along the path toward achieving the end of reason, so long as this is not directly contrary to morality, even if I might be able to do better as far as I am personally concerned. The only thing I am absolutely not permitted to do is what completely violates morality.

I will now address two questions that intrude at this point.

The first question is as follows: how is it that so many people, who otherwise wish to be regarded as righteous and not unintelligent, defend white lies [*Notlügen*] and seek in every way possible to make excuses for the same? The reason is as follows: when, in our present era, people train [*ausbilden*] their mind and their natural character in a manner in keeping with this same era, such culture [*Kultur*] – which, however, is by no means achieved through freedom – places them in the position that was described in more detail above (§ 16, III). Their empirical I is supposed to have dominion over the world, without any regard for the freedom of others; they want to make the world happy, to fill it with bliss, and to keep it from all harm, and they want to do this in accordance with *their* concepts of happiness and unhappiness. This is their main goal. But, because of that weakness with which our own era is so rightly reproached, they do not possess the resoluteness [*Kraft des Entschlusses*] required in order to realize their arbitrary ends by means of force, which is what a vigorous character relies upon; they therefore decide to accomplish their ends by means of cunning. This inner way of thinking then also determines their theoretical system, assuming that they are not the sort of philosophers who are able to proceed from the absolutely highest principles. They proceed from a fact within themselves, that is, from their drive to lay down the law [for everyone], combined with their lack of the courage required in order to execute the law forcefully; from this point on they proceed consistently. That some of them nevertheless depart from their own theory when it comes to acting is to be explained as follows: something else prevents them from employing their own principle, something that also lies within them, but that lies too deep to be able to exercise any influence upon their reasoning: namely, the natural feeling of honor [*Ehrgefühl*] [IV, 287].

The second question to which we are led by the preceding is the following: what is the source of that inner shame regarding oneself that evinces itself even more in the case of a lie than in that of any other unconscionable wrongdoing? The reason is as follows: the frame of

273

mind of the liar is the one described above. He wants to subordinate the other person to his intentions. Now he does this by deceitfully and only apparently subordinating himself to the other's intentions, by appearing to agree with the other's plan, by approving the other's intentions and appearing to further the same. In doing this, he places himself in contradiction with himself; he subjects himself to the person whom he does not dare to oppose openly; he behaves in a cowardly fashion. A lie always in every case involves cowardice. Nothing, however, dishonors us more in our own eyes than lack of courage.

In addition, defending white lies and lying in general for the sake of some good end or another is without a doubt the most absurd and at the same time the most perverted thing that has ever been heard of among human beings. It is the most absurd [for the following reason]: you tell me that you have convinced yourself that a white lie is permissible. If I am supposed to believe you when you tell me this, then I must at the same time not believe it when you say it; for I cannot know if, in saying this to me, you may not be employing this same maxim against me for the sake of some laudable end – for who may know all your ends? –; and thus I cannot know whether your assurance that you deem a white lie to be permissible is not itself an instance of a white lie. Anyone who actually had such a maxim could neither wish to admit that he had it nor wish to make it into a maxim for others; instead, he would have to conceal it carefully within himself and wish to reserve it for himself alone. Once communicated, it would annihilate itself. Once it has become known that a person has such a maxim, then no reasonable person can believe him any longer; for no one is able to know such a person's secret ends nor able to judge whether he might now be in one of those situations in which a lie is permitted – but if no one believes him, then no one will be deceived by him [IV, 288]. Now it is undoubtedly sheer nonsense to ask anyone to believe something that, if and when it is believed, annuls itself.

Defense of white lies is also the most perverted thing possible among human beings. In defending a white lie a person discloses his own, thoroughly corrupt way of thinking. The true root of your perversion lies in the fact that such a lie *even occurred* to you as a possible way of escaping certain predicaments and that you are now able seriously to consider whether one might not be allowed to avail oneself of such a means of escape. Nature contains no drive toward lying; it proceeds directly toward enjoyment. Nor is the moral mode of thinking acquainted with lying. The thought of lying requires something positively evil: a *deliberate search* for some crooked path that will allow one to avoid proceeding along the straight path that offers itself to us. (What has just been said should be compared with our earlier derivation of human lying, above, pp. 194–195.) The possibility of such an escape route does not even occur to an honest person; and hence the concept of lying would never have entered into the system of human concepts simply through the honest person, nor would an investigation into the morality of the white lie have entered into ethics.

Our thoughts on this subject can be made clearer with the help of common classroom examples. A human being who is being persecuted by an enemy with a drawn sword hides himself in your presence. His enemy arrives and asks you where he is. If you tell the truth, then an innocent person will be murdered; hence, some would argue, you would have to lie in such a case. How do those who engage in such rash reasoning move so quickly over and beyond the many possibilities that lie before them on the straight path and switch to the crooked one? First of all, why should you tell the person who asks you where the other is hiding *either* the truth *or* a lie? Why not tell him some third thing, something that lies in the middle: namely, that you do not owe him an answer, that he seems to harbor some quite evil intention, that you advise him to abandon this intention of his own free will, and that otherwise you will take up the cause of the persecuted party and will defend him at the risk of your own life – which is, in any case, your absolute obligation? – You reply that if you were to do this then he would turn his wrath [IV, 289] against you. But why, I ask you, do you consider only this single possibility, inasmuch as, among all the things that are possible in this case, there is also a second possibility, namely, that the opponent will be so startled by your just and audacious resistance that he will desist from persecuting his enemy and will become calmer and open to negotiations? But let us suppose that he does attack you. Why is this something you would absolutely seek to avoid? You were obliged in any case to protect the persecuted person at the risk of your own body, for as soon as any human life is in danger you no longer have the right to be concerned about the security of your own life. Thus it is already clearly evident from what you have said that the immediate end of your lie was by no means to save the life of your fellow human being, but simply to save your own skin; moreover, the danger to you was not even an actual danger, but only one of two possibilities. Thus you wanted to lie simply in order to evade the remote possibility of suffering damage. – So let him attack you! Are you defeated in advance by the bare fact of such an attack, which is what you once again seem to be assuming when you overlook the other remaining possibilities? According to your presupposition, the originally persecuted person has been hiding nearby, and now *you* are in danger. He has a universal duty to come to your aid, and now this is his particular duty as well, out of gratitude [to you for not betraying his location]. Why do you so confidently presuppose that he will not do this? But let us assume that *he* does not come to your aid. In this case you have gained some time through your resistance [to his assailant's demands], and other people might happen to arrive and come to your aid. Finally, if none of these things happen and you have to fight all by yourself, why are you so certain that you will be defeated? Do you not count at all upon the force that will be imparted to your body by your firm resolve simply not to tolerate any wrong and by your enthusiasm [*Enthusiasmus*] for the good cause, nor upon the weakness that confusion, along with the consciousness of his own wrongdoing, must impart to your enemy? – In the worst case, you can do no more than die [IV, 290]; but once you are dead it is no longer your responsibility to defend the life of the person who has been attacked, and at the same time you are thereby protected from the danger of lying. Hence death takes precedence over lying; and you never reach the point of telling a lie. You begin with the lie because you have an eye only for what is crooked, and the straight path is not present for you at all.

Considered *positively*, the proposition that our end must include the correctness of other persons' cognition results in the command to promote correct insight on the part of others and actually to communicate to them any truth we ourselves might know.

We now have to display the basis for such a command; and we shall see at once how far it extends, since we can certainly see in advance that this command might not be unrestrictedly valid. I am required to regard the other person as a tool of the moral law. But an effect corresponding to his concept [of what is required by the moral law] will occur only if this other person has a correct cognition of the object upon which he is acting. I owe it to him to promote his efficacy; hence, even without being summoned by him to do this, I owe it to him to communicate correct cognition to him [regarding this object]. Considered by itself, this is already one of my necessary ends. – But to what extent [am I required to do this]? Naturally, [I am required to communicate correct cognition to the other person] only to the extent that the cognition in question has some immediate influence upon his acting, that is, to the extent that this cognition is immediately practical for him. We therefore would have to distinguish between *immediately practical* items of knowledge [*Kenntnissen*] and purely *theoretical* ones. But according to a thoroughgoing transcendental philosophy, all theory is related to practice, and no theory is possible without such a relationship to practice. The distinction in question is therefore a merely relative one. The very same thing that is purely theoretical for one individual or for one era can be practical for another individual or era. Thus, in order to know which truth one owes to a particular individual, one would first have to be able to ascertain which truth happens to be practical for precisely this individual. How can one do this?

This is something that is immediately evident from each individual's acting. Cognition of that upon which a person is acting, is for him, immediately practical, and every other cognition is not. – If, therefore, I see [IV, 291] that my fellow human being is engaged in some action, and if I have some reason to surmise that he is not entirely acquainted with the particular circumstances, or if I know for certain that he has an incorrect view of these circumstances, it is then my duty to correct his error without any further ado and without first waiting to be summoned by him to do this; for he is in danger of doing something that is contrary to his own end, and when I am engaged in the moral way of thinking I am not indifferent to the occurrence of something contrary to one's end. I am by no means permitted to tolerate his error on this point.

Here I have been speaking throughout about immediately practical truth, and I have presupposed that I in particular am summoned to communicate such truth simply because I happen to be the first person [encountered by the other] and the person nearest to him. Furthermore, the view advanced here is not, as was indicated previously with respect to another duty, that one should actively seek out occasions for correcting those who are in error. That is something for which I do not have the time, assuming that I always do what presents itself to me to be done; and as a general matter, our virtue must always naturally consist in acting whenever we are summoned to act, and not, so to speak, in seeking out adventures, for the latter is not a truly virtuous disposition.

It is the duty of a particular estate, namely, the learned estate or the scholars, to seek and to disseminate truth that is purely theoretical, either for the era as such or for most individuals living during that era. The truth in question ought to become practical, but it cannot do this immediately and all at once, for no step along the path leading toward the perfection of humankind may be skipped. This learned estate works on behalf of future eras and, as it were, lays up treasures that will become useful only then. Later on, we will discuss the duties of the scholar.

III

If a rational being is supposed to exercise free efficacy, i.e., if what this rational being thought of in his concept of an end is supposed to occur within experience, then the constitution of everything related to his ends and of everything that has any influence upon them has to continue to remain the way it was when be became aware of the constitution of the same and when he presupposed [IV, 292] this in his concept of this end. If the success of this person's action depends on and is conditioned by the continued existence of something, and if the latter is altered while he is still engaged in acting, then this also alters the effect of his action, and what was supposed to ensue fails to ensue. (For further discussion of this proposition, which, considered by itself, is straightforward enough, see § 11 of my *Natural Right*.)[20] Assuming that I live among several free beings, what is related to my [individual] acting in this way and is, so to speak, the premise of all my acting in the sensible world – inasmuch as it is that from which my acting proceeds and which it presupposes – can itself only be a part of the sensible world. When it is recognized and guaranteed by society, this particular part of the world, the part that is subject to my ends, is called my *property*. (This recognition and guarantee is *juridically* and *humanly* necessary. Without such recognition I could never be certain that I was not, through my own acting, restricting the freedom of others; and thus I could never act with a good conscience. I can undertake to do something with a good conscience only on the condition that *everyone* concede

---

[20] See *FNR*, pp. 103–108 (*SW* III: 113–119; *GA* I/3: 405–410).

to me a sphere for my free acting and assure me that their freedom will not be disturbed by my acting within this sphere. This recognition is provided immediately or directly by the state [*Staat*] in which I live. In my *Natural Right* I have shown how it is provided indirectly by humanity as a whole.)²¹

The first duty of everyone who has acquired insight into the propositions just established is therefore to institute the right of property, which, to be sure, is not something that happens on its own, but has to be introduced intentionally, in accordance with a concept. Moreover, it is also everyone's duty to acquire some property; for it is everyone's duty to act freely, and so long as one does not possess some property of one's own one cannot act without incessantly remaining in doubt whether one may not be disturbing the freedom of others. This constitutes, albeit in a preliminary manner, a more detailed determination of the propositions put forward above, namely, that a state ought to be established and that each individual ought to belong to it. The freedom of everyone else is, for me, an end that is absolutely commanded by the moral law. A condition for the freedom of the other person is that he possess some property and that he preserve it in an undamaged condition [IV, 293]. Since the latter [viz., the other person's possession of property] is itself the condition for a conditioned end [viz., the other's freedom], it is my end as well.

Considered *negatively*, this disposition of the moral law results in a prohibition against *damaging the property of another person, diminishing it in any way, or rendering the use of the same more difficult to its owner.*

First of all, I am not supposed to employ someone else's property for my own advantage by means of robbery, theft, fraud, or cunning deception – all of which are already prohibited on account of their form, that is, on account of the way of acting they involve: the former as a violent attack upon life and limb, the other three as instances of falseness and lying. Here, however, we are considering only the content of the action: the mere fact that they all involve taking another person's property. This is forbidden because it infringes upon the freedom of the person who is robbed. He was counting upon continuing to have disposition over what was taken from him, and he made his plans accordingly. If he now has to do without this completely, this narrows

---

²¹ See *FNR*, p. 106 (*SW* III: 116–117; *GA* 1/3: 407).

his sphere of efficacy, decreases his physical power, and reduces his causality; if he has to regain these things that were taken from him, then the progress of his efficacious acting is, at a minimum, retarded, and he is forced to re-do what he had done already. – This proposition could be and actually has been objected to in the name of that immoral ethics [*Sittenlehre*] that always pretends to be engaged in furthering good ends in order to excuse evil means, and which has been given the name "Jesuit" morals [*Moral*] (though this is not to say that all Jesuits have such morals nor that no one has them but Jesuits). I maintain that [a proponent of] such an ethics would object as follows: "If what was taken from the person in question is not spoiled in any manner but is only used, then this does not interfere with the furthering of reason's end, which ought to be the ultimate goal of all our acting; moreover, if, let us say, the new property owner were to employ it in a better manner than it would have been employed by the first person [from whom it was taken], then this advances reason's end. What if the person who took the property knew that the original owner would make some harmful use of it, whereas he himself intended to use it in a very praiseworthy way [IV, 294], for the greater glory of God and the greater service to his neighbors: would he not then, according to your own principles, be acting quite rightly?" To this I would respond as follows: I am commanded to promote the cause of the good only conditionally, that is, to the extent that it lies within my sphere and stands in my legitimate power, and I am absolutely forbidden to infringe upon the freedom of others. In such a case [i.e. in the case just cited by the proponent of "Jesuit morals"], my goal would be to act in accordance with what is legal, at the cost of what is moral. In its subordination of alleged legality to morality Jesuit morals remains true to itself and thereby betrays the truth about itself: namely, that it is not really concerned even with legality as such, but with something entirely different: its own advantage. One cannot will legality at all, except for the sake of morality. – The only reason one does not defend theft and deception of others for the sake of some alleged good ends as obstinately as one defends white lies is because our way of thinking regarding this subject has been shaped differently by our civil constitution, which places all its emphasis on the preservation of property and which has imposed severe punishment on any transgressions in this area. One may assume that a New Zealander, whose way of thinking has not been shaped in the same manner by this constitution, steals for a good end, in the same way we lie for one.

We are also prohibited [by this negative disposition of the moral law] from *damaging* someone else's property, either intentionally, with an evil will, or from carelessness; and this for the same reason [that we are forbidden to steal]: because this would hinder the other person's free use of his own property, and hence would hinder his freedom as such.

As far as intentional damage is concerned, this cannot be defended at all, even by means of sophistry; it is absolutely immoral. As for damage inflicted as a result of carelessness, it is my duty to apply the same care to the preservation of someone else's property that I apply to the preservation of my own; in both cases this is my end for the same reason and to the same degree, namely, as a means for furthering the dominion of reason.

Finally [IV, 293], I am forbidden to make it more difficult for another to make free use of his own property. The reason for this prohibition is clear. This property has an end: it is something he can employ freely in order to further his own ends, the aim of which, I have to assume, is the realization of the dominion of reason. To hinder the free use of property is to abolish the end of all property, and thus, in its essence, amounts to the same thing as robbery. It is no excuse to say that in hindering the other's use of his own property I was seeking to prevent some evil and harmful use of the same.

I am always obliged to make some *reparation* [*Ersatz*] for what was removed or spoiled, in short, for any damage to [the property of] another person. Without such reparation there is no pardoning, that is, no reconciliation with myself. This can be rigorously proven as follows: anyone who thinks in a moral manner certainly does not wish to damage anyone else's property. But the consequences of such damage will continue until complete reparation has been made. Thus, as surely as I return to the moral way of thinking, I just as surely want to eliminate these consequences and thereby abolish the action itself [through which the property of the other was damaged]; and if this is what I will then I have to do everything in my power to achieve this end.

Considered *positively*, the proposition that the property of others is an end for me, since it is a condition of their formal and rightful freedom, contains the following commands:

(a) Every human who has arrived at the age where he is able to use his own reason ought to possess some property. The proof of this is contained in what was said above. He must be able to act freely; his action necessarily proceeds from certain starting points, certain objects in the sensible world, which are the first tools of his activity; but these tools must not belong to anyone else but him, because otherwise he could never be sure that [, in using these tools,] he would not be disturbing someone else's freedom.

That everyone possess some property is, first of all, a concern of the state. Strictly speaking, there is no rightful property in a state in which even a single citizen does not possess some property ("property" in the proper sense of the word, in which this term signifies an exclusive sphere for free acting in general, and thus designates not only objects but [IV, 296] also exclusive rights to engage in certain actions). For each person owns his property only to the extent that this has been recognized by everyone else; but they cannot have recognized this unless he in turn has from his side recognized their property; and therefore they [all] have to possess some property. A person without property of his own has not renounced the property of others, and he is fully justified in laying claim to the latter. This is how the matter looks from a [strictly] juridical perspective. – Thus it is the first duty of anyone who is able to convince himself of this truth to do everything in his power to see to it that this same truth is recognized and observed by the state.

Until that happens, however – and why should it not finally happen? –, it is everyone's duty to provide with property anyone whom he knows to be without property; in other words, *beneficence* [*Wohltätigkeit*] is a duty. This is, as everyone can see, a conditioned duty; one would not have such a duty if the state had done what it ought to do.

One should carefully note that beneficence consists in procuring for the person without property some property, a stable position in some estate [*einen festen Stand*], a secure and enduring existence. One ought to seek to assist another individual or several individuals, if one can do so, in a fundamental way and in an enduring manner: procure some appointment for a person without an office; procure some work for a person without a job; lend something or give something to a person who has lost his livelihood, so that he can once again secure his own livelihood; raise orphans or help to raise them, etc. In short, perform as many works of beneficence as one can, and do them thoroughly, rather than simply botching and bungling them here and there. Only then is our beneficence rational, circumspective, and purposive. The proof of this is contained in the very concept of beneficence: everyone ought to have some property, this is the goal of beneficence.

The ordinary practice of almsgiving is a quite ambiguous good deed. All that a person who gives alms that do not help in a thorough manner can reasonably be saying is the following: "I do not want to help you, or I cannot help you. Turn to others; and I will give you this gift so that you can stay alive until then." The dutifulness of almsgiving arises from the duty to preserve the life of our fellow human beings [IV, 297]. – A claim for assistance from one's fellow human beings can have no other end than to acquire some position [*Stand*] or property from private persons, since this has been denied one by the state. It is simply intolerable that human beings should have no other end in begging for alms than obtaining alms, and that they should make begging into an estate [*Stand*]. If the state should tolerate such a situation, then it is the duty of every private person to do all he can to frustrate the achievement of such an end and by no means to further it through thoughtless tender-heartedness and poorly understood duty. It goes without saying that one has to be certain before one's own conscience that one is not denying this benefit out of avarice and natural hard-heartedness and only pretending to do this on the basis of this higher principle. That this is not the case can easily be gathered from the fact that a person performs those works of reasonable benefi-cence described above whenever the occasion for doing so might present itself. (How far do those deviate from reason and truth who make almsgiving a religious exercise and who tolerate begging and even pro-mote it so that believers will never lack occasions to do good deeds – as though there were ever any lack of such occasions!)

How far does the duty of beneficence extend? Is it sufficient to exercise this duty only to the extent that it does not cause us the least inconvenience, and is it enough to give away only what we ourselves cannot use? By no means. One owes it to oneself to make some cuts, to restrict one's expenses, to be more frugal, economical, and industrious so that one will then be able to be beneficent – for a person without property has a claim to our property.

I will add the following in order to prevent anyone from inverting this proposition and concluding that the poor person is permitted to extort [*erzwingen*] support. He is indeed permitted to extort this from the state, were he able to do so. It is a goal of both the poor and the rich to work for a situation in which the state will finally be brought to the point of knowing and performing its duty. But so far as single individuals are concerned, another person can never judge [IV, 298] whether this is the duty of these individuals, whether they are in a position to perform this duty, or whether they may not be prevented from doing so by other, higher duties.

(b) Everyone is supposed to keep what is his, for otherwise his formal freedom would be disturbed. Hence it is my duty to protect another person's property against any attack, even if I am not summoned to do this, and to do so to the same extent to which I would defend my own property; for the defense of both is a duty for the same reason: both are means for promoting the dominion of reason. – And I have a duty to do this regardless of whether the attack comes from some irrational natural force (fire and water) or occurs through the injustice of rational beings, and regardless of whether the latter occurs by means of force or by means of cunning and deception. Since the security of the property of others ought to be just as much my end as is the security of my own, it is immediately clear that I must undertake to defend the property of others even if this endangers the security of my own. We will consider in the following section how far this duty extends and to what extent I am obliged to defend the property of others even if this endangers my own life.

(c) Property is an object of duty because it is a condition and tool of freedom. One of the ends of a morally good human being is that other human beings should have as much freedom as he does – i.e., as much force and causality in the sensible world – in order thereby to promote the dominion of reason; hence it is the duty of an ethical person to increase the *usefulness of the property* of others. What one requires in order to act with great efficacy is not primarily a broad range of means, but rather that the means one already possesses should be entirely in one's own power and that one should be able to accomplish through these means whatever one wills to accomplish. What renders a person free and independent is not a massive body but one that has been trained [*ein geübter*] and stands completely under the dominion of the will; similarly, it is not a large property, but one that is well-ordered, easy to oversee, and applicable at once to every possible end that makes one free and independent. Just as it is our duty to bring our own property into such a condition, so it is our duty to aim for the same with respect to the property of others – by providing them with good counsel and assistance, though this is something we are not permitted to force upon another person [IV, 299], or by surrendering to the other person something that is of more use to him in his situation than it would be to us. In short, it is our duty to be *obliging* [*Dienstfertigkeit*], but the incentive for this must never be some thoughtless kindheartedness but rather the clearly conceived end of furthering as much as possible the causality of reason. It is our duty to decline requests if, according to our own best insight, granting them would do more harm than good to the person making them, though such refusal should be accompanied by reasonable arguments [*Vorstellungen*] meant to correct his concepts and to get him to withdraw this desire [for assistance] of his own free will.

(d) The entire sensible world is supposed to come under the dominion of reason, to be the tool of reason in the hands of rational beings. – But everything in this sensible world is connected with everything else; hence no part of it stands entirely and without restriction under the dominion of reason unless all the parts do so. Applied to the present topic, this means that everything useable in the [sensible] world must be used, and since it can be used purposively only by becoming property, it must become property. It is an end of the morally good person to see that this happens. – Just as everyone ought to have some property, so ought every object to be the property of some human being.

Reason's dominion over the sensible world is particularly well founded through the exercise of the last two prescriptions. By means of the first prescription – that everyone should care and work not only for the use of his own property and for achieving his own private ends, but for the most purposive use of the property of everyone and for the achievement of the particular ends of everyone, and that the activity of everyone should be furthered just as one furthers one's own activity – reason is unified; it becomes one and the same will in the minds of everyone, no matter how different they might be empirically. By means of the second prescription [– every object in the sensible world should be someone's property –] all of nature is comprehended and grasped under this unified will [*diesen Einen Willen*]. Reason is at one with itself, and the sensible world is subordinated to it. – This is the end that has been set for us [IV, 300].

§24

Duties in the case of conflict concerning the freedom of rational beings

There is no conflict concerning the freedom of rational beings *simply as such*; i.e., there is no contradiction involved in the simple fact that several such beings are free in the same sensible world. There is only one case in which the possibility of the freedom of several individuals, the coexistence of two rational individuals, is eliminated by nature itself, and we will discuss this below; but even if such a case actually does occur and does not need to be dealt with simply for the sake of the completeness of the system, it can still be asserted that it occurs very rarely indeed. – A conflict of this sort, not a conflict between free beings as such [*zwischen dem Freisein überhaupt*], but one between specific free actions of rational beings, arises only when one of these beings employs his freedom in a manner contrary to right and duty in order to suppress the freedom of another free being. – All of this will be dealt with in more detail in what follows.

First of all:

(1) *All* [of these rational beings] ought to be free. The employment of freedom by several individuals ought not to hamper itself mutually nor contradict itself. This is an absolute demand of the moral law, and thus it is everyone's duty to further the coexistence of the freedom of all. – But this coexistence is possible only insofar as each individual freely (since he is supposed to be free and to remain so) restricts the employment of his own freedom to a certain sphere, a sphere that all others have conceded to him alone, while he in turn leaves everything else to be divided among the others. Thus, without hampering the freedom of anyone else, everyone is free within his portion of one and the same sensible world. This idea is realized in the state, which, moreover, employs compulsory means [*Zwang*] to keep each individual within his own boundaries, since one cannot count on the good will of all. Our duty with regard to the state was discussed above [IV, 301].

The state itself employs compulsory means in order to preserve the order that it has introduced among individuals. Thus, if a conflict arises between several individuals' employment of freedom, it is the business of the state to settle this conflict and the duty of each individual to leave this to the state. Thus it is by no means evident how there could be any talk about the duties of individuals concerning the conflict of the freedom of several individuals. On the contrary, it would seem that everyone has already adequately satisfied his duty with regard to this point in advance by participating in the establishment of a state and by subjecting himself to it.

The state, however, cannot always immediately settle such conflicts; and this is when the duty of the private person enters the picture.

In this manner we have, for the time being, obtained the proposition that all of the duties with which we are here concerned are duties that apply only where the state cannot be of any help and only to the extent that it cannot be of any help. What this means will become clear when we discuss the individual cases.

(2) Here I would like to add another preliminary remark. It is all the same whether it is *my own* freedom or the freedom of my fellow human being that is endangered by someone else's illegitimate employment of freedom; this makes no difference at all for the purposes of our investigation and does not justify a division of the same, for, as has often been pointed out, the freedom of the other is commended to my care for the same reason my own freedom is commended to my care – and to the same degree. There is no difference between the duty of self-defense and the duty of defending others; both are the same duty to defend freedom as such.

(3) Freedom, as we have now seen, is conditioned by the body, by life, and by property. To be sure, in order to employ freedom one also requires cognition of the truth, but there can arise no conflict among the cognitions of several individuals, since the truth is not divisible in the manner of bodies and goods but is one and the same and is common to all; each individual does not possess his own truth, as he possesses his own body and his own particular property – [IV, 302]. Conflict may arise concerning the preservation of the bodies and the lives of several individuals, as well as concerning the preservation of the property of several individuals. Finally, there can also arise a conflict between the preservation of life and limb on the one hand and the preservation of property on the other. What is one's duty in all of these cases? These are the questions we must now answer.

(A) There is [let us say] a conflict regarding the preservation of the life and limb of several individuals. First of all:

α It may seem that the *preservation of my own* life and the *preservation of someone else's life* cannot coexist with one another, and not because of any injustice on my part or on the part of the other person, but rather, as a result of some disposition [*Verfügung*] of nature. Nature appears in this case to have withdrawn the possibility that both [of our lives] can exist together. – I will not cite any examples. This is the case that was discussed in the Doctrine of Right under the title "right of necessity" or "makeshift law" [*Notrecht*].[22] (There it was concluded that in such a

---

[22] See *FNR*, p. 220 (*SW* III: 252; *GA* 1/4: 53).

case no right whatsoever holds, and since no other kind of law applies to this domain, everyone is referred to his own arbitrary will [*Willkür*].)

This same matter is decided very differently by the moral law. I absolutely ought to preserve my own life, as a tool of the moral law. For the same reason I also ought to preserve the life of the other person, which we are here assuming to be in danger. The moral law commands each of these things equally unconditionally. Both of us are to be regarded as tools of the moral law, and only as such are we objects of duty. In accordance with the natural drive, of course, I have a preference for myself, but this drive must be left entirely out of the calculation; according to the moral law, neither of us has priority, for before this law we are equally means of one and the same reason.

According to our presupposition, the only way I can fulfill the command of the moral law (namely, the command that I preserve myself) is at the cost of the other person's life, and this is prohibited by the moral law. In such a situation every command of the law is opposed by a prohibition of this same law [IV, 303]; hence the two commands cancel each other. The law remains completely silent, and since my actions are supposed to be animated by nothing but the moral law, I ought not to do anything at all, but should calmly await the outcome.

Our proof included the proposition, "we are both tools of the moral law *in the same way*." The latter claim has been disputed, and this has led to the theory that one ought to investigate which person might be the better tool of the moral law. [This has led some to conclude that] the older person ought to sacrifice himself for the younger one, and the less skilled and less eminent person ought to sacrifice himself for the more skilled and more eminent one. – To this I respond as follows: it is simply impossible to judge from whose preservation more or less good will follow, for the finite understanding has no voice when it comes to determining what will and what will not prove to be more advantageous in a certain situation, and every argument of this sort is impertinent and presumptuous. This is a decision that must be left to the rational governance of the world – which is something that one believes in from this [moral] point of view. Finite understanding knows only that at each moment of one's life one ought to do what duty calls upon one to do at that moment, without worrying about how much good will follow from doing this and how this might happen. If someone's life is preserved, then some good ought to follow from this, for the world is governed by the highest wisdom and goodness. If someone perishes, this is not his own fault; he did what he could, and the rest is the responsibility of the moral law that governs the world – if there could be such a thing as responsibility in the case of the moral law itself.

Yet [someone might object:] if both of us calmly await the outcome we will both perish, whereas otherwise one of us could be saved. – First of all, neither of us knows that this is so. Even if *we* do not see any means of rescue, there might still be one. – But even if we both were to perish, then what? Our preservation is by no means the final end; only the fulfillment of the moral law is the final end. If we perish, then this was the will of the moral law; it has been fulfilled, and our final end has been achieved [IV, 304].

β Suppose that the bodies and lives of several of my fellow human beings are in danger. I ought to save them; but I cannot save them all, or at least I cannot save them all at once. How shall I choose whom to save?

My end is and necessarily must be to rescue them all; for all of them are tools of the moral law, and on this point there is no distinction to be made among them. Now if I want to rescue all of them, I will first help those who are in the greatest present danger, because these individuals could not preserve themselves at all without immediate assistance from others. They may be in more urgent danger either on account of their situation or because of their own weakness and helplessness, as is the case, for example, with children, sick people and old people. If it should turn out to be the case that, among those [who require my immediate assistance] there are some whose care and guidance is quite specifically committed to me [and is my responsibility] – *my own people* [*die Meinigen*] – , then these must have preference. But one should note that this preference is not based on natural, pathognomic love[23] or on any concern for my own happiness. All such motives are reprehensible. Instead, I have this preference because I have a particular duty to rescue these people, and because a particular duty always takes precedence over a universal one. If no such grounds for deciding are present, then I should rescue the first person I can rescue, the first person I see. – There is no place here for sophistry regarding the greater importance of this or that life, since I can know nothing about this.

---

[23] Fichte's term "pathognomic love" [*pathognomisch Lieb*] is the equivalent of the term, "pathological love," a term that is to be found in Kant and others. Both terms signify a form of love that is based on feeling rather than upon respect grounded in reason.

γ [Or suppose that] my body and life come under violent attack from a hostile and unjust source, or that someone else comes under such an attack, for this must make no difference to me: to what extent am I in this case permitted to endanger the life of the assailant in defending either myself or someone else? It is an absolute duty to defend the life of the person who is attacked (whether it is *I* who am attacked or someone else, and therefore I will consider both of these possibilities together, under this single term); but this does not mean that it therefore ceases to be my duty to spare and to preserve the life of the assailant. Hence it can never be my end to *kill* the assailant but only to *disarm* him. I will therefore call upon the assistance of others if they are in the vicinity and thereby call upon the help of the state. I will simply repel the hostile attack to [IV, 305] the best of my ability, without placing the assailant himself in danger. If I am unable to do this, then I will lame him or wound him or something similar, but always in such a manner that his death is never my end. Should it nevertheless happen that he is killed, then this is something that happens by accident, despite my intention to the contrary; I am not responsible for it.

One might object to this in the manner of many moralists who have argued that, in acting in this manner, I have nevertheless endangered the assailant's life. Limiting ourselves purely to my own person, that is to the case when I am the only one under attack (since such an argument conflicts too sharply with ordinary moral feelings in the case of an attack upon someone else), [one might still ask the following question:] why do I not die myself rather than place the other's life in danger? In order to refute such an objection thoroughly and convincingly, I will compare this situation with the emergency or makeshift situation [*Notfall*] that was described above [in section α]. In the latter case I had a duty to preserve my own life, just as I do in the case we are now considering; but [in the case considered in section β] I was not permitted to save my own life at the cost of another person's life. The first major difference between these two cases is this: if I should follow a certain course of action in the emergency situation, I am convinced that this will actually result in the death of the other person; whereas in the situation we are now considering the other person need not perish, nor is he supposed to perish. In the first case, the life of the other person is in the hands of nature, which, I am convinced, will certainly rob him of his life as soon as I act in a certain way. In the second case, the life of the other person is subject to my power, a power governed by a freely modifiable concept of an end. I by no means wish to kill the other person, nor do I presuppose nor foresee that I will do so. – The decisive point, however, is that my duty to act in the latter case is based not only upon my obligation to preserve my own life, but also on my obligation simply not to tolerate something that is obviously prohibited by the moral law: namely, my own murder or that of some other person. A morally good person is not permitted, at any price, to allow something to occur that is absolutely prohibited by the moral law, for his will is precisely the will of the moral law itself. There is nothing parallel to this in the previously discussed emergency situation; nothing immoral has to be prevented in this case, for nothing immoral occurs [IV, 306].

My duty to compel [*Zwangspflicht*] the other person ceases as soon as he has been disarmed. From this point on, I can oppose him only with rational arguments. What remains to be done in order to promote the general safety – as an example for others, or in order to insure that he will never again do anything similar – is a matter left to the state, into whose hands this other person now falls. The state is his judge, not I nor any other private person.

(B) [Or let us imagine that] there is a conflict involved in preserving the property of several different people, and it seems that preserving the property of any one of them requires the destruction of that of the others.

[Let us suppose that] my property and someone else's property are simultaneously endangered. – In this case, my property will necessarily have priority; for I will naturally notice the danger to it first, and thus I will first apprehend that I am required by the moral law to save my own property, and a person already attending to his own particular business may not attend to any other business at the same time. Naturally, I am also presupposing that the other person, who is in the same danger I am in, will do the same thing I am doing. – But I have to be certain before my own conscience that this priority that I assign to saving my own property is actually based on a feeling of duty and not at all upon self-love. I have to rescue what is mine not as "mine," but as the common possession [*Gemeingut*] of reason. Whether this is indeed the sense in which I have saved my own property will become quite apparent if, afterwards, I actually do consider it in this manner and if I am prepared to employ it to aid and support the injured party and am ready to share with him as much as I can of the property that was saved.

The mere *possibility* that my property might be endangered does not relieve me of the duty to save the *actually* endangered property of someone else. This is clearly shown by the following: so long as the danger to my own property remains merely possible, I have no work to do, and I would therefore have to be idle; but I am never supposed to remain at rest when duty commands.

It is absolutely contrary to duty to protect one's own property at the cost of the property of others, to deflect some danger that threatens our property by shifting it – whether entirely or in part – to someone else. If the danger had threatened him, then he would have had to deal with it [IV, 307], and we would have had to help him do this; now, however, it threatens not him but us. The morally good person sees in this fact a decree of providence. He combats the danger as well as he can, but he does not transfer to someone else something that providence has sent to *him*.

Life goes beyond property; for life is the condition of property but not vice versa: property is not the condition of life. Thus it is better to save the lives of our fellow human beings than to save their property or our own. Furthermore, it is better to secure our own life than to save our property or theirs – if, that is, the attack in question comes merely from an irrational force of nature. We will consider to what extent the situation might be different, and on what grounds this might be the case, were the attack to come from the injustice of rational beings.

(C) [Finally, let us consider the following case]: my property or that of someone else is violently attacked by rational beings. Here we are not concerned solely with preserving property, as in the case of a danger arising from irrational nature, but with thwarting something that violates the requirements of right and duty. The will of the moral law is the will of the morally good human being himself; hence what the former prohibits, the latter cannot and is not permitted to tolerate. – We therefore have an absolute duty to prevent robbery *to the extent that it is absolutely contrary to the moral law*, and everyone can categorically assert that he is against robbery. – One must not lose sight of the latter restriction, however: an attack upon someone else's property is absolutely contrary to the moral law solely to the extent that the assailant has recognized the item in question as property and therefore finds himself in a contractual relationship regarding this property with the owner of the same. Thus, if such an attack is carried out on a citizen of a state by one of his fellow citizens or by a citizen of a state at peace with one's own state, then it is immoral and is absolutely contrary to right; but the attack is not absolutely immoral if it is carried out by an armed enemy, for in this case the warring states are engaged in dispute over what is right, and from the perspective of external right it is problematic which state is right [IV, 308]. In this case, therefore, neither party has the right of jurisdiction, since the other party does not recognize his tribunal.

I ought to prevent robbery, and I am absolutely commanded to do so. But what means am I permitted to employ for this end? To what extent am I permitted to use force or to endanger my own life or even that of another person [in order to prevent a robbery]?

α On the one hand, it may be the case that the state is able to help, if not right away, then at least after the fact. In this case, the unjust action can be entirely annihilated by the state; hence I have a duty in such a case not to do anything immediately and not to endanger either myself or the assailant, but simply to bring this matter to the attention of the state. My duty to do this, however, is itself conditioned; later on we will determine what these conditions are and what must precede my filing of a complaint [*Klage*].

A case of this sort can occur either if the property that is taken is of such a kind as to be recognizable and immediately safeguarded by the state or if the assailant is someone known to us. In the latter case, however, it is necessary, and consequently it is also a duty, to avail oneself of the proofs required by the state.

β [On the other hand,] it may be that neither of these two situations prevails; and thus if I do not immediately resist [the assailant] then, so far as I can foresee, his unjust intention will be accomplished and will succeed. In this case I have a duty to resist forcibly, albeit in accordance with those prudential rules that have been recommended for the defense of one's life and limb. If the assailant fights back, this will produce a struggle for life and limb. My life will then be under attack, and this matter will now be subject to the previously indicated rules that apply to such a situation. In such a case I will no longer be defending my property, but rather my life itself, which I defend at the risk of the other person's life.

To this one might object as follows: it is I who have brought things to this pass. By forcibly resisting, I myself have transformed a struggle over mere property into one for life and limb. – My response to this is as follows [IV, 309]: in such a case, not only am I not permitted to endure the theft calmly, but it would be contrary to duty for me to permit this. I could not count on the fact that my assailant would not allow himself to be driven away; nor was I permitted to count on this fact, for I always have to expect that things will happen in accordance with the moral law, and not contrary to the same. But it goes without saying that, before resisting his attack, I will have employed rational arguments to try to persuade him to abandon his intention [of robbing me]. That a fight for life and limb has arisen is entirely the fault of my assailant; he should have allowed himself be deterred from his undertaking by my resistance.

γ The disposition of the moral law with respect to the grievance filed with the state, not only in the cases indicated but in general, is as follows:

Where the law requires that I inform [on someone who has broken the law], it is my duty to inform, since obedience to the state is a duty.

Some things are left up to my own arbitrary will, and this indicates the natural limits of the state; in the domain of private affairs that occur inside the house and with respect to absolute property[24] the proposition "where there is no plaintiff, there is no judge." In those cases where filing a complaint depends upon my arbitrary will, the moral mode of thinking demands that I do not file a complaint right away. The reason for this is as follows: the state does not concern itself with convincing anyone; whether one does or does not recognize the correctness and justice of its decision, one still has to subject oneself to it, and it is enforced with physical power. To this extent the state treats human beings not as rational beings but as mere forces of nature that have to be constrained within their boundaries; and it is entirely right to do this, for this is why the state was instituted. When it comes to *private matters*, the state acts in my name; for it acts when I authorize and call upon it to do so, and it would not act in these circumstances if I had not called upon it to do so. What it does must therefore be ascribed to me. Yet *I* am supposed to treat a fellow human being as a rational being, and not simply as a mere force of nature, if, that is, I am to make any progress with him in the situation described above [in the preceding section α].

---

[24] In *FNR* Fichte distinguishes between "absolute" and "relative" property. The former includes personal property, such as "money and similar valuables," whereas the latter includes "fields, gardens, houses, civil licenses, etc." The owner of "absolute" property possesses "the substance" of the same, whereas the owner of "relative" property possesses only the right to use the property in question. According to Fichte, only the latter sort of property is subject to supervision by the state. (See *FNR*, p. 222 [*SW* III, 255; *GA* I/4: 55].)

Thus, before filing a complaint, I have a responsibility to continue to employ rational arguments in order to see [IV, 310] if I cannot perhaps thereby lead my adversary to realize that he is doing wrong and then come to a voluntary decision to make amends for this wrong.

If such arguments are of no avail, then I have a duty to file a complaint, for the unjust action simply ought not to succeed, but must instead be thwarted. – One might ask the following questions: at what point in time do I come to know that my arguments will be of no avail? Indeed, how can I ever know that they will be of no avail? Might it therefore not always remain my duty to continue to press these arguments relentlessly? My answer is as follows: here we are dealing with restitution and reparation. The latter has to be performed at some point of time, and thus I can allow myself and the other a certain, specific period of time [for rational argumentation]. – If, after I have filed my complaint, the state forces him to provide reparation and recompense, I can always continue to employ rational arguments afterwards in order to get him to recognize the legitimacy and rationality of a certain course of action, even though he can no longer act upon this realization, and in order to bring him to subordinate his will to justice, to which hitherto only his external acting had been coercively subordinated – and indeed, it is my duty to do this.

Prior to any legal proceedings, during the course of such proceedings, and following the conclusion of the same, I therefore ought always to regard and treat my adversary as a rational and moral person. So too, as we have seen above, I also ought to seek to preserve the other person as a potential tool of the moral law, even if I am engaged with him in a struggle for life and limb. This provides us with an occasion to talk about love for one's enemies, a subject concerning which, taken by itself, nothing particular would need to be said, since, as we will see, all that needs to be said about this is already contained in the universal principles already established. I will touch upon this point merely in order to clear up a few misunderstandings concerning it.

δ Pathognomic love, that is, the specific attraction toward one person or another, is not an ethical matter, but is something purely natural. Such love ought not to be and is not permitted to become an incentive for our actions. There is virtual unanimity that this is not the sort of love we are commanded to have for our enemies [IV, 311]. If some people say that such love for one's enemies is not commanded simply because it is not possible, then it is only the reason they offer for this conclusion [and not the conclusion itself] that is wrong. Why should such love not be possible? Might we not be able to feel a particular attraction, stemming from some natural ground, for a person who may hate us and persecute us because this attraction is not mutual? The only reason this sort of love is not commanded is *because* it is not ethical at all and is not subject to our free and arbitrary will but is instead based purely on a natural drive.

But it is also an error to assert, from the other side, that what is commanded by this command [to love one's enemy] is not any inner disposition [*Gesinnung*] toward the enemy, but only some external action: that one simply ought to act *as if* one loved the enemy, regardless of how one might feel about him in one's heart. This is wrong, because no action is moral that does not issue from an inner disposition. If this were the case, then all that would be commanded with respect to the enemy would be mere legality, which is never commanded immediately by the moral law.

Here, in brief, is how this matter is to be resolved: within the domain of the moral law, I should view my fellow human beings only as tools of reason. But I ought to and I have to view everyone without exception in this manner, even if someone's present actions could lead one to infer the opposite. Even if a person is not now a tool of the moral law, I am never permitted to give up hope that he will be able to become such a tool, as has been sufficiently shown above. This also holds in the case of my enemy. I ought to love him; i.e., I ought to believe him to be capable of improvement. And I ought to demonstrate this love through my deeds; i.e., I ought to work as much as I can toward his improvement.

Moreover, and this is particularly noteworthy, an ethical human being has no personal enemies at all and recognizes no such enemies. Nothing whatsoever is adverse to him; he is not hostile toward anything and does not seek to prevent anything – except evil, simply because it is evil. It does not matter to him in the least whether the evil in question happens to be directed against him or against someone else, for he is for himself absolutely nothing more than everyone else is for him: a tool of the moral law [IV, 312]. There is no reason why he should think any worse of someone who happens to stand precisely in his way than of someone who happens to stand in the way of any good cause whatsoever, and no reason why he should give up hope any sooner in the former case than in the latter. A person who feels an insult more because it is directed precisely at him is sure to be an egotist and is still far removed from the truly moral disposition.

(D) Even though we do not have to consider the duty of truthfulness in the present section, inasmuch as there can arise no conflict concerning this duty, we do have to consider here something that springs from the duty of truthfulness: *honor and a good reputation.*

Understood in a moral sense, honor and a good reputation consist in the opinion of others concerning us, namely, their opinion that it is indeed possible that, in our actions in general and especially in our interactions with them, we intend to do nothing but what is right and good. It follows from what has already been said above that everyone ought to have this opinion of everyone else, for everyone ought to regard everyone else as a potential tool of the moral law. Everyone ought to have such an opinion of everyone else until the opposite has, for the time being, been demonstrated, and even then one ought not to give up hope that the human being in question might still be able to adopt this maxim [or morality]. Our influence on others is conditioned by this opinion they have of us, and thus it is our duty to preserve and to defend it. – Resolute indifference toward any bad rumors that are spread concerning us shows indifference and contempt toward those human beings upon whom we are still supposed to have some effect; it is an expression of indifference and coldness toward our moral vocation and therefore a most reprehensible way of thinking. It requires no special effort to become indifferent toward the judgments of others from the purely natural perspective. In order not to assign too much worth to the judgments of human beings, one need only look a bit more closely at them as they usually are. But a moral human being simply does not allow such low esteem [of his fellow human beings] to arise within him [IV, 313]; he always sees in human beings more what they *ought* to be and what they *ought* to become than what they actually are.

If someone has attacked our honor, and if we can defend it only by disseminating some disadvantageous information about him, then it is our duty to do so. It is, for example, our duty to say and to prove that the other one did not speak the truth [about us]. The situation here is similar to that of defending life and property against an unjust attack: we ought to defend our life and property, even if this endangers our assailant.

§25

The duty to spread and to promote morality immediately

So far we have seen that we have a duty to protect and to promote the formal freedom of our fellow human beings, for we are obliged to regard everyone with a human face as a tool of the moral law. Other human beings as such, more especially their freedom, are objects of duty for us only insofar as the latter is presupposed; otherwise they would be nothing for us but mere irrational objects, which we could deal with however we wished and would be permitted to subjugate as means for our own ends. Thus, just as surely as we act upon them at all, we are required to regard other humans as moral beings, and how we act in relation to them is determined solely by our regard for them as moral beings. From this it is already clear that we must make an effort to insure that this is the correct way of regarding them and that they really do employ their freedom, which we are supposed to preserve and to promote, in order to further the end of reason [IV, 314]. This same conclusion can also be very easily proven at once. The will of a morally good human being is the will of the moral law itself. The latter, however, wills that all human beings should be moral, and thus this is also what the morally good person must will. But the will of the latter cannot be helpless and lacking in force, for the morally good person, considered as an individual and to the extent that he exercises any force within the sensible world, is a tool of the moral law. He will therefore necessarily seek with all his might to realize [*realisieren*, that is to make real] what he must necessarily will.

Thus it is by no means difficult to prove that we have an absolute and universal duty to spread and to promote morality outside ourselves. It is, however, a bit more difficult to indicate how this might be possible.

Nothing should be called moral except what occurs as a result of one's own free decision, without involving the slightest compulsion or the least external motive. It would thus appear to be impossible to communicate morality, inasmuch as it would seem to be impossible for one human being to be able to render any external help at all to another in such matters. The demand to spread morality therefore seems entirely empty and impossible to obey. All we seem to be left with are impotent wishes, for how could we advance morality other than by means of some sensible [*sinnliche*] influence, and how could any sensible influence ever set freedom in motion? And indeed, as we will now show, this is undeniably true in several respects.

I

First of all, it can never occur to anyone with a moral disposition to employ compulsory means in order to make human beings virtuous – by announcing rewards or punishments, which will either be dispensed by oneself, as for example in the case of the state, or by some other overpowering ruler, or which one promises or threatens in the name of an almighty being, whose confidence one claims to enjoy. All actions motivated by anything of this sort possess absolutely no moral value. Since people still seek to weaken and to limit this claim and endeavor to maintain, on one pretext or another, a [IV, 315] system of virtue based on reward and punishment, I will now provide a rigorous proof of the same.

Every drive for happiness is based upon the natural drive: I will this or that object because my nature contains a certain drive; I do not will this or that because my nature includes an aversion toward the same. Now if one avails oneself of the drive in question in order to get me to engage in certain actions, one does this by making these actions conditions for satisfying this natural drive. In such a case the satisfaction of my natural drive quite obviously remains *the ultimate end* of my actions; the actions themselves are only a means for attaining this end, and this is the only way I view them. This, however, constitutes the very essence of immorality: that the ultimate end of my acting is to satisfy the natural drive. In contrast, the [moral] law demands that I entirely subordinate this same drive [*Trieb*] to a higher impulse [*Antrieb*]. By proceeding in this manner, therefore, one has by no means made me moral but has instead only further confirmed me in my immorality by sanctioning the latter through something called ethics [*Sittenlehre*], which one claims to be the highest and most holy matter of all and trains me in by means of exercise.[25] One thereby annihilates all hope for morality inasmuch as one replaces it with immorality itself and thereby completely eradicates morality, along with any tendency toward it or inkling concerning it. – This way of dealing with human beings is exactly the same as the method

---

[25] *Und durch Übung recht ausbildet.*

we employ when dealing with animals. We take advantage of one of the animal's instincts in order to attach to it the particular abilities that we wish to develop; and so too with human beings: [by treating them in this manner] we would be aiming simply to *train* but not to *cultivate* them.[26]

One should therefore abstain once and for all from all those vague, as well as shallow and harmful, excuses that eradicate all true morality from the ground up, such as: "the reward is not supposed to be the virtuous person's sole end, but only *one* of his ends" [IV, 316], or "the reward is not supposed to be the *main* end but only a *secondary* one." By no means; the reward is not supposed to be one's end *at all*. Every action that is done out of hope for reward or fear of punishment is absolutely immoral.

One should not say, "we want to take advantage of this means only in the beginning, until we have thereby succeeded in rendering human beings more capable of true morality." By employing such a means you do not by any means begin to cultivate a moral disposition; instead, you merely continue to spread the old, immoral one, and you nourish and care for it quite diligently. Furthermore, your entire pretense that human beings, no matter what state they may be in, are incapable of pure morality is a sheer fiction, and your distinction between a pure and an impure morality is utterly absurd. There are not two moralities but only one; and a morality that is not pure, that does not proceed solely from the representation of duty, is no morality at all. – For what we are concerned with here is only the [*moral*] *disposition*, and by no means with whether this disposition is completely or incompletely *carried out* in actual acting. –

II

It is equally impossible to force morality upon anyone through theoretical conviction. First of all, theoretical conviction itself cannot be forced upon anyone – a true proposition that explains many phenomena in the human being and that academic philosophers rarely take to heart, because to do so would disturb them in their illusion that they are capable of improving and converting human beings by means of syllogisms. No one is convinced who does not delve into himself [*in sich selbst*

---

[26] *Ihn nur zu dressieren, nicht zu kultivieren.*

hineingeht] and feel inwardly the consent of his own self to the truth that has been presented, a consent that is an affect of the heart and by no means a conclusion of the understanding. Such attentiveness to ourselves depends upon our freedom, and the consent itself is therefore freely given and never forced. (This is not to say that one could freely convince oneself of anything one wishes. One can convince oneself and others only of the truth, but even in this case, one does not *have to* convince oneself of the truth [IV, 317]; instead, this is something that depends on one's own good will. Conviction is an action of reason, through which it *subordinates* itself to the truth through an act of its own self-activity; it is not a passive state of reason. To be convinced of propositions that infringe upon our passions presupposes the dominion of a good will, which can therefore not in turn be produced by conviction.)

III

We nevertheless have to continue our consideration of efficacious action by means of rational grounds, which cannot have any influence at all except through theoretical reasoning, and we have so far found at least this much: that such influence already presupposes in its object the principle of the good, and hence it would never be possible to promote morality if this principle could not confidently be presupposed at every point.

And in fact we can here point to something ineradicable within human nature, something to which the cultivation of virtue [*Bildung zur Tugend*] can always be attached, namely, the affect of respect. This affect may lie in the soul unused and undeveloped, but it can never be extirpated from the soul, nor can it be directed toward an object alien to itself. Sensible pleasure [*Sinnenlust*] can be loved, sought after, and desired, and one can feel delight in its enjoyment; but one never can respect it; this affect [of respect] has no application whatsoever to sensible pleasure. – But as soon as this affect finds its object it expresses itself unavoidably; everything worthy of respect is most certainly respected. The first rule for spreading morality will therefore be the following: show your fellow human beings things worthy of respect. And we can hardly show them anything better suited to this purpose than our own moral way of thinking and our own moral conduct. From this there follows the duty to set a *good example*. – I will return to this point, and I will now proceed to consider the conclusions that follow therefrom. – The first step of moral cultivation is the development of respect [IV, 318].

IV

As soon as a human being is required to respect something outside of himself he begins to develop a drive to respect himself. Just as soon as the affect of respect has been developed through something outside of us, the drive to self-respect becomes just as ineradicable from human nature as is self-love. No human being can bear coldly despising himself or can calmly regard himself as an unworthy and miserable human being; but it is equally impossible for anyone who is despicable to respect himself.

The moral state of a human being is often in no way improved by this means [that is, by inducing a lack of respect for oneself], but is more often even made considerably worse. There are two ways one might try to evade the unbearable pain of self-contempt, and one often attempts to employ them both at the same time. [On the one hand], a human being seeks to flee from himself because he is afraid of himself. He avoids looking within himself because this will reveal nothing but wrenching objects. Simply in order to evade himself, he seeks to distract himself all the more among the objects of the outer world. He deadens his conscience. But [on the other hand], since he is unable to help himself completely by this means, he [also] seeks to rid himself of any respect that has been forced from him for anything outside of himself and thereby to rid himself of the contempt for himself that this produces; he attempts to do this by persuading himself that his respect is merely folly and fanatical enthusiasm, that nothing whatsoever is worthy of respect, is noble and sublime, that everything is only semblance and illusion, that no human being is any better than he himself and neither is human nature as such. – It would be in vain to attempt to refute such a system on the basis of rational grounds. It has its basis not in the understanding but in the heart. This basis within the heart must first be removed; the people in question have to be helped to overcome their fear and shame regarding themselves. They are separated from everything good only because they are separated from themselves. One must first reconcile them with themselves; i.e., one has to show them [IV, 319] that they are by no means so lacking in all that is good as they themselves believe. The first thing one has to do is lead them to the good principle within themselves.

Immorality thus consists either in complete crudeness [*Rohheit*] or in despair over oneself. In the first case, the crudeness must be cultivated by the means already indicated: that is, simply by teaching the human being in question to respect something. In the second case, one should show the human being in question that other people are at least not so despairing over him [as he is over himself]; one should get him to notice the confidence that others place in him, and, if one comes into closer contact with him, one should make him aware of the hidden good within him. A person in whom others show confidence will soon acquire some confidence in himself; a person over whom everyone else despairs must surely begin to despair over himself.

Thus everything in our theory coheres with everything else, and one part meshes with another. It was already established above that it is absolutely contrary to duty to despair inwardly over the possibility of improving any human being whatsoever. The same thing that there presented itself as an inner duty and as regulative of our external actions now presents itself once again as a means for furthering the end that has been assigned to us, and it also becomes a duty to make a resolute outer display of this inner confidence.

The good principle, which is present in all human beings and cannot be eradicated in anyone, is precisely the possibility of being able to respect something unselfishly [*uneigennützig*], without any regard to what is advantageous [to oneself], hence for an utterly *a priori* reason. Furthermore, this good principle is the drive to want to respect oneself, and it is also the impossibility that anyone could sink so low as to despise himself coldly and calmly. It is this principle to which we should lead others. We should show them that this is the principle that underlies their own conduct. To those, such as Helvetius[27] and those like him, who flatly deny the possibility of an unselfish drive in a human being, we would address ourselves as follows: you report to us that you have discovered that human beings are driven only by selfishness and that they deceive themselves grossly if they view themselves capable of acting on any other impulses. Well, that may be good for you; make the best use you can of this discovery, and proceed along your way [IV, 320]. But

---

[27] Helvétius maintains in *De l'esprit* that self-love alone governs all human pursuits.

303

why do you communicate your discovery to us? What might you have to gain from communicating this discovery, or which loss might it help you prevent, given that all human beings, and thus you yourself as well, are capable of acting only from self-interest [*Eigennutz*]? If that illusion causes harm, at least it does not cause any harm to you, since, as you assure us, you have completely rid yourself of this illusion. And as for any harm it might do to us, how does that harm you, and what do you care if others around you come to harm? Rejoice instead, and reap as much profit for yourself from this as possible. As far as we can see, moreover, it would be immediately useful to you if everyone else but you were to remain in the grip of this error; and if you were consistent, you would have to do everything in your power to uphold it and to spread it. This would provide you with a means for winning us over for your secret ends, under the pretext of virtue and public utility [*Gemeinnützigkeit*]. But it will not be so easy for you to do this if you straightforwardly announce to us that your ultimate end is your own private end. In short, since you cannot gain anything by communicating your discovery, your assertion contradicts itself. –

Furthermore, the manner in which you communicate your discovery to us shows that you are not so entirely indifferent to whether we accept it or not; on the contrary, you make it your earnest business to convince us, and you defend your proposition as vigorously as possible. What could be the origin of this interest [on your part]? If the fanatical enthusiasm in question is actually as despicable as you assert, then why do you oppose it with so much warmth and power? Why not allow it to collapse on its own? – If you were driven by nothing other than self-interest, then the way you proceed would simply be incomprehensible. What could this be that drives you? It will not be difficult to reveal this to you.

The reason you care so much about convincing us of your opinion is not so that we can orient our actions accordingly, for this would be very inconvenient for you [IV, 321], but rather, so that our conviction will help confirm yours. Regardless of what you say, you yourself are not quite so certain about this matter, and you wish to employ our conviction in order to supplement and perfect your own insufficient conviction.

But, I also ask you, why do you want to be so entirely certain about this matter? If the incentive for your actions is pure self-interest, then what would you gain from such complete certainty? Here again, you are inconsistent. You want to be certain on this point, because otherwise you would have to despise yourself, would have to regard yourself as worse than other human beings, as worse and more base than is implied by your own nature. What you want, therefore, is to be able to respect yourself. You possess within yourself a higher principle for your way of acting than mere self-interest; you are better than you yourself think.

As for you others, you who are not in this situation, who do not reveal your heart's opinion to others, but lock it up carefully within yourselves and, when you act, pretend to have honorable ends that you do not have: why do you do this? If you do this only in order to deceive your fellow human beings, in order to be able the better to use them for furthering your own ends, then you indeed recognize – precisely through your own way of acting – that other people possess a higher and nobler incentive than self-interest, since you avail yourself of this, build upon it, and base your calculations upon it. Once again then, your opinion that there is in human nature nothing higher than self-interest contradicts your own way of proceeding, which presupposes something higher and indeed succeeds only on this presupposition. At least in the case of acting, where a human being's inner nature [*das Innere*] reveals itself in the most certain manner, you cannot fail to recognize a higher principle in human beings; but this is a principle you can only have derived from yourself, from your own profound inner sensation, and only subsequently transferred to others. Hence you too are not as lacking in all that is good as you believed.

In summary, there is no human being with even the slightest level of cultivation – here we are not talking about crudely natural human beings [IV, 322], the cultivation of whom we have already discussed above – who does not sometimes perform actions that cannot be explained on the basis of the mere principle of egotistic self-love or on the presupposition that others act upon this principle. It is to these actions and to the principle underlying them that one must direct the attention of those who deny the possibility of acting out of anything other than self-interest.

Against this proposition one might raise a point that we ourselves established above: namely, that theoretical conviction cannot be forced. So how could one be confident that one can convince the other person that there is indeed still something good in him? In order to respond to such an objection, let me add that in this case one can indeed be confident about this, since the heart of the person who has to be convinced is already inclined in advance toward what we are expounding. One can be sure that everyone very much wants to be able to respect himself, if only that were possible. Thus one can be quite sure that one will receive the approval of the other person if one can show him that he at least possesses predispositions that are worthy of respect.

By proceeding gradually, a moral mode of thinking can be erected on this foundation.

V

We now return to a point left undeveloped above. We said previously that in order to develop the affect of respect in human beings one has to show them something worthy of respect, but there is no better available means for doing this than by means of one's own good example. – From this there follows *the duty to set a good example*.

This duty is very often regarded quite incorrectly, as though, merely for the sake of setting a good example, one could be bound to do something that one would otherwise not have had to do (such as going to church, taking communion, and the like). But as we have already seen above, in the domain of the moral law there are no indifferent actions; this law encompasses and determines absolutely everything that can occur through freedom. I absolutely must do what is commanded of me, and do it for its own sake, regardless of any example I might set [IV, 323]. I am absolutely not permitted to do anything I am prohibited from doing, and once again without regard for setting an example. Something contrary to duty will necessarily set a bad example; and nothing good ever arises from something immoral. But I can do no more than is commanded of me, because duty already lays claim to all my powers and all my time. There can therefore be no actions solely for the ultimate end of setting a good example nor actions that occur only for this reason. The duty to set a good example absolutely does not concern the *matter* or *content* of our actions. But perhaps it may concern their *form*, and this is indeed the case.

The moral law only makes it a duty that what is commanded should happen; insofar as this law is concerned only with the sheer action, it does not itself decide whether this action is to happen publicly or secretly, accompanied by some announcement of the principles according to which it happens or unaccompanied by such an announcement.

But if we are responsible for setting a good example then this is no longer a matter of indifference; the maximal *publicity* of our maxims and actions is in this case commanded of us. (To be sure, setting a good example is not supposed to do anything more than help induce respect for virtue – and this is all it can do.)

Let us begin by discussing the *inner* character of such *publicity*. The intent of the same is to induce respect for what is worthy of respect. Respect, however, cannot be coerced nor artificially induced; instead, it offers itself freely and unnoticed. Consequently, the virtuous person is not permitted to allow his intent [to set a good example] to be noticed; and since he ought to allow everything that is in his heart to be noticed and since others will indeed notice what is actually in his heart, he must have no such intent at all with respect to specific individuals. He allows what is innermost in his heart to express itself outwardly in a completely natural manner, without doing anything more in order to attract the attention of others to this.

This is the external character of the sincere man [*des offenen Mannes*]. He continues straight along his path, on every occasion he talks and acts precisely in accordance with the promptings of his heart and in a manner he considers to be dutiful, without glancing to the left or to the right in order to see whether anyone is observing him or not and without eavesdropping or asking what others might say about his manner of acting [IV, 324], for he does not have time for that; his time is taken up with fulfilling his duty. For that very reason, however, he never hides, because he has just as little time to worry about secrecy and concealment. If he is being judged, however, he responds to every judgment and defends himself so long as he is convinced that the charge against him is unjust, and he does not excuse his action if he is shown to have done wrong. – There is certainly no more beautiful trait in a human character than sincerity [*Offenheit*] and no more dangerous one than concealment [*Verstecktheit*]. A direct and sincere frame of mind [*Sinn*] at least leads to righteousness, even if it does not itself constitute the latter; but a person who hides himself has a secret fear of the truth, some sort of deep defect that he does not want to have discovered. Such a person cannot readily be improved until he has rid himself of this fear of truth.

A hypocrite is a person whose end is to be noticed. Whether in others or in ourselves (and it is the latter case that is usually most important to us), one can distinguish this character trait from sincerity by the following feature: the hypocrite usually engages in preparations that are by no means necessary for achieving his end and that therefore can only have the intention of calling attention to themselves; the sincere man does nothing more than happens to be required for achieving his end.

The sincere man affirms this publicity, first of all, concerning his maxims. His ruling maxim ought to be to do his duty simply for the sake of duty. Now he makes absolutely no secret out of this latter motive. It is quite despicable to be ashamed of one's subordination to something higher and larger – as if it were subordination to a superstition – and to want to establish oneself as God of the universe. But it is just as despicable to want to give some other name to what one has done for others from a feeling of duty, or at least ought to have done, to ascribe such acts to "special friendship," "partiality," "generosity," "grace," and the like.

This same publicity is present in the sincere person's acting, as is already self-evident from the publicity of his maxims [IV, 325], since these are not maxims if they are not put into actions, and since there is no way to convince anyone that these actually are our maxims other than by acting. Mere virtuous chatter is of no use and does not set a good but only a very bad example, inasmuch as it strengthens disbelief in virtue. The sincere man shows himself to be particularly consistent in this regard: his deeds are like his words.

Overview of particular duties

§26

The relation of particular duties to universal ones; and subdivisions of the particular duties

Regarding the relation of the particular [*besonderen*] to the universal [*allgemeinen*] duties, we need only point out the following:

The sole duty of everyone is to further the end of reason; the latter comprehends within itself all other ends; particular duties are duties only to the extent that they refer to the achievement of this main end.

I ought to exercise the particular duty of my estate and profession not simply because I am supposed to do so, but because this allows me to promote the advance of reason from my present position. I ought to view a particular duty as a means for accomplishing the universal duty of all human beings, and absolutely not as a end [in its own right]; and in fulfilling the particular obligations of my estate and profession I do my duty purely and solely insofar as I fulfill these particular obligations *for the sake of duty in general.* The proposition [IV, 326], "everyone shall do his duty by honestly fulfilling the particular obligations of his estate," must therefore be understood with the following restriction: "– to the extent that he fulfills these obligations solely out of and for the sake of duty." This is because one can think of many other motives that might move a human being to engage in the most diligent observation of his obligations: e.g., a natural predilection and inclination for his profession, fear of reproach and punishment, ambition, and the like. A person who is driven by such motives may do *what* he is supposed to do and he may act legally, but he will not be doing this *in the manner* he ought to be doing it; he will not be acting *morally.* Whether someone actually fulfills *his duty* within his estate is therefore something that he alone can calculate, before the witness of his own conscience. The preceding remark has concerned the necessary *form* of the will with regard to the particular duties.

We still have to add another remark, this one concerning the *matter* or *content* of the will with regard to the particular duties, and this will also provide us with a criterion that will allow anyone to recognize whether or not he satisfies his obligations to his estate out of a love for duty, to wit: if one's estate and profession are absolutely not ends in themselves, but only means for reaching an end, then it is impermissible and contrary to duty to sacrifice one's virtue to one's estate and profession, since it is absurd to put the means before the end.

The work prescribed by one's estate and profession, as well as the rights that render such work possible, can from time to time come into conflict with the end of reason. In this case, a person whose ultimate end is his estate and profession and who therefore pursues the latter for reasons other than from a feeling of duty will still continue to pursue this end, because he is acquainted with no higher point of view whatsoever and knows only that he is supposed to do and to say this and that. But a person who regards his estate and his profession as a means will in such cases [of conflict between the end of reason and the requirements of his profession and estate] certainly not continue to pursue them, because now they no longer serve to advance the end [of reason] but hinder it instead. In the course of the investigation that follows I will apply this general remark to the particular duties of individual estates and professions and show what it implies for each. In this manner this remark itself will also become clearer [IV, 327].

The subdivisions of our overview of the particular duties must be based on the subdivisions of those particular human relations that are called estates. Relationships among human beings are, to begin with, either *natural*, i.e., relationships based upon some natural arrangement, or *artificial*, i.e., relationships based on a contingent and free determination of the will. – In the language of ordinary life one often hears the terms *estate* and *profession* linked. The first word obviously indicates something more fixed[28] and enduring than the second, which includes freedom and the mutual interaction of free beings as one of its distinguishing features. Thus, solely for the purpose of *our present* investigation, we may call the former *estate* and the second *profession* – though I introduce this distinction without thereby wishing to assert that this is how these terms are understood in ordinary language or as if I wanted to prescribe laws for linguistic usage. –

§27

Duties of human beings according to their particular natural estate

There are only two natural relationships among rational, sensible human beings and both of these are based on the natural arrangement for the propagation of the species: the relationship of *spouses to each other*, and the relationship of *parents and children*. We have dealt in detail with both of these relationships in our *Natural Right*.[29] Here we will only summarize briefly what was said there; for further discussion of this subject our readers are referred to this work [IV, 328].

---

[28] The German term *Stand*, rendered here as "estate," literally means "stand."

[29] See *FNR*, "Outline of Family Right," pp. 264–319 (*SW* III: 304–369; *GA* I/4: 95–149).

(A) The relationship of spouses

I

As already noted, the relationship of spouses is based on the arrangement of nature into two different sexes for the propagation of the species. Here as everywhere, the means employed by nature for achieving its end in free beings is a natural drive; and the relation of this particular drive to freedom is the same as that of all natural drives, which is a topic that was adequately discussed above. The drive itself can neither be generated nor annihilated by freedom; it is given. Nature's end is achieved only insofar as some action of the free being is immediately produced by the drive in question – and this is a rule that holds more strictly in the case of the natural drive for the union of the sexes than in the case of any other natural drive. A concept can only permit this drive to operate, or prevent it from transforming itself into an action; it cannot eradicate the drive, nor can it put itself in the place of the drive in such a way that the action would be grounded *immediately* in the concept of an end instead of being grounded in the drive and merely *mediated* by the concept. Humankind is not propagated in accordance with concepts as a result of free decisions of the will.

At first glance, therefore, it would seem that the very same thing would have to be said about the satisfaction of this natural drive that was said earlier about the satisfaction of natural drives in general: the drive must actually be present and not be a need that is, so to speak, feigned by the power of the imagination. The satisfaction of this drive is permitted only as a means for its end. The proximate end in this case is the propagation of the species. This end must in turn be related to our highest and final end, namely, that reason should have dominion. But an entirely different, less physical aspect of this drive will also reveal itself, and to this extent the command that one permit oneself to satisfy this drive only as a means for propagating the species [IV, 329] must already be restricted in a preliminary manner so that if this end [of propagating the species] fails to be achieved by satisfying this drive the responsibility for this failure must at least not be assigned to us.

II

If the natural drive required nothing more than the activity of two people, then our investigation would be finished and there would be no conjugal relationship and no duties pertaining to the same. The conditions under which one is permitted to act when summoned to do so by a natural drive are well-known, and we were just reminded of these; and it is not particularly difficult to think that it is permissible for two persons to engage in free mutual interaction with each other, just as long as they have both consented to this.

But things are different in the case now before us. The particular arrangement of nature is such that within the community of the sexes for the purposes of propagating the species only one sex behaves in an active manner while the behavior of the other is entirely passive. (One will find a more detailed specification of this arrangement and of the basis for the same in my *Natural Right*.)[30] The most tender relationships among human beings arise from this unique foundation.

It is impossible that in a rational being there could be a drive to behave only passively, a drive simply to surrender oneself, as a mere object to be used, to some foreign influence. Sheer passivity stands in outright contradiction to reason and abolishes the latter. Consequently, just as surely as a woman possesses reason and just as surely as reason has exercised any influence upon the formation of her character, her sexual drive cannot appear as a drive for a state of mere passivity, but must transform itself equally into a drive for activity. Notwithstanding the arrangement of nature, which must still continue to exist alongside this drive, the woman's drive can only be to satisfy a man and not herself – a drive to surrender herself not for her own sake, but for the sake of the other person. Such a drive is called *love*. Love is nature and reason in their most original union.

One cannot say that it is a woman's duty to love, because love includes within itself a natural drive that does not depend on freedom. But one can say that where there is even the slightest predisposition toward morality [IV, 330], the natural drive cannot appear other than in the shape of love. In its raw state, a woman's sexual drive is the most repugnant and disgusting thing that exists in nature, and at the same

---

[30] See *FNR*, 264ff. (*SW* III: 95ff.; *GA* I/4: 95ff.).

time it indicates the absolute absence of all morality. The lack of a chaste heart [*Unkeuschheit des Herzens*] in a woman, which consists precisely in the sexual drive expressing itself in her directly, even if for other reasons it never erupts in actions, is the foundation of all vice. In contrast, female purity and chastity, which consists precisely in her sexual drive never manifesting itself as such but only in the shape of love, is the source of everything noble and great in the female soul. For a woman chastity is the principle of all morality.

III

If a woman submits to a man out of love, from this there arises with moral necessity a *marriage*.

Let us consider this first of all from the side of the woman. In giving herself, she gives herself entirely, along with all her powers, her strengths, and her will – in short, her empirical I – and she gives herself *forever*. First of all, [she gives herself] *entirely*: she gives her personality; if she were to exempt anything from this subjugation, then what she had exempted would have to have a higher worth for her than her own person, which would amount to the utmost disdain for and debasement of the latter, which is something that simply could not coexist with the moral way of thinking. In addition, she gives herself *forever*, or at least that is what she presupposes. Her surrender occurs out of love, and this can coexist with morality only on the presupposition that she has lost herself completely – both her life and her will, without holding back anything whatsoever – to her loved one, and that she could not exist except as his. But if, in the hour of giving herself, she were still able to think of herself as being at some other time anything other than his, then she would not feel herself to be compelled [to surrender herself], and this would violate the presupposition in question and abolish morality [IV, 331].

The concept of marriage (in the sense just indicated) is already contained in the mere concept of love, and to say that a moral woman can give herself only to love is the same as saying that she can give herself only under the presupposition of a marriage.

Let us now consider this matter from the side of the man. The entire ethical character of the woman is based on the conditions just indicated. But no human being may demand the sacrifice of a human character. Therefore, a man can accept his wife's submission only under those conditions on which alone she can submit herself to him; otherwise he would not be treating her as a moral being but as a mere thing. – Even if a woman were to offer herself on other conditions, the man could not accept her subjugation, and in this case the legal principle, "no wrong happens to a person who is treated in accordance with his own will," does not hold. We are not permitted to make any use of another person's immorality – in this case, it is absolute depravity – without also being held responsible for the other's offense.

It follows from these propositions that satisfaction of the sexual drive is permitted only within marriage (in the previously indicated sense of the word). Such satisfaction outside of marriage is completely degrading for a woman's ethical character, and for a man it involves his participation in this crime, as well as his utilization of an animalistic inclination. From a moral point of view, no union of two persons of both sexes for the satisfaction of their [sexual] drive is possible except in a complete and indissoluble marriage. Within marriage, however, the union of the sexes, which in itself carries the stamp of animal crudeness, obtains an entirely different character, one that is worthy of a rational being. It becomes the complete fusion of two rational individuals into one: unconditional surrender on the part of the woman, a vow of the most sincere tenderness and magnanimity on the part of the man. Female purity remains even in marriage, and only in marriage does it remain unblemished: the woman always gives herself only from love, and even the natural drive of the man, which he otherwise might very well permit himself to avow, receives a different shape; it becomes love in return [IV, 332].

This relationship between the spouses extends throughout all their mutual relations, and its intimacy grows with the duration of the marriage. The woman can never cease to depend entirely on her husband nor to lose herself in him without holding anything back, for otherwise she relinquishes her dignity in her own eyes and has to believe that what motivated her to subjugate herself [to her husband] was her own sexual drive, since it could not have been love. Nor can the man cease to return to her everything that she has given him, and more; he does this in order to be worthy of respect and noble, because not only her worldly fate but even her confidence in her own character depend upon his conduct. – There are no commands that need to be mentioned regarding the conjugal relationship. If the latter is the kind of relationship it ought to be, then it is a command unto itself; if it is not, then it constitutes a single, continuous crime, which is incapable of improvement by means of ethical rules.

I wish to indicate only one implication [of the preceding]:

It is the absolute vocation of every individual of both sexes to enter into marriage. The physical human being is neither a man nor a woman, but is both; and the same is true of the moral human being. The human character has several sides, and its most noble ones are precisely those that can be developed only in marriage: the woman's devoted love; the man's magnanimity, which sacrifices everything for his companion; the necessity of being worthy of honor, if not for one's own sake, then for that of one's spouse; true friendship – friendship is possible only in marriage, but there it ensues necessarily – ; paternal and maternal feelings, and so on. The original striving of the human being is egotistic; within marriage, even nature leads him to forget himself in another person, and the conjugal union of both sexes is the only way of improving the human being by natural means. An unmarried person is only half a human being.

To be sure, no woman can be told, "you ought to love," and no man can be told, "you ought to be loved and to love in return," because this is something that does not depend entirely upon freedom. This, however, can be put forward as an absolute command: namely, that it must not, to the best of our knowledge, be because of us that we remain unmarried [IV, 333]. A clearly conceived intention never to marry is absolutely contrary to duty. It is a great misfortune to remain unmarried through no fault of one's own; to remain unmarried through one's own fault is a great fault. – One is not permitted to sacrifice this end to other ends, such as service to the church, the aims of the state or the family, the calm of a life devoted to speculation, and the like; for the end of being a complete human being is higher than any other end.

(B) The relationship of parents and children and the reciprocal duties arising therefrom

Here we are not discussing the reciprocal duties of older people in general and children in general, considered as uneducated and inexperienced human beings. Much could surely be said on this topic, but this is not the topic of our present investigation. We are instead discussing the reciprocal duties of parents and the specific children they have engendered. This relationship is not based upon a freely designed concept but upon an arrangement of nature, and it is necessary to present this relationship and to develop an ethical relationship from it.

I

Between a father and his child there is absolutely no natural connection that is guided by freedom and consciously established. The act of generation, upon which some philosophers want to ground rights and duties, is an act that, as such, occurs without freedom and consciousness, and it produces no cognition of the one who is generated by this act. – Such a connection is, however, consciously established between a mother and her child. The fruit is first nourished in her body, and her own preservation is bound up with the preservation and health of this fruit – and, indeed, she is personally conscious of this. She knows to which object she gives this enduring [IV, 334], constantly recurring care, and in this way she becomes accustomed to viewing the life of the same as a part of her own life. The birth of the child is accompanied by pain and danger to the life of the mother. For the mother, the appearance of the child is at the same time the end of her pains, which is necessarily a joyful moment. The animal union of mother and child continues for a while longer since the child's nourishment is prepared within the mother, and the mother feels that it is no less a need for her to provide this nourishment than it is a need of the child to accept it. The mother preserves her child from need, as is also the case among animals.

Now it absolutely violates the dignity of a rational being to be driven by a purely natural instinct. To be sure, the instinct in question cannot and ought not to be eradicated, but in its union with reason and freedom it will appear in a different guise [*Gestalt*], just as we saw occur above in the case of the sexual drive of the woman. What could this guise be? According to the mere arrangement of nature, the need of the child was itself a physical need of the mother. If we posit a being with consciousness and freedom, then this purely natural drive will be transformed into a sensation and an affect; the place that was previously occupied by a physical need will now be occupied by a need of the *heart*, the freely elected need to make the preservation of the child her own need. This is the affect of *compassion* and *pity*. As in the case of love, one can hardly say that maternal compassion is a duty; instead, it necessarily arises from the original union of the natural drive with reason. One can, however, say of both love and maternal compassion that they condition the possibility of all morality. If a woman is incapable of any sensation of maternal tenderness, one could undoubtedly say of her that she does not rise above the level of animality. Freedom enters the picture only afterward, and along with freedom there appears a command of duty. A mother has to be expected to open herself to these sensations, to strengthen them within herself, and to suppress everything that could infringe upon them.

Disregarding everything that is brought about by our civil constitution, [public] opinion, the power of [IV, 335] imagination, and the like, the father's love of his child is only an *indirect* or *mediated* love. It arises from his love for the [child's] mother. Conjugal tenderness makes it a joy and a duty for him to share in the sensations of his spouse, and this is how love for his child and care for its preservation arise in the father.

The first duty of both parents with respect to the child that is generated from their union is to care for its preservation.

II

Here I am presupposing, as would be the case if we were more faithful to nature – and we were able to be more faithful to her – , that the man and the woman always live together, work together, etc., and hence that they also live together with their child, since the child has to remain under their eyes for the sake of its preservation. Since humans being are only too inclined to transfer the concept of reason and freedom to everything outside them, the father and mother could also be expected to transfer to their child this concept of reason and freedom and to treat the child in accordance with this presupposition, and in this case it could not fail to happen that traces of reason would, when summoned by this mutual interaction, manifest themselves in the child.

In accordance with the necessary concepts of free beings, freedom also pertains to well-being; and, since the parents love their child and therefore desire its well-being, they could not wish to rob it of freedom as such. But since they are, at the same time, watching over its preservation, as an end commanded by nature and by duty, they can encourage and admit freedom only to the extent that this is compatible with the child's preservation.

This is the first concept of education [*Erziehung*], or, as one could call this part of education in particular, the first concept of *discipline*

[*Zucht*]. It is the parents' duty to preserve their child; it is [also] their duty to protect and encourage the child's freedom. To the extent that the latter could infringe upon the former, it is their duty to subordinate the [child's] employment of freedom to their highest end with respect to the child: i.e., discipline is a duty.

Very soon the duty to provide a higher education enters the picture: education for morality [IV, 336].

The parents have discovered the freedom of the child, though for the time being the freedom in question is purely formal; but every free being is capable of morality and is supposed to be cultivated thereto, and this also applies to their child. Because the physical preservation of the child is imposed exclusively on the parents, they must have the child with them; and thus they alone are the ones who can provide the child with a moral education.

The following [duties] are contained in this [universal] duty of moral education: first of all, [the parents have a duty] to cultivate the powers of the child in a purposive manner, so that it can be a good tool for furthering the end of reason; hence, [they have a duty] to produce [in the child a certain degree of] *skill*. (In passing, we should mention that it cannot be our intention on this occasion to provide an exhaustive treatment of the theory of education.) This then is the proper end of education, to the extent that it depends on art and rules: to develop and to cultivate the pupil's free powers. Finally, there is the duty to provide the cultivated freedom of the pupil with some direction, and this can occur only in the same general way that morality is promoted outside of us at all, as was discussed above.

III

Now what is the mutual relationship of the parents and the children in the context of education?

It is often the parents' duty to restrict the freedom of their children, in part for the sake of their preservation. They must not tolerate any use of freedom that would threaten the preservation of their children. Another reason they need to restrict their children's freedom is for the sake of cultivating their skills. In connection with the latter the parents must admonish them to engage in actions that have such cultivation as their end and to avoid others that have no connection either with the primary end of preservation or with the secondary end of cultivation, because such actions are superfluous and are nothing but a waste of time and force. They must not restrict their children's freedom for the sake of morality; for something is moral only to the extent that it is done or not done freely [IV, 337].

The question concerning the parents' right to restrict the freedom of their children can hardly arise. I have to protect the formal freedom of every human being, because I must consider every person to be a fully cultivated being with respect to morality, and I must consider each person's freedom to be a means for furthering reason's end. I cannot be the judge of the other person, for he is my equal. I do not, however, regard my child as a fully cultivated moral being; instead, I regard my child as someone who first has to be cultivated, and this is precisely how my child is given to me by virtue of my duty to educate him. Thus, the very same end that requires me to protect the freedom of those who are equal to me also requires that I restrict the freedom of my child.

It is the duty of parents to restrict the freedom of their children to the extent that their use of it could be disadvantageous to the end of education – but only to that extent. Any other restriction is contrary to duty, for it is contrary to the end [of reason]. It is, after all, *the freedom* of the children that is supposed to be cultivated; hence they have to have freedom, if the cultivation of the same is to be possible. Parents ought not, out of mere willfulness [*Eigensinn*], to prohibit their children from doing certain things, in order, as they say, to break their will. The only will that ought to be broken is a will that is contrary to the end of education. But the children ought to possess a will as such. One is educating free beings and not machines without a will, to be used by the first person who lays hold of them. On this matter, however, the parents alone are their own sole judge; they have to come to terms with themselves about this in the court of their own conscience.

If compulsion is the only means that can be found for subjugating the children to the end of education, then the parents have the right of compulsion, and it is then their duty to compel their children, if this is indeed the only way to achieve the end required by duty.

If the child is compelled, then it is and remains a mere object upon which the parents act. It possesses freedom only in the sphere where the compulsion ends, and this freedom is to be viewed as the result of the actions of the parents. Hence the actions of the children do not possess the least morality, for they are compelled [IV, 338].

But morality is supposed to be developed within the child; hence something must remain that is the result of the child's own freedom, and this remainder is the child's *free obedience*. Such free obedience consists in the children doing voluntarily what the parents command, without any use of compulsory means or fear of the same, and voluntarily abstaining from what the parents prohibit, *because* they have prohibited it or commanded it; for if the children themselves are so convinced of the goodness and purposiveness of what is commanded of them, and if they are so convinced of this that their own inclination already drives them to do what is commanded of them by their parents, then this is a case not of obedience but of insight. Obedience is not based on any particular insight into the goodness of whatever happens to be commanded, but on a childlike belief in the higher wisdom and goodness of the parents as such.

Just as one cannot say that love or a woman's compassion is a duty, so one cannot say that this childlike obedience is a duty; but such obedience issues from a predisposition toward morality as such and toward a dutiful disposition. Moreover, if the children are treated right then such obedience will occur all by itself, for it can be based on nothing but respect and submissiveness before superiority of mind and morality – a superiority that is as yet not comprehended, but only obscurely felt –, along with a love of such superiority of mind and morality and a desire to share in it as well. This is the source of obedience; and if anything demonstrates that there is goodness in human nature, then it is such obedience.

Once obedience is present, it can be strengthened and augmented by means of freedom; specifically, the child can give himself over to those considerations and sensations that augment obedience, and it is from this perspective and only now that obedience becomes a *duty of the children*. – It is the sole duty of the children; it develops sooner than other moral feelings, for it is the root of all morality. Later on, [even] after morality becomes possible within the sphere that has been left free by the parents, obedience still remains the highest duty. The child is not permitted to want to be free outside this sphere [IV, 339].

(In the child, obedience is an imitation [*Nachbildung*] of the moral way of thinking in its entirety, and that is why it is more important than anything else; for the child relates to the command and person of its parents in the same way a cultivated human being relates to the moral law as such and to the executor of the same, God. We ought simply to do what duty commands, without trying to calculate the consequences; and yet, simply in order to be able to do what duty commands, we must necessarily assume that the consequences will turn out well in God's hands. In Christianity, God is represented by the image of the father, and this is fine. Yet one should not content oneself with talking forever and ceaselessly about God's goodness, but should at the same time also be mindful of our obedience toward God and of our childlike submission to his will, without any sophistry or calculation; and such submission should not occur merely in our sensations, as a means of consoling ourselves, but should be expressed above all in our courageous execution of our obligations, regardless of the consequences that we, in our shortsightedness, may believe ourselves to have discovered. Inculcation [*Ausbildung*] of such obedience is the sole means by which parents can immediately produce a moral disposition in their child; hence it is quite properly their duty to admonish them to obey. – It is therefore an utterly false maxim, one which we owe, like so many other ills, to the once prevailing eudaemonism, that one should want to compel the child to do anything only by means of rational grounds and on the basis of the child's own insight into the same. In addition to the other reasons for objecting to this maxim, there is the fact that it is self-contradictory, inasmuch as it expects that one's children will possess a good deal more reason than one expects of oneself; for adults also act largely on the basis of inclination and not on the basis of rational grounds.)

We still have to address here the question concerning the limits of unconditional obedience on the part of the children and the limits of the parents' demand for such obedience. (All obedience is both *unconditional* and blind, for otherwise it would not be obedience – because it is blind with regard to a particular person. Blind obedience "in general" is not possible; obedience is necessarily grounded on some personal conviction [IV, 340] regarding the higher wisdom and goodness of the person we are obeying.)

The question just posed can have two different meanings. On the one hand, one can inquire concerning the extension, that is, the sphere of actions, in which a child ought to obey its parents and *the extent to which* the child should obey them; on the other, one can ask how far into the future this duty on the part of the child extends, that is, *how long* a child is supposed to obey its parents and whether there is not some point in time when the child is set free, and, if so, when this might be.

If the question is understood in the former sense, then it is a question raised either by the child or by the parents. The child ought not to raise such a question, and it is precisely in this prohibition that we find the answer to our question: the child is supposed to obey, and its obedience consists precisely in not wanting to be any more free than its parents allow it to be. The necessary boundary of the child's obedience is something that only the parents can judge; the child cannot judge this at all, inasmuch as the child has submitted itself obediently to its parents. – It is utterly contradictory to say, as one sometimes hears it said, that the child is supposed to obey in all matters in which it is fair to require such obedience [*in billigen Stücke*]. A person who obeys only when it is [in his view] fair to be asked to do so, does not obey at all; for in order to do this he must make a judgment about what is fair and what is not. If he does what is "fair" as such, then he acts on the basis of his own conviction and not out of obedience. Whether the obedience that is demanded is fair or not is something for which the parents will have to answer in accordance with their own conscience; they cannot allow themselves to be judged before the tribunal of the child. – "But what," someone might proceed to ask, "if the parents were to command that their child do something immoral?" To this I would respond as follows: either the immorality of the command reveals itself only after careful investigation or else it is immediately obvious. The first case cannot occur [in this situation], for the obedient child does not presuppose that its parents could command it to do something evil. If the second case should occur, then from that moment on the basis of [the child's] obedience, i.e., belief in the higher morality of the parents, is removed, and any further obedience would now be contrary to duty. This is also what happens when the existing immorality and shamefulness of the parents' way of living [IV, 341] is immediately obvious to the children. In such a case, no obedience on the part of the children and no education through the parents is possible.

If it is the parents who raise the question indicated above [concerning the extent to which their children should obey them], which is more appropriate, then the answer is as follows: do not issue any commands unless you are personally and conscientiously convinced that these commands, in accordance with your highest convictions, are aimed at the end of education. You have no inner, moral right to demand any further obedience.

If the question concerns the duration of the [child's] duty of obedience, then the answer is as follows:

First of all, obedience is demanded for the sake of education; but education is a means to an end; and the means falls away once the end has been achieved. The end of education was to make the child's forces useful for furthering the end of reason in some field and in some manner. The child itself cannot be the judge of whether this end has been achieved, for the child concedes higher insight to its parents. One possibility, therefore, is that the parents themselves, employing their own free will and according to their own estimation, will decide that this end has been achieved and will set the child free.

A second possibility is that success itself will decide whether the end of education, the [child's] usefulness [for the end of reason], has been attained. This is a matter of which the state is an extremely competent judge. Thus, if the state grants some office to the son, it thereby judges that his education is completed. Moreover, the judgment of the state binds the parents juridically; they have to subordinate themselves to this judgment without appeal. It [also] binds them morally; they ought to subordinate themselves to it for the sake of duty. –

A third and final possibility is that education is no longer possible at all, and this is surely the case following the marriage of the children. [Following marriage,] the daughter subordinates herself entirely to the man and depends upon his will, and therefore she cannot depend any longer upon the will of others, including that of her parents [IV, 242]. The son assumes the responsibility of caring for the fate of his spouse, completely in accordance with her wishes, and therefore he cannot be determined any longer by the wishes of others, including those of his parents.

IV

Even after the children have been set free, a particular moral relationship continues to hold between them and their parents.

If we assume, as we have been presupposing, that the parents were the educators of their children, then they are familiar with their entire character, because they have seen it arise before their own eyes and have cultivated it. They are more familiar with their children's character than the children themselves are capable of being. Hence they remain their children's best counselors, and this therefore remains the duty of the parents in particular, more than that of any other human beings. – This is an important point, since otherwise there would be no *particular* relationship [between parents and children], but only a *universal* relationship, according to which it is a duty to give good advice to every human being. It is, I maintain, a lasting particular duty of the parents to advise their children, for it is precisely here that their counsel is most appropriately employed. It is the children's duty to listen more attentively to the counsel of their parents than to any other counsel and to consider it more diligently. To be sure, they no longer have a duty of obedience [toward their parents]; they are dismissed from this duty and are able to act only according to their own conviction; but they continue to have this duty to listen attentively and then to reflect upon their parent's advice. – The parents retain the duty of *solicitude*, the children that of childlike *deference*. (Deference consists precisely in this: one presupposes that the other person possesses higher wisdom and takes pains to find all his counsels to be wise and good. It betrays a lack of deference to dismiss out of hand what another person says.)

Moreover, there remains between parents and children the *particular* duty of mutual aid and support for one another. The children continue to retain in their parents their best guides and counselors; the parents retain in their children their own work, that which they have cultivated for the world, and in this way they can still sufficiently satisfy their [IV, 343] duties toward the world, even after their own deaths.

Duties of human beings within a particular profession

§28

Subdivisions of possible human professions

We have already explained above what a profession means as such. There are all sorts of things that pertain to the furthering of reason's end. An individual's profession is that portion of this end that a single individual takes it upon himself quite specifically to further. – We have also pointed out the maxim according to which one has to choose one's profession: not in accordance with inclination but in accordance to duty.

The proper object of the end of reason is always the community of rational beings. One either acts immediately upon this community of rational beings, or else one acts upon nature for the sake of this community. – There is no efficacious acting upon nature simply for the sake of nature; the ultimate end of acting efficaciously upon nature is always human beings. – This provides the basis for the chief subdivisions of all possible human professions. The former [that is, those professions that act directly upon other human beings] could be called the higher professions, and the latter [that is, those that involve acting directly upon nature for the sake of the human community] could be called the lower ones. On this same basis, one could also divide human beings into two classes [*Klassen*], a higher and a lower one.

First of all, how many ways can a human being as a rational being be acted upon immediately? [IV, 344].

What is primary and highest in a human being – though not what is most noble in him – is cognition, the primordial matter of his entire intellectual [*geistig*] life. It is cognition that guides one in one's actions. The best disposition may indeed retain its inner worth, but it does not lead to the realization of reason's end if cognition is incorrect. Thus, the first way one can work upon the human community is to work to cultivate its theoretical insight. This is the profession of the *learned person* or the scholar [*des Gelehrten*]. Hence we will have to begin by discussing the duties of the scholar.[31]

Insight, however, is and always remains simply a means to an end. In the absence of a good will, insight alone does not provide one with any inner worth; insight without good will is of very little use to the

---

[31] "The Duties of the Scholar" was a perennial subject of special interest for Fichte. When he first arrived at Jena, in the summer of 1794, he began a year-long series of public lectures entitled "Morality for Scholars," the first five of which were published that same summer under the title "Some Lectures concerning the Scholar's Vocation." (These lectures are available in English in *EPW*, pp. 144–184 [*SW* VI: 291–346; *GA* I/3: 25–68].) Ten years later, when Fichte taught for a year at the Prussian university in Erlangen, he delivered a new set of public lectures on this same theme. (These are available in English under the title "The Nature of the Scholar and its Manifestations" in Vol. I of *The Popular Works of Johann Gottlieb Fichte*, trans. William Smith, 4th edn [Bristol: Thoemmes, 1999], pp. 147–317 [*SW* VI: 349–447; *GA* I/8: 59–139]. Fichte lectured one last time on this topic in Berlin during the Summer Semester of 1811.

community of rational beings. But cognition itself does not necessarily produce a good will; this is a fundamental proposition, which was highlighted above. There thus remains the particular task of working immediately to improve the will of the community. This is accomplished by the church, which is itself precisely the community of rational beings, and it accomplishes this by means of its servants, the so-called clerics [*Geistliche*], who should more correctly be called "moral educators of the people" [*moralische Volkserzieher*]. Thus, the second topic we will have to discuss is the duties of these teachers of the people [*Volkslehrer*]. – Between these two, the scholar, who has to cultivate the understanding, and the teacher of the people, who has to cultivate the will, there stands the aesthetic artist, who cultivates the aesthetic sense, which serves in a human being as a unifying link between the understanding and the will. In passing, we will add some remarks concerning the duties of the latter.

If human beings are to exercise a mutual influence upon one another, then, prior to anything else, their legal relationship has to be assured. This is a condition for any society. – The institution through which this occurs is called the *state*, and we will have to discuss the duties of the state official [*Staatsbeamter*]. This will conclude what we have to say about the higher class of the people [*höhere Volksklasse*].

The life of a human being and his efficacy within the sensible world is conditioned by certain connections he has with matter [IV, 345]. If human beings are to cultivate themselves for morality, then they must live; and the conditions for their life in material nature must be supplied, to the extent that these conditions are in the control of human beings. This is the way in which the most insignificant occupation, the one that is considered to be the lowest, is connected with the further-ance of reason's end. Such an occupation is related to the preservation and free activity of moral beings, and it is thereby sanctified just as much as the highest occupation.

Nature can be to some degree directed and supported in its produc-tion of what serves us as nourishment, as shelter, and as tools for our activities. This is the profession of the farmers, who direct the organi-zation of nature and whose profession, viewed from that angle, is sublime. In some cases all that has to be done is to gather products that are produced without having to be tended and cared for, and this is done by miners, fishermen, hunters, and the like. All of these, taken together with the farmers, could be called *producers*. – In other cases the raw product must be further fashioned for human ends, and it thereby becomes an artifact or product of art. This is the profession of the craftsmen, artisans, and factory workers, whom I would like to call collectively artisans [*Künstler*], since they all make products of art. (But they have to be distinguished from the aesthetic artist.) Among human beings there must [also] take place some exchange of the many things they need. It would be quite appropriate if there were a particular profession of certain human beings to see to this exchange. This is the profession of the merchants. The duties of the different branches of the lower classes are very much the same, and thus we will only have to discuss in a general way the duties of the lower classes of the people [*niederen Volksklasse*] [IV, 346].

§29

Duties of the scholar

If one regards all the human beings on earth in the manner one ought to view them from the moral standpoint, namely, as one single family – which is also what they ought gradually to become in actuality –, then one can assume that this family also possesses a single system of cognition, which expands and perfects itself from age to age. Just as in the case of an individual, so too does the whole species become more sagacious as the years go by and develop itself by means of experience.

The cognition of each age is supposed to mark an advance, and the learned estate exists precisely in order to raise cognition to a higher level.

First of all, the scholars are the depositories, the archives as it were, of the culture of the age; and they are not merely the depositories of the mere results [of research], which, as such, are also to be encountered among non-scholars, albeit in a dispersed fashion, but they are also in possession of the principles [on which these results are based]. They know not only that something possesses a certain character, but they also know how human beings arrived at a cognition of this and how this cognition coheres with the rest of their cognitions. The latter is necessary because scholars are supposed to advance cognition, which means, among other things, that they also ought to correct existing cognition; but one cannot see that the latter deviates from the truth unless one is acquainted with the principles from which it is derived. – The first thing that follows from this is that a scholar ought to have an historical acquaintance with the progress of science up to his own age and be familiar with the principles employed by the same.

In addition, the scholar ought to contribute to the progress of this mind of the community, either by correcting the same, which is also a way of expanding cognition (for a person who is rid of an error also gains knowledge), or by drawing new inferences from what is already known [IV, 347].

It is not merely for himself that the scholar engages in research, corrects [prevailing cognition], and makes discoveries: he does this for the community, and only because of this does his research become something moral and only in this way does he become, within his own field of research, someone who does his duty and serves the community. – The scholar has an immediate effect only upon the learned public; and then, in the manner with which we are familiar, these results spread from the latter to the community as a whole.

It is hardly necessary to point out explicitly that the scholar's way of thinking can be called moral with respect to its form only if he actually devotes himself to the sciences out of a love of duty and with the insight that, in devoting himself to science, he is satisfying a duty toward humanity. Here we are asking simply, *What* is he supposed to do? This can be answered on the basis of what was said above. The scholar ought to be familiar with the object of the culture of his age, and he also ought to advance it further. He must sincerely seek to accomplish the latter, for only in that way can he actually acquire any worth of his own. But even if it should happen that he is unable to make such an advance, he still must at least have had the firm will, the zeal, and the industriousness required in order to make such an advance. If this is so, then his existence will still not have been in vain, for he at least will have kept science alive during his age, and he is thus a link in the chain through which culture is transmitted. To have animated the spirit of inquiry is also a true and important service.

The proper virtue of the scholar is a strict love of truth. He is supposed to advance humankind's cognition and not simply to play with it. Like every virtuous person, the scholar ought to forget himself in his end. What purpose is supposed to be served by presenting glittering paradoxes or by further defending and maintaining any errors one might happen to have let slip? [One does this] only in order to sustain one's own egotism. Ethics wholly disapproves of this, and prudence would have to disapprove of it as well; for only what is true and good persists in humanity, whereas what is false fades away, no matter how much it might glitter in the beginning [IV, 348].

§30
Duties of the moral teachers of the people

I

Human beings, taken together, constitute a single moral community. It is the dutiful disposition of each person to spread morality outside of himself to the best of his ability and knowledge, i.e., to see to it that everyone has the same disposition he has; for everyone necessarily holds his own way of thinking to be the best, since otherwise it would be contrary to conscience to continue to think in that way. For the same reason, every other person also considers his own way of thinking, which differs from ours, to be the best. It follows from this that the overall end of the moral community as a whole is to produce unanimity concerning matters of morality. This is the ultimate end of all reciprocal interaction between moral beings.

When regarded from this point of view, society is called the *church*. – Hence the church is not a particular community, as has often been argued, but is merely a particular way of looking at the same single human society at large. Everyone belongs to the church to the extent that they have the correct, moral way of thinking, and everyone ought to belong to it.

II

This universal duty of everyone to fashion [*bearbeiten*] everyone morally can be transferred to a particular estate, and it is transferred to it – not in such a way that this transfer releases anyone entirely of his duty to work for the improvement of others whenever the opportunity to do so presents itself, but only in such a way that one no longer *explicitly has to make such improvement of others his own particular end* [IV, 349]. Those who belong to this estate are to that extent officials, servants of the church. – Everyone is supposed to cultivate everyone; hence the person to whom this duty is transferred cultivates in *the name of everyone*. He must proceed from that concerning which we are all in agreement, from the symbol or creed. (We have already discussed this above, where we reached this same conclusion by a different route.)[32] He must then proceed toward that concerning which we all ought to be in agreement. Hence he must see farther than the single individuals; he must have mastered the best and most secure results of the moral culture of his age, and it is toward this that he has to lead these individuals. Hence he is and necessarily ought to be a scholar in this particular field. – Everyone ought to be in accord; but they also ought to remain in accord throughout the course of their advancement; hence the moral teacher of the people must always precede them in such a way that everyone can follow him. To be sure, he elevates himself as quickly as possible, but only so quickly as to make it possible to advance everyone in union with one another, and not just one or another single individual. If, in his presentation, he rushes ahead of the culture of everyone, then he is no longer addressing everyone; nor does he speak in the name of everyone, but rather in his name. Of course, he may speak in his own name as a private person or as a member of the republic of scholars, to which he, as a private person, presents any results he has obtained through his own reason. But when he speaks as a servant of the church, he does not represent his own person but the community.

III

Morality develops itself freely and by means of purely rational education in the context of social intercourse and solely from the human heart. As we observed above, it cannot be artificially produced by means of theoretical conviction or anything similar. Some sense for morality is presupposed by our public educational institutions [*Bildungsanstalten*], and it is from this sense for morality that the cleric must necessarily proceed; it is this alone that first makes his office possible and upon which it is built. Immoral human beings do not have a church, nor do they have anyone to represent them with regard to their duties toward the church [IV, 350]. – From this it follows that it can by no means be the aim of public religious institutions to construct theoretical proofs

---

[32] See above, § 18, sect. V.

and a system of ethics [*Gebäude der Sittenlehre*] or to speculate at all about the principles [of the same]. The community does not conduct such proofs for itself, for, just as certainly as it is a community, it already believes [in morality]. Its belief is a fact, and to develop such belief from *a priori* principles is a concern only of scholars. The end of public moral presentations [*Vorstellungen*] can therefore only be to animate and to strengthen this sense that is already universally present, to remove anything that could make it waver inwardly or could prevent it from manifesting itself outwardly in actions. But there is nothing that could have such an effect except doubt concerning whether the final end of morality can be furthered at all, doubt concerning whether there actually is any progress with respect to goodness, or doubt concerning whether this entire disposition is not some sort of fanatical enthusiasm directed at a non-entity. The only thing that could animate and strengthen this [moral] disposition is a firm belief that the furthering of the end of reason is indeed possible and that such progress toward what is better occurs necessarily. Examined more closely, however, the belief in question is a belief in God and immortality. If there is no God, then the furtherance of the good does not proceed in accordance with any rule, for no such rule is contained in the course of nature, which makes no reference whatsoever to freedom; nor is any such rule within the power of finite beings, and for the same reason: because human beings act only with natural force. To maintain that this [furtherance of the good] is nevertheless something that proceeds necessarily and in accordance with a rule is thus to maintain that there is a God. – So too, we cannot advance in a deliberate manner toward our ultimate end unless we endure eternally, for our goal cannot be reached at any time.

The teacher of the people thus deals mainly with articles of faith or belief. This does not mean that he deduces them *a priori*. Belief follows immediately from the moral disposition, and the teacher of the people necessarily presupposes both the latter and the former; however, he animates the belief in question, and he does this precisely by presupposing that one is acquainted with it, and in this way he directs human beings toward God and eternity – [IV, 351]. It is an enormous advantage for human beings who have an external church that they become accustomed to relating even the most humble activities in which they may be engaged to the most sublime thought attainable by a human being: to God and eternity.

So too is it the office of the teacher of the people to instruct the community regarding the determinate application of the concept of duty, the love of which he rightly presupposes in them. All of them would like to live rationally and ethically, but they do not quite know how to set about doing this nor what pertains thereto: this is the presupposition from which the teacher proceeds. Just as all single individuals, if they were united in a single person and if they could speak, would each contribute what he knows about this subject, so too does the teacher of the people speak in the name of them all. "What should one do in order to put oneself into this or that frame of mind, which, as such, forms a part of the dutiful way of thinking?" – He answers this and similar questions. His instruction is as such quite practical and is designed for immediate application.

Generally speaking, *he does not prove and does not engage in polemics*: these are his main rules. For the teacher of the people presupposes that the articles of faith are already known and accepted and that the will is already well disposed. In a gathering of believers, it is entirely inappropriate for him to squash those who deride religion, to terrify obdurate sinners, or to harangue the community as a band of evil rogues. One would think that such people would not attend such a gathering, and any one of them who did attend would have already offered thereby a public confession of his belief and of his good will. – Moreover, the teacher speaks in the name and in the place of the community, but not in that of God, for he himself stands under God, just as the people do, and he, like them, is only a poor sinner in the eyes of God. This is also why he also speaks just as they would speak: as a counselor, not as a lawgiver; on the basis of experience, not on the basis of principles [IV, 352].

IV

As was just indicated, the teacher of the people does not deal in front of the community with resolute non-believers and with those who do not recognize and respect duty (for this alone constitutes true disbelief); instead, he deals with such people *individually* [*im besonderen*]. We have already indicated above how such people are to be dealt with. The teacher should lead them back into themselves; he should teach them to respect themselves more highly than they may have respected themselves until now. At the basis of disbelief there is always a concealed contempt for oneself and despair over oneself. This basis has to be eradicated, and what rests on it will then disappear on its own.

This is how the teacher of the people should conduct himself with regard to all the particular moral needs of individuals: he should always be prepared to offer advice regarding anything pertinent. He should also seek out the person who does not seek him out, but – and this is the most important point – he should do this with modesty and with respect for the human dignity and for the self-sufficiency of every person. He will become an advisor regarding matters of conscience only if someone explicitly makes him such an advisor. He has no right to impose himself.

V

The proper and characteristic duty of the teacher of the people is to set a good example. He does not provide such an example simply for his own sake, but for the sake of the entire community that he represents.

The belief of the community is largely based on his belief and is, strictly speaking, for the most part nothing other than a belief in his belief. In the eyes of the single individuals he is not actually this particular person but is for them instead the actual representative of the moral community, of the church as a whole. He is supposed to present what he presents not as something he has learned as a scholar and discovered by means of speculation, but as something he has drawn from his own inner experience; and they believe it precisely because everything in this domain is only the result of experience. If his life contradicts [what he presents in his teaching], then no one will believe in his experience [IV, 353]; and, since the latter was something they could only believe in, inasmuch he was neither able nor supposed to supplement his experience with theoretical proofs, no one will actually believe anything whatsoever that he says.

§31

Duties of the fine artist

Since I have discussed the relationship of the scholar and of the moral teacher of the people to the cultivation of humanity, this gives me an occasion to discuss along the way – if only for the sake of completeness – the fine artist [*ästhetische Künstler*], who exercises an equally great, albeit not immediately noticeable influence on this cultivation. In addition, our age demands that everyone do all he can to raise and to discuss this topic.

Unlike the scholar, fine art [*schöne Kunst*] does not cultivate only the understanding; and unlike the moral teacher of the people, it does not cultivate only the heart. Instead, it cultivates the entire unified human being. It addresses itself neither to the understanding nor to the heart, but to the mind [*Gemüt*] as a whole, in the unity of its powers [*Vermögen*]. It constitutes a third power, composed of the other two. Perhaps one cannot express what fine art does in any better way than by saying that *it makes the transcendental point of view the ordinary point of view*. – The philosopher elevates himself and others to this point of view by means of work and in accordance with a rule. The beautiful spirit [*der schöne Geist*] occupies this viewpoint without thinking of it in any determinate manner; he is acquainted with no other viewpoint. He elevates those who open themselves to his influence to this same viewpoint, and he does that just as unnoticeably, so that they are not even aware of the transition [IV, 354].

Let me make myself clearer: from the transcendental point of view, the world is something that is made; from the ordinary point of view, it is something that is given; from the aesthetic point of view, the world is given, but only under the aspect of how it was made. The world, the world that is actually given, i.e., *nature* (for that is all I am talking about here), has two sides: it is a product of our limitation, and it is a product of our free acting – though, to be sure, a product of an *ideal* acting (and not, as it were, of our real efficacious acting). Looked at as a product of our limitation, it is itself limited on all sides; looked at as a product of our free acting, it is itself free on all sides. The first way of looking at the world is the ordinary way; the second is the aesthetic way. For example, every shape in space is to be viewed as a limitation imposed by a neighboring body; [or else] it is to be viewed as a manifestation of the inner fullness and power of the very body that has this shape. A person who proceeds in accordance with this first way of looking sees only distorted, pressed, and anxious forms; he sees ugliness. A person who proceeds in accordance with the second way of looking at things sees the vigorous fullness of nature; he sees life and upward striving; he sees beauty. It is the same with what is highest: the moral law commands absolutely and suppresses all natural inclinations; a person who looks at it in this way relates himself to it as a slave. But the moral law is at the same time the I itself; it comes from the inner depth of our own being [*Wesen*], and when we obey it we are still obeying only ourselves. A person who views the moral law in the latter way views it aesthetically. The beautiful mind sees everything from the side of beauty; he sees everything as free and alive.

I am not here discussing the grace and serenity that this way of looking at things confers upon our entire life. Here I want only to indicate what this aesthetic way of looking at things can contribute to cultivating and ennobling us for our ultimate vocation.

Where then is the world of the beautiful spirit? [It lies] within, within humanity, and nowhere else. Fine art thus leads a human being into himself and makes him feel at home there. It tears him loose from nature as something given and depicts him as self-sufficient and existing for himself alone. Our ultimate end, however, is the self-sufficiency of reason.

Aesthetic sense is not virtue; for the moral law demands self-sufficiency in accordance with *concepts*, while the former arises on its own, without any concepts. It is nevertheless a preparation for virtue; it prepares the ground for it, and when morality comes upon the scene [IV, 355] it finds that half the work – liberation from the bonds of sensibility – has already been accomplished.

Aesthetic cultivation is thus most efficaciously related to furthering the end of reason, and duties can be formulated regarding the same. One cannot make it anyone's duty to care for the aesthetic cultivation of humanity, for, as we have seen, the aesthetic sense does not depend upon freedom and cannot be cultivated by means of concepts. In the name of ethics, however, one can prohibit anyone from hindering such cultivation or from doing his best to make such cultivation impossible by spreading a lack of taste. For everyone can have taste, and taste can be freely cultivated; hence everyone can know what is contrary to taste. By spreading a lack of any taste for aesthetic beauty, one does not leave human beings in a state of indifference, as it were, a state in which they might still expect some future cultivation; instead, one "miscultivates" or deforms [*verbilden*] them.

Two rules can be stated regarding this matter.

(1) [A rule] for all human beings: do not make yourself into an artist against the will of nature; and this is something that always occurs against the will of nature so long as it does not occur because of a

natural impetus but is forced in accordance with a freely taken intention. It is absolutely true that an artist is born an artist. A genius is
reined in by a rule, but no rule can make a genius – precisely because it is
a rule and therefore aims at limitation, but not at freedom.

(2) [A rule] for the true artist: guard yourself against becoming a slave
to the taste of your age, whether from self-interest or from a desire for
current fame. Strive to depict the ideal that hovers before your soul, and
forget everything else. The artist should be inspired only by the sacred-
ness of his profession; all he needs to learn is that in applying his talent
he does not serve human beings, but only serves his own duty. If he
learns this he will soon come to view his own art with entirely different
eyes; he will become a better human being and a better artist as well.
The common saying, "*what is beautiful is what pleases*," is as harmful in
art as it is in morality [IV, 356]. To be sure, what pleases cultivated
humanity, and only that, is beautiful; but so long as humanity is not yet
cultivated – and when will it ever be so? – what is most lacking in taste
may often please people because it is in fashion, and the most excellent
work of art may fail to find any approval because the age has not yet
developed the sense with which it would have to be apprehended.

§32

Duties of the state official

According to the above, the constitution of the state is to be viewed as a
product of the communal will that has expressed itself through an explicit
or an implicit contract. As was shown above, implicit agreement and
subjugation to certain institutions count the same as explicit agreement
in cases of necessity [*im Notfalle*]. – Whatever the state permits in the
communal sphere of everyone's freedom can be done with a good conscience by anyone, for according to our presupposition, one's fellow
citizens have given up their freedom to precisely this extent. Lacking the
permission of the state, one must fear that one is infringing upon the
freedom of others every time one acts freely within this communal sphere.

The state official – and here I am concerned particularly with the
higher officials of the state, the ones who participate in legislation and
whose decisions cannot be appealed – is nothing but an administrator of
this communal will. His office is instituted and his duties are assigned to

him by all of the [other] estates, and he does not have the right to change the constitution unilaterally. It is a matter of conscience for him to regard himself in this manner, for it is precisely and only within the form of the constitution that has been entrusted to him that anyone at all can act with a good conscience [IV, 357]. If he alters the constitution arbitrarily and in a manner such that opposition against this alteration makes itself heard, then he thereby afflicts everyone's conscience and forces them to hesitate between obedience to him and their duties toward the freedom of everyone else.

There is, however, a rule issuing from pure reason regarding the social contract. The positive rule, which the state official has to administer, can depart considerably from the rule based on pure reason: the former can be harsh; it can be unjust. How should the state official conduct himself when faced with such a conflict? This question has already been largely answered by what was said above.

First of all, the official is certainly permitted to take it upon himself to administer this positive constitution, which, according to his own conviction, fails to measure up completely to the purely rational constitution. It is even his duty to do this if he has otherwise been called upon to do so; for there has to be some constitution or another, since otherwise society, along with that for which society exists – progress toward what is better – would not exist. According to our presupposition, however, the constitution that now exists is in accord with the will of everyone, though everyone is permitted to give up and to relinquish what is his by right. But reason still demands that the social bond should gradually approximate that bond that is the only rightful one, and this is also what is demanded by the arrangement of nature. Thus a governor [*Regent*] who has to govern the state with this end in mind must be acquainted with the latter [that is, he must be acquainted with what constitutes a rightful bond in accordance with reason]. According to what was said above, a person who elevates himself above ordinary experience by means of concepts is called a scholar; hence the state official must be a scholar within his own field. Plato says that no prince could rule well who did not participate in the ideas,[33] and this is exactly what we are saying here.

The state official is necessarily familiar with the following: he is familiar with the constitution to which he is obliged, as well as with

---

[33] *Republic* 519 b 7–c 2.

the explicit or implicit contracts upon which this constitution rests. He is also familiar with the state constitution as it ought to be, that is, with the ideal constitution. Finally, he is acquainted with the path that humanity in general, and especially his own people [*Volk*], has to follow in order to participate in this ideal constitution [IV, 358].

The state official's manner of governance can be described by the following brief formula: he should absolutely enforce whatever is demanded by absolute right [*Recht*], that is, whatever is demanded by natural right, without any mitigation or forbearance. If something is demanded only by the written, positive law [*Recht*], then he should enforce this only to the extent that he is able to consider it to be the enduring product of the will of all the interested parties. – Allow me to make myself clearer: as far as the first case [of absolute right] is concerned, it is an utterly false proposition that the government is instituted to serve the best interests of those who are governed. (*Salus populi suprema lex esto.*)[34] What is right is because it ought to be; it exists absolutely, and it ought to be enforced even if no one were to benefit from this. (*Fiat justitia, et pereat mundus.*)[35] With respect to the latter [positive law or right], it is not, as has already been noted, contrary to natural right that someone should give up his own right for the advantage of someone else. (*Volenti non fit injuria.*)[36] It is, however, absolutely contrary to right that anyone should be forced to relinquish his own right. Consequently, if there should arise general and loud protest against a law [*Gesetz*] that is in itself unjust, and which could be [considered] just only under the presupposition of consent, it is then the governor's absolute duty to renounce this law, no matter how loudly those who profit from the injustice in question might complain about a violation of the contract. If there is no protest, then he can enforce the law in good conscience. – (Since these principles are easily misunderstood, and since such misunderstanding might result in a dangerous misuse of the same principles, I will now determine them in a bit more detail. To the extent that the state contract establishes reciprocal rights toward persons it is a contract not between individuals but between estates. For example, where the nobility has exclusive possession of the

---

[34] "The welfare of the people shall be the highest law."
[35] "Let there be justice, and may the world perish."
[36] "No wrong is done to a person who is willing."

highest state offices and of the real property in land [*des reinen Landeigentums*] – under the title of "manorial estates" [*Rittergüter*], inasmuch as other goods are for the most part not real property – this is due to a largely implicit contract with the estate of the *burghers* [*Bürgerstand*], for the latter tolerate this situation and make their arrangements accordingly, namely, by acquiring for themselves skills for other things. In this way, everything remains in order, and if a governor were to suspend [IV, 359] such a constitution unilaterally and without being summoned to do so, then he would be acting despotically and utterly contrary to right. He is bound by duty to this constitution, and the nobility has submitted to him under the condition that he uphold it. If an individual burgher, without first announcing his intention [to appeal to natural right] and after having already approved of this constitution by means of his behavior, encroaches upon the presumptive rights of the nobility, then he is punishable, and he would be rightly punished in accordance with the positive law that he has recognized by his silence up until now. Such a person is by no means to be judged in accordance with natural right, which he ought to have reclaimed publicly and *prior to the deed* and not merely after the deed had been committed. Surely he wanted to avail himself of the advantages of the positive law, so how can he afterward lay claim to another law, one that is opposed to the positive law? If, as is fitting, an individual burgher duly reclaims his [natural] right with the governor and thereby suspends his contract with the nobility, then through this same act of reclamation he also suspends at the same time his contract with his own estate, in unison with which he had concluded the original contract [that he now wishes to abrogate]. He is no longer a party to the contract and thus must also renounce any advantages accruing to him therefrom, such as the right to engage in commerce, if it should be the case that this is a right that belongs only to the estate of the burghers. Now what does someone who does this really desire? He desires to be accepted into the estate of the nobility, and by right this has to be granted to him so long as his external circumstances permit it. – Single individuals who complain about an infringement of the constitution must therefore be permitted to change their estate. This is the only way to redress the wrong in response to their reclamation [of their natural right]. Any tolerable state simply must make it easy for someone to change his estate; the opposite is absolutely contrary to right, and no governor can tolerate such a situation in good conscience. Indentured servitude (*glebae adscriptio*[37]), for example, and the prohibition against certain estates pursuing university studies are absolutely contrary to right. – But if the entire estate of the burghers, or even a very large majority of them, were to reclaim its natural right [IV, 360], it would then be the governor's absolute duty to undertake a revision of the legislation in this regard, regardless of whether the nobility agrees to this or not. If the advantaged estates were wise, they would never let things come to such a point of reclamation [of rights], but would gradually give up their privileges on their own accord.)

Contracts of this kind [such as indentured servitude] continue because of the ignorance and helplessness of the disadvantaged estates, because they lack any knowledge of their rights and are unskilled in exercising them. As the level of culture rises and as culture spreads more widely such privileges will cease, and it is the end of both nature and of reason that they should cease and that there should arise a complete equality of all citizens according to *birth* – but equality only in this respect, for once one goes on to choose a profession, differences are once again introduced. The spread of culture is thus the end of both nature and of reason. Culture is the foundation of all improvement; therefore it is absolutely contrary to right and to duty to bring its progress to a halt or to allow it to be brought to a halt by estates with an interest in darkness. – *Obscurantism* is, among other things, a crime against the state as it ought to be. – Supporting enlightenment is a matter of conscience for a governor who is acquainted with his vocation.

One of the highest determinations of the state constitution, as demanded by pure reason, is that the governor is responsible to the people, and most actual states differ from this ideal of reason precisely because they have not instituted this responsibility [of the governor to the people]. To be sure, the governor of such an [actual] state, who [nevertheless] governs according to ideas, cannot actually discharge this responsibility that is demanded by reason, for there is no one to whom he might discharge it; but he still governs *as though* he were responsible [to the people], in a manner such that he is always ready to give an account of himself if this should be demanded.

---

[37] "Belonging to the soil," i.e., serfdom [*Leibeigenschaft*].

Everything we have said so far applies to the supreme power [in the state], whether that is conferred upon a single person or divided among several who recognize no higher judge above themselves (such as the nation [*Nation*], if the latter were capable of sitting in judgment). A subordinate official is strictly bound to the letter of the law [IV, 361]. Hardly anything conflicts more directly with the end of the state than a subordinate official setting himself up as an interpreter of the law. This always creates an injustice, since the losing party is judged by a law that the judge has created through his own interpretation only after the deed [that he is judging]. – It is also true that the laws should not be of the kind that allow themselves to be interpreted and turned and twisted; indeterminateness of its laws is a very great ill for a state. – If someone objects to the positive law on the basis of natural right, then, to be sure, the subordinate official ought not to enforce the positive law; but in this case he should do nothing immediately except delegate this matter to the highest authority, understood as the legislative power.

In summary, every state constitution is rightful and can be served with good conscience, so long as it does not make it impossible to progress toward what is better, both in general and for single individuals. The only constitution that is utterly contrary to right is a constitution the end of which is to preserve everything just as it now is.

§33
Duties of the lower classes of the people

As we have already seen above, the vocation of the lower classes of the people is to operate immediately upon irrational nature for the sake of rational beings in order to make the former suitable for the ends of the latter.

According to my presupposition, I have to deal here not with the lower classes of the people immediately, but rather with those whose task it is to cultivate them. I will therefore describe only the disposition to which the lower classes of the people are to be raised [IV, 362].

(1) The dignity of every human being, his self-respect and, along with this, his morality, depends upon his being able to relate his own occupation [*Geschäft*] to the end of reason – or, which means the same, to God's end with respect to human beings – and on his being able to say, "what I am doing is God's will." This is something that the

members of the lower classes of the people are fully entitled to say. Even if they are not the pinnacle of empirical humanity, they are surely the pillars of the same. How could the scholar do research, the teacher of the people teach, or the state official govern if they could not live in the first place?

The dignity of these [lower] estates only increases if one considers – and allows them to consider – that humanity's progress toward the better has always depended on these estates in particular, and it will continue to do so. If humanity is to make any considerable advance, then it must waste as little time and power as possible on mechanical work; nature must become mild, matter must become pliant, everything must become such that, with only a little effort, it will grant human beings what they need and the struggle against nature will no longer be such a pressing matter.

For the sake of this vocation, it is the absolute duty of the lower classes to perfect and to advance their trade, since the progress of humanity as such is conditioned thereby. It is the duty of every individual in these classes at least to strive to satisfy this demand, for only in this way can he pay for his place in the series of rational beings. Otherwise he is merely a member of the series of those who transmit his trade. – (Some authors have asserted that the inventor of the plough possesses far greater merit than, e.g., the discoverer of a merely theoretical proposition in geometry.[38] This claim has recently provoked vehement opposition, and unjustly so, in my opinion. Such opposition reveals more of the disposition of a scholar than that of a human being. Both parties are equally right and equally wrong. Neither of these two inventions [IV, 363], along with what belongs to them, mechanical work and science, have any *absolute* worth; they possess a relative worth in relation to the end of reason. Both inventions are therefore of approximately equal worth. What determines the higher worth of an inventor is not his success but his disposition.)

The lower classes of the people can hardly satisfy their duty to advance their trade without the guidance of the higher classes, who

---

[38] Fichte here groups together the *discoverer* of a mathematical theorem and the *inventor* of an agricultural implement because the German term *Erfinden* carried both meanings in the late eighteenth century.

are in immediate possession of the cognitions [required for such an advance]. Hence it is

(2) *the duty of the lower classes of the people to honor the members of the higher classes.* Here I am not talking about the submissiveness they owe the administrator of the laws, as such, nor of the obedience and confidence they owe to the teacher of the people, as such; for these are universal duties. Instead, I am talking about the respect they ought to have for the scholar and the artist, even outside their respective offices, as *more highly cultivated* human beings. Such respect does not consist in external demonstrations of honor nor in silent and slavish respect, but in presupposing that these are men who understand more and who see farther than they themselves do, and [thus] that their counsel and their suggestions for improving this or that procedure – some branch of business, of domestic life, of education, and so on – may very well be based on truth and insight. Such respect is not to be rendered in blind faith or silent obedience, for the people are not obliged to do this, but in the form of simple attentiveness and with the preliminary assumption that the suggestions in question might well be reasonable and worthy of further examination. – In short, the respect we are talking about here is the very same frame of mind that we showed above to be appropriate on the part of adult children with regard to their parents. – This kind of deference depends upon free deliberation and reflection, and hence one can make it a duty – not, to be sure, an immediate duty [of respect], but a duty to engage in the kind of reflection that fosters such respect – [iv, 364]. It is immediately evident that if the lower classes reject out of hand any proposals for improvement that they may receive from the higher classes, then they will never advance any further.

Yet one must also bear in mind that it is almost always the fault of the higher classes themselves that they are denied such deference; indeed, this is something that depends very largely upon the respect the higher classes themselves demonstrate for the lower classes. – One should respect their freedom, for no one is in a position to command them to do anything unless he is their superior and only to this extent – and even then one is in a position only to counsel them. One should show respect for their affairs and let them see that one recognizes the dignity of the same. If one wants to act upon them, one should come down to their level. There is no more pointless vanity than to want to appear learned in front of those who are not learned. They do not know how to appreciate this. – The rule for dealing with them – which is at the same time the rule for any popular discourse – is as follows: one should by no means proceed from principles they cannot understand nor proceed in such a manner that they cannot follow the course of one's thoughts; instead, one should, as much as possible, connect everything one has to say to them to their own experience.

The correct relationship between the higher and lower classes, the appropriate mutual interaction between the two, is, as such, the true underlying support upon which the improvement of the human species rests. The higher classes constitute the mind of the single large whole of humanity; the lower classes constitute its limbs; the former are the thinking and designing [*Entwerfende*] part, the latter the executive part. A body is healthy when every movement ensues immediately and without hindrance just as soon as the will has been determined, and it remains healthy to the extent that the understanding continuously shows equal care for the preservation of all its limbs. It is the same with the human community. If this relationship is as it is supposed to be, then the right relationship among the other estates will soon come about by itself. If the lower estates continue to become more cultivated – and they will advance in this way if they listen to the counsel of the higher estates – [IV, 365], then the statesman will no longer look down upon the scholar as an idle dreamer, since the statesman himself will be driven over the course of time to realize the scholar's ideas and will find that they are always confirmed within experience; nor will the scholar continue to despise the statesman as a mindless exponent of empirical reality [*Empiriker*]. Furthermore, the scholar and the so-called cleric will also cease quarreling with each other – whether in several persons or, as is often the case, within one and the same person – , because the common man will become ever more capable of advancing with the culture of the age.

There is no more appropriate manner in which I could end this book than by calling attention to this chief point upon which the improvement of our species, as the final end of all ethics, rests.

Glossary

German–English

Abhängigkeit	dependence
ableiten	to derive
Abneigung	aversion
abschreiben	to take away
Absicht	aim, intent
absolut	absolute
Absolutheit	absoluteness
Achtung	respect
Affekt	affect
Agilität	agility
Akt	act
allgemein	universal, general
allmählich	gradual, gradually
Amt	office
anerkennen	to recognize
Anforderung	demand
angemessen	suitable
Angewöhnung	habituation
anknüpfen	to attach
Anknüpfung	attachment
Anlage	predisposition
annähern	to approximate, to approach
Annahme	assumption, supposition
annehmen	to assume
Anschauung	intuition

Ansicht	view, aspect
Anstoß	check, impulse
Anstrengung	exertion
Antrieb	stimulus
Anwendbarkeit	applicability
Art	kind
sich aufdringen	to impose itself
auffassen	to apprehend
Aufforderung	summons
Aufgabe	task, problem
aufgeben	to assign
aufheben	to annul, to suspend
aufstellen	to exhibit
Ausbildung	training
Ausführung	execution
ausgehen	to proceed from, to continue
Äußerung	manifestation
Ausspruch	expression
Ausübung	exercise
autonom	autonomous
Autonomie	autonomy
beabsichtigen	to intend
Beamter	official
bearbeiten	to fashion
Bedeutung	meaning
bedingen	to condition
Bedingung	condition
Bedürfnis	need
Befolgung	observance
befördern	to further, to promote
Befreiung	liberation
Befriedigung	satisfaction
Begebenheit	occurrence
Begehren	desiring
begehren	to desire
Begierde	desire
begreifen	to comprehend

346

begrenzt	bounded
Begrenztheit	boundedness
Begrenzung	bounding
Begriff	concept
Behandlung	treatment
beharrlich	persistent
Behauptung	assertion, claim
beilegen	to attribute
Beimischung	admixture
Belehrung	instruction
Benennung	designation
Beobachtung	observation
Berechnung	calculation
Beruf	profession
beschaffen	constituted
Beschaffenheit	constitution, state, property
Beschäftigung	occupation
beschränken	to limit
Beschränktheit	limitedness
Beschränkung	limitation
beschreiben	to describe
besonderer	particular
Besonnenheit	thoughtful self-awareness, circumspection
Bestandteil	component, component part
bestehen	to subsist, to continue to exist
Bestehen	subsistence
bestimmbar	determinable
Bestimmtheit	determinacy, determinateness
Bestimmung	determination, vocation
bestimmt	determinate, determined
Betragen	conduct
Beurteilung	adjudication
Beweglichkeit	mobility
Bewegungsgrund	motive, motive for action
Beweis	proof
Bewußtsein	consciousness
Bezeichnung	designation

Biedermann	honorable person
Bild	image
bilden	to cultivate
Bildung	cultivation, formation
Bildungstrieb	formative drive
Böses	evil
Bosheit	malice
Botmäßigkeit	sway, control
bürgerlich	civil
Bürgervertrag	civil contract
charakterisieren	to characterize
darstellen	to present
Darstellung	presentation
Dauer	duration
dauernd	continuing
Denkart	way of thinking
Denkweise	manner of thinking
Disposition	disposition
dressieren	to train
dulden	to tolerate
Egoismus	egotism
egoistisch	egotistic
Ehrerbietigkeit	deference
Eigennutz	self-interest
eigennützig	selfish, self-interested
Eigenschaft	property
Eigensinn	willfulness
Eigentum	property
einbilden	to imagine
Einbildungskraft	power of imagination
Einheit	unity
Einrichtung	arrangement, institution, constitution
Einschränkung	restriction
Einwirkung	influence
einzeln	singular
Empfindbarkeit	sensitivity
empfindend	sensitive

Empfindung	sensation
endlich	finite
Endlichkeit	finitude
Endzweck	final end
Entäußerung	externalization
entgegengesetzt	opposite, opposing, posited in opposition
Entgegengesetzte	opposites
entgegensetzen	to counterposit, to posit in opposition
Entgegensetzung	opposition
Entscheidung	decision
Entschluß	resolve, resolution
entwerfen	to design
Entwicklung	development
Erfahrung	experience
erfolgen	to ensue
Erfüllung	filling, fullfillment
sich ergeben	to submit
Ergebung	submission
erhaben	sublime
Erhabenheit	sublimity
erhalten	to preserve, to sustain
Erhaltung	preservation
Erhebung	elevation
erhoben	elevated
erkennbar	cognizable
erkennen	to cognize
Erkenntnis	cognition
Erlaubnis	permission
Erörterung	exposition
erregen	to excite
Ersatz	reparation, replacement
erscheinen	to appear
Erscheinung	appearance
erwarten	to expect
Erweiterung	extension
Erzeugung	generation
erziehen	to educate

Erziehung	education
faktisch	factual
Faktum	fact
Feigheit	cowardice
feindselig	malevolent
festgesetzt	fixed
finden	to find
Folge	consequence
fordern	to demand
Forderung	demand
Fortdauer	continuation
Fortpflanzung	propogation
Freiheit	freedom
Freisein	being free, free being
freitätig	freely active
fremd	foreign
fremdartig	heterogeneous
Freude	joy
fühlen	to feel
Gebiet	domain
Gebot	command, precept
gebunden	bound, constrained
Gebundenheit	constrained state
gefallen	to please
gefesselt	fettered
Gefühl	feeling
Gegensatz	contrary
Gegensetzung	opposition
Gegenstand	object
Gegenteil	opposite, contrary
Gegner	adversary
Gehorsam	obedience
Geist	spirit, mind
geistig	spiritual, mental
geistiges Wesen	spiritual being
Gelehrter	scholar
gelehrter Stand	learned estate

gemein	common
Gemeingut	common good or possession
gemeinsam	common
Gemeinschaft	community
gemeinschaftlich	communal
Gemeinwesen	commonwealth
Gemütszustand	mental state
Genuß	enjoyment
gerecht	just
Geschäft	business
Geschicklichkeit	skillfulness, skill
geschickt	able
Geschlecht	sex
Gesellschaft	society
Gesetz	law
Gesetzgebung	legislation
Gesetzmäßigkeit	lawfulness
Gesichtspunkt	viewpoint, point of view
Gesinnung	disposition
Gestalt	shape
gewähren	to provide
Gewalt	force, power
Gewalttätigkeit	violence
Gewerbe	trade
Gewissen	conscience
gewissenlos	unconscionable
Glaube	belief, faith
Glaubensartikel	article of faith
Gleichgewicht	balance
Gleichgültigkeit	indifference
Glied	member, element
Glückseligkeit	happiness
Gnade	grace
greiflich	tangible
Grenze	boundary
Grenzpunkt	boundary point
Größe	magnitude

großmütig	magnanimous
Grund	ground, reason, basis
Grundlage	foundation
Grundtrieb	fundamental drive
gültig	valid
Gültigkeit	validity
Güte	goodness
Handeln	acting
handeln	to act
Handlung	action
Hang	propensity
heilig	holy
heiligen	to sanctify
Hemmung	restraint
herausgreifen	to select
Herrschaft	dominion, reign
herrschen	to have dominion, to reign, to rule
hervorbringen	to produce
sich hingeben	to surrender
Hirngespinst	fancy
Hochschätzung	high esteem
das Ich	the I
Ichheit	I-hood
Idee	idea
Inhalt	content
innig	heartfelt
intellektuell	intellectual
Intelligenz	intellect, intelligence
Kausalität	causality
kennen	to be acquainted with, to be familiar with
Klage	complaint
Klasse	class
Klugheit	prudence
konsequent	consistent
konstituieren	to constitute
Kraft	force
kultivieren	to cultivate

Kunst	art
Künstler	artist, artisan
Kunstprodukt	artifact, product of art
Lehre	doctrine, theory
Lehrsatz	theorem
Leib	body
leiden	to suffer
Leiden	passivity, state of passivity, suffering
leidend	passive
Leidenschaft	passion
Leitfaden	guiding thread
letztes Zweck	ultimate end
Lust	pleasure
Macht	might
Mannigfältigkeit	manifold
Materie	matter, content, material content
Mehrheit	plurality
Mensch	human being
Menschengeschlecht	human species, humanity
Menschheit	humanity
Merkmal	distinguishing feature, feature
Mißbrauch	abuse
Mitleid	compassion
mittelbar	mediate, indirect
Moralität	morality
Mutmaßung	conjecture
Nachbeterei	parroting
Nachbild	copy
nachbilden	to copy, to imitate
nachdenken	to meditate, to reflect
nachweisen	to demonstrate
Nation	nation
Naturanlage	natural disposition
Naturtrieb	natural drive
Naturwesen	natural being
Neigung	inclination
Nicht-Ich	the Not-I

Norm	norm
Notstaat	makeshift state, state of necessity
Notwendigkeit	necessity
Oberer	superior
Oberherrschaft	supremacy
Objekt	object
Obrigkeit	authority
offen	sincere
ohnmächtig	impotent
Pfaffentum	priestcraft
Pflicht	duty
pflichtgemäß	in accordance with duty
pflichtmäßig	dutiful
pflichtwidrig	contrary to duty
planmäßig	methodical
prädestiniert	predestined
prästabiliert	pre-established
Quantum	quantum, amount
Rang	rank
Räsonnement	argumentation, reasoning
realisieren	to realize (to make real)
Realität	reality
Recht	right, law
rechtlich	righteous
Rechtschaffenheit	righteousness
reell	real
Regent	governor
regieren	to govern
Reiz	attraction
Richtung	direction
Ruhe	repose, state of repose
Satz	proposition
schätzen	to assess
Schein	illusion
Schicksal	fate
schlechthin	purely and simply, absolutely
Schluß	conclusion, inference

schonen	to preserve
Schranke	limit
Schuld	guilt
Schuldigkeit	obligation
schwanken	to waver
Schwärmerei	fanatical ethusiasm
schweben	to hover
Sehnen	longing
Sein	being
Selbstbestimmung	self-determination
selbständig	self-sufficient
Selbständigkeit	self-sufficiency
Selbsttätigkeit	self-activity
Seligkeit	blessedness
setzen	to posit
Sicherheit	security
Sinn	sense
Sinnenwelt	sensible world
Sinnesart	mind-set
sinnlich	sensible, sensory
Sinnlichkeit	sensibility
Sinnlosigkeit	mindlessness
Sitten	morals
Sittengesetz	moral law
Sittenlehre	ethics (i.e. the philosophical theory of morality)
sittlich	ethical
sollen	ought, should, to be supposed to
Sollen, des	the ought
Sorgfalt	solicitude
Sprung	leap
Staatsbeamter	state official
Staatsverfassung	state constitution
Staatsvertrag	state contract
Stand	estate
stetig	continuous
Stimmung	frame of mind, mood
Stoff	stuff

straffbar	punishable
sträflich	blameable
Straflichkeit	blameworthiness
streben	to strive
Streben	striving
Substanz	substance
Symbol	symbol, creed
Tat	deed, act
tätig	active
Tätigkeit	activity
Tatkraft	active force
Tatsache	fact
tauglich	fit
Tendenz	tendency
Theorie	theory
träge	indolent
Trägheit	laziness, inertia
Trennung	separation
Trieb	drive
Triebfeder	incentive
tugendhaft	virtuous
Tun	doing
übereinstimmend	harmonizing
Übereinstimmung	accord, correspondence
Übergang	transition, movement of transition
Übergehen	transition, movement of transition
übertragen	to transfer
Überzeugung	conviction
Übung	exercise
Umfang	extent, sphere
umfassen	to include
Unabhängigkeit	independence
unaufhörlich	incessant
unbedingt	unconditional
unbegreiflich	inconceivable
Unbestimmbarkeit	indeterminability
Unbestimmtheit	indeterminacy, indeterminateness

Undank	ingratitude
Unding	absurdity
Uneigennützigkeit	unselfishness
unendlich	infinite
Unendlichkeit	infinity
unerlaubt	impermissible
Unkeuschheit	sexual depravity
unleidlich	intolerable
Unlust	displeasure
Unmäßigkeit	intemperance
unmittelbar	immediate, direct
unmoralisch	immoral
Unrecht	injustice
Unruhe	disquiet
Unsittlichkeit	immorality
Unsterblichkeit	immortality
Untätigkeit	inactivity
untauglich	unfit
unterdrücken	to suppress
untergeordnet	subordinated [to]
unterlassen	to refrain from, to abstain
Unterlassung	abstention
unterordnen	to subordinate
Unterricht	instruction
Unterschied	difference
unterwerfen	to subjugate, to subordinate
Unterwerfung	subjugation
Unterwürfigkeit	submissiveness
unverdorben	uncorrupted
Unvermögen	incapability
unvernünftig	irrational
Unwissenheit	ignorance
Urbestimmung	original determination
Ursache	cause
Ursprung	origin
ursprünglich	original
Urteilskraft	power of judgment

Urtrieb	original drive
Verachtung	contempt
verändern	to change
Veranstaltung	arrangement
verbinden	to combine, to connect
Verbindlichkeit	obligatory character
Verbot	prohibition
verbreiten	to spread
Verdienst	merit
verdorben	depraved
vereinigen	to unify, to unite
vereinigt	unified
Vereinigung	union, unification
Verfahren	procedure
Verfassung	constitution
Verfügung	regulation
Vergehen	wrongdoing
Vergnügen	delight
Verhinderung	hindrance
Verkehrtheit	perversion
Verkettung	concatenation
Verleugnung	renunciation
vermittelt	mediated
Vermögen	power, capacity
Vernichtung	annihilation
Vernunft	reason
Vernüntelei	sophistry
vernünftig	reasonable
Vernünftigkeit	rationality
Vernunftwesen	rational being
Verordnung	prescription
verschieden	different
Verschiedenheit	diversity
Verschmelzung	fusion
Verschuldung	guiltiness
Verstand	understanding
verständlich	comprehensible

Vervollkommnung	perfecting
verwerflich	objectionable
Verzweiflung	despair
Volk	people, nation
Volkslehrer	teacher of the people
Vorbild	pre-figuration, model
Vorhandensein	presence
vorläufig	preliminary
vorstellen	to represent
Vorstellen	representing, act of representing
Vorstellung	representation
vortrefflich	splendid
Wahl	choice
wählen	to choose
Wahrnehmung	perception
wechselseitig	mutual, reciprocal
Wechselwirkung	reciprocal interaction, interaction
wehmütig	sad
Weltregierung	governance of the world
Werkzeug	tool
Wert	value
Wertachtung	esteem
Werthaltung	estimation
Wesen	essence, being, nature
widersinnig	absurd
Widerstand	resistance
Widerstreit	conflict
Wille	will
Willensakt	act of willing
Willkür	(power of) choice, arbitrary choice
willkürlich	arbitrary, based on free choice
wirken	act efficaciously, effectuate, effect
wirklich	actual
Wirklichkeit	actuality
Wirksamkeit	efficacy, efficacious action
Wirkung	effective operation, effect
wissen	to know

Wissen	knowledge
Wissenschaft	science
Wohltätigkeit	beneficence
wollen	to will
Wollen	willing, act of willing
Wollung	volition
Wollüstling	voluptuary
Würde	dignity
Zeichen	sign
zerstören	to destroy
Ziel	goal
Zucht	discipline
zufällig	contingent
Zufriedenheit	contentment
Zumutung	intimation
Zunötigung	constraint
zusammenfallen	to coincide
zusammenstimmen	to harmonize
Zusammenstimmung	harmony, agreement
zusammentreffen	to come together, to concur
Zusammentreffen	concurrence
zuschreiben	to ascribe
zusehen	to look on
Zustand	state, condition
Zwang	compulsion, constraint
Zweck	end
zweckmäßig	purposive, appropriate
Zweckmäßigkeit	purposiveness

English–German

able	*geschickt*
absolute	*absolut, schlechthin*
absoluteness	*Absolutheit*
abstention	*Unterlassung*
absurd	*widersinnig*
absurdity	*Unding*
abuse	*Mißbrauch*

accord	*Übereinstimmung*
to be acquainted with	*kennen*
the act	*Akt*
to act	*handeln*
to act efficaciously	*wirken*
act of willing	*Willensakt*
what is acted upon	*das Behandelte*
the acting	*Handeln*
action	*Handlung*
active	*tätig*
active force	*Tatkraft*
activity	*Tätigkeit*
actual	*wirklich*
actuality	*Wirklichkeit*
adjudication	*Beurteilung*
admixture	*Beimischung*
adversary	*Gegner*
affect	*Affekt*
agility	*Agilität*
agreement	*Zusammenstimmung*
aim	*Absicht*
amount	*Quantum*
animality	*Tierheit*
annihilation	*Vernichtung*
to annul	*aufheben*
to appear	*erscheinen*
appearance	*Erscheinung, Anschein*
applicability	*Anwendbarkeit*
to apprehend	*auffassen*
to approach	*annähern*
to approximate	*annähern*
arbitrary	*willkürlich*
arbitrary choice	*Willkür*
argumentation	*Räsonnement*
arrangement	*Veranstaltung*
art	*Kunst*
article of faith	*Glaubensartikel*

articulation	*Artikulation*
artifact	*Kunstprodukt*
artisan	*Künstler*
artist	*Künstler*
to ascribe	*zuschreiben*
aspect	*Ansicht*
to assess	*schätzen*
assertion	*Behauptung*
to assume	*annehmen*
assumption	*Annahme*
to attach	*anknüpfen*
attachment	*Anknüpfung*
attraction	*Reiz*
to attribute	*beilegen*
authority	*Obrigkeit*
autonomous	*autonom*
autonomy	*Autonomie*
aversion	*Abneigung*
being	*Sein, Wesen*
being free	*Freisein*
belief	*Glaube*
blamable	*sträflich*
blameworthiness	*Straflichkeit*
blessedness	*Seligkeit*
body	*Leib*
bound	*gebunden*
bounded	*begrenzt*
boundary	*Grenze*
boundary line	*Grenzlinie*
boundary point	*Grenzpunkt*
boundedness	*Begrenztheit*
bounding	*Begrenzung*
business	*Geschäft*
calculation	*Berechnung*
causality	*Kausalität*
cause	*Ursache*
to change	*verändern*

to characterize	*charakterisieren*
check	*Anstoß*
choice	*Wahl*
to choose	*wählen*
circumspection	*Besonnenheit*
civil	*bürgerlich*
civil contract	*Bürgervertrag*
claim	*Behauptung*
class	*Klasse*
cognition	*Erkenntnis*
cognizable	*erkennbar*
to cognize	*erkennen*
to coincide	*zusammenfallen*
to come together	*zusammentreffen*
command	*Gebot*
common	*gemeinsam, gemein*
common good	*Gemeingut*
common possession	*Gemeingut*
commonwealth	*Gemeinwesen*
communal	*gemeinschaftlich*
community	*Gemeinschaft*
compassion	*Mitleid*
component part	*Bestandteil*
to comprehend	*begreifen*
comprehensibility	*Begreiflichkeit*
comprehensible	*verständlich*
compulsion	*Zwang*
concatenation	*Verkettung*
concept	*Begriff*
conclusion	*Schluß*
condition	*Bedingung*
to condition	*bedingen*
conduct	*Betragen*
conjecture	*Mutmaßung*
connection	*Verbindung*
conscience	*Gewissen*
consciousness	*Bewußtsein*

consequence	*Folge*
consistent	*konsequent*
to constitute	*konstituieren*
constituted	*beschaffen*
constitution	*Beschaffenheit, Einrichtung, Verfassung* (of a state)
constrained state	*Gebundenheit*
constraint	*Zwang, Zunötigung*
contempt	*Verachtung*
content	*Inhalt, Materie*
contentment	*Zufriedenheit*
contingent	*zufällig*
continuation	*Fortdauer*
continuing	*dauernd, fortdauernd*
continuous	*stetig*
contrary	*Gegenteil*
contrary to duty	*pflichtwidrig*
contrast	*Gegensatz*
control	*Botmäßigkeit*
conviction	*Überzeugung*
copy	*Nachbild*
correspondence	*Übereinstimmung*
to counterposit	*entgegensetzen*
cowardice	*Feigheit*
creed	*Glaubensbekenntnis, Symbol*
to cultivate	*bilden, kultivieren*
cultivation	*Bildung*
culture	*Kultur, Bildung*
decision	*Entscheidung*
deed	*Tat*
deference	*Ehrerbietigkeit*
delight	*Vergnügen*
demand	*Anforderung, Forderung*
to demand	*fordern*
to demonstrate	*nachweisen*
dependence	*Abhängigkeit*
depraved	*verdorben*

to derive	*ableiten*
to describe	*beschreiben*
description	*Beschreibung*
design	*Entwerfung*
to design	*entwerfen*
designation	*Benennung, Bezeichnung*
desire	*Begierde*
to desire	*begehren*
to destroy	*zerstören*
determinable	*bestimmbar*
determinacy	*Bestimmtheit*
determinate	*bestimmt*
determinateness	*Bestimmtheit*
determination	*Bestimmung*
determined	*bestimmt*
difference	*Unterschied*
different	*verschieden*
dignity	*Würde*
direct	*unmittelbar*
direction	*Richtung*
discipline	*Zucht*
displeasure	*Unlust*
disposition	*Gesinnung*
disquiet	*Unruhe*
diversity	*Verschiedenheit*
doctrine	*Lehre*
doing	*Tun*
domain	*Gebiet*
dominion	*Herrschaft*
drive	*Trieb*
to drive	*treiben*
duration	*Dauer*
dutiful	*pflichtmäßig*
duty	*Pflicht*
education	*Erziehung*
effect	*Wirkung, Effekt*
to effect	*wirken*

effectuate	*bewirken*
efficacy	*Wirksamkeit*
elevated	*erhoben*
elevation	*Erhebung*
elucidation	*Erörterung*
to endure	*dauern, ertragen*
enjoyment	*Genuß*
essence	*Wesen*
essential	*wesentlich*
estate	*Stand*
estimation	*Werthaltung*
ethical	*sittlich*
ethics	*Sittenlehre*
evil	*Böses*
to excite	*erregen*
execution	*Ausführung*
exercise	*Ausübung, Übung*
exertion	*Anstrengung*
to exhibit	*aufstellen*
exhibition	*Aufstellung*
existence	*Existenz, Dasein*
to expect	*erwarten*
experience	*Erfahrung*
exposition	*Erörterung*
expression	*Ausspruch*
extension	*Erweiterung*
extent	*Umfang*
externalization	*Entäußerung*
fact	*Tatsache, Faktum*
factual	*faktisch*
faith	*Glaube*
to be familiar with	*erkennen*
fanatical enthusiasm	*Schwärmerei*
fancy	*Hirngespinst*
to fashion	*bearbeiten*
fate	*Schicksal*
feature	*Merkmal*

to feel	*fühlen*
feeling	*Gefühl*
fettered	*gefesselt*
filling	*Erfüllung*
final end	*Endzweck*
fine art	*schöne Kunst*
finite	*endlich*
finitude	*Endlichkeit*
fit	*tauglich*
fixed	*festgesetzt*
force	*Kraft, Gewalt*
foreign	*fremd*
to form	*bilden*
formally	*formaliter*
formation	*Bildung*
formative drive	*Bildungstrieb*
foundation	*Grundlage*
free being	*Freisein*
free choice	*freie Willkür, Willkür*
freedom	*Freiheit*
freely active	*freitätig*
fullfillment	*Erfüllung*
fundamental drive	*Grundtrieb*
fusion	*Verschmelzung*
general	*allgemein*
generation	*Erzeugung*
goal	*Ziel*
goodness	*Güte*
to govern	*regieren*
governance of the world	*Weltregierung*
governor	*Regent*
grace	*Gnade*
gradual	*allmählich*
ground	*Grund, Boden*
guiding thread	*Leitfaden*
guilt	*Schuld*
guiltiness	*Verschuldung*

habituation	*Angewöhnung*
happiness	*Glückseligkeit*
harmonizing	*übereinstimmend*
harmony	*Harmonie, Zusammenstimmung*
to have dominion	*herrschen*
heartfelt	*innig*
heterogeneous	*fremdartig*
heteronomous	*heteronom*
high esteem	*Hochschätzung*
holy	*heilig*
honorable person	*Biedermann*
to hover	*schweben*
human being	*Mensch*
humanity	*Menschheit, Menschengeschlecht*
the I	*das Ich*
ideal	*ideal*
ignorance	*Unwissenheit*
I-hood	*Ichheit*
illusion	*Schein*
image	*Bild*
to imagine	*einbilden*
immediate	*unmittelbar*
immoral	*unmoralisch*
immorality	*Unsittlichkeit*
immortality	*Unsterblichkeit*
impermissible	*unerlaubt*
impetus	*Antrieb*
to impose itself	*sich aufdringen*
impotent	*ohnmächtig*
impulse	*Anstoß*
in accordance with duty	*pflichtgemäß*
inactivity	*Untätigkeit*
incapability	*Unvermögen*
incentive	*Triebfeder*
incessant	*unaufhörlich*
inclination	*Neigung*
to include	*umfassen*

inconceivable	*unbegreiflich*
independence	*Unabhängigkeit, Selbständigkeit*
indeterminability	*Unbestimmbarkeit*
indeterminateness	*Unbestimmtheit*
indifference	*Gleichgültigkeit*
indolent	*träge*
inertia	*Trägheit*
inference	*Schluß*
infinite	*unendlich*
infinity	*Unendlichkeit*
influence	*Einwirkung*
ingratitude	*Undank*
injustice	*Unrecht*
institution	*Einrichtung*
instruction	*Belehrung, Unterricht*
intellect	*Intelligenz*
intellectual	*intellektuell*
intelligence	*Intelligenz*
intemperance	*Unmäßigkeit*
to intend	*beabsichtigen*
intent	*Absicht*
interaction	*Wechselwirkung*
intimation	*Zumutung*
intolerable	*unleidlich*
intuition	*Anschauung*
involuntary	*unfreiwillig*
inward	*innerlich*
irrational	*unvernünftig*
joy	*Freude*
just	*gerecht*
kind	*Art*
to know	*wissen*
knowledge	*Wissen*
law	*Gesetz*
lawfulness	*Gesetzmäßigkeit*
laziness	*Trägheit*
leap	*Sprung*

learned estate	*gelehrter Stand*
legislation	*Gesetzgebung*
liberation	*Befreiung*
limit	*Schranke*
to limit	*beschränken*
limitation	*Beschränkung*
limited	*beschränkt*
limitedness	*Beschränktheit*
longing	*Sehnen*
to look on	*zusehen*
magnanimous	*großmütig*
magnitude	*Größe*
makeshift state	*Notstaat*
malevolent	*feindselig*
malice	*Bosheit*
manifestation	*Äußerung*
manifold	*mannigfaltig*
manner of thinking	*Denkweise*
material	*material, materiell*
matter	*Materie*
meaning	*Sinn, Bedeutung*
mediate	*mittelbar*
mediated	*vermittelt*
mediately	*mittelbar*
to meditate	*nachdenken*
mental	*geistig*
mental state	*Gemütszustand*
merit	*Verdienst*
methodical	*planmäßig*
might	*Macht*
mind	*Geist, Gemüt*
mindlessness	*Sinnlosigkeit*
mind-set	*Sinnesart*
mobility	*Beweglichkeit*
model	*Vorbild*
mood	*Stimmung*
moral	*moralisch*

moral law	*Sittengesetz*
moral sense	*moralischer Sinn*
moral system	*Moralsystem*
morality	*Sittlichkeit, Moralität*
morals	*Moral, Sitten*
motive	*Beweggrund, Bewegungsgrund*
mutual	*wechselseitig*
natural being	*Naturwesen*
natural disposition	*Naturanlage*
natural drive	*Naturtrieb*
necessity	*Notwendigkeit*
need	*Bedürfnis*
norm	*Norm*
the Not-I	*Nicht-Ich*
obedience	*Gehorsam*
object	*Gegenstand, Objekt*
objectionable	*verwerflich*
obligation	*Schuldigkeit*
obligatory character	*Verbindlichkeit*
observance	*Befolgung*
observation	*Beobachtung*
occupation	*Beschäftigung*
occurrence	*Begebenheit*
office	*Amt*
official	*Beamter*
ommission	*Unterlassung*
opposite	*entgegengesetzt*
opposite	*Gegenteil*
opposites	*Entgegengesetzte*
opposition	*Gegensetzung, Entgegensetzung*
oppression	*Unterdrückung*
oppressor	*Unterdrücker*
ordinary	*gemein*
origin	*Ursprung*
original	*ursprünglich*
original determination	*Urbestimmung*
ought	*sollen*

the ought	*das Sollen*
particular	*besonderer*
parroting	*Nachbeterei*
passion	*Leidenschaft*
passive	*leidend*
passivity	*Leiden*
to perceive	*wahrnehmen*
perception	*Wahrnehmung*
perfecting	*Vervollkommnung*
permission	*Erlaubnis*
persistent	*beharrlich*
perversion	*Verkehrtheit*
to please	*gefallen*
pleasure	*Lust*
plurality	*Mehrheit*
to posit	*setzen*
power	*Vermögen, Gewalt*
power of cognition	*Erkenntnisvermögen*
power of desire	*Begehrungsvermögen*
power of feeling	*Gefühlsvermögen*
power of judgment	*Urteilskraft*
power of thinking	*Denkvermögen*
power of imagination	*Einbildungskraft*
precept	*Gebot*
predestined	*prädestiniert*
predisposition	*Anlage*
pre-established	*prästabiliert*
pre-figuration	*Vorbild*
preliminary	*vorläufig*
prescription	*Verordnung*
presence	*Vorhandensein*
to present	*darstellen*
presentation	*Darstellung*
to preserve	*erhalten, schonen*
preservation	*Erhaltung*
priestcraft	*Pfaffentum*
principle	*Prinzip, Grundsatz*

problem	*Aufgabe*
procedure	*Verfahren*
to produce	*hervorbringen*
product of art	*Kunstprodukt*
product of nature	*Naturprodukt*
profession	*Beruf*
prohibition	*Verbot*
proof	*Beweis*
propagation	*Fortpflanzung*
propensity	*Hang*
property	*Eigenschaft, Beschaffenheit, Eigentum*
proposition	*Satz*
to provide	*gewähren*
prudence	*Klugheit*
purposive	*zweckmäßig*
purposiveness	*Zweckmäßigkeit*
quantum	*Quantum*
rank	*Rang*
rational being	*Vernunftwesen*
rationality	*Vernünftigkeit*
real	*reell*
reality	*Realität*
to realize, to make real	*realisieren*
reason	*Vernunft, Grund, Vernunftgrund*
reasonable	*vernünftig*
reasoning	*Räsonnement*
reciprocal	*gegenseitig*
reciprocal interaction	*gegenseitige Wechselwirkung, Wechselwirkung*
to recognize	*anerkennen*
to reflect	*reflektieren, nachdenken*
reflection	*Reflexion, Überlegung*
ro refrain from	*unterlassen*
regulation	*Verfügung*
to reign	*herrschen*
relation	*Beziehung, Verhältnis*
relationship	*Verhältnis, Beziehung*
renunciation	*Verleugnung*

repose	*Ruhe*
to represent	*vorstellen*
representation	*Vorstellung*
(act of) representing	*Vorstellen*
resistance	*Widerstand*
resolution	*Entschluss*
respect	*Achtung*
to respect	*achten*
restraint	*Hemmung*
restriction	*Einschränkung*
right	*Recht*
righteous	*rechtlich*
righteousness	*Rechtschaffenheit*
to rule	*herrschen*
sad	*wehmütig*
to sanctify	*heiligen*
satisfaction	*Befriedigung*
scholar	*Gelehrter*
science	*Wissenschaft*
security	*Sicherheit*
to select	*herausgreifen*
self-activity	*Selbsttätigkeit*
self-conceit	*Eigendünkel*
self-determination	*Selbstbestimmung*
self-interest	*Eigennutz*
self-sufficiency	*Selbständigkeit*
self-sufficient	*selbständig*
selfish	*eigennützig*
selfishness	*Eigennützigkeit*
sensation	*Empfindung*
sensibility	*Sinnlichkeit*
sensible	*sinnlich*
sensible world	*Sinnenwelt*
sensitive	*empfindend*
sensitivity	*Empfindbarkeit*
sensory	*sinnlich*
separation	*Trennung*

sex	*Geschlecht*
sexual depravity	*Unkeuschheit*
shape	*Gestalt*
sign	*Zeichen*
sincere	*offen*
singular	*einzeln*
skillfulness	*Geschicklichkeit*
society	*Gesellschaft*
solicitude	*Sorgfalt*
sophistry	*Vernünftelei*
sphere	*Umfang*
spirit	*Geist*
spiritual	*geistig*
spiritual being	*geistiges Wesen*
splendid	*vortrefflich*
spontaneity	*Spontaneität*
to spread	*verbreiten*
standpoint	*Standpunkt*
state	*Zustand, Beschaffenheit, Staat*
state constitution	*Staatsverfassung*
state contract	*Staatsvertrag*
state official	*Staatsbeamter*
state of necessity	*Notstaat*
to strive	*streben*
striving	*Streben*
stuff	*Stoff*
subjugation	*Unterwerfung*
sublime	*erhaben*
sublimity	*Erhabenheit*
submissiveness	*Unterwürfigkeit*
to subsist	*bestehen*
subsistence	*Bestehen*
substance	*Substanz*
to suffer	*leiden*
suffering	*Leiden*
suitable	*angemessen*
summons	*Aufforderung*

superior	*oberer*
supposition	*Annahme*
supremacy	*Oberherrschaft*
to suspend	*aufheben*
to sustain	*erhalten*
sway	*Botmäßigkeit*
symbol	*Symbol*
tangible	*greiflich*
task	*Aufgabe*
teacher of the people	*Volkslehrer*
tendency	*Tendenz*
theorem	*Lehrsatz*
thoughtful self-awareness	*Besonnenheit*
to tolerate	*dulden*
tool	*Werkzeug*
trade	*Gewerbe*
to train	*dressieren, ausbilden*
training	*Ausbildung*
to transfer	*übertragen*
transition	*Übergang, Übergehen*
treatment	*Behandlung*
ultimate end	*letzte Zweck*
unconditional	*unbedingt*
uncorrupted	*unverdorben*
understanding	*Verstand*
undeterminability	*Unbestimmbarkeit*
undetermined	*unbestimmt*
unfit	*untauglich*
unification	*Vereinigung*
unified	*vereinigt*
to unify	*vereinigen*
union	*Vereinigung*
to unite	*vereinigen*
unity	*Einheit*
universal	*allgemein*
unselfishness	*Uneigenützigkeit*
valid	*gültig*

validity	*Gültigkeit*
value	*Wert*
view	*Ansicht*
viewpoint	*Gesichtspunkt*
violence	*Gewalttätigkeit*
virtuous	*tugendhaft*
vocation	*Bestimmung*
volition	*Wollung*
voluptuary	*Wollüstling*
to waver	*schwanken*
will	*Wille*
to will	*wollen*
worth	*Wert*

Index

378

Cambridge texts in the history of philosophy

Titles published in the series thus far

Nietzsche *Writings from the Late Notebooks* (edited by Rüdiger Bittner, translated by Kate Sturge)

Novalis *Fichte Studies* (edited by Jane Kneller)

Schleiermacher *Hermeneutics and Criticism* (edited by Andrew Bowie)

Schleiermacher *Lectures on Philosophical Ethics* (edited by Robert Louden, translated by Louise Adey Huish)

Schleiermacher *On Religion: Speeches to its Cultured Despisers* (edited by Richard Crouter)

Schopenhauer *Prize Essay on the Freedom of the Will* (edited by Günter Zöller)

Sextus Empiricus *Against the Logicians* (edited by Richard Bett)

Sextus Empiricus *Outlines of Scepticism* (edited by Julia Annas and Jonathan Barnes)

Shaftesbury, *Characteristics of Men, Manners, Opinions, Times* (edited by Lawrence Klein)

Adam Smith, *The Theory of Moral Sentiments* (edited by Knud Haakonssen)

Voltaire *Treatise on Tolerance and Other Writings* (edited by Simon Harvey)